Advanced Python Programming

Build high performance, concurrent, and multi-threaded apps
with Python using proven design patterns

Dr. Gabriele Lanaro
Quan Nguyen
Sakis Kasampalis

BIRMINGHAM - MUMBAI

Advanced Python Programming

First Published: February 2019
Production Reference: 2280219

Published by Packt Publishing Ltd.
Livery Place, 35 Livery Street
Birmingham, B3 2PB, U.K.

ISBN 978-1-83855-121-6

www.packtpub.com

`mapt.io`

Mapt is an online digital library that gives you full access to over 5,000 books and videos, as well as industry-leading tools to help you plan your personal development and advance your career. For more information, please visit our website.

Why Subscribe?

- Spend less time learning and more time coding with practical eBooks and Videos from over 4,000 industry professionals

- Improve your learning with Skill Plans built especially for you

- Get a free eBook or video every month

- Mapt is fully searchable

- Copy and paste, print, and bookmark content

Packt.com

Did you know that Packt offers eBook versions of every book published, with PDF and ePub files available? You can upgrade to the eBook version at `www.packt.com` and as a print book customer, you are entitled to a discount on the eBook copy. Get in touch with us at `customercare@packtpub.com` for more details.

At `www.packt.com`, you can also read a collection of free technical articles, sign up for a range of free newsletters, and receive exclusive discounts and offers on Packt books and eBooks.

Contributors

About the Authors

Dr. Gabriele Lanaro is passionate about good software and is the author of the chemlab and chemview open source packages. His interests span machine learning, numerical computing visualization, and web technologies. In 2013, he authored the first edition of the book High Performance Python Programming. He has been conducting research to study the formation and growth of crystals using medium and large-scale computer simulations. In 2017, he obtained his PhD in theoretical chemistry.

Quan Nguyen is a Python enthusiast and data scientist. Currently, he works as a data analysis engineer at Micron Technology, Inc. With a strong background in mathematics and statistics, Quan is interested in the fields of scientific computing and machine learning. With data analysis being his focus, Quan also enjoys incorporating technology automation into everyday tasks through programming. Quan's passion for Python programming has led him to be heavily involved in the Python community. He started as a primary contributor for the Python for Scientists and Engineers book and various open source projects on GitHub. Quan is also a writer for the Python software foundation and an occasional content contributor for DataScience.com (part of Oracle).

Sakis Kasampalis is a software engineer living in the Netherlands. He is not dogmatic about particular programming languages and tools; his principle is that the right tool should be used for the right job. One of his favorite tools is Python because he finds it very productive. Sakis has also technically reviewed the Mastering Object-oriented Python and Learning Python Design Patterns books, both published by Packt Publishing.

Packt Is Searching for Authors Like You

If you're interested in becoming an author for Packt, please visit authors.packtpub.com and apply today. We have worked with thousands of developers and tech professionals, just like you, to help them share their insight with the global tech community. You can make a general application, apply for a specific hot topic that we are recruiting an author for, or submit your own idea.

Table of Contents

Preface

This Learning Path shows you how to leverage the power of both native and third-party Python libraries for building robust and responsive applications. You will learn about profilers and reactive programming, concurrency and parallelism, as well as tools for making your apps quick and efficient. You will discover how to write code for parallel architectures using TensorFlow and Theano, and use a cluster of computers for large-scale computations using technologies such as Dask and PySpark. With the knowledge of how Python design patterns work, you will be able to clone objects, secure interfaces, dynamically choose algorithms, and accomplish much more in high performance computing.

By the end of this Learning Path, you will have the skills and confidence to build engaging models that quickly offer efficient solutions to your problems.

This Learning Path includes content from the following Packt products:

- Python High Performance - Second Edition by Dr. Gabriele Lanaro
- Mastering Concurrency in Python by Quan Nguyen
- Mastering Python Design Patterns by Sakis Kasampalis

Who This Book Is For

This Learning Path is specially designed for Python developers who want to build high-performance applications and learn about single core and multi-core programming, distributed concurrency, and Python design patterns. Some experience with Python programming language will help you get the most out of this Learning Path.

What This Book Covers

Chapter 1, Benchmark and Profiling, will teach you how to assess the performance of Python programs and practical strategies on how to identify and isolate the slow sections of your code.

Chapter 2, Pure Python Optimizations, discusses how to improve your running times by order of magnitudes using the efficient data structures and algorithms available in the Python standard library and pure-Python third-party modules.

Chapter 3, Fast Array Operations with NumPy and Pandas, is a guide to the NumPy and Pandas packages. Mastery of these packages will allow you to implement fast numerical algorithms with an expressive, concise interface.

Chapter 4, C Performance with Cython, is a tutorial on Cython, a language that uses a Python-compatible syntax to generate efficient C code.

Chapter 5, Exploring Compilers, covers tools that can be used to compile Python to efficient machine code. The chapter will teach you how to use Numba, an optimizing compiler for Python functions, and PyPy, an alternative interpreter that can execute and optimize Python programs on the fly.

Chapter 6, Implementing Concurrency, is a guide to asynchronous and reactive programming. We will learn about key terms and concepts, and demonstrate how to write clean, concurrent code using the asyncio and RxPy frameworks.

Chapter 7, Parallel Processing, is an introduction to parallel programming on multi-core processors and GPUs. In this chapter, you will learn to achieve parallelism using the multiprocessing module and by expressing your code using Theano and Tensorflow.

Chapter 8, Advanced Introduction to Concurrent and Parallel Programming, introduces you to the concept of concurrency, and demonstrates an instance in which concurrent programming can improve significantly the speed of a Python program.

Chapter 9, Amdahl's Law, takes a theoretical approach and discusses the limitations of concurrency in improving the speed of applications. We will take a look at what concurrency truly provides and how we can best incorporate it.

Chapter 10, *Working with Threads in Python*, introduces the formal definition of threading and covers a different approach to implementing threading in a Python program. In this chapter, we will also discuss a major element in concurrent programming—the concept of synchronization.

Chapter 11, *Using the with Statement in Threads*, combines the concept of context management with threading in the overall context of concurrent programming in Python. We will be introduced to the main idea behind context management and how it is used in various programming practices, including threading.

Chapter 12, *Concurrent Web Requests*, covers one of the main applications of concurrent programming: web scraping. It also covers the concept of web scraping, along with other relevant elements, before discussing how threading can be applied to web scraping programs in order to achieve significant speedup.

Chapter 13, *Working with Processes in Python*, shows the formal definition of multiprocessing and how Python supports it. We will also learn more about the key differences between threading and multiprocessing, which are often confused with one another.

Chapter 14, *Reduction Operators in Processes*, pairs the concepts of reduction operations and multiprocessing together as a concurrent programming practice. This chapter will go over the theoretical foundation of reduction operations and how it is relevant to multiprocessing as well as programming in general.

Chapter 15, *Concurrent Image Processing*, goes into a specific application of concurrency: image processing. The basic ideas behind image processing, in addition to some of the most common processing techniques, are discussed. We will, of course, see how concurrency, specifically multiprocessing, can speed up the task of image processing.

Chapter 16, *Introduction to Asynchronous Programming*, considers the formal concept of asynchronous programming as one of the three major concurrent programming models aside from threading and multiprocessing. We will learn how asynchronous programming is fundamentally different from the two mentioned, but can still speedup concurrent applications.

Chapter 17, *Implementing Asynchronous Programming in Python*, goes in depth into the API that Python provides to facilitate asynchronous programming. Specifically, we will learn about the `asyncio` module, which is the main tool for implementing asynchronous programming in Python, and the general structure of an asynchronous application.

Chapter 18, Building Communication Channels with asyncio, combines the knowledge obtained regarding asynchronous programming covered in previous chapters with the topic of network communication. Specifically, we will look into using the `aiohttp` module as a tool to make asynchronous HTTP requests to web servers, as well as the `aiofile` module that implements asynchronous file reading/writing.

Chapter 19, Deadlocks, introduces the first of the problems that are commonly faced in concurrent programming. We will learn about the classical dining philosophers problem as an example of how deadlocks can cause concurrent programs to stop functioning. This chapter will also cover a number of potential approaches to deadlocks as well as relevant concepts, such as livelocks and distributed deadlocks.

Chapter 20, Starvation, considers another common problem in concurrent applications. The chapter uses the narrative of the classical readers-writers problem to explain the concept of starvation and its causes. We will, of course, also discuss potential solutions to these problems via hands-on examples in Python.

Chapter 21, Race Conditions, addresses arguably the most well-known concurrency problem: race conditions. We will also discuss the concept of a critical section, which is an essential element in the context of race conditions specifically, and concurrent programming in general. The chapter will then cover mutual exclusion as a potential solution for this problem.

Chapter 22, The Global Interpreter Lock, introduces the infamous GIL, which is considered the biggest challenge in concurrent programming in Python. We will learn about the reason behind GIL's implementation and the problems that it raises. This chapter concludes with some thoughts regarding how Python programmers and developers should think about and interact with the GIL.

Chapter 23, The Factory Pattern, will teach you how to use the Factory design pattern (Factory Method and Abstract Factory) to initialize objects, and also covers the benefits of using the Factory design pattern instead of direct object instantiation.

Chapter 24, The Builder Pattern, will teach you how to simplify the object creation process for cases typically composed of several related objects. We will review real-world examples and use cases, and then implement the builder pattern in developing a pizza-ordering application.

Chapter 25, *Other Creational Patterns*, will teach you how to handle other object creation situations with techniques such as creating a new object that is a full copy (hence, named clone) of an existing object, a technique offered by the Prototype pattern. You will also learn about the Singleton pattern.

Chapter 26, *The Adapter Pattern*, will teach you how to make your existing code compatible with a foreign interface (for example, an external library) with minimal changes. Specifically, we will we see how you can achieve interface conformance using the adapter pattern without modifying the source code of the incompatible model.

Chapter 27, *The Decorator Pattern*, will teach you how to enhance the functionality of an object without using inheritance. We will mention several categories of cross-cutting concerns, and specifically demonstrate memoization in this view. We will also describe how decorators can help us to keep our functions clean, without sacrificing performance.

Chapter 28, *The Bridge Pattern*, will teach you how to externalize an object's implementation details from its class hierarchy to another object class hierarchy. This chapter encourages the idea of preferring composition over inheritance.

Chapter 29, *The Facade Pattern*, will teach you how to create a single entry point to hide the complexity of a system. We will cover the basic use cases of facade and an implementation of the interface used by a multiserver operating system.

Chapter 30, *Other Structural Patterns*, will teach you the Flyweight, Model-View-Controller and Proxy patterns. With the Flyweight pattern, you will learn to reuse objects from an object pool to improve the memory usage and possibly the performance of your applications. The Model-View-Controller (MVC) pattern is used in application development (desktop, web) to improve maintainability by avoiding mixing the business logic with the user interface. And with the Proxy pattern, you provide a special object that acts as a surrogate or placeholder for another object to control access to it and reduce complexity and/or improve performance.

Chapter 31, *The Chain of Responsibility Pattern*, will teach another technique to improve the maintainability of your applications by avoiding mixing the business logic with the user interface.

Chapter 32, *The Command Pattern*, will teach you how to encapsulate operations (such as undo, copy, paste) as objects, to improve your application. Among the advantages of this technique, the object that invokes the command is decoupled from the object that performs it.

Chapter 33, *The Observer Pattern*, will teach you how to send a request to multiple receivers.

To Get the Most out of This Book

The software in this book is tested on Python version 3.5 and on Ubuntu version 16.04. However, majority of the examples can also be run on the Windows and Mac OS X operating systems. Also, it is useful to know about advanced syntax and new syntax introduced in the Python 3 releases. You might also want to learn about idiomatic Python programming, by checkout out resources on Internet about the topic, if needed.

The recommended way to install Python and the associated libraries is through the Anaconda distribution, which can be downloaded from `https://www.continuum.io/downloads`, for Linux, Windows, and Mac OS X. Chapters in this book might discuss the use of external libraries or tools that have to be installed via a package manager such as pip and Anaconda, and specific instructions on how to install those libraries are included in their corresponding chapters.

Additionally, make sure you have installed SQLite 3.22.0 or later from `https://www.sqlite.org/download.html` and RabbitMQ 3.7.7 from `https://www.rabbitmq.com/download.html`.

Download the Example Code Files

You can download the example code files for this book from your account at `www.packt.com`. If you purchased this book elsewhere, you can visit `www.packt.com/support` and register to have the files emailed directly to you.

You can download the code files by following these steps:

1. Log in or register at `www.packt.com`.
2. Select the **SUPPORT** tab.
3. Click on **Code Downloads & Errata**.
4. Enter the name of the book in the **Search** box and follow the onscreen instructions.

Once the file is downloaded, please make sure that you unzip or extract the folder using the latest version of:

- WinRAR/7-Zip for Windows
- Zipeg/iZip/UnRarX for Mac
- 7-Zip/PeaZip for Linux

The code bundle for the book is also hosted on GitHub at `https://github.com/PacktPublishing/AdvancedPythonProgramming`. In case there's an update to the code, it will be updated on the existing GitHub repository.

We also have other code bundles from our rich catalog of books and videos available at `https://github.com/PacktPublishing/`. Check them out!

Conventions Used

There are a number of text conventions used throughout this book.

`CodeInText`: Indicates code words in text, database table names, folder names, filenames, file extensions, pathnames, dummy URLs, user input, and Twitter handles. Here is an example: "In the `Musician` class, the main action is performed by the `play()` method."

A block of code is set as follows:

```
class Musician:
    def __init__(self, name):
        self.name = name
    def __str__(self):
  return f'the musician {self.name}'
    def play(self):
        return 'plays music'
```

Bold: Indicates a new term, an important word, or words that you see onscreen. For example, words in menus or dialog boxes appear in the text like this. Here is an example: "A **remote proxy**, which acts as the local representation of an object that really exists in a different address space (for example, a network server)."

Warnings or important notes appear like this.

Tips and tricks appear like this.

The answers to the questions posed in this book can be found in the appendix.

Get in Touch

Feedback from our readers is always welcome.

General feedback: If you have questions about any aspect of this book, mention the book title in the subject of your message and email us at customercare@packtpub.com.

Errata: Although we have taken every care to ensure the accuracy of our content, mistakes do happen. If you have found a mistake in this book, we would be grateful if you would report this to us. Please visit www.packt.com/submit-errata, selecting your book, clicking on the Errata Submission Form link, and entering the details.

Piracy: If you come across any illegal copies of our works in any form on the Internet, we would be grateful if you would provide us with the location address or website name. Please contact us at copyright@packt.com with a link to the material.

If you are interested in becoming an author: If there is a topic that you have expertise in and you are interested in either writing or contributing to a book, please visit authors.packtpub.com.

Reviews

Please leave a review. Once you have read and used this book, why not leave a review on the site that you purchased it from? Potential readers can then see and use your unbiased opinion to make purchase decisions, we at Packt can understand what you think about our products, and our authors can see your feedback on their book. Thank you!

For more information about Packt, please visit packt.com.

Benchmarking and Profiling 1

Recognizing the slow parts of your program is the single most important task when it comes to speeding up your code. Luckily, in most cases, the code that causes the application to slow down is a very small fraction of the program. By locating those critical sections, you can focus on the parts that need improvement without wasting time in micro-optimization.

Profiling is the technique that allows us to pinpoint the most resource-intensive spots in an application. A **profiler** is a program that runs an application and monitors how long each function takes to execute, thus detecting the functions in which your application spends most of its time.

Python provides several tools to help us find these bottlenecks and measure important performance metrics. In this chapter, we will learn how to use the standard `cProfile` module and the `line_profiler` third-party package. We will also learn how to profile an application's memory consumption through the `memory_profiler` tool. Another useful tool that we will cover is *KCachegrind*, which can be used to graphically display the data produced by various profilers.

Benchmarks are small scripts used to assess the total execution time of your application. We will learn how to write benchmarks and how to accurately time your programs.

The list of topics we will cover in this chapter is as follows:

- General principles of high performance programming
- Writing tests and benchmarks
- The Unix `time` command
- The Python `timeit` module
- Testing and benchmarking with `pytest`
- Profiling your application
- The `cProfile` standard tool
- Interpreting profiling results with KCachegrind

- `line_profiler` and `memory_profiler` tools
- Disassembling Python code through the `dis` module

Designing your application

When designing a performance-intensive program, the very first step is to write your code without bothering with small optimizations:

"Premature optimization is the root of all evil."

- Donald Knuth

In the early development stages, the design of the program can change quickly and may require large rewrites and reorganizations of the code base. By testing different prototypes without the burden of optimization, you are free to devote your time and energy to ensure that the program produces correct results and that the design is flexible. After all, who needs an application that runs fast but gives the wrong answer?

The mantras that you should remember when optimizing your code are as follows:

- **Make it run**: We have to get the software in a working state, and ensure that it produces the correct results. This exploratory phase serves to better understand the application and to spot major design issues in the early stages.
- **Make it right**: We want to ensure that the design of the program is solid. Refactoring should be done before attempting any performance optimization. This really helps separate the application into independent and cohesive units that are easier to maintain.
- **Make it fast**: Once our program is working and is well structured, we can focus on performance optimization. We may also want to optimize memory usage if that constitutes an issue.

In this section, we will write and profile a *particle simulator* test application. The **simulator** is a program that takes some particles and simulates their movement over time according to a set of laws that we impose. These particles can be abstract entities or correspond to physical objects, for example, billiard balls moving on a table, molecules in gas, stars moving through space, smoke particles, fluids in a chamber, and so on.

Computer simulations are useful in fields such as Physics, Chemistry, Astronomy, and many other disciplines. The applications used to simulate systems are particularly performance-intensive and scientists and engineers spend an inordinate amount of time optimizing these codes. In order to study realistic systems, it is often necessary to simulate a very high number of bodies and every small increase in performance counts.

In our first example, we will simulate a system containing particles that constantly rotate around a central point at various speeds, just like the hands of a clock.

The necessary information to run our simulation will be the starting positions of the particles, the speed, and the rotation direction. From these elements, we have to calculate the position of the particle in the next instant of time. An example system is shown in the following figure. The origin of the system is the (0, 0) point, the position is indicated by the **x, y** vector and the velocity is indicated by the **vx, vy** vector:

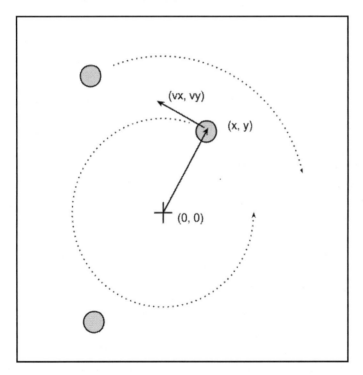

The basic feature of a circular motion is that the particles always move perpendicular to the direction connecting the particle and the center. To move the particle, we simply change the position by taking a series of very small steps (which correspond to advancing the system for a small interval of time) in the direction of motion, as shown in the following figure:

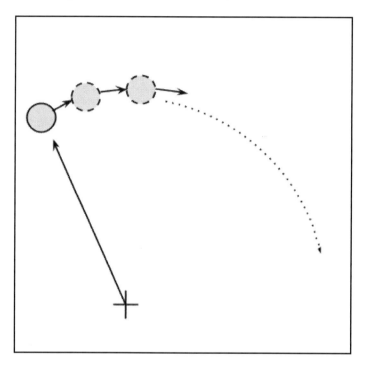

We will start by designing the application in an object-oriented way. According to our requirements, it is natural to have a generic `Particle` class that stores the particle positions, x and y, and their angular velocity, `ang_vel`:

```
class Particle:
    def __init__(self, x, y, ang_vel):
        self.x = x
        self.y = y
        self.ang_vel = ang_vel
```

Note that we accept positive and negative numbers for all the parameters (the sign of `ang_vel` will simply determine the direction of rotation).

Another class, called `ParticleSimulator`, will encapsulate the laws of motion and will be responsible for changing the positions of the particles over time. The `__init__` method will store a list of `Particle` instances and the `evolve` method will change the particle positions according to our laws.

We want the particles to rotate around the position corresponding to the x=0 and y=0 coordinates, at a constant speed. The direction of the particles will always be perpendicular to the direction from the center (refer to the first figure of this chapter). To find the direction of the movement along the *x* and *y* axes (corresponding to the Python `v_x` and `v_y` variables), it is sufficient to use these formulae:

```
v_x = -y / (x**2 + y**2)**0.5
v_y = x / (x**2 + y**2)**0.5
```

If we let one of our particles move, after a certain time *t*, it will reach another position following a circular path. We can approximate a circular trajectory by dividing the time interval, *t*, into tiny time steps, *dt*, where the particle moves in a straight line tangentially to the circle. The final result is just an approximation of a circular motion. In order to avoid a strong divergence, such as the one illustrated in the following figure, it is necessary to take very small time steps:

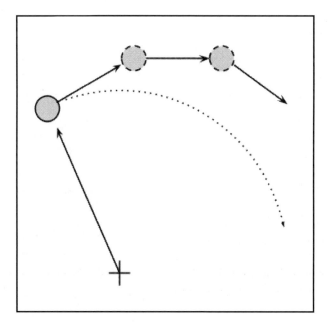

In a more schematic way, we have to carry out the following steps to calculate the particle position at time t:

1. Calculate the direction of motion (v_x and v_y).
2. Calculate the displacement (d_x and d_y), which is the product of time step, angular velocity, and direction of motion.
3. Repeat steps 1 and 2 for enough times to cover the total time t.

The following code shows the full `ParticleSimulator` implementation:

```
class ParticleSimulator:

    def __init__(self, particles):
        self.particles = particles

    def evolve(self, dt):
        timestep = 0.00001
        nsteps = int(dt/timestep)
        for i in range(nsteps):
            for p in self.particles:
                # 1. calculate the direction
                norm = (p.x**2 + p.y**2)**0.5
                v_x = -p.y/norm
                v_y = p.x/norm

                # 2. calculate the displacement
                d_x = timestep * p.ang_vel * v_x
                d_y = timestep * p.ang_vel * v_y

                p.x += d_x
                p.y += d_y
                # 3. repeat for all the time steps
```

We can use the `matplotlib` library to visualize our particles. This library is not included in the Python standard library, and it can be easily installed using the `pip install matplotlib` command.

Alternatively, you can use the Anaconda Python distribution (`https://store.continuum.io/cshop/anaconda/`) that includes `matplotlib` and most of the other third-party packages used in this book. Anaconda is free and is available for Linux, Windows, and Mac.

To make an interactive visualization, we will use the `matplotlib.pyplot.plot` function to display the particles as points and the `matplotlib.animation.FuncAnimation` class to animate the evolution of the particles over time.

The `visualize` function takes a particle `ParticleSimulator` instance as an argument and displays the trajectory in an animated plot. The steps necessary to display the particle trajectory using the `matplotlib` tools are as follows:

- Set up the axes and use the `plot` function to display the particles. `plot` takes a list of *x* and *y* coordinates.
- Write an initialization function, `init`, and a function, `animate`, that updates the *x* and *y* coordinates using the `line.set_data` method.
- Create a `FuncAnimation` instance by passing the `init` and `animate` functions plus the `interval` parameters, which specify the update interval, and `blit`, which improves the update rate of the image.
- Run the animation with `plt.show()`:

```python
from matplotlib import pyplot as plt
from matplotlib import animation

def visualize(simulator):

    X = [p.x for p in simulator.particles]
    Y = [p.y for p in simulator.particles]

    fig = plt.figure()
    ax = plt.subplot(111, aspect='equal')
    line, = ax.plot(X, Y, 'ro')
    # Axis limits
    plt.xlim(-1, 1)
    plt.ylim(-1, 1)

    # It will be run when the animation starts
    def init():
        line.set_data([], [])
        return line, # The comma is important!

    def animate(i):
        # We let the particle evolve for 0.01 time units
        simulator.evolve(0.01)
        X = [p.x for p in simulator.particles]
        Y = [p.y for p in simulator.particles]

        line.set_data(X, Y)
        return line,
```

```
# Call the animate function each 10 ms
anim = animation.FuncAnimation(fig,
                               animate,
                               init_func=init,
                               blit=True,
                               interval=10)
plt.show()
```

To test things out, we define a small function, `test_visualize`, that animates a system of three particles rotating in different directions. Note that the third particle completes a round three times faster than the others:

```
def test_visualize():
    particles = [Particle(0.3, 0.5, 1),
                 Particle(0.0, -0.5, -1),
                 Particle(-0.1, -0.4, 3)]

    simulator = ParticleSimulator(particles)
    visualize(simulator)

if __name__ == '__main__':
    test_visualize()
```

The `test_visualize` function is helpful to graphically understand the system time evolution. In the following section, we will write more test functions to properly verify program correctness and measure performance.

Writing tests and benchmarks

Now that we have a working simulator, we can start measuring our performance and tune-up our code so that the simulator can handle as many particles as possible. As a first step, we will write a test and a benchmark.

We need a test that checks whether the results produced by the simulation are correct or not. Optimizing a program commonly requires employing multiple strategies; as we rewrite our code multiple times, bugs may easily be introduced. A solid test suite ensures that the implementation is correct at every iteration so that we are free to go wild and try different things with the confidence that, if the test suite passes, the code will still work as expected.

Our test will take three particles, simulate them for 0.1 time units, and compare the results with those from a reference implementation. A good way to organize your tests is using a separate function for each different aspect (or unit) of your application. Since our current functionality is included in the `evolve` method, our function will be named `test_evolve`. The following code shows the `test_evolve` implementation. Note that, in this case, we compare floating point numbers up to a certain precision through the `fequal` function:

```python
def test_evolve():
    particles = [Particle( 0.3,  0.5, +1),
                 Particle( 0.0, -0.5, -1),
                 Particle(-0.1, -0.4, +3)]

    simulator = ParticleSimulator(particles)

    simulator.evolve(0.1)

    p0, p1, p2 = particles

    def fequal(a, b, eps=1e-5):
        return abs(a - b) < eps

    assert fequal(p0.x,  0.210269)
    assert fequal(p0.y,  0.543863)

    assert fequal(p1.x, -0.099334)
    assert fequal(p1.y, -0.490034)

    assert fequal(p2.x,  0.191358)
    assert fequal(p2.y, -0.365227)

if __name__ == '__main__':
    test_evolve()
```

A test ensures the correctness of our functionality but gives little information about its running time. A benchmark is a simple and representative use case that can be run to assess the running time of an application. Benchmarks are very useful to keep score of how fast our program is with each new version that we implement.

We can write a representative benchmark by instantiating a thousand `Particle` objects with random coordinates and angular velocity, and feed them to a `ParticleSimulator` class. We then let the system evolve for 0.1 time units:

```python
from random import uniform

def benchmark():
    particles = [Particle(uniform(-1.0, 1.0),
```

```
                              uniform(-1.0, 1.0),
                              uniform(-1.0, 1.0))
                  for i in range(1000)]

        simulator = ParticleSimulator(particles)
        simulator.evolve(0.1)

    if __name__ == '__main__':
        benchmark()
```

Timing your benchmark

A very simple way to time a benchmark is through the Unix time command. Using the time command, as follows, you can easily measure the execution time of an arbitrary process:

```
    $ time python simul.py
real    0m1.051s
user    0m1.022s
sys     0m0.028s
```

 The time command is not available for Windows. To install Unix tools, such as time, on Windows you can use the cygwin shell, downloadable from the official website (http://www.cygwin.com/). Alternatively, you can use similar PowerShell commands, such as Measure-Command (https://msdn.microsoft.com/en-us/powershell/reference/5.1/microsoft.powershell.utility/measure-command), to measure execution time.

By default, time displays three metrics:

- real: The actual time spent running the process from start to finish, as if it was measured by a human with a stopwatch
- user: The cumulative time spent by all the CPUs during the computation
- sys: The cumulative time spent by all the CPUs during system-related tasks, such as memory allocation

Note that sometimes user + sys might be greater than real, as multiple processors may work in parallel.

time also offers richer formatting options. For an overview, you can explore its manual (using the man time command). If you want a summary of all the metrics available, you can use the -v option.

The Unix time command is one of the simplest and more direct ways to benchmark a program. For an accurate measurement, the benchmark should be designed to have a long enough execution time (in the order of seconds) so that the setup and tear-down of the process is small compared to the execution time of the application. The user metric is suitable as a monitor for the CPU performance, while the real metric also includes the time spent in other processes while waiting for I/O operations.

Another convenient way to time Python scripts is the timeit module. This module runs a snippet of code in a loop for *n* times and measures the total execution times. Then, it repeats the same operation *r* times (by default, the value of *r* is 3) and records the time of the best run. Due to this timing scheme, timeit is an appropriate tool to accurately time small statements in isolation.

The timeit module can be used as a Python package, from the command line or from *IPython*.

IPython is a Python shell design that improves the interactivity of the Python interpreter. It boosts tab completion and many utilities to time, profile, and debug your code. We will use this shell to try out snippets throughout the book. The IPython shell accepts **magic commands**--statements that start with a % symbol--that enhance the shell with special behaviors. Commands that start with %% are called **cell magics**, which can be applied on multi-line snippets (termed as **cells**).

IPython is available on most Linux distributions through pip and is included in Anaconda.

You can use IPython as a regular Python shell (ipython), but it is also available in a Qt-based version (ipython qtconsole) and as a powerful browser-based interface (jupyter notebook).

In IPython and command-line interfaces, it is possible to specify the number of loops or repetitions with the −n and −r options. If not specified, they will be automatically inferred by timeit. When invoking timeit from the command line, you can also pass some setup code, through the −s option, which will execute before the benchmark. In the following snippet, the IPython command line and Python module version of timeit are demonstrated:

```
# IPython Interface
$ ipython
In [1]: from simul import benchmark
In [2]: %timeit benchmark()
1 loops, best of 3: 782 ms per loop

# Command Line Interface
$ python -m timeit -s 'from simul import benchmark' 'benchmark()'
10 loops, best of 3: 826 msec per loop

# Python Interface
# put this function into the simul.py script

import timeit
result = timeit.timeit('benchmark()',
 setup='from __main__ import benchmark',
 number=10)

# result is the time (in seconds) to run the whole loop
result = timeit.repeat('benchmark()',
 setup='from __main__ import benchmark',
 number=10,
 repeat=3)
# result is a list containing the time of each repetition (repeat=3 in this
case)
```

Note that while the command line and IPython interfaces automatically infer a reasonable number of loops n, the Python interface requires you to explicitly specify a value through the number argument.

Better tests and benchmarks with pytest-benchmark

The Unix `time` command is a versatile tool that can be used to assess the running time of small programs on a variety of platforms. For larger Python applications and libraries, a more comprehensive solution that deals with both testing and benchmarking is `pytest`, in combination with its `pytest-benchmark` plugin.

In this section, we will write a simple benchmark for our application using the `pytest` testing framework. For the interested reader, the `pytest` documentation, which can be found at `http://doc.pytest.org/en/latest/`, is the best resource to learn more about the framework and its uses.

 You can install `pytest` from the console using the `pip install pytest` command. The benchmarking plugin can be installed, similarly, by issuing the `pip install pytest-benchmark` command.

A testing framework is a set of tools that simplifies writing, executing, and debugging tests and provides rich reports and summaries of the test results. When using the `pytest` framework, it is recommended to place tests separately from the application code. In the following example, we create the `test_simul.py` file, which contains the `test_evolve` function:

```python
from simul import Particle, ParticleSimulator

def test_evolve():
    particles = [Particle( 0.3,  0.5, +1),
                 Particle( 0.0, -0.5, -1),
                 Particle(-0.1, -0.4, +3)]

    simulator = ParticleSimulator(particles)

    simulator.evolve(0.1)
    p0, p1, p2 = particles

    def fequal(a, b, eps=1e-5):
        return abs(a - b) < eps

    assert fequal(p0.x, 0.210269)
    assert fequal(p0.y, 0.543863)

    assert fequal(p1.x, -0.099334)
    assert fequal(p1.y, -0.490034)
```

```
assert fequal(p2.x,  0.191358)
assert fequal(p2.y, -0.365227)
```

The `pytest` executable can be used from the command line to discover and run tests contained in Python modules. To execute a specific test, we can use the `pytest path/to/module.py::function_name` syntax. To execute `test_evolve`, we can type the following command in a console to obtain simple but informative output:

```
$ pytest test_simul.py::test_evolve

platform linux -- Python 3.5.2, pytest-3.0.5, py-1.4.32, pluggy-0.4.0
rootdir: /home/gabriele/workspace/hiperf/chapter1, inifile: plugins:
collected 2 items

test_simul.py .

=========================== 1 passed in 0.43 seconds
===========================
```

Once we have a test in place, it is possible for you to execute your test as a benchmark using the `pytest-benchmark` plugin. If we change our `test` function so that it accepts an argument named `benchmark`, the `pytest` framework will automatically pass the `benchmark` resource as an argument (in `pytest` terminology, these resources are called *fixtures*). The benchmark resource can be called by passing the function that we intend to benchmark as the first argument, followed by the additional arguments. In the following snippet, we illustrate the edits necessary to benchmark the `ParticleSimulator.evolve` function:

```
from simul import Particle, ParticleSimulator

def test_evolve(benchmark):
    # ... previous code
    benchmark(simulator.evolve, 0.1)
```

To run the benchmark, it is sufficient to rerun the `pytest`
`test_simul.py::test_evolve` command. The resulting output will contain detailed
timing information regarding the `test_evolve` function, as shown:

```
========================================= test session starts =========================================
platform linux -- Python 3.5.2, pytest-3.0.5, py-1.4.32, pluggy-0.4.0
benchmark: 3.0.0 (defaults: timer=time.perf_counter disable_gc=False min_rounds=5 min_time=5.00us max_time=1.00s cal
ibration_precision=10 warmup=False warmup_iterations=100000)
rootdir: /home/gabriele/workspace/hiperf/chapter1, inifile:
plugins: benchmark-3.0.0
collected 2 items

test_simul.py .


------------------------------------------- benchmark: 1 tests -------------------------------------------
Name (time in ms)        Min       Max     Mean   StdDev   Median      IQR  Outliers(*)  Rounds  Iterations
---------------------------------------------------------------------------------------------------------
test_evolve          29.4716   41.1791  30.4622   2.0234  29.9630   0.7376          2;2      34           1
---------------------------------------------------------------------------------------------------------

(*) Outliers: 1 Standard Deviation from Mean; 1.5 IQR (InterQuartile Range) from 1st Quartile and 3rd Quartile.
========================================= 1 passed in 2.52 seconds =========================================
```

For each test collected, `pytest-benchmark` will execute the benchmark function several
times and provide a statistic summary of its running time. The output shown earlier is very
interesting as it shows how running times vary between runs.

In this example, the benchmark in `test_evolve` was run `34` times (column `Rounds`), its
timings ranged between `29` and `41` ms (`Min` and `Max`), and the `Average` and `Median` times
were fairly similar at about `30` ms, which is actually very close to the best timing obtained.
This example demonstrates how there can be substantial performance variability between
runs, and that when taking timings with one-shot tools such as `time`, it is a good idea to
run the program multiple times and record a representative value, such as the minimum or
the median.

`pytest-benchmark` has many more features and options that can be used to take accurate
timings and analyze the results. For more information, consult the documentation at `http:/`
`/pytest-benchmark.readthedocs.io/en/stable/usage.html`.

Finding bottlenecks with cProfile

After assessing the correctness and timing the execution time of the program, we are ready to identify the parts of the code that need to be tuned for performance. Those parts are typically quite small compared to the size of the program.

Two profiling modules are available through the Python standard library:

- **The** `profile` **module**: This module is written in pure Python and adds a significant overhead to the program execution. Its presence in the standard library is because of its vast platform support and because it is easier to extend.
- **The** `cProfile` **module**: This is the main profiling module, with an interface equivalent to `profile`. It is written in C, has a small overhead, and is suitable as a general purpose profiler.

The `cProfile` module can be used in three different ways:

- From the command line
- As a Python module
- With IPython

`cProfile` does not require any change in the source code and can be executed directly on an existing Python script or function. You can use `cProfile` from the command line in this way:

```
$ python -m cProfile simul.py
```

This will print a long output containing several profiling metrics of all of the functions called in the application. You can use the `-s` option to sort the output by a specific metric. In the following snippet ,the output is sorted by the `tottime` metric, which will be described here:

```
$ python -m cProfile -s tottime simul.py
```

The data produced by `cProfile` can be saved in an output file by passing the `-o` option. The format that `cProfile` uses is readable by the `stats` module and other tools. The usage of the `-o` option is as follows:

```
$ python -m cProfile -o prof.out simul.py
```

The usage of cProfile as a Python module requires invoking the `cProfile.run` function in the following way:

```
from simul import benchmark
import cProfile


cProfile.run("benchmark()")
```

You can also wrap a section of code between method calls of a `cProfile.Profile` object, as shown:

```
from simul import benchmark
import cProfile


pr = cProfile.Profile()
pr.enable()
benchmark()
pr.disable()
pr.print_stats()
```

cProfile can also be used interactively with IPython. The `%prun` magic command lets you profile an individual function call, as illustrated:

```
● ● ●   IPython: chapter1/codes
(hperf) → codes ipython
Python 3.5.2 |Continuum Analytics, Inc.| (default, Jul  2 2016, 17:53:06)
Type "copyright", "credits" or "license" for more information.

IPython 5.1.0 -- An enhanced Interactive Python.
?           -> Introduction and overview of IPython's features.
%quickref -> Quick reference.
help        -> Python's own help system.
object?     -> Details about 'object', use 'object??' for extra details.

In [1]: from simul import benchmark

In [2]: %prun benchmark()
        707 function calls in 1.231 seconds

  Ordered by: internal time

  ncalls  tottime  percall  cumtime  percall filename:lineno(function)
       1    1.230    1.230    1.230    1.230 simul.py:21(evolve)
       1    0.000    0.000    0.001    0.001 simul.py:118(<listcomp>)
     300    0.000    0.000    0.000    0.000 random.py:342(uniform)
     100    0.000    0.000    0.000    0.000 simul.py:10(__init__)
     300    0.000    0.000    0.000    0.000 {method 'random' of '_random.Random' objects}
       1    0.000    0.000    1.231    1.231 {built-in method builtins.exec}
       1    0.000    0.000    1.231    1.231 <string>:1(<module>)
       1    0.000    0.000    1.231    1.231 simul.py:117(benchmark)
       1    0.000    0.000    0.000    0.000 simul.py:18(__init__)
       1    0.000    0.000    0.000    0.000 {method 'disable' of '_lsprof.Profiler' objects}

In [3]:
```

The `cProfile` output is divided into five columns:

- `ncalls`: The number of times the function was called.
- `tottime`: The total time spent in the function without taking into account the calls to other functions.
- `cumtime`: The time in the function including other function calls.
- `percall`: The time spent for a single call of the function--it can be obtained by dividing the total or cumulative time by the number of calls.
- `filename:lineno`: The filename and corresponding line numbers. This information is not available when calling C extensions modules.

The most important metric is `tottime`, the actual time spent in the function body excluding subcalls, which tell us exactly where the bottleneck is.

Unsurprisingly, the largest portion of time is spent in the `evolve` function. We can imagine that the loop is the section of the code that needs performance tuning. `cProfile` only provides information at the function level and does not tell us which specific statements are responsible for the bottleneck. Fortunately, as we will see in the next section, the `line_profiler` tool is capable of providing line-by-line information of the time spent in the function.

Analyzing the `cProfile` text output can be daunting for big programs with a lot of calls and subcalls. Some visual tools aid the task by improving navigation with an interactive, graphical interface.

KCachegrind is a **Graphical User Interface (GUI)** useful to analyze the profiling output emitted by `cProfile`.

 KCachegrind is available in the Ubuntu 16.04 official repositories. The Qt port, QCacheGrind, can be downloaded for Windows from `http://sourceforge.net/projects/qcachegrindwin/`. Mac users can compile QCacheGrind using Mac Ports (`http://www.macports.org/`) by following the instructions present in the blog post at `http://blogs.perl.org/users/rurban/2013/04/install-kachegrind-on-macosx-with-ports.html`.

KCachegrind can't directly read the output files produced by `cProfile`. Luckily, the `pyprof2calltree` third-party Python module is able to convert the `cProfile` output file into a format readable by KCachegrind.

You can install `pyprof2calltree` from the Python Package Index using the command `pip install pyprof2calltree`.

To best show the KCachegrind features, we will use another example with a more diversified structure. We define a `recursive` function, `factorial`, and two other functions that use `factorial`, named `taylor_exp` and `taylor_sin`. They represent the polynomial coefficients of the Taylor approximations of `exp(x)` and `sin(x)`:

```python
def factorial(n):
    if n == 0:
        return 1.0
    else:
        return n * factorial(n-1)

def taylor_exp(n):
    return [1.0/factorial(i) for i in range(n)]

def taylor_sin(n):
    res = []
    for i in range(n):
        if i % 2 == 1:
            res.append((-1)**((i-1)/2)/float(factorial(i)))
        else:
            res.append(0.0)
    return res

def benchmark():
    taylor_exp(500)
    taylor_sin(500)

if __name__ == '__main__':
    benchmark()
```

To access profile information, we first need to generate the `cProfile` output file:

```
$ python -m cProfile -o prof.out taylor.py
```

Then, we can convert the output file with `pyprof2calltree` and launch KCachegrind:

```
$ pyprof2calltree -i prof.out -o prof.calltree
$ kcachegrind prof.calltree # or qcachegrind prof.calltree
```

The output is shown in the following screenshot:

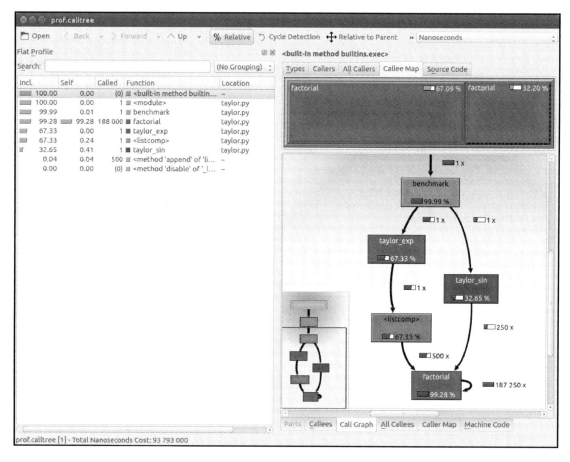

The preceding screenshot shows the KCachegrind user interface. On the left, we have an output fairly similar to cProfile. The actual column names are slightly different: **Incl.** translates to cProfile module's cumtime and **Self** translates to tottime. The values are given in percentages by clicking on the **Relative** button on the menu bar. By clicking on the column headers, you can sort them by the corresponding property.

On the top right, a click on the **Callee Map** tab will display a diagram of the function costs. In the diagram, the time percentage spent by the function is proportional to the area of the rectangle. Rectangles can contain sub-rectangles that represent subcalls to other functions. In this case, we can easily see that there are two rectangles for the factorial function. The one on the left corresponds to the calls made by taylor_exp and the one on the right to the calls made by taylor_sin.

On the bottom right, you can display another diagram, the *call graph*, by clicking on the **Call Graph** tab. A call graph is a graphical representation of the calling relationship between the functions; each square represents a function and the arrows imply a calling relationship. For example, `taylor_exp` calls `factorial` **500** times, and `taylor_sin` calls factorial **250** times. KCachegrind also detects recursive calls: `factorial` calls itself **187250** times.

You can navigate to the **Call Graph** or the **Caller Map** tab by double-clicking on the rectangles; the interface will update accordingly, showing that the timing properties are relative to the selected function. For example, double-clicking on `taylor_exp` will cause the graph to change, showing only the contribution of `taylor_exp` to the total cost.

 Gprof2Dot (`https://github.com/jrfonseca/gprof2dot`) is another popular tool used to produce call graphs. Starting from output files produced by one of the supported profilers, it will generate a `.dot` diagram representing the call graph.

Profile line by line with line_profiler

Now that we know which function we have to optimize, we can use the `line_profiler` module that provides information on how time is spent in a line-by-line fashion. This is very useful in situations where it's difficult to determine which statements are costly. The `line_profiler` module is a third-party module that is available on the Python Package Index and can be installed by following the instructions at `https://github.com/rkern/line_profiler`.

In order to use `line_profiler`, we need to apply a `@profile` decorator to the functions we intend to monitor. Note that you don't have to import the `profile` function from another module as it gets injected in the global namespace when running the `kernprof.py` profiling script. To produce profiling output for our program, we need to add the `@profile` decorator to the `evolve` function:

```
@profile
def evolve(self, dt):
    # code
```

The `kernprof.py` script will produce an output file and will print the result of the profiling on the standard output. We should run the script with two options:

- `-l` to use the `line_profiler` function
- `-v` to immediately print the results on screen

The usage of `kernprof.py` is illustrated in the following line of code:

```
$ kernprof.py -l -v simul.py
```

It is also possible to run the profiler in an IPython shell for interactive editing. You should first load the `line_profiler` extension that will provide the `lprun` magic command. Using that command, you can avoid adding the `@profile` decorator:

```
IPython: chapter1/codes

In [1]: %load_ext line_profiler

In [2]: from simul import benchmark, ParticleSimulator

In [3]: %lprun -f ParticleSimulator.evolve benchmark()
Timer unit: 1e-06 s

Total time: 8.66675 s
File: /home/gabriele/workspace/hiperf/chapter1/codes/simul.py
Function: evolve at line 21

Line #      Hits         Time  Per Hit   % Time  Line Contents
==============================================================
    21                                           def evolve(self, dt):
    22         1            2      2.0      0.0       timestep = 0.00001
    23         1            4      4.0      0.0       nsteps = int(dt/timestep)
    24
    25     10001        12561      1.3      0.1       for i in range(nsteps):
    26   1010000       867457      0.9     10.0           for p in self.particles:
    27
    28   1000000      1859312      1.9     21.5               norm = (p.x**2 + p.y**2)**0.5
    29   1000000       972028      1.0     11.2               v_x = (-p.y)/norm
    30   1000000       921008      0.9     10.6               v_y = p.x/norm
    31
    32   1000000       982441      1.0     11.3               d_x = timestep * p.ang_vel * v_x
    33   1000000       974838      1.0     11.2               d_y = timestep * p.ang_vel * v_y
    34
    35   1000000      1058183      1.1     12.2               p.x += d_x
    36   1000000      1018915      1.0     11.8               p.y += d_y

In [4]:
```

The output is quite intuitive and is divided into six columns:

- `Line #`: The number of the line that was run
- `Hits`: The number of times that line was run
- `Time`: The execution time of the line in microseconds (`Time`)
- `Per Hit`: Time/hits
- `% Time`: Fraction of the total time spent executing that line
- `Line Contents`: The content of the line

By looking at the percentage column, we can get a pretty good idea of where the time is spent. In this case, there are a few statements in the `for` loop body with a cost of around 10-20 percent each.

Optimizing our code

Now that we have identified where exactly our application is spending most of its time, we can make some changes and assess the change in performance.

There are different ways to tune up our pure Python code. The way that produces the most remarkable results is to improve the *algorithms* used. In this case, instead of calculating the velocity and adding small steps, it will be more efficient (and correct as it is not an approximation) to express the equations of motion in terms of radius, r, and angle, alpha, (instead of x and y), and then calculate the points on a circle using the following equation:

```
x = r * cos(alpha)
y = r * sin(alpha)
```

Another way lies in minimizing the number of instructions. For example, we can precalculate the `timestep * p.ang_vel` factor that doesn't change with time. We can exchange the loop order (first we iterate on particles, then we iterate on time steps) and put the calculation of the factor outside the loop on the particles.

The line-by-line profiling also showed that even simple assignment operations can take a considerable amount of time. For example, the following statement takes more than 10 percent of the total time:

```
v_x = (-p.y)/norm
```

We can improve the performance of the loop by reducing the number of assignment operations performed. To do that, we can avoid intermediate variables by rewriting the expression into a single, slightly more complex statement (note that the right-hand side gets evaluated completely before being assigned to the variables):

```
p.x, p.y = p.x - t_x_ang*p.y/norm, p.y + t_x_ang * p.x/norm
```

This leads to the following code:

```
def evolve_fast(self, dt):
    timestep = 0.00001
    nsteps = int(dt/timestep)

    # Loop order is changed
    for p in self.particles:
        t_x_ang = timestep * p.ang_vel
        for i in range(nsteps):
            norm = (p.x**2 + p.y**2)**0.5
            p.x, p.y = (p.x - t_x_ang * p.y/norm,
                        p.y + t_x_ang * p.x/norm)
```

After applying the changes, we should verify that the result is still the same by running our test. We can then compare the execution times using our benchmark:

```
$ time python simul.py # Performance Tuned
real    0m0.756s
user    0m0.714s
sys     0m0.036s

$ time python simul.py # Original
real    0m0.863s
user    0m0.831s
sys     0m0.028s
```

As you can see, we obtained only a modest increment in speed by making a pure Python micro-optimization.

The dis module

Sometimes it's not easy to estimate how many operations a Python statement will take. In this section, we will dig into the Python internals to estimate the performance of individual statements. In the CPython interpreter, Python code is first converted to an intermediate representation, the **bytecode**, and then executed by the Python interpreter.

To inspect how the code is converted to bytecode, we can use the `dis` Python module (`dis` stands for disassemble). Its usage is really simple; all that is needed is to call the `dis.dis` function on the `ParticleSimulator.evolve` method:

```
import dis
from simul import ParticleSimulator
dis.dis(ParticleSimulator.evolve)
```

This will print, for each line in the function, a list of bytecode instructions. For example, the `v_x = (-p.y)/norm` statement is expanded in the following set of instructions:

```
29              85 LOAD_FAST                5 (p)
                88 LOAD_ATTR                4 (y)
                91 UNARY_NEGATIVE
                92 LOAD_FAST                6 (norm)
                95 BINARY_TRUE_DIVIDE
                96 STORE_FAST               7 (v_x)
```

`LOAD_FAST` loads a reference of the `p` variable onto the stack and `LOAD_ATTR` loads the `y` attribute of the item present on top of the stack. The other instructions, `UNARY_NEGATIVE` and `BINARY_TRUE_DIVIDE`, simply do arithmetic operations on top-of-stack items. Finally, the result is stored in `v_x` (`STORE_FAST`).

By analyzing the `dis` output, we can see that the first version of the loop produces 51 bytecode instructions while the second gets converted into 35 instructions.

The `dis` module helps discover how the statements get converted and serves mainly as an exploration and learning tool of the Python bytecode representation.

To improve our performance even further, we can keep trying to figure out other approaches to reduce the amount of instructions. It's clear, however, that this approach is ultimately limited by the speed of the Python interpreter and it is probably not the right tool for the job. In the following chapters, we will see how to speed up interpreter-limited calculations by executing fast specialized versions written in a lower level language (such as C or Fortran).

Profiling memory usage with memory_profiler

In some cases, high memory usage constitutes an issue. For example, if we want to handle a huge number of particles, we will incur a memory overhead due to the creation of many `Particle` instances.

The `memory_profiler` module summarizes, in a way similar to `line_profiler`, the memory usage of the process.

 The `memory_profiler` package is also available on the Python Package Index. You should also install the `psutil` module (`https://github.com/giampaolo/psutil`) as an optional dependency that will make `memory_profiler` considerably faster.

Just like `line_profiler`, `memory_profiler` also requires the instrumentation of the source code by placing a `@profile` decorator on the function we intend to monitor. In our case, we want to analyze the `benchmark` function.

We can slightly change `benchmark` to instantiate a considerable amount (100000) of `Particle` instances and decrease the simulation time:

```
def benchmark_memory():
    particles = [Particle(uniform(-1.0, 1.0),
                          uniform(-1.0, 1.0),
                          uniform(-1.0, 1.0))
                 for i in range(100000)]

    simulator = ParticleSimulator(particles)
    simulator.evolve(0.001)
```

We can use `memory_profiler` from an IPython shell through the `%mprun` magic command as shown in the following screenshot:

```
IPython: chapter1/codes

IPython 5.1.0 -- An enhanced Interactive Python.
?           -> Introduction and overview of IPython's features.
%quickref -> Quick reference.
help        -> Python's own help system.
object?     -> Details about 'object', use 'object??' for extra details.

In [1]: %load_ext memory_profiler

In [2]: from simul import benchmark_memory

In [3]: %mprun -f benchmark_memory benchmark_memory()
Filename: /home/gabriele/workspace/hiperf/chapter1/codes/simul.py

Line #    Mem usage    Increment   Line Contents
================================================
   142     37.8 MiB     0.0 MiB    def benchmark_memory():
   143     61.5 MiB    23.7 MiB        particles = [Particle(uniform(-1.0, 1.0),
   144                                                        uniform(-1.0, 1.0),
   145                                                        uniform(-1.0, 1.0))
   146     61.5 MiB     0.0 MiB                   for i in range(100000)]
   147
   148     61.5 MiB     0.0 MiB        simulator = ParticleSimulator(particles)
   149     61.5 MiB     0.0 MiB        simulator.evolve(0.001)

In [4]:
```

It is possible to run `memory_profiler` from the shell using the `mprof` run command after adding the `@profile` decorator.

From the `Increment` column, we can see that 100,000 `Particle` objects take `23.7 MiB` of memory.

1 MiB (mebibyte) is equivalent to 1,048,576 bytes. It is different from 1 MB (*megabyte*), which is equivalent to 1,000,000 bytes.

We can use __slots__ on the Particle class to reduce its memory footprint. This feature saves some memory by avoiding storing the variables of the instance in an internal dictionary. This strategy, however, has a drawback--it prevents the addition of attributes other than the ones specified in __slots__ :

```python
class Particle:
    __slots__ = ('x', 'y', 'ang_vel')

    def __init__(self, x, y, ang_vel):
        self.x = x
        self.y = y
        self.ang_vel = ang_vel
```

We can now rerun our benchmark to assess the change in memory consumption, the result is displayed in the following screenshot:

```
● ● ●   IPython: chapter1/codes

IPython 5.1.0 -- An enhanced Interactive Python.
?          -> Introduction and overview of IPython's features.
%quickref -> Quick reference.
help       -> Python's own help system.
object?    -> Details about 'object', use 'object??' for extra details.

In [1]: %load_ext memory_profiler

In [2]: from simul import benchmark_memory

In [3]: %mprun -f benchmark_memory benchmark_memory()
Filename: /home/gabriele/workspace/hiperf/chapter1/codes/simul.py

Line #    Mem usage    Increment   Line Contents
================================================
   142     38.0 MiB     0.0 MiB    def benchmark_memory():
   143     51.7 MiB    13.7 MiB        particles = [Particle(uniform(-1.0, 1.0),
   144                                                        uniform(-1.0, 1.0),
   145                                                        uniform(-1.0, 1.0))
   146     51.7 MiB     0.0 MiB                    for i in range(100000)]
   147
   148     51.7 MiB     0.0 MiB        simulator = ParticleSimulator(particles)
   149     51.7 MiB     0.0 MiB        simulator.evolve(0.001)

In [4]: ▊
```

By rewriting the Particle class using __slots__, we can save about 10 MiB of memory.

Summary

In this chapter, we introduced the basic principles of optimization and applied those principles to a test application. When optimizing, the first thing to do is test and identify the bottlenecks in the application. We saw how to write and time a benchmark using the `time` Unix command, the Python `timeit` module, and the full-fledged `pytest-benchmark` package. We learned how to profile our application using `cProfile`, `line_profiler`, and `memory_profiler`, and how to analyze and navigate the profiling data graphically with KCachegrind.

In the next chapter, we will explore how to improve performance using algorithms and data structures available in the Python standard library. We will cover scaling, sample usage of several data structures, and learn techniques such as caching and memoization.

Pure Python Optimizations

2

As mentioned in the last chapter, one of the most effective ways of improving the performance of applications is through the use of better algorithms and data structures. The Python standard library provides a large variety of ready-to-use algorithms and data structures that can be directly incorporated in your applications. With the tools learned from this chapter, you will be able to use the right algorithm for the task and achieve massive speed gains.

Even though many algorithms have been around for quite a while, they are especially relevant in today's world as we continuously produce, consume, and analyze ever increasing amounts of data. Buying a larger server or microoptimizing can work for some time, but achieving better scaling through algorithmic improvement can solve the problem once and for all.

In this chapter, we will understand how to achieve better scaling using standard algorithms and data structures. More advanced use cases will also be covered by taking advantage of third-party libraries. We will also learn about tools to implement caching, a technique used to achieve faster response times by sacrificing some space on memory or on disk.

The list of topics to be covered in this chapter is as follows:

- Introduction to computational complexity
- Lists and deques
- Dictionaries
- How to build an inverted index using a dictionary
- Sets
- Heaps and priority queues
- Implementing autocompletion using tries
- Introduction to caching
- In-memory caching with the `functools.lru_cache` decorator
- On-disk cache with `joblib.Memory`
- Fast and memory-efficient loops with comprehensions and generators

Useful algorithms and data structures

Algorithmic improvements are especially effective in increasing performance because they typically allow the application to scale better with increasingly large inputs.

Algorithm running times can be classified according to their computational complexity, a characterization of the resources required to perform a task. Such classification is expressed through the Big-O notation, an upper bound on the operations required to execute the task, which usually depends on the input size.

For example, incrementing each element of a list can be implemented using a `for` loop, as follows:

```
input = list(range(10))
for i, _ in enumerate(input):
    input[i] += 1
```

If the operation does not depend on the size of the input (for example, accessing the first element of a list), the algorithm is said to take constant, or $O(1)$, time. This means that, no matter how much data we have, the time to run the algorithm will always be the same.

In this simple algorithm, the `input[i] += 1` operation will be repeated 10 times, which is the size of the input. If we double the size of the input array, the number of operations will increase proportionally. Since the number of operations is proportional to the input size, this algorithm is said to take $O(N)$ time, where N is the size of the input array.

In some instances, the running time may depend on the structure of the input (for example, if the collection is sorted or contains many duplicates). In these cases, an algorithm may have different best-case, average-case, and worst-case running times. Unless stated otherwise, the running times presented in this chapter are considered to be average running times.

In this section, we will examine the running times of the main algorithms and data structures that are implemented in the Python standard library, and understand how improving running times results in massive gains and allows us to solve large-scale problems with elegance.

You can find the code used to run the benchmarks in this chapter in the `Algorithms.ipynb` notebook, which can be opened using Jupyter.

Lists and deques

Python lists are ordered collections of elements and, in Python, are implemented as resizable arrays. An array is a basic data structure that consists of a series of contiguous memory locations, and each location contains a reference to a Python object.

Lists shine in accessing, modifying, and appending elements. Accessing or modifying an element involves fetching the object reference from the appropriate position of the underlying array and has complexity $O(1)$. Appending an element is also very fast. When an empty list is created, an array of fixed size is allocated and, as we insert elements, the slots in the array are gradually filled up. Once all the slots are occupied, the list needs to increase the size of its underlying array, thus triggering a memory reallocation that can take $O(N)$ time. Nevertheless, those memory allocations are infrequent, and the time complexity for the append operation is referred to as amortized $O(1)$ time.

The list operations that may have efficiency problems are those that add or remove elements at the beginning (or somewhere in the middle) of the list. When an item is inserted, or removed, from the beginning of a list, all the subsequent elements of the array need to be shifted by a position, thus taking $O(N)$ time.

In the following table, the timings for different operations on a list of size 10,000 are shown; you can see how insertion and removal performances vary quite dramatically if performed at the beginning or at the end of the list:

Code	N=10000 (µs)	N=20000 (µs)	N=30000 (µs)	Time
list.pop()	0.50	0.59	0.58	$O(1)$
list.pop(0)	4.20	8.36	12.09	$O(N)$
list.append(1)	0.43	0.45	0.46	$O(1)$
list.insert(0, 1)	6.20	11.97	17.41	$O(N)$

In some cases, it is necessary to efficiently perform insertion or removal of elements both at the beginning and at the end of the collection. Python provides a data structure with those properties in the `collections.deque` class. The word **deque** stands for double-ended queue because this data structure is designed to efficiently put and remove elements at the beginning and at the end of the collection, as it is in the case of queues. In Python, deques are implemented as doubly-linked lists.

Deques, in addition to `pop` and `append`, expose the `popleft` and `appendleft` methods that have $O(1)$ running time:

Code	N=10000 (µs)	N=20000 (µs)	N=30000 (µs)	Time
`deque.pop()`	0.41	0.47	0.51	$O(1)$
`deque.popleft()`	0.39	0.51	0.47	$O(1)$
`deque.append(1)`	0.42	0.48	0.50	$O(1)$
`deque.appendleft(1)`	0.38	0.47	0.51	$O(1)$

Despite these advantages, deques should not be used to replace regular lists in most cases. The efficiency gained by the `appendleft` and `popleft` operations comes at a cost: accessing an element in the middle of a deque is a $O(N)$ operation, as shown in the following table:

Code	N=10000 (µs)	N=20000 (µs)	N=30000 (µs)	Time
`deque[0]`	0.37	0.41	0.45	$O(1)$
`deque[N - 1]`	0.37	0.42	0.43	$O(1)$
`deque[int(N / 2)]`	1.14	1.71	2.48	$O(N)$

Searching for an item in a list is generally a $O(N)$ operation and is performed using the `list.index` method. A simple way to speed up searches in lists is to keep the array sorted and perform a binary search using the `bisect` module.

The `bisect` module allows fast searches on sorted arrays. The `bisect.bisect` function can be used on a sorted list to find the index to place an element while maintaining the array in sorted order. In the following example, we can see that if we want to insert the 3 element in the array while keeping `collection` in sorted order, we should put 3 in the third position (which corresponds to index 2):

```
insert bisect
collection = [1, 2, 4, 5, 6]
bisect.bisect(collection, 3)
# Result: 2
```

This function uses the binary search algorithm that has $O(log(N))$ running time. Such a running time is exceptionally fast, and basically means that your running time will increase by a constant amount every time you *double* your input size. This means that if, for example, your program takes 1 second to run on an input of size 1000, it will take 2 seconds to process an input of size 2000, 3 seconds to process an input of size 4000, and so on. If you had 100 seconds, you could theoretically process an input of size 10^{33}, which is larger than the number of atoms in your body!

If the value we are trying to insert is already present in the list, the bisect.bisect function will return the location *after* the already present value. Therefore, we can use the bisect.bisect_left variant, which returns the correct index in the following way (taken from the module documentation at https://docs.python.org/3.5/library/bisect.html):

```
def index_bisect(a, x):
    'Locate the leftmost value exactly equal to x'
    i = bisect.bisect_left(a, x)
    if i != len(a) and a[i] == x:
    return i
    raise ValueError
```

In the following table, you can see how the running time of the bisect solution is barely affected at these input sizes, making it a suitable solution when searching through very large collections:

Code	N=10000 (µs)	N=20000 (µs)	N=30000 (µs)	Time
list.index(a)	87.55	171.06	263.17	$O(N)$
index_bisect(list, a)	3.16	3.20	4.71	$O(log(N))$

Dictionaries

Dictionaries are extremely versatile and extensively used in the Python language. Dictionaries are implemented as hash maps and are very good at element insertion, deletion, and access; all these operations have an average $O(1)$ time complexity.

In Python versions up to 3.5, dictionaries are unordered collections. Since Python 3.6, dictionaries are capable of maintaining their elements by order of insertion.

A hash map is a data structure that associates a set of key-value pairs. The principle behind hash maps is to assign a specific index to each key so that its associated value can be stored in an array. The index can be obtained through the use of a `hash` function; Python implements hash functions for several data types. As a demonstration, the generic function to obtain hash codes is `hash`. In the following example, we show you how to obtain the hash code given the `"hello"` string:

```python
hash("hello")
# Result: -1182655621190490452

# To restrict the number to be a certain range you can use
# the modulo (%) operator
hash("hello") % 10
# Result: 8
```

Hash maps can be tricky to implement because they need to handle collisions that happen when two different objects have the same hash code. However, all the complexity is elegantly hidden behind the implementation and the default collision resolution works well in most real-world scenarios.

Access, insertion, and removal of an item in a dictionary scales as $O(1)$ with the size of the dictionary. However, note that the computation of the hash function still needs to happen and, for strings, the computation scales with the length of the string. As string keys are usually relatively small, this doesn't constitute a problem in practice.

A dictionary can be used to efficiently count unique elements in a list. In this example, we define the `counter_dict` function that takes a list and returns a dictionary containing the number of occurrences of each value in the list:

```python
def counter_dict(items):
    counter = {}
    for item in items:
        if item not in counter:
            counter[item] = 1
        else:
            counter[item] += 1
    return counter
```

The code can be somewhat simplified using `collections.defaultdict`, which can be used to produce dictionaries where each new key is automatically assigned a default value. In the following code, the `defaultdict(int)` call produces a dictionary where every new element is automatically assigned a zero value, and can be used to streamline the counting:

```
from collections import defaultdict
def counter_defaultdict(items):
    counter = defaultdict(int)
    for item in items:
        counter[item] += 1
    return counter
```

The `collections` module also includes a `Counter` class that can be used for the same purpose with a single line of code:

```
from collections import Counter
counter = Counter(items)
```

Speed-wise, all these ways of counting have the same time complexity, but the `Counter` implementation is the most efficient, as shown in the following table:

Code	N=1000 (µs)	N=2000 (µs)	N=3000 (µs)	Time
`Counter(items)`	51.48	96.63	140.26	O(N)
`counter_dict(items)`	111.96	197.13	282.79	O(N)
`counter_defaultdict(items)`	120.90	238.27	359.60	O(N)

Building an in-memory search index using a hash map

Dictionaries can be used to quickly search for a word in a list of documents, similar to a search engine. In this subsection, we will learn how to build an inverted index based on a dictionary of lists. Let's say we have a collection of four documents:

```
docs = ["the cat is under the table",
        "the dog is under the table",
        "cats and dogs smell roses",
        "Carla eats an apple"]
```

A simple way to retrieve all the documents that match a query is to scan each document and test for the presence of a word. For example, if we want to look up the documents where the word `table` appears, we can employ the following filtering operation:

```
matches = [doc for doc in docs if "table" in doc]
```

This approach is simple and works well when we have one-off queries; however, if we need to query the collection very often, it can be beneficial to optimize querying time. Since the per-query cost of the linear scan is $O(N)$, you can imagine that a better scaling will allow us to handle much larger document collections.

A better strategy is to spend some time preprocessing the documents so that they are easier to find at query time. We can build a structure, called the **inverted index**, that associates each word in our collection with the list of documents where that word is present. In our earlier example, the word "table" will be associated to the "the cat is under the table" and "the dog is under the table" documents; they correspond to indices 0 and 1.

Such a mapping can be implemented by going over our collection of documents and storing in a dictionary the index of the documents where that term appears. The implementation is similar to the counter_dict function, except that, instead of accumulating a counter, we are growing the list of documents that match the current term:

```
# Building an index
index = {}
for i, doc in enumerate(docs):
    # We iterate over each term in the document
    for word in doc.split():
        # We build a list containing the indices
        # where the term appears
        if word not in index:
            index[word] = [i]
        else:
            index[word].append(i)
```

Once we have built our index, doing a query involves a simple dictionary lookup. For example, if we want to return all the documents containing the term table, we can simply query the index, and retrieve the corresponding documents:

```
results = index["table"]
result_documents = [docs[i] for i in results]
```

Since all it takes to query our collection is a dictionary access, the index can handle queries with time complexity $O(1)$! Thanks to the inverted index, we are now able to query any number of documents (as long as they fit in memory) in constant time. Needless to say, indexing is a technique widely used to quickly retrieve data not only in search engines, but also in databases and any system that requires fast searches.

Note that building an inverted index is an expensive operation and requires you to encode every possible query. This is a substantial drawback, but the benefits are great and it may be worthwhile to pay the price in terms of decreased flexibility.

Sets

Sets are unordered collections of elements, with the additional restriction that the elements must be unique. The main use-cases where sets are a good choice are membership tests (testing if an element is present in the collection) and, unsurprisingly, set operations such as union, difference, and intersection.

In Python, sets are implemented using a hash-based algorithm just like dictionaries; therefore, the time complexities for addition, deletion, and test for membership scale as $O(1)$ with the size of the collection.

Sets contain only unique elements. An immediate use case of sets is the removal of duplicates from a collection, which can be accomplished by simply passing the collection through the set constructor, as follows:

```
# create a list that contains duplicates
x = list(range(1000)) + list(range(500))
# the set *x_unique* will contain only
# the unique elements in x
x_unique = set(x)
```

The time complexity for removing duplicates is $O(N)$, as it requires to read the input and put each element in the set.

Sets expose a number of operations like union, intersection, and difference. The union of two sets is a new set containing all the elements of both the sets; the intersection is a new set that contains only the elements in common between the two sets, and the difference is a new set containing the element of the first set that are not contained in the second set. The time complexities for these operations are shown in the following table. Note that since we have two different input sizes, we will use the letter S to indicate the size of the first set (called s), and T to indicate the size of the second set (called t):

Code	Time
s.union(t)	$O(S + T)$
s.intersection(t)	$O(min(S, T))$
s.difference(t)	$O(S)$

An application of set operations are, for example, Boolean queries. Going back to the inverted index example of the previous subsection, we may want to support queries that include multiple terms. For example, we may want to search for all the documents that contain the words `cat` and `table`. This kind of a query can be efficiently computed by taking the intersection between the set of documents containing `cat` and the set of documents containing `table`.

In order to efficiently support those operations, we can change our indexing code so that each term is associated to a set of documents (rather than a list). After applying this change, calculating more advanced queries is a matter of applying the right set operation. In the following code, we show the inverted index based on sets and the query using set operations:

```python
# Building an index using sets
index = {}
for i, doc in enumerate(docs):
    # We iterate over each term in the document
    for word in doc.split():
        # We build a set containing the indices
        # where the term appears
        if word not in index:
            index[word] = {i}
        else:
            index[word].add(i)
# Querying the documents containing both "cat" and "table"
index['cat'].intersection(index['table'])
```

Heaps

Heaps are data structures designed to quickly find and extract the maximum (or minimum) value in a collection. A typical use-case for heaps is to process a series of incoming tasks in order of maximum priority.

One can theoretically use a sorted list using the tools in the `bisect` module; however, while extracting the maximum value will take $O(1)$ time (using `list.pop`), insertion will still take $O(N)$ time (remember that, even if finding the insertion point takes $O(log(N))$ time, inserting an element in the middle of a list is still a $O(N)$ operation). A heap is a more efficient data structure that allows for insertion and extraction of maximum values with $O(log(N))$ time complexity.

In Python, heaps are built using the procedures contained in the `heapq` module on an underlying list. For example, if we have a list of 10 elements, we can reorganize it into a heap with the `heapq.heapify` function:

```
import heapq

collection = [10, 3, 3, 4, 5, 6]
heapq.heapify(collection)
```

To perform the insertion and extraction operations on the heap, we can use the `heapq.heappush` and `heapq.heappop` functions. The `heapq.heappop` function will extract the minimum value in the collection in $O(log(N))$ time and can be used in the following way:

```
heapq.heappop(collection)
# Returns: 3
```

Similarly, you can push the integer 1, with the `heapq.heappush` function, as follows:

```
heapq.heappush(collection, 1)
```

Another easy-to-use option is the `queue.PriorityQueue` class that, as a bonus, is thread and process-safe. The `PriorityQueue` class can be filled up with elements using the `PriorityQueue.put` method, while `PriorityQueue.get` can be used to extract the minimum value in the collection:

```
from queue import PriorityQueue

queue = PriorityQueue()
for element in collection:
    queue.put(element)

queue.get()
# Returns: 3
```

If the maximum element is required, a simple trick is to multiply each element of the list by −1. In this way, the order of the elements will be inverted. Also, if you want to associate an object (for example, a task to run) to each number (which can represent the priority), one can insert tuples of the `(number, object)` form; the comparison operator for the tuple will be ordered with respect to its first element, as shown in the following example:

```
queue = PriorityQueue()
queue.put((3, "priority 3"))
queue.put((2, "priority 2"))
queue.put((1, "priority 1"))
```

```
queue.get()
# Returns: (1, "priority 1")
```

Tries

A perhaps less popular data structure, very useful in practice, is the trie (sometimes called prefix tree). Tries are extremely fast at matching a list of strings against a prefix. This is especially useful when implementing features such as search-as-you type and autocompletion, where the list of available completions is very large and short response times are required.

Unfortunately, Python does not include a trie implementation in its standard library; however, many efficient implementations are readily available through PyPI. The one we will use in this subsection is `patricia-trie`, a single-file, pure Python implementation of trie. As an example, we will use `patricia-trie` to perform the task of finding the longest prefix in a set of strings (just like autocompletion).

As an example, we can demonstrate how fast a trie is able to search through a list of strings. In order to generate a large amount of unique random strings, we can define a function, `random_string`. The `random_string` function will return a string composed of random uppercase characters and, while there is a chance to get duplicates, we can greatly reduce the probability of duplicates to the point of being negligible if we make the string long enough. The implementation of the `random_string` function is shown as follows:

```python
from random import choice
from string import ascii_uppercase

def random_string(length):
    """Produce a random string made of *length* uppercase ascii
    characters"""
    return ''.join(choice(ascii_uppercase) for i in range(length))
```

We can build a list of random strings and time how fast it searches for a prefix (in our case, the "AA" string) using the `str.startswith` function:

```python
strings = [random_string(32) for i in range(10000)]
matches = [s for s in strings if s.startswith('AA')]
```

List comprehension and `str.startwith` are already very optimized operations and, on this small dataset, the search takes only a millisecond or so:

```python
%timeit [s for s in strings if s.startswith('AA')]

1000 loops, best of 3: 1.76 ms per loop
```

Now, let's try using a trie for the same operation. In this example, we will use the `patricia-trie` library that is installable through `pip`. The `patricia.trie` class implements a variant of the trie data structure with an interface similar to a dictionary. We can initialize our trie by creating a dictionary from our list of strings, as follows:

```
from patricia import trie
strings_dict = {s:0 for s in strings}
# A dictionary where all values are 0
strings_trie = trie(**strings_dict)
```

To query `patricia-trie` for a matching prefix, we can use the `trie.iter` method, which returns an iterator over the matching strings:

```
matches = list(strings_trie.iter('AA'))
```

Now that we know how to initialize and query a trie, we can time the operation:

```
%timeit list(strings_trie.iter('AA'))
10000 loops, best of 3: 60.1 µs per loop
```

If you look closely, the timing for this input size is **60.1 µs**, which is about 30 times faster (1.76 ms = 1760 µs) than linear search! The speed up is so impressive because of the better computational complexity of the trie prefix search. Querying a trie has a time complexity $O(S)$, where S is the length of the longest string in the collection, while the time complexity of a simple linear scan is $O(N)$, where N is the size of the collection.

Note that if we want to return all the prefixes that match, the running time will be proportional to the number of results that match the prefix. Therefore, when designing timing benchmarks, care must be taken to ensure that we are always returning the same number of results.

The scaling properties of a trie versus a linear scan for datasets of different sizes that contains ten prefix matches are shown in the following table:

Algorithm	N=10000 (µs)	N=20000 (µs)	N=30000 (µs)	Time
Trie	17.12	17.27	17.47	$O(S)$
Linear scan	1978.44	4075.72	6398.06	$O(N)$

An interesting fact is that the implementation of `patricia-trie` is actually a single Python file; this clearly shows how simple and powerful a clever algorithm can be. For extra features and performance, other C-optimized trie libraries are also available, such as `datrie` and `marisa-trie`.

Caching and memoization

Caching is a great technique used to improve the performance of a wide range of applications. The idea behind caching is to store expensive results in a temporary location, called cache, that can be located in memory, on-disk, or in a remote location.

Web applications make extensive use of caching. In a web application, it often happens that users request a certain page at the same time. In this case, instead of recomputing the page for each user, the web application can compute it once and serve the user the already rendered page. Ideally, caching also needs a mechanism for invalidation so that if the page needs to be updated, we can recompute it before serving it again. Intelligent caching allows web applications to handle increasing number of users with less resources. Caching can also be done preemptively, such as the later sections of the video get buffered when watching a video online.

Caching is also used to improve the performance of certain algorithms. A great example is computing the Fibonacci sequence. Since computing the next number in the Fibonacci sequence requires the previous number in the sequence, one can store and reuse previous results, dramatically improving the running time. Storing and reusing the results of the previous function calls in an application is usually termed as **memoization**, and is one of the forms of caching. Several other algorithms can take advantage of memoization to gain impressive performance improvements, and this programming technique is commonly referred to as **dynamic programming**.

The benefits of caching, however, do not come for free. What we are actually doing is sacrificing some space to improve the speed of the application. Additionally, if the cache is stored in a location on the network, we may incur transfer costs and general time needed for communication. One should evaluate when it is convenient to use a cache and how much space we are willing to trade for an increase in speed.

Given the usefulness of this technique, the Python standard library includes a simple in-memory cache out of the box in the `functools` module. The `functools.lru_cache` decorator can be used to easily cache the results of a function. In the following example, we create a function, `sum2`, that prints a statement and returns the sum of two numbers. By running the function twice, you can see that the first time the `sum2` function is executed the `"Calculating ..."` string is produced, while the second time the result is returned without running the function:

```
from functools import lru_cache

@lru_cache()
def sum2(a, b):
    print("Calculating {} + {}".format(a, b))
    return a + b

print(sum2(1, 2))
# Output:
# Calculating 1 + 2
# 3

print(sum2(1, 2))
# Output:
# 3
```

The `lru_cache` decorator also provides other basic features. To restrict the size of the cache, one can set the number of elements that we intend to maintain through the `max_size` argument. If we want our cache size to be unbounded, we can specify a value of `None`. An example usage of `max_size` is shown here:

```
@lru_cache(max_size=16)
def sum2(a, b):
    ...
```

In this way, as we execute `sum2` with different arguments, the cache will reach a maximum size of 16 and, as we keep requesting more calculations, new values will replace older values in the cache. The `lru` prefix originates from this strategy, which means least recently used.

The `lru_cache` decorator also adds extra functionalities to the decorated function. For example, it is possible to examine the cache performance using the `cache_info` method, and it is possible to reset the cache using the `cache_clear` method, as follows:

```
sum2.cache_info()
# Output: CacheInfo(hits=0, misses=1, maxsize=128, currsize=1)
sum2.cache_clear()
```

As an example, we can see how a problem, such as computing the fibonacci series, may benefit from caching. We can define a `fibonacci` function and time its execution:

```
def fibonacci(n):
    if n < 1:
        return 1
    else:
        return fibonacci(n - 1) + fibonacci(n - 2)

# Non-memoized version
%timeit fibonacci(20)
100 loops, best of 3: 5.57 ms per loop
```

The execution takes 5.57 ms, which is very high. The scaling of the function written in this way has poor performance; the previously computed fibonacci sequences are not reused, causing this algorithm to have an exponential scaling of roughly $O(2^N)$.

Caching can improve this algorithm by storing and reusing the already-computed fibonacci numbers. To implement the cached version, it is sufficient to apply the `lru_cache` decorator to the original `fibonacci` function. Also, to design a proper benchmark, we need to ensure that a new cache is instantiated for every run; to do this, we can use the `timeit.repeat` function, as shown in the following example:

```
import timeit
setup_code = '''
from functools import lru_cache
from __main__ import fibonacci
fibonacci_memoized = lru_cache(maxsize=None)(fibonacci)
'''

results = timeit.repeat('fibonacci_memoized(20)',
                        setup=setup_code,
                        repeat=1000,
                        number=1)
print("Fibonacci took {:.2f} us".format(min(results)))
# Output: Fibonacci took 0.01 us
```

Even though we changed the algorithm by adding a simple decorator, the running time now is much less than a microsecond. The reason is that, thanks to caching, we now have a linear time algorithm instead of an exponential one.

The lru_cache decorator can be used to implement simple in-memory caching in your application. For more advanced use cases, third-party modules can be used for more powerful implementation and on-disk caching.

Joblib

A simple library that, among other things, provides a simple on-disk cache is joblib. The package can be used in a similar way as lru_cache, except that the results will be stored on disk and will persist between runs.

> The joblib module can be installed from PyPI using the pip install joblib command.

The joblib module provides the Memory class that can be used to memoize functions using the Memory.cache decorator:

```
from joblib import Memory
memory = Memory(cachedir='/path/to/cachedir')

@memory.cache
def sum2(a, b):
    return a + b
```

The function will behave similar to lru_cache, with the exception that the results will be stored on-disk in the directory specified by the cachedir argument during Memory initialization. Additionally, the cached results will persist over subsequent runs!

The Memory.cache method also allows to limit recomputation only when certain arguments change, and the resulting decorated function supports basic functionalities to clear and analyze the cache.

Perhaps the best `joblib` feature is that, thanks to intelligent hashing algorithms, it provides efficient memoization of functions that operate on `numpy` arrays, and is particularly useful in scientific and engineering applications.

Comprehensions and generators

In this section, we will explore a few simple strategies to speed up Python loops using comprehension and generators. In Python, comprehension and generator expressions are fairly optimized operations and should be preferred in place of explicit for-loops. Another reason to use this construct is readability; even if the speedup over a standard loop is modest, the comprehension and generator syntax is more compact and (most of the times) more intuitive.

In the following example, we can see that both the list comprehension and generator expressions are faster than an explicit loop when combined with the `sum` function:

```python
def loop():
    res = []
    for i in range(100000):
        res.append(i * i)
    return sum(res)

def comprehension():
    return sum([i * i for i in range(100000)])

def generator():
    return sum(i * i for i in range(100000))

%timeit loop()
100 loops, best of 3: 16.1 ms per loop
%timeit comprehension()
100 loops, best of 3: 10.1 ms per loop
%timeit generator()
100 loops, best of 3: 12.4 ms per loop
```

Just like lists, it is possible to use `dict` comprehension to build dictionaries slightly more efficiently and compactly, as shown in the following code:

```python
def loop():
    res = {}
    for i in range(100000):
        res[i] = i
    return res
```

```
def comprehension():
    return {i: i for i in range(100000)}
%timeit loop()
100 loops, best of 3: 13.2 ms per loop
%timeit comprehension()
100 loops, best of 3: 12.8 ms per loop
```

Efficient looping (especially in terms of memory) can be implemented using iterators and functions such as `filter` and `map`. As an example, consider the problem of applying a series of operations to a list using list comprehension and then taking the maximum value:

```
def map_comprehension(numbers):
    a = [n * 2 for n in numbers]
    b = [n ** 2 for n in a]
    c = [n ** 0.33 for n in b]
    return max(c)
```

The problem with this approach is that for every list comprehension, we are allocating a new list, increasing memory usage. Instead of using list comprehension, we can employ generators. Generators are objects that, when iterated upon, compute a value on the fly and return the result.

For example, the `map` function takes two arguments--a function and an iterator--and returns a generator that applies the function to every element of the collection. The important point is that the operation happens only *while we are iterating*, and not when `map` is invoked!

We can rewrite the previous function using `map` and by creating intermediate generators, rather than lists, thus saving memory by computing the values on the fly:

```
def map_normal(numbers):
    a = map(lambda n: n * 2, numbers)
    b = map(lambda n: n ** 2, a)
    c = map(lambda n: n ** 0.33, b)
    return max(c)
```

We can profile the memory of the two solutions using the `memory_profiler` extension from an IPython session. The extension provides a small utility, `%memit`, that will help us evaluate the memory usage of a Python statement in a way similar to `%timeit`, as illustrated in the following snippet:

```
%load_ext memory_profiler
numbers = range(1000000)
%memit map_comprehension(numbers)
peak memory: 166.33 MiB, increment: 102.54 MiB
%memit map_normal(numbers)
peak memory: 71.04 MiB, increment: 0.00 MiB
```

As you can see, the memory used by the first version is `102.54 MiB`, while the second version consumes `0.00 MiB`! For the interested reader, more functions that return generators can be found in the `itertools` module, which provides a set of utilities designed to handle common iteration patterns.

Summary

Algorithmic optimization can improve how your application scales as we process increasingly large data. In this chapter, we demonstrated use-cases and running times of the most common data structures available in Python, such as lists, deques, dictionaries, heaps, and tries. We also covered caching, a technique that can be used to trade some space, in memory or on-disk, in exchange for increased responsiveness of an application. We also demonstrated how to get modest speed gains by replacing for-loops with fast constructs, such as list comprehensions and generator expressions.

In the subsequent chapters, we will learn how to improve performance further using numerical libraries such as `numpy`, and how to write extension modules in a lower-level language with the help of *Cython*.

3
Fast Array Operations with NumPy and Pandas

NumPy is the *de facto* standard for scientific computing in Python. It extends Python with a flexible multidimensional array that allows fast and concise mathematical calculations.

NumPy provides common data structures and algorithms designed to express complex mathematical operations using a concise syntax. The multidimensional array, `numpy.ndarray`, is internally based on C arrays. Apart from the performance benefits, this choice allows NumPy code to easily interface with the existing C and FORTRAN routines; NumPy is helpful in bridging the gap between Python and the legacy code written using those languages.

In this chapter, we will learn how to create and manipulate NumPy arrays. We will also explore the NumPy broadcasting feature used to rewrite complex mathematical expressions in an efficient and succinct manner.

Pandas is a tool that relies heavily on NumPy and provides additional data structures and algorithms targeted toward data analysis. We will introduce the main Pandas features and its usage. We will also learn how to achieve high performance from Pandas data structures and vectorized operations.

The topics covered in this chapter are as follows:

- Creating and manipulating NumPy arrays
- Mastering NumPy's broadcasting feature for fast and succinct vectorized operations
- Improving our particle simulator with NumPy
- Reaching optimal performance with `numexpr`
- Pandas fundamentals
- Database-style operations with Pandas

Getting started with NumPy

The NumPy library revolves around its multidimensional array object, `numpy.ndarray`. NumPy arrays are collections of elements of the same data type; this fundamental restriction allows NumPy to pack the data in a way that allows for high-performance mathematical operations.

Creating arrays

You can create NumPy arrays using the `numpy.array` function. It takes a list-like object (or another array) as input and, optionally, a string expressing its data type. You can interactively test array creation using an IPython shell, as follows:

```
import numpy as np
a = np.array([0, 1, 2])
```

Every NumPy array has an associated data type that can be accessed using the `dtype` attribute. If we inspect the `a` array, we find that its `dtype` is `int64`, which stands for 64-bit integer:

```
a.dtype
# Result:
# dtype('int64')
```

We may decide to convert those integer numbers to float type. To do this, we can either pass the dtype argument at array initialization or cast the array to another data type using the astype method. The two ways to select a data type are shown in the following code:

```
a = np.array([1, 2, 3], dtype='float32')
a.astype('float32')
# Result:
# array([ 0.,   1.,   2.], dtype-float32)
```

To create an array with two dimensions (an array of arrays), we can perform the initialization using a nested sequence, as follows:

```
a = np.array([[0, 1, 2], [3, 4, 5]])
print(a)
# Output:
# [[0 1 2]
#  [3 4 5]]
```

The array created in this way has two dimensions, which are called **axes** in NumPy's jargon. An array formed in this way is like a table that contains two rows and three columns. We can access the axes using the ndarray.shape attribute:

```
a.shape
# Result:
# (2, 3)
```

Arrays can also be reshaped as long as the product of the shape dimensions is equal to the total number of elements in the array (that is, the total number of elements is conserved). For example, we can reshape an array containing 16 elements in the following ways: (2, 8), (4, 4), or (2, 2, 4). To reshape an array, we can either use the ndarray.reshape method or assign a new value to the ndarray.shape tuple. The following code illustrates the use of the ndarray.reshape method:

```
a = np.array([0, 1, 2, 3, 4, 5, 6, 7, 8,
              9, 10, 11, 12, 13, 14, 15])
a.shape
# Output:
# (16,)

a.reshape(4, 4)  # Equivalent: a.shape = (4, 4)
# Output:
# array([[ 0,  1,  2,  3],
#        [ 4,  5,  6,  7],
#        [ 8,  9, 10, 11],
#        [12, 13, 14, 15]])
```

Thanks to this property, you can freely add dimensions of size one. You can reshape an array with 16 elements to (16, 1), (1, 16), (16, 1, 1), and so on. In the next section, we will extensively use this feature to implement complex operations through *broadcasting*.

NumPy provides convenience functions, shown in the following code, to create arrays filled with zeros, ones, or with no initial value (in this case, their actual value is meaningless and depends on the memory state). Those functions take the array shape as a tuple and, optionally, its dtype:

```
np.zeros((3, 3))
np.empty((3, 3))
np.ones((3, 3), dtype='float32')
```

In our examples, we will use the numpy.random module to generate random floating point numbers in the (0, 1) interval. The numpy.random.rand will take a shape and return an array of random numbers with that shape:

```
np.random.rand(3, 3)
```

Sometimes it is convenient to initialize arrays that have the same shape as that of some other array. For that purpose, NumPy provides some handy functions, such as zeros_like, empty_like, and ones_like. These functions can be used as follows:

```
np.zeros_like(a)
np.empty_like(a)
np.ones_like(a)
```

Accessing arrays

The NumPy array interface is, on a shallow level, similar to that of Python lists. NumPy arrays can be indexed using integers and iterated using a for loop:

```
A = np.array([0, 1, 2, 3, 4, 5, 6, 7, 8])
A[0]
# Result:
# 0

[a for a in A]
# Result:
# [0, 1, 2, 3, 4, 5, 6, 7, 8]
```

In NumPy, array elements and sub-arrays can be conveniently accessed by using multiple values separated by commas inside the subscript operator, `[]`. If we take a `(3,3)` array (an array containing three triplets), and we access the element with index `0`, we obtain the first row, as follows:

```
A = np.array([[0, 1, 2], [3, 4, 5], [6, 7, 8]])
A[0]
# Result:
# array([0, 1, 2])
```

We can index the row again by adding another index separated by a comma. To get the second element of the first row, we can use the `(0, 1)` index. An important observation is that the `A[0, 1]` notation is actually a shorthand for `A[(0, 1)]`, that is, we are actually indexing using a *tuple*! Both the versions are shown in the following snippet:

```
A[0, 1]
# Result:
# 1

# Equivalent version using tuple
A[(0, 1)]
```

NumPy allows you to slice arrays into multiple dimensions. If we slice on the first dimension, we can obtain a collection of triplets, shown as follows:

```
A[0:2]
# Result:
# array([[0, 1, 2],
#        [3, 4, 5]])
```

If we slice the array again on the second dimension with `0:2`, we are basically extracting the first two elements from the collection of triplets shown earlier. This results in an array of shape `(2, 2)`, shown in the following code:

```
A[0:2, 0:2]
# Result:
# array([[0, 1],
#        [3, 4]])
```

Intuitively, you can update the values in the array using both numerical indexes and slices. An example is illustrated in the following code snippet:

```
A[0, 1] = 8
A[0:2, 0:2] = [[1, 1], [1, 1]]
```

Indexing with the slicing syntax is very fast because, unlike lists, it doesn't produce a copy of the array. In NumPy's terminology, it returns a *view* of the same memory area. If we take a slice of the original array, and then we change one of its values, the original array will be updated as well. The following code illustrates an example of this feature:

```
a= np.array([1, 1, 1, 1])
a_view = a[0:2]
a_view[0] = 2
print(a)
# Output:
# [2 1 1 1]
```

It is important to be extra careful when mutating NumPy arrays. Since views share data, changing the values of a view can result in hard-to-find bugs. To prevent side effects, you can set the `a.flags.writeable = False` flag, which will prevent accidental mutation of the array or any of its views.

We can take a look at another example that shows how the slicing syntax can be used in a real-world setting. We define an `r_i` array, shown in the following line of code, which contains a set of 10 coordinates (x, y). Its shape will be `(10, 2)`:

```
r_i = np.random.rand(10, 2)
```

If you have a hard time distinguishing arrays that differ in the axes order, for example between an a array of shape `(10, 2)` and `(2, 10)`, it is useful to think that every time you say the word *of*, you should introduce a new dimension. An array with ten elements *of* size two will be `(10, 2)`. Conversely, an array with two elements *of* size ten will be `(2, 10)`.

A typical operation we may be interested in is the extraction of the *x* component from each coordinate. In other words, you want to extract the `(0, 0)`, `(1, 0)`, `(2, 0)`, and so on items, resulting in an array with shape `(10,)`. It is helpful to think that the first index is *moving* while the second one is *fixed* (at `0`). With this in mind, we will slice every index on the first axis (the moving one) and take the first element (the fixed one) on the second axis, as shown in the following line of code:

```
x_i = r_i[:, 0]
```

On the other hand, the following expression will keep the first index fixed and the second index moving, returning the first (x, y) coordinate:

```
r_0 = r_i[0, :]
```

Slicing all the indexes over the last axis is optional; using `r_i[0]` has the same effect as `r_i[0, :]`.

NumPy allows you to index an array using another NumPy array made of either integer or Boolean values--a feature called *fancy indexing*.

If you index an array (say, a) with another array of integers (say, `idx`), NumPy will interpret the integers as indexes and will return an array containing their corresponding values. If we index an array containing 10 elements with `np.array([0, 2, 3])`, we obtain an array of shape `(3,)` containing the elements at positions 0, 2, and 3. The following code gives us an illustration of this concept:

```
a = np.array([9, 8, 7, 6, 5, 4, 3, 2, 1, 0])
idx = np.array([0, 2, 3])
a[idx]
# Result:
# array([9, 7, 6])
```

You can use fancy indexing on multiple dimensions by passing an array for each dimension. If we want to extract the `(0, 2)` and `(1, 3)` elements, we have to pack all the indexes acting on the first axis in one array, and the ones acting on the second axis in another. This can be seen in the following code:

```
a = np.array([[0, 1, 2], [3, 4, 5],
              [6, 7, 8], [9, 10, 11]])
idx1 = np.array([0, 1])
idx2 = np.array([2, 3])
a[idx1, idx2]
```

You can also use normal lists as index arrays, but not tuples. For example, the following two statements are equivalent:

```
a[np.array([0, 1])] # is equivalent to
a[[0, 1]]
```

However, if you use a tuple, NumPy will interpret the following statement as an index on multiple dimensions:

```
a[(0, 1)] # is equivalent to
a[0, 1]
```

The index arrays are not required to be one-dimensional; we can extract elements from the original array in any shape. For example, we can select elements from the original array to form a (2,2) array, as shown:

```
idx1 = [[0, 1], [3, 2]]
idx2 = [[0, 2], [1, 1]]
a[idx1, idx2]
# Output:
# array([[ 0,   5],
#        [10,   7]])
```

The array slicing and fancy-indexing features can be combined. This is useful, for instance, when we want to swap the *x* and *y* columns in a coordinate array. In the following code, the first index will be running over all the elements (a slice) and, for each of those, we extract the element in position 1 (the *y*) first and then the one in position 0 (the *x*):

```
r_i = np.random(10, 2)
r_i[:, [0, 1]] = r_i[:, [1, 0]]
```

When the index array is of the `bool` type, the rules are slightly different. The `bool` array will act like a *mask*; every element corresponding to `True` will be extracted and put in the output array. This procedure is shown in the following code:

```
a = np.array([0, 1, 2, 3, 4, 5])
mask = np.array([True, False, True, False, False, False])
a[mask]
# Output:
# array([0, 2])
```

The same rules apply when dealing with multiple dimensions. Furthermore, if the index array has the same shape as the original array, the elements corresponding to `True` will be selected and put in the resulting array.

Indexing in NumPy is a reasonably fast operation. Anyway, when speed is critical, you can use the slightly faster `numpy.take` and `numpy.compress` functions to squeeze out a little more performance. The first argument of `numpy.take` is the array we want to operate on, and the second is the list of indexes we want to extract. The last argument is `axis`; if not provided, the indexes will act on the flattened array; otherwise, they will act along the specified axis:

```
r_i = np.random(100, 2)
idx = np.arange(50) # integers 0 to 50

%timeit np.take(r_i, idx, axis=0)
1000000 loops, best of 3: 962 ns per loop
```

```
%timeit r_i[idx]
100000 loops, best of 3: 3.09 us per loop
```

The similar, but faster version for Boolean arrays is numpy.compress, which works in the same way. The use of numpy.compress is shown as follows:

```
In [51]: idx = np.ones(100, dtype='bool') # all True values
In [52]: %timeit np.compress(idx, r_i, axis=0)
1000000 loops, best of 3: 1.65 us per loop
In [53]: %timeit r_i[idx]
100000 loops, best of 3: 5.47 us per loop
```

Broadcasting

The true power of NumPy lies in its fast mathematical operations. The approach used by NumPy is to avoid stepping into the Python interpreter by performing element-wise calculation using optimized C code. **Broadcasting** is a clever set of rules that enables fast array calculations for arrays of similar (but not equal!) shape.

Whenever you do an arithmetic operation on two arrays (like a product), if the two operands have the same shape, the operation will be applied in an element-wise fashion. For example, upon multiplying two shape (2,2) arrays, the operation will be done between pairs of corresponding elements, producing another (2, 2) array, as shown in the following code:

```
A = np.array([[1, 2], [3, 4]])
B = np.array([[5, 6], [7, 8]])
A * B
# Output:
# array([[ 5, 12],
#        [21, 32]])
```

If the shapes of the operands don't match, NumPy will attempt to match them using broadcasting rules. If one of the operands is a *scalar* (for example, a number), it will be applied to every element of the array, as the following code illustrates:

```
A * 2
# Output:
# array([[2, 4],
#        [6, 8]])
```

If the operand is another array, NumPy will try to match the shapes starting from the last axis. For example, if we want to combine an array of shape (3, 2) with one of shape (2,), the second array will be repeated three times to generate a (3, 2) array. In other words, the array is *broadcasted* along a dimension to match the shape of the other operand, as shown in the following figure:

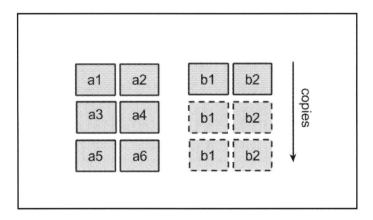

If the shapes mismatch, for example, when combining a (3, 2) array with a (2, 2) array, NumPy will throw an exception.

If one of the axis's size is 1, the array will be repeated over this axis until the shapes match. To illustrate that point, consider that we have an array of the following shape:

```
5, 10, 2
```

Now, consider that we want to broadcast it with an array of shape (5, 1, 2); the array will be repeated on the second axis 10 times, which is shown as follows:

```
5, 10, 2
5,  1, 2 → repeated
- - - -
5, 10, 2
```

Earlier, we saw that it is possible to freely reshape arrays to add axes of size 1. Using the numpy.newaxis constant while indexing will introduce an extra dimension. For instance, if we have a (5, 2) array and we want to combine it with one of shape (5, 10, 2), we can add an extra axis in the middle, as shown in the following code, to obtain a compatible (5, 1, 2) array:

```
A = np.random.rand(5, 10, 2)
B = np.random.rand(5, 2)
A * B[:, np.newaxis, :]
```

This feature can be used, for example, to operate on all possible combinations of the two arrays. One of these applications is the *outer product*. Consider that we have the following two arrays:

```
a = [a1, a2, a3]
b = [b1, b2, b3]
```

The outer product is a matrix containing the product of all the possible combinations (i, j) of the two array elements, as shown in the following snippet:

```
a x b = a1*b1, a1*b2, a1*b3
        a2*b1, a2*b2, a2*b3
        a3*b1, a3*b2, a3*b3
```

To calculate this using NumPy, we will repeat the [a1, a2, a3] elements in one dimension, the [b1, b2, b3] elements in another dimension, and then take their element-wise product, as shown in the following figure:

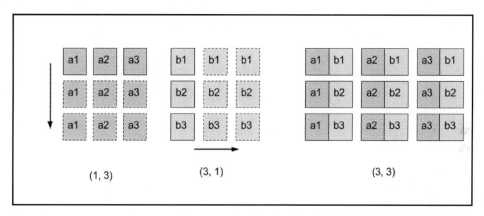

Using code, our strategy will be to transform the a array from shape (3,) to shape (3, 1), and the b array from shape (3,) to shape (1, 3). The two arrays are broadcasted in the two dimensions and get multiplied together using the following code:

```
AB = a[:, np.newaxis] * b[np.newaxis, :]
```

This operation is very fast and extremely effective as it avoids Python loops and is able to process a high number of elements at speeds comparable with pure C or FORTRAN code.

Mathematical operations

NumPy includes the most common mathematical operations available for broadcasting, by default, ranging from simple algebra to trigonometry, rounding, and logic. For instance, to take the square root of every element in the array, we can use numpy.sqrt, as shown in the following code:

```
np.sqrt(np.array([4, 9, 16]))
# Result:
# array([2., 3., 4.])
```

The comparison operators are useful when trying to filter certain elements based on a condition. Imagine that we have an array of random numbers from 0 to 1, and we want to extract all the numbers greater than 0.5. We can use the > operator on the array to obtain a bool array, as follows:

```
a = np.random.rand(5, 3)
a > 0.3
# Result:
# array([[ True, False,  True],
#        [ True,  True,  True],
#        [False,  True,  True],
#        [ True,  True, False],
#        [ True,  True, False]], dtype=bool)
```

The resulting bool array can then be reused as an index to retrieve the elements greater than 0.5:

```
a[a > 0.5]
print(a[a>0.5])
# Output:
# [ 0.9755  0.5977  0.8287  0.6214  0.5669  0.9553  0.5894
0.7196  0.9200  0.5781  0.8281 ]
```

NumPy also implements methods such as ndarray.sum, which takes the sum of all the elements on an axis. If we have an array of shape (5, 3), we can use the ndarray.sum method to sum the elements on the first axis, the second axis, or over all the elements of the array, as illustrated in the following snippet:

```
a = np.random.rand(5, 3)
a.sum(axis=0)
# Result:
# array([ 2.7454,  2.5517,  2.0303])

a.sum(axis=1)
# Result:
```

```
# array([ 1.7498,   1.2491,   1.8151,   1.9320,   0.5814])

a.sum() # With no argument operates on flattened array
# Result:
# 7.3275
```

Note that by summing the elements over an axis, we eliminate that axis. From the preceding example, the sum on the axis 0 produces an array of shape (3,), while the sum on the axis 1 produces an array of shape (5,).

Calculating the norm

We can review the basic concepts illustrated in this section by calculating the *norm* of a set of coordinates. For a two-dimensional vector, the norm is defined as follows:

```
norm = sqrt(x**2 + y**2)
```

Given an array of 10 coordinates (x, y), we want to find the norm of each coordinate. We can calculate the norm by taking these steps:

1. Square the coordinates, obtaining an array that contains (x**2, y**2) elements.
2. Sum those with numpy.sum over the last axis.
3. Take the square root, element-wise, with numpy.sqrt.

The final expression can be compressed in a single line:

```
r_i = np.random.rand(10, 2)
norm = np.sqrt((r_i ** 2).sum(axis=1))
print(norm)
# Output:
# [ 0.7314   0.9050   0.5063   0.2553   0.0778   0.9143   1.3245
0.9486   1.010   1.0212]
```

Rewriting the particle simulator in NumPy

In this section, we will optimize our particle simulator by rewriting some parts of it in NumPy. We found, from the profiling we did in Chapter 1, *Benchmarking and Profiling*, that the slowest part of our program is the following loop contained in the ParticleSimulator.evolve method:

```
for i in range(nsteps):
```

```
for p in self.particles:

    norm = (p.x**2 + p.y**2)**0.5
    v_x = (-p.y)/norm
    v_y = p.x/norm

    d_x = timestep * p.ang_vel * v_x
    d_y = timestep * p.ang_vel * v_y

    p.x += d_x
    p.y += d_y
```

You may have noticed that the body of the loop acts solely on the current particle. If we had an array containing the particle positions and angular speed, we could rewrite the loop using a broadcasted operation. In contrast, the loop's steps depend on the previous step and cannot be parallelized in this way.

It is natural then, to store all the array coordinates in an array of shape (nparticles, 2) and the angular speed in an array of shape (nparticles,), where nparticles is the number of particles. We'll call those arrays r_i and ang_vel_i:

```
r_i = np.array([[p.x, p.y] for p in self.particles])
ang_vel_i = np.array([p.ang_vel for p in self.particles])
```

The velocity direction, perpendicular to the vector (x, y), was defined as follows:

```
v_x = -y / norm
v_y = x / norm
```

The norm can be calculated using the strategy illustrated in the *Calculating the norm* section under the *Getting started with NumPy* heading:

```
norm_i = ((r_i ** 2).sum(axis=1))**0.5
```

For the $(-y, x)$ components, we first need to swap the x and y columns in r_i and then multiply the first column by -1, as shown in the following code:

```
v_i = r_i[:, [1, 0]] / norm_i
v_i[:, 0] *= -1
```

To calculate the displacement, we need to compute the product of v_i, ang_vel_i, and timestep. Since ang_vel_i is of shape (nparticles,), it needs a new axis in order to operate with v_i of shape (nparticles, 2). We will do that using numpy.newaxis, as follows:

```
d_i = timestep * ang_vel_i[:, np.newaxis] * v_i
r_i += d_i
```

Outside the loop, we have to update the particle instances with the new coordinates, *x* and *y*, as follows:

```
for i, p in enumerate(self.particles):
    p.x, p.y = r_i[i]
```

To summarize, we will implement a method called `ParticleSimulator.evolve_numpy` and benchmark it against the pure Python version, renamed as `ParticleSimulator.evolve_python`:

```
def evolve_numpy(self, dt):
    timestep = 0.00001
    nsteps = int(dt/timestep)

    r_i = np.array([[p.x, p.y] for p in self.particles])
    ang_vel_i = np.array([p.ang_vel for p in self.particles])

    for i in range(nsteps):

        norm_i = np.sqrt((r_i ** 2).sum(axis=1))
        v_i = r_i[:, [1, 0]]
        v_i[:, 0] *= -1
        v_i /= norm_i[:, np.newaxis]
        d_i = timestep * ang_vel_i[:, np.newaxis] * v_i
        r_i += d_i

        for i, p in enumerate(self.particles):
            p.x, p.y = r_i[i]
```

We also update the benchmark to conveniently change the number of particles and the simulation method, as follows:

```
def benchmark(npart=100, method='python'):
    particles = [Particle(uniform(-1.0, 1.0),
                          uniform(-1.0, 1.0),
                          uniform(-1.0, 1.0))
                          for i in range(npart)]

    simulator = ParticleSimulator(particles)

    if method=='python':
        simulator.evolve_python(0.1)

    elif method == 'numpy':
        simulator.evolve_numpy(0.1)
```

Let's run the benchmark in an IPython session:

```
from simul import benchmark
%timeit benchmark(100, 'python')
1 loops, best of 3: 614 ms per loop
%timeit benchmark(100, 'numpy')
1 loops, best of 3: 415 ms per loop
```

We have some improvement, but it doesn't look like a huge speed boost. The power of NumPy is revealed when handling big arrays. If we increase the number of particles, we will note a more significant performance boost:

```
%timeit benchmark(1000, 'python')
1 loops, best of 3: 6.13 s per loop
%timeit benchmark(1000, 'numpy')
1 loops, best of 3: 852 ms per loop
```

The plot in the following figure was produced by running the benchmark with different particle numbers:

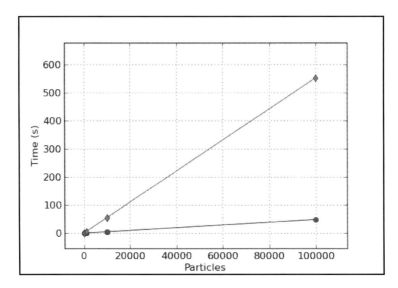

The plot shows that both the implementations scale linearly with particle size, but the runtime in the pure Python version grows much faster than the NumPy version; at greater sizes, we have a greater NumPy advantage. In general, when using NumPy, you should try to pack things into large arrays and group the calculations using the broadcasting feature.

Reaching optimal performance with numexpr

When handling complex expressions, NumPy stores intermediate results in memory. David M. Cooke wrote a package called `numexpr`, which optimizes and compiles array expressions on the fly. It works by optimizing the usage of the CPU cache and by taking advantage of multiple processors.

Its usage is generally straightforward and is based on a single function-- `numexpr.evaluate`. The function takes a string containing an array expression as its first argument. The syntax is basically identical to that of NumPy. For example, we can calculate a simple `a + b * c` expression in the following way:

```
a = np.random.rand(10000)
b = np.random.rand(10000)
c = np.random.rand(10000)
d = ne.evaluate('a + b * c')
```

The `numexpr` package increases the performances in almost all cases, but to get a substantial advantage, you should use it with large arrays. An application that involves a large array is the calculation of a *distance matrix*. In a particle system, a distance matrix contains all the possible distances between the particles. To calculate it, we should first calculate all the vectors connecting any two particles `(i, j)`, as follows:

```
x_ij = x_j - x_i
y_ij = y_j - y_i.
```

Then, we calculate the length of this vector by taking its norm, as in the following code:

```
d_ij = sqrt(x_ij**2 + y_ij**2)
```

We can write this in NumPy by employing the usual broadcasting rules (the operation is similar to the outer product):

```
r = np.random.rand(10000, 2)
r_i = r[:, np.newaxis]
r_j = r[np.newaxis, :]
d_ij = r_j - r_i
```

Finally, we calculate the norm over the last axis using the following line of code:

```
d_ij = np.sqrt((d_ij ** 2).sum(axis=2))
```

Rewriting the same expression using the `numexpr` syntax is extremely easy. The `numexpr` package doesn't support slicing in its array expression; therefore, we first need to prepare the operands for broadcasting by adding an extra dimension, as follows:

```
r = np.random(10000, 2)
r_i = r[:, np.newaxis]
r_j = r[np.newaxis, :]
```

At that point, we should try to pack as many operations as possible in a single expression to allow a significant optimization.

Most of the NumPy mathematical functions are also available in `numexpr`. However, there is a limitation--the reduction operations (the ones that reduce an axis, such as sum) have to happen last. Therefore, we have to first calculate the sum, then step out of `numexpr`, and finally calculate the square root in another expression:

```
d_ij = ne.evaluate('sum((r_j - r_i)**2, 2)')
d_ij = ne.evaluate('sqrt(d_ij)')
```

The `numexpr` compiler will avoid redundant memory allocation by not storing intermediate results. When possible, it will also distribute the operations over multiple processors. In the `distance_matrix.py` file, you will find two functions that implement the two versions: `distance_matrix_numpy` and `distance_matrix_numexpr`:

```
from distance_matrix import (distance_matrix_numpy,
                             distance_matrix_numexpr)
%timeit distance_matrix_numpy(10000)
1 loops, best of 3: 3.56 s per loop
%timeit distance_matrix_numexpr(10000)
1 loops, best of 3: 858 ms per loop
```

By simply converting the expressions to use `numexpr`, we were able to obtain a 4.5x increase in performance over standard NumPy. The `numexpr` package can be used every time you need to optimize a NumPy expression that involves large arrays and complex operations, and you can do so with minimal changes in the code.

Pandas

Pandas is a library originally developed by Wes McKinney, which was designed to analyze datasets in a seamless and performant way. In recent years, this powerful library has seen an incredible growth and huge adoption by the Python community. In this section, we will introduce the main concepts and tools provided in this library, and we will use it to increase performance of various usecases that can't otherwise be addressed with NumPy's vectorized operations and broadcasting.

Pandas fundamentals

While NumPy deals mostly with arrays, Pandas main data structures are `pandas.Series`, `pandas.DataFrame`, and `pandas.Panel`. In the rest of this chapter, we will abbreviate `pandas` with `pd`.

The main difference between a `pd.Series` object and an `np.array` is that a `pd.Series` object associates a specific *key* to each element of an array. Let's see how this works in practice with an example.

Let's assume that we are trying to test a new blood pressure drug, and we want to store, for each patient, whether the patient's blood pressure improved after administering the drug. We can encode this information by associating to each subject ID (represented by an integer), `True` if the drug was effective, and `False` otherwise.

We can create a `pd.Series` object by associating an array of keys, the patients, to the array of values that represent the drug effectiveness. The array of keys can be passed to the `Series` constructor using the `index` argument, as shown in the following snippet:

```
import pandas as pd
patients = [0, 1, 2, 3]
effective = [True, True, False, False]

effective_series = pd.Series(effective, index=patients)
```

Associating a set of integers from 0 to *N* to a set of values can technically be implemented with `np.array`, since, in this case, the key will simply be the position of the element in the array. In Pandas, keys are not limited to integers but can also be strings, floating point numbers, and also generic (hashable) Python objects. For example, we can easily turn our IDs into strings with little effort, as shown in the following code:

```
patients = ["a", "b", "c", "d"]
effective = [True, True, False, False]

effective_series = pd.Series(effective, index=patients)
```

An interesting observation is that, while NumPy arrays can be thought of as a contiguous collection of values similar to Python lists, the Pandas `pd.Series` object can be thought of as a structure that maps keys to values, similar to Python dictionaries.

What if you want to store the initial and final blood pressure for each patient? In Pandas, one can use a `pd.DataFrame` object to associate multiple data to each key.

`pd.DataFrame` can be initialized, similarly to a `pd.Series` object, by passing a dictionary of columns and an index. In the following example, we will see how to create a `pd.DataFrame` containing four columns that represent the initial and final measurements of systolic and dyastolic blood pressure for our patients:

```
patients = ["a", "b", "c", "d"]

columns = {
  "sys_initial": [120, 126, 130, 115],
  "dia_initial": [75, 85, 90, 87],
  "sys_final": [115, 123, 130, 118],
  "dia_final": [70, 82, 92, 87]
}
df = pd.DataFrame(columns, index=patients)
```

Equivalently, you can think of a `pd.DataFrame` as a collection of `pd.Series`. In fact, it is possible to directly initialize a `pd.DataFrame`, using a dictionary of `pd.Series` instances:

```
columns = {
  "sys_initial": pd.Series([120, 126, 130, 115], index=patients),
  "dia_initial": pd.Series([75, 85, 90, 87], index=patients),
  "sys_final": pd.Series([115, 123, 130, 118], index=patients),
  "dia_final": pd.Series([70, 82, 92, 87], index=patients)
}
df = pd.DataFrame(columns)
```

To inspect the content of a pd.DataFrame or pd.Series object, you can use the pd.Series.head and pd.DataFrame.head methods, which print the first few rows of the dataset:

```
effective_series.head()
# Output:
# a True
# b True
# c False
# d False
# dtype: bool

df.head()
# Output:
#     dia_final  dia_initial  sys_final  sys_initial
# a          70           75        115          120
# b          82           85        123          126
# c          92           90        130          130
# d          87           87        118          115
```

Just like a pd.DataFrame can be used to store a collection of pd.Series, you can use a pd.Panel to store a collection of pd.DataFrames. We will not cover the usage of pd.Panel as it is not used as often as pd.Series and pd.DataFrame. To learn more about pd.Panel, ensure that you refer to the excellent documentation at http://pandas.pydata.org/pandas-docs/stable/dsintro.html#panel.

Indexing Series and DataFrame objects

Retrieving data from a pd.Series, given its *key*, can be done intuitively by indexing the pd.Series.loc attribute:

```
effective_series.loc["a"]
# Result:
# True
```

It is also possible to access the elements, given its *position* in the underlying array, using the pd.Series.iloc attribute:

```
effective_series.iloc[0]
# Result:
# True
```

You can also use the `pd.Series.ix` attribute for mixed access. If the key is not an integer, it will try to match by key, otherwise it will extract the element at the position indicated by the integer. A similar behavior will take place when you access the `pd.Series` directly. The following example demonstrates these concepts:

```
effective_series.ix["a"] # By key
effective_series.ix[0]   # By position

# Equivalent
effective_series["a"] # By key
effective_series[0]   # By position
```

Note that if the index is made of integers, this method will fall back to the key-only method (like `loc`). To index by position in this scenario, the `iloc` method is your only option.

Indexing `pd.DataFrame` works in a similar way. For example, you can use `pd.DataFrame.loc` to extract a row by key, and you can use `pd.DataFrame.iloc` to extract a row by position:

```
df.loc["a"]
df.iloc[0]
# Result:
# dia_final 70
# dia_initial 75
# sys_final 115
# sys_initial 120
# Name: a, dtype: int64
```

An important aspect is that the return type in this case is a `pd.Series`, where each column is a new key. In order to retrieve a specific row and column, you can use the following code. The `loc` attribute will index both row and column by key, while the `iloc` version will index row and column by an integer:

```
df.loc["a", "sys_initial"] # is equivalent to
df.loc["a"].loc["sys_initial"]

df.iloc[0, 1] # is equivalent to
df.iloc[0].iloc[1]
```

Indexing a `pd.DataFrame` using the `ix` attribute is convenient to mix and match index and location-based indexing. For example, retrieving the `"sys_initial"` column for the row at position 0 can be accomplished as follows:

```
df.ix[0, "sys_initial"]
```

Retrieving a column from a `pd.DataFrame` by name can be achieved by regular indexing or attribute access. To retrieve a column by position, you can either use `iloc` or use the `pd.DataFrame.column` attribute to retrieve the name of the column:

```
# Retrieve column by name
df["sys_initial"] # Equivalent to
df.sys_initial

# Retrieve column by position
df[df.columns[2]] # Equivalent to
df.iloc[:, 2]
```

The mentioned methods also support more advanced indexing similar to those of NumPy, such as `bool`, lists, and `int` arrays.

Now it's time for some performance considerations. There are some differences between an index in Pandas and a dictionary. For example, while the keys of a dictionary cannot contain duplicates, Pandas indexes can contain repeated elements. This flexibility, however, comes at a cost--if we try to access an element in a non-unique index, we may incur substantial performance loss--the access will be $O(N)$, like a linear search, rather than $O(1)$, like a dictionary.

A way to mitigate this effect is to sort the index; this will allow Pandas to use a binary search algorithm with a computational complexity of $O(log(N))$, which is much better. This can be accomplished using the `pd.Series.sort_index` function, as in the following code (the same applies for `pd.DataFrame`):

```
# Create a series with duplicate index
index = list(range(1000)) + list(range(1000))

# Accessing a normal series is a O(N) operation
series = pd.Series(range(2000), index=index)

# Sorting the will improve look-up scaling to O(log(N))
series.sort_index(inplace=True)
```

The timings for the different versions are summarized in the following table:

Index type	N=10000	N=20000	N=30000	Time
Unique	12.30	12.58	13.30	$O(1)$
Non unique	494.95	814.10	1129.95	$O(N)$
Non unique (sorted)	145.93	145.81	145.66	$O(log(N))$

Database-style operations with Pandas

You may have noted that the "tabular" data is similar to what is usually stored in a database. A database is usually indexed using a primary key, and the various columns can have different data types, just like in a pd.DataFrame.

The efficiency of the index operations in Pandas makes it suitable for database style manipulations, such as counting, joining, grouping, and aggregations.

Mapping

Pandas supports element-wise operations just like NumPy (after all, pd.Series stores their data using np.array). For example, it is possible to apply transformation very easily on both pd.Series and pd.DataFrame:

```
np.log(df.sys_initial)  # Logarithm of a series
df.sys_initial ** 2     # Square a series
np.log(df)              # Logarithm of a dataframe
df ** 2                 # Square of a dataframe
```

You can also perform element-wise operations between two pd.Series in a way similar to NumPy. An important difference is that the operands will be matched by key, rather than by position; if there is a mismatch in the index, the resulting value will be set to NaN. Both the scenarios are exemplified in the following example:

```
# Matching index
a = pd.Series([1, 2, 3], index=["a", "b", "c"])
b = pd.Series([4, 5, 6], index=["a", "b", "c"])
a + b
# Result:
# a 5
# b 7
# c 9
# dtype: int64

# Mismatching index
b = pd.Series([4, 5, 6], index=["a", "b", "d"])
# Result:
# a 5.0
# b 7.0
# c NaN
# d NaN
# dtype: float64
```

For added flexibility, Pandas exposes the map, apply, and applymap methods that can be used to apply specific transformations.

The pd.Series.map method can be used to execute a function to each value and return a pd.Series containing each result. In the following example, we show how to apply the superstar function to each element of a pd.Series:

```
a - pd.Series([1, 2, 3], index=["a", "b", "c"])
def superstar(x):
    return '*' + str(x) + '*'
a.map(superstar)

# Result:
# a *1*
# b *2*
# c *3*
# dtype: object
```

The pd.DataFrame.applymap function is the equivalent of pd.Series.map, but for DataFrames:

```
df.applymap(superstar)
# Result:
#    dia_final  dia_initial  sys_final  sys_initial
# a      *70*         *75*      *115*         *120*
# b      *82*         *85*      *123*         *126*
# c      *92*         *90*      *130*         *130*
# d      *87*         *87*      *118*         *115*
```

Finally, the pd.DataFrame.apply function can apply the passed function to each column or each row, rather than element-wise. The selection can be performed with the argument axis, where a value of 0 (the default) corresponds to columns, and 1 corresponds to rows. Also, note that the return value of apply is a pd.Series:

```
df.apply(superstar, axis=0)
# Result:
# dia_final *a 70nb 82nc 92nd 87nName: dia...
# dia_initial *a 75nb 85nc 90nd 87nName: dia...
# sys_final *a 115nb 123nc 130nd 118nName:...
# sys_initial *a 120nb 126nc 130nd 115nName:...
# dtype: object

df.apply(superstar, axis=1)
# Result:
# a *dia_final 70ndia_initial 75nsys_f...
# b *dia_final 82ndia_initial 85nsys_f...
# c *dia_final 92ndia_initial 90nsys_f...
```

```
# d *dia_final 87ndia_initial 87nsys_f...
# dtype: object
```

Pandas also supports efficient `numexpr`-style expressions with the convenient `eval` method. For example, if we want to calculate the difference in the final and initial blood pressure, we can write the expression as a string, as shown in the following code:

```
df.eval("sys_final - sys_initial")
# Result:
# a -5
# b -3
# c 0
# d 3
# dtype: int64
```

It is also possible to create new columns using the assignment operator in the `pd.DataFrame.eval` expression. Note that, if the `inplace=True` argument is used, the operation will be applied directly on the original `pd.DataFrame`; otherwise, the function will return a new dataframe. In the next example, we compute the difference between `sys_final` and `sys_initial`, and we store it in the `sys_delta` column:

```
df.eval("sys_delta = sys_final - sys_initial", inplace=False)
# Result:
#       dia_final    dia_initial    sys_final    sys_initial    sys_delta
# a            70             75          115            120           -5
# b            82             85          123            126           -3
# c            92             90          130            130            0
# d            87             87          118            115            3
```

Grouping, aggregations, and transforms

One of the most appreciated features of Pandas is the simple and concise expression of data analysis pipelines that requires grouping, transforming, and aggregating the data. To demonstrate this concept, let's extend our dataset by adding two new patients to whom we didn't administer the treatment (this is usually called a *control group*). We also include a column, `drug_admst`, which records whether the patient was administered the treatment:

```
patients = ["a", "b", "c", "d", "e", "f"]

columns = {
    "sys_initial": [120, 126, 130, 115, 150, 117],
    "dia_initial": [75, 85, 90, 87, 90, 74],
    "sys_final": [115, 123, 130, 118, 130, 121],
    "dia_final": [70, 82, 92, 87, 85, 74],
    "drug_admst": [True, True, True, True, False, False]
```

```
    }

    df = pd.DataFrame(columns, index=patients)
```

At this point, we may be interested to know how the blood pressure changed between the two groups. You can group the patients according to drug_amst using the pd.DataFrame.groupby function. The return value will be the DataFrameGroupBy object, which can be iterated to obtain a new pd.DataFrame for each value of the drug_admst column:

```
df.groupby('drug_admst')
for value, group in df.groupby('drug_admst'):
    print("Value: {}".format(value))
    print("Group DataFrame:")
    print(group)
# Output:
# Value: False
# Group DataFrame:
#     dia_final   dia_initial   drug_admst   sys_final   sys_initial
# e          85            90        False         130           150
# f          74            74        False         121           117
# Value: True
# Group DataFrame:
#     dia_final   dia_initial   drug_admst   sys_final   sys_initial
# a          70            75         True         115           120
# b          82            85         True         123           126
# c          92            90         True         130           130
# d          87            87         True         118           115
```

Iterating on the DataFrameGroupBy object is almost never necessary, because, thanks to method chaining, it is possible to calculate group-related properties directly. For example, we may want to calculate mean, max, or standard deviation for each group. All those operations that summarize the data in some way are called aggregations and can be performed using the agg method. The result of agg is another pd.DataFrame that relates the grouping variables and the result of the aggregation, as illustrated in the following code:

```
df.groupby('drug_admst').agg(np.mean)
#               dia_final   dia_initial   sys_final   sys_initial
# drug_admst
# False             79.50         82.00       125.5        133.50
# True              82.75         84.25       121.5        122.75
```

It is also possible to perform processing on the DataFrame groups that do not represent a summarization. One common example of such an operation is filling in missing values. Those intermediate steps are called *transforms.*

We can illustrate this concept with an example. Let's assume that we have a few missing values in our dataset, and we want to replace those values with the average of the other values in the same group. This can be accomplished using a transform, as follows:

```
df.loc['a','sys_initial'] = None
df.groupby('drug_admst').transform(lambda df: df.fillna(df.mean()))
#       dia_final    dia_initial    sys_final    sys_initial
# a            70             75          115      123.666667
# b            82             85          123      126.000000
# c            92             90          130      130.000000
# d            87             87          118      115.000000
# e            85             90          130      150.000000
# f            74             74          121      117.000000
```

Joining

Joins are useful to aggregate data that is scattered among different tables. Let's say that we want to include the location of the hospital in which patient measurements were taken in our dataset. We can reference the location for each patient using the H1, H2, and H3 labels, and we can store the address and identifier of the hospital in a hospital table:

```
hospitals = pd.DataFrame(
  { "name" : ["City 1", "City 2", "City 3"],
    "address" : ["Address 1", "Address 2", "Address 3"],
    "city": ["City 1", "City 2", "City 3"] },
  index=["H1", "H2", "H3"])

hospital_id = ["H1", "H2", "H2", "H3", "H3", "H3"]
df['hospital_id'] = hospital_id
```

Now, we want to find the city where the measure was taken for each patient. We need to *map* the keys from the hospital_id column to the city stored in the hospitals table.

This can surely be implemented in Python using dictionaries:

```
hospital_dict = {
  "H1": ("City 1", "Name 1", "Address 1"),
  "H2": ("City 2", "Name 2", "Address 2"),
  "H3": ("City 3", "Name 3", "Address 3")
}
cities = [hospital_dict[key][0]
            for key in hospital_id]
```

This algorithm runs efficiently with an $O(N)$ time complexity, where N is the size of `hospital_id`. Pandas allows you to encode the same operation using simple indexing; the advantage is that the join will be performed in heavily optimized Cython and with efficient hashing algorithms. The preceding simple Python expression can be easily converted to Pandas in this way:

```
cities = hospitals.loc[hospital_id, "city"]
```

More advanced joins can also be performed with the `pd.DataFrame.join` method, which will produce a new `pd.DataFrame` that will attach the hospital information for each patient:

```
result = df.join(hospitals, on='hospital_id')
result.columns
# Result:
# Index(['dia_final', 'dia_initial', 'drug_admst',
# 'sys_final', 'sys_initial',
# 'hospital_id', 'address', 'city', 'name'],
# dtype='object')
```

Summary

In this chapter, we learned how to manipulate NumPy arrays and how to write fast mathematical expressions using array broadcasting. This knowledge will help you write more concise, expressive code and, at the same time, to obtain substantial performance gains. We also introduced the `numexpr` library to further speed up NumPy calculations with minimal effort.

Pandas implements efficient data structures that are useful when analyzing large datasets. In particular, Pandas shines when the data is indexed by non-integer keys and provides very fast hashing algorithms.

NumPy and Pandas work well when handling large, homogenous inputs, but they are not suitable when the expressions grow complex and the operations cannot be expressed using the tools provided by these libraries. In such cases, we can leverage Python capabilities as a glue language by interfacing it with C using the Cython package.

C Performance with Cython

4

Cython is a language that extends Python by supporting the declaration of types for functions, variables, and classes. These typed declarations enable Cython to compile Python scripts to efficient C code. Cython can also act as a bridge between Python and C as it provides easy-to-use constructs to write interfaces to external C and C++ routines.

In this chapter, we will learn the following things:

- Cython syntax basics
- How to compile Cython programs
- How to use **static typing** to generate fast code
- How to efficiently manipulate arrays using typed **memoryviews**
- Optimizing a sample particle simulator
- Tips on using Cython in the Jupyter notebook
- The profiling tools available for Cython

While a minimum knowledge of C is helpful, this chapter focuses only on Cython in the context of Python optimization. Therefore, it doesn't require any C background.

Compiling Cython extensions

The Cython syntax is, by design, a superset of Python. Cython can compile, with a few exceptions, most Python modules without requiring any change. Cython source files have the `.pyx` extension and can be compiled to produce a C file using the `cython` command.

Our first Cython script will contain a simple function that prints `Hello, World!` as the output.

Create a new `hello.pyx` file containing the following code:

```
def hello():
    print('Hello, World!')
```

The `cython` command will read `hello.pyx` and generate the `hello.c` file:

```
$ cython hello.pyx
```

To compile `hello.c` to a Python extension module, we will use the GCC compiler. We need to add some Python-specific compilation options that depend on the operating system. It's important to specify the directory that contains the header files; in the following example, the directory is `/usr/include/python3.5/`:

```
$ gcc -shared -pthread -fPIC -fwrapv -O2 -Wall -fno-strict-aliasing -lm -
I/usr/include/python3.5/ -o hello.so hello.c
```

 To find your Python include directory, you can use the `distutils` utility: `sysconfig.get_python_inc`. To execute it, you can simply issue the following `python -c "from distutils import sysconfig; print(sysconfig.get_python_inc())"` command.

This will produce a file called `hello.so`, a C extension module that is directly importable into a Python session:

```
>>> import hello
>>> hello.hello()
Hello, World!
```

Cython accepts both Python 2 and Python 3 as input and output languages. In other words, you can compile a Python 3 script `hello.pyx` file using the `-3` option:

```
$ cython -3 hello.pyx
```

The generated `hello.c` can be compiled without any changes to Python 2 and Python 3 by including the corresponding headers with the `-I` option, as follows:

```
$ gcc -I/usr/include/python3.5 # ... other options
$ gcc -I/usr/include/python2.7 # ... other options
```

A Cython program can be compiled in a more straightforward way using `distutils`, the standard Python packaging tool. By writing a `setup.py` script, we can compile the `.pyx` file directly to an extension module. To compile our `hello.pyx` example, we can write a minimal `setup.py` containing the following code:

```
from distutils.core import setup
```

```
from Cython.Build import cythonize

setup(
    name='Hello',
    ext_modules = cythonize('hello.pyx')
)
```

In the first two lines of the preceding code, we import the `setup` function and the `cythonize` helper. The `setup` function contains a few key-value pairs that specify the name of the application and the extensions that need to be built.

The `cythonize` helper takes either a string or a list of strings containing the Cython modules we want to compile. You can also use glob patterns using the following code:

```
cythonize(['hello.pyx', 'world.pyx', '*.pyx'])
```

To compile our extension module using `distutils`, you can execute the `setup.py` script using the following code:

```
$ python setup.py build_ext --inplace
```

The `build_ext` option tells the script to build the extension modules indicated in `ext_modules`, while the `--inplace` option tells the script to place the `hello.so` output file in the same location as the source file (instead of a build directory).

Cython modules can also be automatically compiled using `pyximport`. All that's needed is a call to `pyximport.install()` at the beginning of your script (or you need to issue the command in your interpreter). After doing that, you can import `.pyx` files directly and `pyximport` will transparently compile the corresponding Cython modules:

```
>>> import pyximport
>>> pyximport.install()
>>> import hello # This will compile hello.pyx
```

Unfortunately, `pyximport` will not work for all kinds of configurations (for example, when they involve a combination of C and Cython files), but it comes handy for testing simple scripts.

Since version 0.13, IPython includes the `cythonmagic` extension to interactively write and test a series of Cython statements. You can load the extensions in an IPython shell using `load_ext`:

```
%load_ext Cython
```

Once the extension is loaded, you can use the `%%cython` *cell magic* to write a multiline Cython snippet. In the following example, we define a `hello_snippet` function that will be compiled and added to the IPython session namespace:

```
%%cython
def hello_snippet():
    print("Hello, Cython!")

hello_snippet()
Hello, Cython!
```

Adding static types

In Python, a variable can be associated to objects of different types during the execution of the program. While this feature is desirable as it makes the language flexible and dynamic, it also adds a significant overhead to the interpreter as it needs to look up type and methods of the variables at runtime, making it difficult to perform various optimizations. Cython extends the Python language with explicit type declarations so that it can generate efficient C extensions through compilation.

The main way to declare data types in Cython is through `cdef` statements. The `cdef` keyword can be used in multiple contexts, such as variables, functions, and extension types (statically-typed classes).

Variables

In Cython, you can declare the type of a variable by prepending the variable with `cdef` and its respective type. For example, we can declare the `i` variable as a 16 bit integer in the following way:

```
cdef int i
```

The `cdef` statement supports multiple variable names on the same line along with optional initialization, as seen in the following line:

```
cdef double a, b = 2.0, c = 3.0
```

Typed variables are treated differently in comparison to regular variables. In Python, variables are often described as *labels* that refer to objects in memory. For example, we could assign the value `'hello'` to the `a` variable at any point in the program without restriction:

```
a = 'hello'
```

The a variable holds a reference to the 'hello' string. We can also freely assign another value (for example, the integer 1) to the same variable later in the code:

```
a = 1
```

Python will assign the integer 1 to the a variable without any problem.

Typed variables behave quite differently and are usually described as *data containers:* we can only store values that fit into the container that is determined by its data type. For example, if we declare the a variable as int, and then we try to assign it to a double, Cython will trigger an error, as shown in the following code:

```
%%cython
cdef int i
i = 3.0

# Output has been cut
...cf4b.pyx:2:4 Cannot assign type 'double' to 'int'
```

Static typing makes it easy for the compiler to perform useful optimizations. For example, if we declare a loop index as int, Cython will rewrite the loop in pure C without needing to step into the Python interpreter. The typing declaration guarantees that the type of the index will always be int and cannot be overwritten at runtime so that the compiler is free to perform the optimizations without compromising the program correctness.

We can assess the speed gain in this case with a small test case. In the following example, we implement a simple loop that increments a variable 100 times. With Cython, the example function can be coded as follows:

```
%%cython
def example():
    cdef int i, j=0
    for i in range(100):
        j += 1
    return j

example()
# Result:
# 100
```

We can compare the speed of an analogous, untyped, pure Python loop:

```
def example_python():
    j=0
    for i in range(100):
```

```
            j += 1
        return j

    %timeit example()
    10000000 loops, best of 3: 25 ns per loop
    %timeit example_python()
    100000 loops, best of 3: 2.74 us per loop
```

The speedup obtained by implementing this simple type declaration is a whopping 100x! This works because the Cython loop has first been converted to pure C and then to efficient machine code, while the Python loop still relies on the slow interpreter.

In Cython, it is possible to declare a variable to be of any standard C type, and it is also possible to define custom types using classic C constructs, such as struct, enum, and typedef.

An interesting example is that if we declare a variable to be of the object type, the variable will accept any kind of Python object:

```
    cdef object a_py
    # both 'hello' and 1 are Python objects
    a_py = 'hello'
    a_py = 1
```

Note that declaring a variable as object has no performance benefits as accessing and operating on the object will still require the interpreter to look up the underlying type of the variable and its attributes and methods.

Sometimes, certain data types (such as float and int numbers) are compatible in the sense that they can be converted into each other. In Cython, it is possible to convert (*cast*) between types by surrounding the destination type between pointy brackets, as shown in the following snippet:

```
    cdef int a = 0
    cdef double b
    b = <double> a
```

Functions

You can add type information to the arguments of a Python function by specifying the type in front of each of the argument names. Functions specified in this way will work and perform like regular Python functions, but their arguments will be type-checked. We can write a max_python function, which returns the greater value between two integers:

```
def max_python(int a, int b):
    return a if a > b else b
```

A function specified in this way will perform type-checking and treat the arguments as typed variables, just like in cdef definitions. However, the function will still be a Python function, and calling it multiple times will still need to switch back to the interpreter. To allow Cython for function call optimizations, we should declare the type of the return type using a cdef statement:

```
cdef int max_cython(int a, int b):
    return a if a > b else b
```

Functions declared in this way are translated to native C functions and have much less overhead compared to Python functions. A substantial drawback is that they can't be used from Python, but only from Cython, and their scope is restricted to the same Cython file unless they're exposed in a definition file (refer to the *Sharing declarations* section).

Fortunately, Cython allows you to define functions that are both callable from Python and translatable to performant C functions. If you declare a function with a cpdef statement, Cython will generate two versions of the function: a Python version available to the interpreter, and a fast C function usable from Cython. The cpdef syntax is equivalent to cdef, shown as follows:

```
cpdef int max_hybrid(int a, int b):
    return a if a > b else b
```

Sometimes, the call overhead can be a performance issue even with C functions, especially when the same function is called many times in a critical loop. When the function body is small, it is convenient to add the inline keyword in front of the function definition; the function call will be replaced by the function body itself. Our max function is a good candidate for *inlining*:

```
cdef inline int max_inline(int a, int b):
    return a if a > b else b
```

Classes

We can define an extension type using the cdef class statement and declaring its attributes in the class body. For example, we can create an extension type--Point--as shown in the following code, which stores two coordinates (*x*, *y*) of the double type:

```
cdef class Point
    cdef double x
    cdef double y
```

```
def __init__(self, double x, double y):
    self.x = x
    self.y = y
```

Accessing the declared attributes in the class methods allows Cython to bypass expensive Python attribute look-ups by direct access to the given fields in the underlying C `struct`. For this reason, attribute access in typed classes is an extremely fast operation.

To use the `cdef class` in your code, you need to explicitly declare the type of the variables you intend to use at compile time. You can use the extension type name (such as `Point`) in any context where you will use a standard type (such as `double`, `float`, and `int`). For example, if we want a Cython function that calculates the distance from the origin (in the example, the function is called `norm`) of a `Point`, we have to declare the input variable as `Point`, as shown in the following code:

```
cdef double norm(Point p):
    return (p.x**2 + p.y**2)**0.5
```

Just like typed functions, typed classes have some limitations. If you try to access an extension type attribute from Python, you will get an `AttributeError`, as follows:

```
>>> a = Point(0.0, 0.0)
>>> a.x
AttributeError: 'Point' object has no attribute 'x'
```

In order to access attributes from Python code, you have to use the `public` (for read/write access) or `readonly` specifiers in the attribute declaration, as shown in the following code:

```
cdef class Point:
    cdef public double x
```

Additionally, methods can be declared with the `cpdef` statement, just like regular functions.

Extension types do not support the addition of extra attributes at runtime. In order to do that, a solution is defining a Python class that is a subclass of the typed class and extends its attributes and methods in pure Python.

Sharing declarations

When writing your Cython modules, you may want to reorganize your most used functions and classes declaration in a separate file so that they can be reused in different modules. Cython allows you to put these components in a *definition file* and access them with `cimport` statements.

Let's say that we have a module with the `max` and `min` functions, and we want to reuse those functions in multiple Cython programs. If we simply write a bunch of functions in a `.pyx` file, the declarations will be confined to the same file.

 Definition files are also used to interface Cython with external C code. The idea is to copy (or, more accurately, translate) the types and function prototypes in the definition file and leave the implementation in the external C code that will be compiled and linked in a separate step.

To share the `max` and `min` functions, we need to write a definition file with a `.pxd` extension. Such a file only contains the types and function prototypes that we want to share with other modules--a *public* interface. We can declare the prototypes of our `max` and `min` functions in a file named `mathlib.pxd`, as follows:

```
cdef int max(int a, int b)
cdef int min(int a, int b)
```

As you can see, we only write the function name and arguments without implementing the function body.

The function implementation goes into the implementation file with the same base name but the `.pyx` extension--`mathlib.pyx`:

```
cdef int max(int a, int b):
    return a if a > b else b

cdef int min(int a, int b):
    return a if a < b else b
```

The `mathlib` module is now importable from another Cython module.

To test our new Cython module, we will create a file named `distance.pyx` containing a function named `chebyshev`. The function will calculate the Chebyshev distance between two points, as shown in the following code. The Chebyshev distance between two coordinates--`(x1, y1)` and `(x2, y2)`--is defined as the maximum value of the difference between each coordinate:

```
max(abs(x1 - x2), abs(y1 - y2))
```

To implement the `chebyshev` function, we will use the `max` function declared in `mathlib.pxd` by importing it with the `cimport` statement, as shown in the following code snippet:

```
from mathlib cimport max

def chebyshev(int x1, int y1, int x2, int y2):
    return max(abs(x1 - x2), abs(y1 - y2))
```

The cimport statement will read `mathlib.pxd` and the `max` definition will be used to generate the `distance.c` file

Working with arrays

Numerical and high performance calculations often make use of arrays. Cython provides an easy way to interact with them, using directly low-level C arrays, or the more general *typed memoryviews*.

C arrays and pointers

C arrays are a collection of items of the same type, stored contiguously in memory. Before digging into the details, it is helpful to understand (or review) how memory is managed in C.

Variables in C are like containers. When creating a variable, a space in memory is reserved to store its value. For example, if we create a variable containing a 64 bit floating point number (`double`), the program will allocate 64 bit (16 bytes) of memory. This portion of memory can be accessed through an address to that memory location.

To obtain the address of a variable, we can use the *address operator* denoted by the & symbol. We can also use the `printf` function, as follows, available in the `libc.stdio` Cython module to print the address of this variable:

```
%%cython
cdef double a
from libc.stdio cimport printf
printf("%p", &a)
# Output:
# 0x7fc8bb611210
```

 Note that the output will only be generated when the aforementioned code is run from a standard python terminal. This limitation of IPython is detailed at https://github.com/ipython/ipython/issues/1230

Memory addresses can be stored in special variables, *pointers*, that can be declared by putting a * prefix in front of the variable name, as follows:

```
from libc.stdio cimport printf
cdef double a
cdef double *a_pointer
a_pointer = &a # a_pointer and &a are of the same type
```

If we have a pointer, and we want to grab the value contained in the address it's pointing at, we can use the *dereference operator* denoted by the * symbol. Be careful, the * used in this context has a different meaning from the * used in the variable declaration:

```
cdef double a
cdef double *a_pointer
a_pointer = &a

a = 3.0
print(*a_pointer) # prints 3.0
```

When declaring a C array, the program allocates enough space to accommodate all the elements requested. For instance, to create an array that has 10 double values (16 bytes each), the program will reserve *16 * 10 = 160* bytes of contiguous space in memory. In Cython, we can declare such arrays using the following syntax:

```
cdef double arr[10]
```

We can also declare a multidimensional array, such as an array with 5 rows and 2 columns, using the following syntax:

```
cdef double arr[5][2]
```

The memory will be allocated in a single block of memory, row after row. This order is commonly referred to as *row-major* and is depicted in the following figure. Arrays can also be ordered *column-major*, as is the case for the FORTRAN programming language:

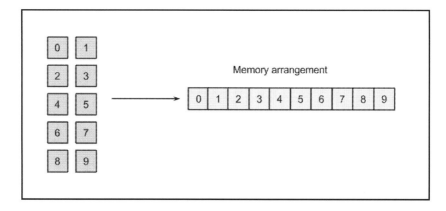

Array ordering has important consequences. When iterating a C array over the last dimension, we access contiguous memory blocks (in our example, 0, 1, 2, 3 ...) while when we iterate on the first dimension, we skip a few positions (0, 2, 4, 6, 8, 1 ...). You should always try to access memory sequentially as this optimizes cache and memory usage.

We can store and retrieve elements from the array using standard indexing; C arrays don't support fancy indexing or slices:

```
arr[0] = 1.0
```

C arrays have many of the same behaviors as pointers. The arr variable, in fact, points to the memory location of the first element of the array. We can verify that the address of the first element of the array is the same as the address contained in the arr variable using the dereference operator, as follows:

```
%%cython
from libc.stdio cimport printf
cdef double arr[10]
printf("%p\n", arr)
printf("%p\n", &arr[0])
# Output
# 0x7ff6de204220
# 0x7ff6de204220
```

Note that the output will only be generated when the aforementioned code is run from a standard python terminal. This limitation of IPython is detailed at `https://github.com/ipython/ipython/issues/1230`

You should use C arrays and pointers when interfacing with the existing C libraries or when you need a fine control over the memory (also, they are very performant). This level of fine control is also prone to mistakes as it doesn't prevent you from accessing the wrong memory locations. For more common use cases and improved safety, you can use NumPy arrays or typed memoryviews.

NumPy arrays

NumPy arrays can be used as normal Python objects in Cython using their already optimized broadcasted operations. However, Cython provides a `numpy` module with better support for direct iteration.

When we normally access an element of a NumPy array, a few other operations take place at the interpreter level causing a major overhead. Cython can bypass those operations and checks by acting directly on the underlying memory area used by NumPy arrays, and thus obtaining impressive performance gains.

NumPy arrays can be declared as the `ndarray` data type. To use the data type in our code, we first need to `cimport` the `numpy` Cython module (which is not the same as the Python NumPy module). We will bind the module to the `c_np` variable to make the difference with the Python `numpy` module more explicit:

```
cimport numpy as c_np
import numpy as np
```

We can now declare a NumPy array by specifying its type and the number of dimensions between square brackets (this is called *buffer syntax*). To declare a two-dimensional array of type `double`, we can use the following code:

```
cdef c_np.ndarray[double, ndim=2] arr
```

Access to this array will be performed by directly operating on the underlying memory area; the operation will avoid stepping into the interpreter, giving us a tremendous speed boost.

In the next example, we will show the usage of typed numpy arrays and compare them with the normal Python version.

We first write the `numpy_bench_py` function that increments each element of `py_arr`. We declare the `i` index as an integer so that we avoid the for-loop overhead:

```
%%cython
import numpy as np
def numpy_bench_py():
    py_arr = np.random.rand(1000)
    cdef int i
    for i in range(1000):
        py_arr[i] += 1
```

Then, we write the same function using the `ndarray` type. Note that after we define the `c_arr` variable using `c_np.ndarray`, we can assign to it an array from the `numpy` Python module:

```
%%cython
import numpy as np
cimport numpy as c_np

def numpy_bench_c():
    cdef c_np.ndarray[double, ndim=1] c_arr
    c_arr = np.random.rand(1000)
    cdef int i

    for i in range(1000):
        c_arr[i] += 1
```

We can time the results using `timeit`, and we can see how the typed version is 50x faster:

```
%timeit numpy_bench_c()
100000 loops, best of 3: 11.5 us per loop
%timeit numpy_bench_py()
1000 loops, best of 3: 603 us per loop
```

Typed memoryviews

C and NumPy arrays as well as the built-in `bytes`, `bytearray`, and `array.array` objects are similar in the sense that they all operate on a contiguous memory area (also called memory *buffer*). Cython provides a universal interface--the *typed memoryview*--that unifies and simplifies the access to all these data types.

A **memoryview** is an object that maintains a reference on a specific memory area. It doesn't actually own the memory, but it can read and change its contents; in other words, it is a *view* on the underlying data. Memoryviews can be defined using a special syntax. For example, we can define a memoryview of int and a two-dimensional memoryview of double in the following way:

```
cdef int[:] a
cdef double[:, :] b
```

The same syntax applies to the declaration of any type in variables, function definitions, class attributes, and so on. Any object that exposes a buffer interface (for example, NumPy arrays, bytes, and array.array objects) will be bound to the memoryview automatically. For example, we can bind the memoryview to a NumPy array using a simple variable assignment:

```
import numpy as np

cdef int[:] arr
arr_np = np.zeros(10, dtype='int32')
arr = arr_np # We bind the array to the memoryview
```

It is important to note that the memoryview does not *own* the data, but it only provides a way to *access* and *change* the data it is bound to; the ownership, in this case, is left to the NumPy array. As you can see in the following example, changes made through the memoryview will act on the underlying memory area and will be reflected in the original NumPy structure (and vice versa):

```
arr[2] = 1 # Changing memoryview
print(arr_np)
# [0 0 1 0 0 0 0 0 0 0]
```

In a certain sense, the mechanism behind memoryviews is similar to what NumPy produces when we slice an array. As we have seen in Chapter 3, *Fast Array Operations with NumPy and Pandas*, slicing a NumPy array does not copy the data but returns a view on the same memory area, and changes to the view will reflect on the original array.

Memoryviews also support array slicing with the standard NumPy syntax:

```
cdef int[:, :, :] a
arr[0, :, :] # Is a 2-dimensional memoryview
arr[0, 0, :] # Is a 1-dimensional memoryview
arr[0, 0, 0] # Is an int
```

To copy data between one memoryview and another, you can use syntax similar to slice assignment, as shown in the following code:

```
import numpy as np

cdef double[:, :] b
cdef double[:] r
b = np.random.rand(10, 3)
r = np.zeros(3, dtype='float64')

b[0, :] = r # Copy the value of r in the first row of b
```

In the next section, we will use the typed memoryviews to declare types for the arrays in our particle simulator.

Particle simulator in Cython

Now that we have a basic understanding of how Cython works, we can rewrite the `ParticleSimulator.evolve` method. Thanks to Cython, we can convert our loops in C, thus removing the overhead introduced by the Python interpreter.

In Chapter 3, *Fast Array Operations with NumPy and Pandas,* we wrote a fairly efficient version of the `evolve` method using NumPy. We can rename the old version as `evolve_numpy` to differentiate it from the new version:

```
def evolve_numpy(self, dt):
    timestep = 0.00001
    nsteps = int(dt/timestep)

    r_i = np.array([[p.x, p.y] for p in self.particles])
    ang_speed_i = np.array([p.ang_speed for p in self.particles])
    v_i = np.empty_like(r_i)

    for i in range(nsteps):
        norm_i = np.sqrt((r_i ** 2).sum(axis=1))

        v_i = r_i[:, [1, 0]]
        v_i[:, 0] *= -1
        v_i /= norm_i[:, np.newaxis]

        d_i = timestep * ang_speed_i[:, np.newaxis] * v_i

        r_i += d_i
```

```
    for i, p in enumerate(self.particles):
        p.x, p.y = r_i[i]
```

We want to convert this code to Cython. Our strategy will be to take advantage of the fast indexing operations by removing the NumPy array broadcasting, thus reverting to an indexing-based algorithm. Since Cython generates efficient C code, we are free to use as many loops as we like without any performance penalty.

As a design choice, we can decide to encapsulate the loop in a function that we will rewrite in a Cython module called `cevolve.pyx`. The module will contain a single Python function, c_evolve, that will take the particle positions, angular velocities, timestep, and number of steps as input.

At first, we are not adding typing information; we just want to isolate the function and ensure that we can compile our module without errors:

```
# file: simul.py
def evolve_cython(self, dt):
    timestep = 0.00001
    nsteps = int(dt/timestep)

    r_i = np.array([[p.x, p.y] for p in self.particles])
    ang_speed_i = np.array([p.ang_speed for p in self.particles])

    c_evolve(r_i, ang_speed_i, timestep, nsteps)

    for i, p in enumerate(self.particles):
        p.x, p.y = r_i[i]

# file: cevolve.pyx
import numpy as np

def c_evolve(r_i, ang_speed_i, timestep, nsteps):
    v_i = np.empty_like(r_i)

    for i in range(nsteps):
        norm_i = np.sqrt((r_i ** 2).sum(axis=1))

        v_i = r_i[:, [1, 0]]
        v_i[:, 0] *= -1
        v_i /= norm_i[:, np.newaxis]
        d_i = timestep * ang_speed_i[:, np.newaxis] * v_i

        r_i += d_i
```

Note that we don't need a return value for `c_evolve` as values are updated in the `r_i` array in-place. We can benchmark the untyped Cython version against the old NumPy version by slightly changing our benchmark function, as follows:

```
def benchmark(npart=100, method='python'):
    particles = [Particle(uniform(-1.0, 1.0),
                          uniform(-1.0, 1.0),
                          uniform(-1.0, 1.0))
                          for i in range(npart)]
    simulator = ParticleSimulator(particles)
    if method=='python':
        simulator.evolve_python(0.1)
    elif method == 'cython':
        simulator.evolve_cython(0.1)
    elif method == 'numpy':
        simulator.evolve_numpy(0.1)
```

We can time the different versions in an IPython shell:

```
%timeit benchmark(100, 'cython')
1 loops, best of 3: 401 ms per loop
%timeit benchmark(100, 'numpy')
1 loops, best of 3: 413 ms per loop
```

The two versions have the same speed. Compiling the Cython module without static typing doesn't have any advantage over pure Python. The next step is to declare the type of all the important variables so that Cython can perform its optimizations.

We can start adding types to the function arguments and see how the performance changes. We can declare the arrays as typed memoryviews containing `double` values. It's worth mentioning that if we pass an array of the `int` or `float32` type, the casting won't happen automatically and we will get an error:

```
def c_evolve(double[:, :] r_i,
             double[:] ang_speed_i,
             double timestep,
             int nsteps):
```

At this point, we can rewrite the loops over the particles and timesteps. We can declare the
i and j iteration indices and the `nparticles` particle number as `int`:

```
cdef int i, j
cdef int nparticles = r_i.shape[0]
```

The algorithm is very similar to the pure Python version; we iterate over the particles and
timesteps, and we compute the velocity and displacement vectors for each particle
coordinate using the following code:

```
for i in range(nsteps):
    for j in range(nparticles):
        x = r_i[j, 0]
        y = r_i[j, 1]
        ang_speed = ang_speed_i[j]

        norm = sqrt(x ** 2 + y ** 2)

        vx = (-y)/norm
        vy = x/norm

        dx = timestep * ang_speed * vx
        dy = timestep * ang_speed * vy

        r_i[j, 0] += dx
        r_i[j, 1] += dy
```

In the preceding code, we added the x, y, ang_speed, norm, vx, vy, dx, and dy variables.
To avoid the Python interpreter overhead, we have to declare them with their
corresponding types at the beginning of the function, as follows:

```
cdef double norm, x, y, vx, vy, dx, dy, ang_speed
```

We also used a function called `sqrt` to calculate the norm. If we use the `sqrt` present in the
math module or the one in numpy, we will again include a slow Python function in our
critical loop, thus killing our performance. A fast `sqrt` is available in the standard C
library, already wrapped in the `libc.math` Cython module:

```
from libc.math cimport sqrt
```

We can rerun our benchmark to assess our improvements, as follows:

```
In [4]: %timeit benchmark(100, 'cython')
100 loops, best of 3: 13.4 ms per loop
In [5]: %timeit benchmark(100, 'numpy')
1 loops, best of 3: 429 ms per loop
```

For small particle numbers, the speed-up is massive as we obtained a 40x performance over the previous version. However, we should also try to test the performance scaling with a larger number of particles:

```
In [2]: %timeit benchmark(1000, 'cython')
10 loops, best of 3: 134 ms per loop
In [3]: %timeit benchmark(1000, 'numpy')
1 loops, best of 3: 877 ms per loop
```

As we increase the number of particles, the two versions get closer in speed. By increasing the particle size to 1000, we already decreased our speed-up to a more modest 6x. This is likely due to the fact that, as we increase the number of particles, the Python for-loop overhead becomes less and less significant compared to the speed of other operations.

Profiling Cython

Cython provides a feature, called *annotated view*, that helps find which lines are executed in the Python interpreter and which are good candidates for ulterior optimizations. We can turn this feature on by compiling a Cython file with the –a option. In this way, Cython will generate an HTML file containing our code annotated with some useful information. The usage of the –a option is as follows:

```
$ cython -a cevolve.pyx
$ firefox cevolve.html
```

The HTML file displayed in the following screenshot shows our Cython file line by line:

```
generated for it.

Raw output: cevolve.c

+01: import numpy as np
 02: cimport cython
 03: from libc.math cimport sqrt
 04:
+05: def c_evolve(double[:, :] r_i,double[:] ang_speed_i,
 06:              double timestep,int nsteps):
 07:     cdef int i
 08:     cdef int j
+09:     cdef int nparticles = r_i.shape[0]
 10:     cdef double norm, x, y, vx, vy, dx, dy, ang_speed
 11:
 12:
+13:     for i in range(nsteps):
+14:         for j in range(nparticles):
+15:             x = r_i[j, 0]
+16:             y = r_i[j, 1]
+17:             ang_speed = ang_speed_i[j]
 18:
+19:             norm = sqrt(x ** 2 + y ** 2)
 20:
+21:             vx = (-y)/norm
+22:             vy = x/norm
       if (unlikely(__pyx_v_norm == 0)) {
         #ifdef WITH_THREAD
         PyGILState_STATE __pyx_gilstate_save = PyGILState_Ensure();
         #endif
         PyErr_SetString(PyExc_ZeroDivisionError, "float division");
         #ifdef WITH_THREAD
         PyGILState_Release(__pyx_gilstate_save);
         #endif
         {__pyx_filename = __pyx_f[0]; __pyx_lineno = 22; __pyx_clineno = __LINE__; goto __pyx_L1_error;}
       }
       __pyx_v_vy = (__pyx_v_x / __pyx_v_norm);
 23:
+24:             dx = timestep * ang_speed * vx
+25:             dy = timestep * ang_speed * vy
 26:
+27:             r_i[j, 0] += dx
+28:             r_i[j, 1] += dy
 29:
```

Each line in the source code can appear in different shades of yellow. A more intense color corresponds to more interpreter-related calls, while white lines are translated to regular C code. Since interpreter calls substantially slow down execution, the objective is to make the function body as white as possible. By clicking on any of the lines, we can inspect the code generated by the Cython compiler. For example, the `v_y = x/norm` line checks that the norm is not 0 and raises a `ZeroDivisionError` if the condition is not verified. The `x = r_i[j, 0]` line shows that Cython checks whether the indexes are within the bounds of the array. You may note that the last line is of a very intense color; by inspecting the code, we can see that this is actually a glitch; the code refers to a boilerplate related to the end of the function.

Cython can shut down checks, such as division by zero, so that it can remove those extra interpreter related calls; this is usually accomplished through compiler directives. There are a few different ways to add compiler directives:

- Using a decorator or a context manager
- Using a comment at the beginning of the file
- Using the Cython command-line options

 For a complete list of the Cython compiler directives, you can refer to the official documentation at http://docs.cython.org/src/reference/ compilation.html#compiler-directives.

For example, to disable bounds checking for arrays, it is sufficient to decorate a function with cython.boundscheck, in the following way:

```
cimport cython

@cython.boundscheck(False)
def myfunction():
    # Code here
```

Alternatively, we can use cython.boundscheck to wrap a block of code into a context manager, as follows:

```
with cython.boundscheck(False):
    # Code here
```

If we want to disable bounds checking for a whole module, we can add the following line of code at the beginning of the file:

```
# cython: boundscheck=False
```

To alter the directives with the command-line options, you can use the -X option as follows:

```
$ cython -X boundscheck=True
```

To disable the extra checks in our c_evolve function, we can disable the boundscheck directive and enable cdivision (this prevents checks for ZeroDivisionError), as in the following code:

```
cimport cython

@cython.boundscheck(False)
@cython.cdivision(True)
def c_evolve(double[:, :] r_i,
```

```
        double[:] ang_speed_i,
        double timestep,
        int nsteps):
```

If we look at the annotated view again, the loop body has become completely white--we removed all traces of the interpreter from the inner loop. In order to recompile, just type `python setup.py build_ext --inplace` again. By running the benchmark, however, we note that we didn't obtain a performance improvement, suggesting that those checks are not part of the bottleneck:

```
In [3]: %timeit benchmark(100, 'cython')
100 loops, best of 3: 13.4 ms per loop
```

Another way to profile Cython code is through the use of the `cProfile` module. As an example, we can write a simple function that calculates the Chebyshev distance between coordinate arrays. Create a `cheb.py` file:

```
import numpy as np
from distance import chebyshev

def benchmark():
    a = np.random.rand(100, 2)
    b = np.random.rand(100, 2)
    for x1, y1 in a:
        for x2, y2 in b:
            chebyshev(x1, x2, y1, y2)
```

If we try profiling this script as-is, we won't get any statistics regarding the functions that we implemented in Cython. If we want to collect profiling information for the `max` and `min` functions, we need to add the `profile=True` option to the `mathlib.pyx` file, as shown in the following code:

```
# cython: profile=True

cdef int max(int a, int b):
    # Code here
```

We can now profile our script with `%prun` using IPython, as follows:

```
import cheb
%prun cheb.benchmark()

# Output:
2000005 function calls in 2.066 seconds

  Ordered by: internal time
```

```
ncalls  tottime  percall  cumtime  percall  filename:lineno(function)
     1    1.664    1.664    2.066    2.066  cheb.py:4(benchmark)
1000000    0.351    0.000    0.401    0.000  {distance.chebyshev}
1000000    0.050    0.000    0.050    0.000  mathlib.pyx:2(max)
     2    0.000    0.000    0.000    0.000  {method 'rand' of
'mtrand.RandomState' objects}
     1    0.000    0.000    2.066    2.066  <string>:1(<module>)
     1    0.000    0.000    0.000    0.000  {method 'disable' of
'_lsprof.Profiler' objects}
```

From the output, we can see that the max function is present and is not a bottleneck. Most of the time seems to be spent in the benchmark function, meaning that the bottleneck is likely the pure Python for-loop. In this case, the best strategy will be rewriting the loop in NumPy or porting the code to Cython.

Using Cython with Jupyter

Optimizing Cython code requires substantial trial and error. Fortunately, Cython tools can be conveniently accessed through the Jupyter notebook for a more streamlined and integrated experience.

You can launch a notebook session by typing jupyter notebook in the command line and you can load the Cython magic by typing %load_ext cython in a cell.

As already mentioned earlier, the %%cython magic can be used to compile and load the Cython code inside the current session. As an example, we may copy the contents of cheb.py into a notebook cell:

```
%%cython
import numpy as np

cdef int max(int a, int b):
    return a if a > b else b

cdef int chebyshev(int x1, int y1, int x2, int y2):
    return max(abs(x1 - x2), abs(y1 - y2))

def c_benchmark():
    a = np.random.rand(1000, 2)
    b = np.random.rand(1000, 2)

    for x1, y1 in a:
        for x2, y2 in b:
            chebyshev(x1, x2, y1, y2)
```

A useful feature of the `%%cython` magic is the `-a` option that will compile the code and produce an annotated view (just like the command line `-a` option) of the source directly in the notebook, as shown in the following screenshot:

```
In [15]: %%cython -a
         import numpy as np

         cdef int max(int a, int b):
             return a if a > b else b

         cdef int chebyshev(int x1, int y1, int x2, int y2):
             return max(abs(x1 - x2), abs(y1 - y2))

         def c_benchmark():
             a = np.random.rand(1000, 2)
             b = np.random.rand(1000, 2)

             for x1, y1 in a:
                 for x2, y2 in b:
                     chebyshev(x1, x2, y1, y2)
```

```
Out[15]:
         Generated by Cython 0.25.2

         Yellow lines hint at Python interaction.
         Click on a line that starts with a "+" to see the C code that Cython generated for it.
          01: # cython: profile=True
         +02: import numpy as np
          03:
         +04: cdef int max(int a, int b):
         +05:     return a if a > b else b
          06:
         +07: cdef int chebyshev(int x1, int y1, int x2, int y2):
         +08:     return max(abs(x1 - x2), abs(y1 - y2))
          09:
         +10: def c_benchmark():
         +11:     a = np.random.rand(1000, 2)
         +12:     b = np.random.rand(1000, 2)
          13:
         +14:     for x1, y1 in a:
         +15:         for x2, y2 in b:
         +16:             chebyshev(x1, x2, y1, y2)
```

This allows you to quickly test different versions of your code and also use the other integrated tools available in Jupyter. For example, we can time and profile the code (provided that we activate the profile directive in the cell) in the same session using tools such as %prun and %timeit. For example, we can inspect the profiling results by taking advantage of the %prun magic, as shown in the following screenshot:

```
In [22]: %prun c_benchmark()
```

```
         2000005 function calls in 1.370 seconds

   Ordered by: internal time

   ncalls  tottime  percall  cumtime  percall filename:lineno(function)
        1    1.127    1.127    1.370    1.370 _cython_magic_c7d6eab16ab5658137c9af8534d5cafb.pyx:10(c_benchma
rk)
  1000000    0.191    0.000    0.243    0.000 _cython_magic_c7d6eab16ab5658137c9af8534d5cafb.pyx:7(chebyshev)
  1000000    0.052    0.000    0.052    0.000 _cython_magic_c7d6eab16ab5658137c9af8534d5cafb.pyx:4(max)
        1    0.000    0.000    1.370    1.370 <string>:1(<module>)
        1    0.000    0.000    1.370    1.370 {built-in method builtins.exec}
        1    0.000    0.000    1.370    1.370 {_cython_magic_c7d6eab16ab5658137c9af8534d5cafb.c_benchmark}
        1    0.000    0.000    0.000    0.000 {method 'disable' of '_lsprof.Profiler' objects}
```

It is also possible to use the line_profiler tool we discussed in Chapter 1, *Benchmarking and Profiling*, directly in the notebook. In order to support line annotations, it is necessary to do the following things:

- Enable the linetrace=True and binding=True compiler directives
- Enable the CYTHON_TRACE=1 flag at compile time

This can be easily accomplished by adding the respective arguments to the %%cython magic, and by setting the compiler directives, as shown in the following code:

```
%%cython -a -f -c=-DCYTHON_TRACE=1
# cython: linetrace=True
# cython: binding=True

import numpy as np

cdef int max(int a, int b):
    return a if a > b else b

def chebyshev(int x1, int y1, int x2, int y2):
    return max(abs(x1 - x2), abs(y1 - y2))

def c_benchmark():
    a = np.random.rand(1000, 2)
    b = np.random.rand(1000, 2)
```

```
    for x1, y1 in a:
        for x2, y2 in b:
            chebyshev(x1, x2, y1, y2)
```

Once the code is instrumented, we can profile using the `%lprun` magic:

```
%lprun -f c_benchmark c_benchmark()
# Output:
Timer unit: 1e-06 s

Total time: 2.322 s
File:
/home/gabriele/.cache/ipython/cython/_cython_magic_18ad8204e9d29650f3b09feb
48ab0f44.pyx
Function: c_benchmark at line 11
```

Line #	Hits	Time	Per Hit	% Time	Line Contents
11					def c_benchmark():
12	1	226	226.0	0.0	a = np.random.rand...
13	1	67	67.0	0.0	b = np.random.rand...
14					
15	1001	1715	1.7	0.1	for x1, y1 in a:
16	1001000	1299792	1.3	56.0	for x2, y2 in b:
17	1000000	1020203	1.0	43.9	chebyshev...

As you can see, a good chunk of time is actually spent in line 16, which is a pure Python loop and a good candidate for further optimization.

The tools available in Jupyter notebook allow for a fast edit-compile-test cycle so that you can quickly prototype and save time when testing different solutions.

Summary

Cython is a tool that bridges the convenience of Python with the speed of C. Compared to C bindings, Cython programs are much easier to maintain and debug, thanks to the tight integration and compatibility with Python and the availability of excellent tools.

In this chapter, we introduced the basics of the Cython language and how to make our programs faster by adding static types to our variables and functions. We also learned how to work with C arrays, NumPy arrays, and memoryviews.

We optimized our particle simulator by rewriting the critical `evolve` function, obtaining a tremendous speed gain. Finally, we learned how to use the annotated view to spot hard-to-find interpreter related calls and how to enable `cProfile` support in Cython. Also, we learned how to take advantage of the Jupyter notebook for integrated profiling and analysis of Cython codes.

In the next chapter, we will explore other tools that can generate fast machine code on the fly, without requiring compilation of our code to C ahead of time.

5
Exploring Compilers

Python is a mature and widely used language and there is a large interest in improving its performance by compiling functions and methods directly to machine code rather than executing instructions in the interpreter. We have already seen a compiler example in Chapter 4, *C Performance with Cython*, where Python code is enhanced with types, compiled to efficient C code, and the interpreter calls are side-stepped.

In this chapter, we will explore two projects--Numba and PyPy--that approach compilation in a slightly different way. **Numba** is a library designed to compile small functions on the fly. Instead of transforming Python code to C, Numba analyzes and compiles Python functions directly to machine code. **PyPy** is a replacement interpreter that works by analyzing the code at runtime and optimizing the slow loops automatically.

These tools are called **Just-In-Time** (**JIT**) compilers because the compilation is performed at runtime rather than before running the code (in other cases, the compiler is called ahead-of-time or AOT).

The list of topics to be covered in this chapter is as follows:

- Getting started with Numba
- Implementing fast functions with native mode compilation
- Understanding and implementing universal functions
- JIT classes
- Setting up PyPy
- Running the particle simulator with PyPy
- Other interesting compilers

Numba

Numba was started in 2012 by Travis Oliphant, the original author of NumPy, as a library for compiling individual Python functions at runtime using the **Low-Level Virtual Machine** (**LLVM**) toolchain.

LLVM is a set of tools designed to write compilers. LLVM is language agnostic and is used to write compilers for a wide range of languages (an important example is the clang compiler). One of the core aspects of LLVM is the intermediate representation (the LLVM IR), a very low-level platform-agnostic language similar to assembly, that can be compiled to machine code for the specific target platform.

Numba works by inspecting Python functions and by compiling them, using LLVM, to the IR. As we have already seen in the last chapter, the speed gains can be obtained when we introduce types for variables and functions. Numba implements clever algorithms to guess the types (this is called type inference) and compiles type-aware versions of the functions for fast execution.

Note that Numba was developed to improve the performance of numerical code. The development efforts often prioritize the optimization of applications that intensively use NumPy arrays.

Numba is evolving really fast and can have substantial improvements between releases and, sometimes, backward incompatible changes. To keep up, ensure that you refer to the release notes for each version. In the rest of this chapter, we will use Numba version 0.30.1; ensure that you install the correct version to avoid any error.

The complete code examples in this chapter can be found in the `Numba.ipynb` notebook.

First steps with Numba

Getting started with Numba is fairly straightforward. As a first example, we will implement a function that calculates the sum of squares of an array. The function definition is as follows:

```
def sum_sq(a):
    result = 0
    N = len(a)
```

```
        for i in range(N):
            result += a[i]
        return result
```

To set up this function with Numba, it is sufficient to apply the nb.jit decorator:

```
from numba import nb

@nb.jit
def sum_sq(a):
    ...
```

The nb.jit decorator won't do much when applied. However, when the function will be invoked for the first time, Numba will detect the type of the input argument, a , and compile a specialized, performant version of the original function.

To measure the performance gain obtained by the Numba compiler, we can compare the timings of the original and the specialized functions. The original, undecorated function can be easily accessed through the py_func attribute. The timings for the two functions are as follows:

```
import numpy as np

x = np.random.rand(10000)

# Original
%timeit sum_sq.py_func(x)
100 loops, best of 3: 6.11 ms per loop

# Numba
%timeit sum_sq(x)
100000 loops, best of 3: 11.7 µs per loop
```

From the previous code, you can see how the Numba version (11.7 µs) is one order of magnitude faster than the Python version (6.11 ms). We can also compare how this implementation stacks up against NumPy standard operators:

```
%timeit (x**2).sum()
10000 loops, best of 3: 14.8 µs per loop
```

In this case, the Numba compiled function is marginally faster than NumPy vectorized operations. The reason for the extra speed of the Numba version is likely that the NumPy version allocates an extra array before performing the sum in comparison with the in-place operations performed by our sum_sq function.

As we didn't use array-specific methods in `sum_sq`, we can also try to apply the same function on a regular Python list of floating point numbers. Interestingly, Numba is able to obtain a substantial speed up even in this case, as compared to a list comprehension:

```
x_list = x.tolist()
%timeit sum_sq(x_list)
1000 loops, best of 3: 199 µs per loop

%timeit sum([x**2 for x in x_list])
1000 loops, best of 3: 1.28 ms per loop
```

Considering that all we needed to do was apply a simple decorator to obtain an incredible speed up over different data types, it's no wonder that what Numba does looks like magic. In the following sections, we will dig deeper and understand how Numba works and evaluate the benefits and limitations of the Numba compiler.

Type specializations

As shown earlier, the `nb.jit` decorator works by compiling a specialized version of the function once it encounters a new argument type. To better understand how this works, we can inspect the decorated function in the `sum_sq` example.

Numba exposes the specialized types using the `signatures` attribute. Right after the `sum_sq` definition, we can inspect the available specialization by accessing the `sum_sq.signatures`, as follows:

```
sum_sq.signatures
# Output:
# []
```

If we call this function with a specific argument, for instance, an array of `float64` numbers, we can see how Numba compiles a specialized version on the fly. If we also apply the function on an array of `float32`, we can see how a new entry is added to the `sum_sq.signatures` list:

```
x = np.random.rand(1000).astype('float64')
sum_sq(x)
sum_sq.signatures
# Result:
# [(array(float64, 1d, C),)]

x = np.random.rand(1000).astype('float32')
sum_sq(x)
sum_sq.signatures
```

```
# Result:
# [(array(float64, 1d, C),), (array(float32, 1d, C),)]
```

It is possible to explicitly compile the function for certain types by passing a signature to the `nb.jit` function.

An individual signature can be passed as a tuple that contains the type we would like to accept. Numba provides a great variety of types that can be found in the `nb.types` module, and they are also available in the top-level `nb` namespace. If we want to specify an array of a specific type, we can use the slicing operator, `[:]`, on the type itself. In the following example, we demonstrate how to declare a function that takes an array of `float64` as its only argument:

```
@nb.jit((nb.float64[:],))
def sum_sq(a):
```

Note that when we explicitly declare a signature, we are prevented from using other types, as demonstrated in the following example. If we try to pass an array, x, as `float32`, Numba will raise a `TypeError`:

```
sum_sq(x.astype('float32'))
# TypeError: No matching definition for argument type(s)
array(float32, 1d, C)
```

Another way to declare signatures is through type strings. For example, a function that takes a `float64` as input and returns a `float64` as output can be declared with the `float64(float64)` string. Array types can be declared using a `[:]` suffix. To put this together, we can declare a signature for our `sum_sq` function, as follows:

```
@nb.jit("float64(float64[:])")
def sum_sq(a):
```

You can also pass multiple signatures by passing a list:

```
@nb.jit(["float64(float64[:])",
         "float64(float32[:])"])
def sum_sq(a):
```

Object mode versus native mode

So far, we have shown how Numba behaves when handling a fairly simple function. In this case, Numba worked exceptionally well, and we obtained great performance on arrays and lists.

The degree of optimization obtainable from Numba depends on how well Numba is able to infer the variable types and how well it can translate those standard Python operations to fast type-specific versions. If this happens, the interpreter is side-stepped and we can get performance gains similar to those of Cython.

When Numba cannot infer variable types, it will still try and compile the code, reverting to the interpreter when the types can't be determined or when certain operations are unsupported. In Numba, this is called **object mode** and is in contrast to the interpreter-free scenario, called **native mode**.

Numba provides a function, called `inspect_types`, that helps understand how effective the type inference was and which operations were optimized. As an example, we can take a look at the types inferred for our `sum_sq` function:

```
sum_sq.inspect_types()
```

When this function is called, Numba will print the type inferred for each specialized version of the function. The output consists of blocks that contain information about variables and types associated with them. For example, we can examine the `N = len(a)` line:

```
# --- LINE 4 ---
#    a = arg(0, name=a)  :: array(float64, 1d, A)
#    $0.1 = global(len: <built-in function len>)  ::
Function(<built-in function len>)
#    $0.3 = call $0.1(a)  :: (array(float64, 1d, A),) -> int64
#    N = $0.3  :: int64

N = len(a)
```

For each line, Numba prints a thorough description of variables, functions, and intermediate results. In the preceding example, you can see (second line) that the argument `a` is correctly identified as an array of `float64` numbers. At `LINE 4`, the input and return type of the `len` function is also correctly identified (and likely optimized) as taking an array of `float64` numbers and returning an `int64`.

If you scroll through the output, you can see how all the variables have a well-defined type. Therefore, we can be certain that Numba is able to compile the code quite efficiently. This form of compilation is called **native mode**.

As a counter example, we can see what happens if we write a function with unsupported operations. For example, as of version 0.30.1, Numba has limited support for string operations.

We can implement a function that concatenates a series of strings, and compiles it as follows:

```
@nb.jit
def concatenate(strings):
    result = ''
    for s in strings:
        result += s
    return result
```

Now, we can invoke this function with a list of strings and inspect the types:

```
concatenate(['hello', 'world'])
concatenate.signatures
# Output: [(reflected list(str),)]
concatenate.inspect_types()
```

Numba will return the output of the function for the `reflected list (str)` type. We can, for instance, examine how line 3 gets inferred. The output of `concatenate.inspect_types()` is reproduced here:

```
# --- LINE 3 ---
#    strings = arg(0, name=strings)  :: pyobject
#    $const0.1 = const(str, )  :: pyobject
#    result = $const0.1  :: pyobject
#    jump 6
# label 6

result = ''
```

You can see how this time, each variable or function is of the generic `pyobject` type rather than a specific one. This means that, in this case, Numba is unable to compile this operation without the help of the Python interpreter. Most importantly, if we time the original and compiled function, we note that the compiled function is about three times *slower* than the pure Python counterpart:

```
x = ['hello'] * 1000
%timeit concatenate.py_func(x)
10000 loops, best of 3: 111 µs per loop

%timeit concatenate(x)
1000 loops, best of 3: 317 µs per loop
```

This is because the Numba compiler is not able to optimize the code and adds some extra overhead to the function call.

As you may have noted, Numba compiled the code without complaints even if it is inefficient. The main reason for this is that Numba can still compile other sections of the code in an efficient manner while falling back to the Python interpreter for other parts of the code. This compilation strategy is called **object mode**.

It is possible to force the use of native mode by passing the `nopython=True` option to the `nb.jit` decorator. If, for example, we apply this decorator to our concatenate function, we observe that Numba throws an error on first invocation:

```
@nb.jit(nopython=True)
def concatenate(strings):
    result = ''
    for s in strings:
        result += s
    return result

concatenate(x)
# Exception:
# TypingError: Failed at nopython (nopython frontend)
```

This feature is quite useful for debugging and ensuring that all the code is fast and correctly typed.

Numba and NumPy

Numba was originally developed to easily increase performance of code that uses NumPy arrays. Currently, many NumPy features are implemented efficiently by the compiler.

Universal functions with Numba

Universal functions are special functions defined in NumPy that are able to operate on arrays of different sizes and shapes according to the broadcasting rules. One of the best features of Numba is the implementation of fast `ufuncs`.

We have already seen some `ufunc` examples in Chapter 3, *Fast Array Operations with NumPy and Pandas*. For instance, the `np.log` function is a `ufunc` because it can accept scalars and arrays of different sizes and shapes. Also, universal functions that take multiple arguments still work according to the broadcasting rules. Examples of universal functions that take multiple arguments are `np.sum` or `np.difference`.

Universal functions can be defined in standard NumPy by implementing the scalar version and using the `np.vectorize` function to enhance the function with the broadcasting feature. As an example, we will see how to write the *Cantor pairing function*.

A pairing function is a function that encodes two natural numbers into a single natural number so that you can easily interconvert between the two representations. The Cantor pairing function can be written as follows:

```
import numpy as np

def cantor(a, b):
    return  int(0.5 * (a + b)*(a + b + 1) + b)
```

As already mentioned, it is possible to create a ufunc in pure Python using the `np.vectorized` decorator:

```
@np.vectorize
def cantor(a, b):
    return  int(0.5 * (a + b)*(a + b + 1) + b)

cantor(np.array([1, 2]), 2)
# Result:
# array([ 8, 12])
```

Except for the convenience, defining universal functions in pure Python is not very useful as it requires a lot of function calls affected by interpreter overhead. For this reason, ufunc implementation is usually done in C or Cython, but Numba beats all these methods by its convenience.

All that is needed to do in order to perform the conversion is using the equivalent decorator, `nb.vectorize`. We can compare the speed of the standard `np.vectorized` version which, in the following code, is called `cantor_py`, and the same function is implemented using standard NumPy operations:

```
# Pure Python
%timeit cantor_py(x1, x2)
100 loops, best of 3: 6.06 ms per loop
# Numba
%timeit cantor(x1, x2)
100000 loops, best of 3: 15 µs per loop
# NumPy
%timeit (0.5 * (x1 + x2)*(x1 + x2 + 1) + x2).astype(int)
10000 loops, best of 3: 57.1 µs per loop
```

You can see how the Numba version beats all the other options by a large margin! Numba works extremely well because the function is simple and type inference is possible.

 An additional advantage of universal functions is that, since they depend on individual values, their evaluation can also be executed in parallel. Numba provides an easy way to parallelize such functions by passing the `target="cpu"` or `target="gpu"` keyword argument to the `nb.vectorize` decorator.

Generalized universal functions

One of the main limitations of universal functions is that they must be defined on scalar values. A generalized universal function, abbreviated `gufunc`, is an extension of universal functions to procedures that take arrays.

A classic example is the matrix multiplication. In NumPy, matrix multiplication can be applied using the `np.matmul` function, which takes two 2D arrays and returns another 2D array. An example usage of `np.matmul` is as follows:

```
a = np.random.rand(3, 3)
b = np.random.rand(3, 3)

c = np.matmul(a, b)
c.shape
# Result:
# (3, 3)
```

As we saw in the previous subsection, a `ufunc` broadcasts the operation over arrays of *scalars*, its natural generalization will be to broadcast over an array of *arrays*. If, for instance, we take two arrays of 3 by 3 matrices, we will expect `np.matmul` to take to match the matrices and take their product. In the following example, we take two arrays containing 10 matrices of shape `(3, 3)`. If we apply `np.matmul`, the product will be applied *matrix-wise* to obtain a new array containing the 10 results (which are, again, `(3, 3)` matrices):

```
a = np.random.rand(10, 3, 3)
b = np.random.rand(10, 3, 3)

c = np.matmul(a, b)
c.shape
# Output
# (10, 3, 3)
```

The usual rules for broadcasting will work in a similar way. For example, if we have an array of (3, 3) matrices, which will have a shape of (10, 3, 3), we can use np.matmul to calculate the matrix multiplication of each element with a single (3, 3) matrix. According to the broadcasting rules, we obtain that the single matrix will be repeated to obtain a size of (10, 3, 3):

```
a = np.random.rand(10, 3, 3)
b = np.random.rand(3, 3) # Broadcasted to shape (10, 3, 3)
c = np.matmul(a, b)
c.shape
# Result:
# (10, 3, 3)
```

Numba supports the implementation of efficient generalized universal functions through the nb.guvectorize decorator. As an example, we will implement a function that computes the euclidean distance between two arrays as a gufunc. To create a gufunc, we have to define a function that takes the input arrays, plus an output array where we will store the result of our calculation.

The nb.guvectorize decorator requires two arguments:

- The types of the input and output: two 1D arrays as input and a scalar as output
- The so called layout string, which is a representation of the input and output sizes; in our case, we take two arrays of the same size (denoted arbitrarily by n), and we output a scalar

In the following example, we show the implementation of the euclidean function using the nb.guvectorize decorator:

```
@nb.guvectorize(['float64[:], float64[:], float64[:]'], '(n), (n) -> ()')
def euclidean(a, b, out):
    N = a.shape[0]
    out[0] = 0.0
    for i in range(N):
        out[0] += (a[i] - b[i])**2
```

There are a few very important points to be made. Predictably, we declared the types of the inputs a and b as float64[:], because they are 1D arrays. However, what about the output argument? Wasn't it supposed to be a scalar? Yes, however, **Numba treats scalar argument as arrays of size 1**. That's why it was declared as float64[:].

Similarly, the layout string indicates that we have two arrays of size (n) and the output is a scalar, denoted by empty brackets--(). However, the array out will be passed as an array of size 1.

Also, note that we don't return anything from the function; all the output has to be written in the out array.

The letter n in the layout string is completely arbitrary; you may choose to use k or other letters of your liking. Also, if you want to combine arrays of uneven sizes, you can use layouts strings, such as (n, m).

Our brand new euclidean function can be conveniently used on arrays of different shapes, as shown in the following example:

```
a = np.random.rand(2)
b = np.random.rand(2)
c = euclidean(a, b) # Shape: (1,)

a = np.random.rand(10, 2)
b = np.random.rand(10, 2)
c = euclidean(a, b) # Shape: (10,)

a = np.random.rand(10, 2)
b = np.random.rand(2)
c = euclidean(a, b) # Shape: (10,)
```

How does the speed of euclidean compare to standard NumPy? In the following code, we benchmark a NumPy vectorized version with our previously defined euclidean function:

```
a = np.random.rand(10000, 2)
b = np.random.rand(10000, 2)

%timeit ((a - b)**2).sum(axis=1)
1000 loops, best of 3: 288 µs per loop

%timeit euclidean(a, b)
10000 loops, best of 3: 35.6 µs per loop
```

The Numba version, again, beats the NumPy version by a large margin!

JIT classes

As of today, Numba doesn't support optimization of generic Python objects. This limitation, however, doesn't have a huge impact on numerical codes as they usually involve arrays and math operations exclusively.

Nevertheless, certain data structures are much more naturally implemented using objects; therefore, Numba provides support for defining classes that can be used and compiled to fast, native code.

Bear in mind that this is one of the newest (almost experimental) features, and it is extremely useful as it allows us to extend Numba to support fast data structures that are not easily implemented with arrays.

As an example, we will show how to implement a simple linked list using JIT classes. A linked list can be implemented by defining a Node class that contains two fields: a value and the next item in the list. As you can see in the following figure, each **Node** connects to the next and holds a value, and the last node contains a broken link, to which we assign a value of **None**:

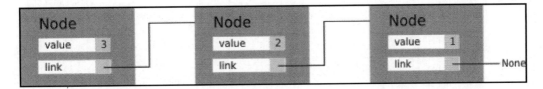

In Python, we can define the Node class as follows:

```
class Node:
    def __init__(self, value):
        self.next = None
        self.value = value
```

We can manage the collection of Node instances by creating another class, called LinkedList. This class will keep track of the head of the list (in the preceding figure, this corresponds to the **Node** with **value 3**). To insert an element in the front of the list, we can simply create a new **Node** and link it to the current head.

In the following code, we develop the initialization function for LinkedList and the LinkedList.push_back method that inserts an element in the front of the list using the strategy outlined earlier:

```
class LinkedList:
    def __init__(self):
```

```
            self.head = None
    def push_front(self, value):
        if self.head == None:
            self.head = Node(value)
        else:
            # We replace the head
            new_head = Node(value)
            new_head.next = self.head
            self.head = new_head
```

For debugging purposes, we can also implement the `LinkedList.show` method that traverses and prints each element in the list. The method is shown in the following snippet:

```
    def show(self):
        node = self.head
        while node is not None:
            print(node.value)
            node = node.next
```

At this point, we can test our `LinkedList` and see whether it behaves correctly. We can create an empty list, add a few elements, and print its content. Note that since we are pushing elements at the front of the list, the last elements inserted will be the first to be printed:

```
lst = LinkedList()
lst.push_front(1)
lst.push_front(2)
lst.push_front(3)
lst.show()
# Output:
# 3
# 2
# 1
```

Finally, we can implement a function, `sum_list`, that returns the sum of the elements in the linked list. We will use this method to time differences between the Numba and pure Python version:

```
@nb.jit
def sum_list(lst):
    result = 0
    node = lst.head
    while node is not None:
```

```
        result += node.value
        node = node.next
    return result
```

If we measure the execution time of the original `sum_list` version and the `nb.jit` version, we see that there is not much difference. The reason is that Numba cannot infer the type of classes:

```
lst = LinkedList()
[lst.push_front(i) for i in range(10000)]

%timeit sum_list.py_func(lst)
1000 loops, best of 3: 2.36 ms per loop

%timeit sum_list(lst)
100 loops, best of 3: 1.75 ms per loop
```

We can improve the performance of `sum_list` by compiling the `Node` and `LinkedList` classes using the `nb.jitclass` decorator.

The `nb.jitclass` decorator takes a single argument that contains the attribute types. In the `Node` class, the attribute types are `int64` for `value` and `Node` for `next`. The `nb.jitclass` decorator will also compile all the methods defined for the class. Before delving into the code, there are two observations that need to be made.

First, the attribute declaration has to be done before the class is defined, but how do we declare a type we haven't defined yet? Numba provides the `nb.deferred_type()` function, which can be used for this purpose.

Second, the `next` attribute can be either `None` or a `Node` instance. This is what is called an optional type, and Numba provides a utility, called `nb.optional`, that lets you declare variables that can be (optionally) `None`.

This `Node` class is illustrated in the following code sample. As you can see, `node_type` is predeclared using `nb.deferred_type()`. The attributes are declared as a list of pairs containing the attribute name and the type (also note the use of `nb.optional`). After the class declaration, we are required to declare the deferred type:

```
node_type = nb.deferred_type()

node_spec = [
    ('next', nb.optional(node_type)),
    ('value', nb.int64)
]
```

```
@nb.jitclass(node_spec)
class Node:
    # Body of Node is unchanged

node_type.define(Node.class_type.instance_type)
```

The `LinkedList` class can be easily compiled, as follows. All that's needed is to define the `head` attribute and to apply the `nb.jitclass` decorator:

```
ll_spec = [
    ('head', nb.optional(Node.class_type.instance_type))
]

@nb.jitclass(ll_spec)
class LinkedList:
    # Body of LinkedList is unchanged
```

We can now measure the execution time of the `sum_list` function when we pass a JIT `LinkedList`:

```
lst = LinkedList()
[lst.push_front(i) for i in range(10000)]

%timeit sum_list(lst)
1000 loops, best of 3: 345 μs per loop

%timeit sum_list.py_func(lst)
100 loops, best of 3: 3.36 ms per loop
```

Interestingly, when using a JIT class from a compiled function, we obtain a substantial performance improvement against the pure Python version. However, using the JIT class from the original `sum_list.py_func` actually results in worse performance. Ensure that you use JIT classes only inside compiled functions!

Limitations in Numba

There are some instances where Numba cannot properly infer the variable types and will refuse to compile. In the following example, we define a function that takes a nested list of integers and returns the sum of the element in every sublist. In this case, Numba will raise `ValueError` and refuse to compile:

```
a = [[0, 1, 2],
     [3, 4],
     [5, 6, 7, 8]]
```

```
@nb.jit
def sum_sublists(a):
    result = []
    for sublist in a:
        result.append(sum(sublist))
    return result

sum_sublists(a)
# ValueError: cannot compute fingerprint of empty list
```

The problem with this code is that Numba is not able to determine the type of the list and fails. A way to fix this problem is to help the compiler determine the right type by initializing the list with a sample element and removing it at the end:

```
@nb.jit
def sum_sublists(a):
    result = [0]
    for sublist in a:
        result.append(sum(sublist))
    return result[1:]
```

Among other features that are not yet implemented in the Numba compiler are function and class definitions, list, set and dict comprehension, generators, the with statement, and try except blocks. Note, however, that many of these features may become supported in the future.

The PyPy project

PyPy is a very ambitious project at improving the performance of the Python interpreter. The way PyPy improves performance is by automatically compiling slow sections of the code at runtime.

PyPy is written in a special language called RPython (rather than C) that allows developers to quickly and reliably implement advanced features and improvements. RPython means *Restricted Python* because it implements a restricted subset of the Python language targeted to the compiler development.

As of today, PyPy version 5.6 supports a lot of Python features and is a possible choice for a large variety of applications.

PyPy compiles code using a very clever strategy, called *tracing JIT compilation*. At first, the code is executed normally using interpreter calls. PyPy then starts to profile the code and identifies the most intensive loops. After the identification takes place, the compiler then observes (*traces*) the operations and is able to compile its optimized, interpreter-free version.

Once an optimized version of the code is present, PyPy is able to run the slow loop much faster than the interpreted version.

This strategy can be contrasted with what Numba does. In Numba, the units of compilation are methods and functions, while the PyPy focus is just slow loops. Overall, the focus of the projects is also very different as Numba has a limited scope for numerical code and requires a lot of instrumentation while PyPy aims at replacing the CPython interpreter.

In this section, we will demonstrate and benchmark PyPy on our particle simulator application.

Setting up PyPy

PyPy is distributed as a precompiled binary that can be downloaded from http://pypy.org/download.html, and it currently supports Python versions 2.7 (beta support in PyPy 5.6) and 3.3 (alpha support in PyPy 5.5). In this chapter, we will demonstrate the usage of the 2.7 version.

Once PyPy is downloaded and unpacked, you can locate the interpreter in the bin/pypy directory relative to the unpacked archive. You can initialize a new virtual environment where we can install additional packages using the following command:

```
$ /path/to/bin/pypy -m ensurepip
$ /path/to/bin/pypy -m pip install virtualenv
$ /path/to/bin/virtualenv my-pypy-env
```

To activate the environment, we will use the following command:

```
$ source my-pypy-env/bin/activate
```

At this point, you can verify that the binary Python is linked to the PyPy executable by typing python -V. At this point, we can go ahead and install some packages we may need. As of version 5.6, PyPy has limited support for software that uses the Python C API (most notably, packages such as numpy and matplotlib). We can go ahead and install them in the usual way:

```
(my-pypy-env) $ pip install numpy matplotlib
```

On certain platforms, installation of `numpy` and `matplotlib` can be tricky. You can skip the installation step and remove any imports on these two packages from the scripts we will run.

Running a particle simulator in PyPy

Now that we have successfully set up the PyPy installation, we can go ahead and run our particle simulator. As a first step, we will time the particle simulator from Chapter 1, *Benchmarking and Profiling*, on the standard Python interpreter. If the virtual environment is still active, you can issue the command deactivate to exit the environment. We can confirm that the Python interpreter is the standard one by using the python -V command:

```
(my-pypy-env) $ deactivate
$ python -V
Python 3.5.2 :: Continuum Analytics, Inc.
```

At this point, we can time our code using the `timeit` command-line interface:

```
$ python -m timeit --setup "from simul import benchmark" "benchmark()"
10 loops, best of 3: 886 msec per loop
```

We can reactivate the environment and run the exact same code from PyPy. On Ubuntu, you may have problems importing the `matplotlib.pyplot` module. You can try issuing the following `export` command to fix the issue or removing the `matplotlib` imports from `simul.py`:

```
$ export MPLBACKEND='agg'
```

Now, we can go ahead and time the code using PyPy:

```
$ source my-pypy-env/bin/activate
Python 2.7.12 (aff251e54385, Nov 09 2016, 18:02:49)
[PyPy 5.6.0 with GCC 4.8.2]

(my-pypy-env) $ python -m timeit --setup "from simul import benchmark"
"benchmark()"
WARNING: timeit is a very unreliable tool. use perf or something else for
real measurements
10 loops, average of 7: 106 +- 0.383 msec per loop (using standard
deviation)
```

Note that we obtained a large, more than eight times, speedup! PyPy, however, warns us that the `timeit` module can be unreliable. We can confirm our timings using the `perf` module, as suggested by PyPy:

```
(my-pypy-env) $ pip install perf
(my-pypy-env) $ python -m perf timeit --setup 'from simul import benchmark'
'benchmark()'
.......
Median +- std dev: 97.8 ms +- 2.3 ms
```

Other interesting projects

Over the years, many projects attempted to improve Python performance through several strategies and, sadly, many of them failed. As of today, there are a few projects that survive and hold the promise for a faster Python.

Numba and PyPy are mature projects that are steadily improving over the years. Features are continuously being added and they hold great promise for the future of Python.

Nuitka is a program developed by Kay Hayen that compiles Python code to C. As of right now (version 0.5.x), it provides extreme compatibility with the Python language and produces efficient code that results in moderate performance improvements over CPython.

Nuitka is quite different than Cython in the sense that it focuses on extreme compatibility with the Python language, and it doesn't extend the language with additional constructs.

Pyston is a new interpreter developed by Dropbox that powers JIT compilers. It differs substantially from PyPy as it doesn't employ a tracing JIT, but rather a method-at-a-time JIT (similar to what Numba does). Pyston, like Numba, is also built on top of the LLVM compiler infrastructure.

Pyston is still in early development (alpha stage) and only supports Python 2.7. Benchmarks show that it is faster than CPython but slower than PyPy; that said, it is still an interesting project to follow as new features are added and compatibility is increased.

Summary

Numba is a tool that compiles fast, specialized versions of Python functions at runtime. In this chapter, we learned how to compile, inspect, and analyze functions compiled by Numba. We also learned how to implement fast NumPy universal functions that are useful in a wide array of numerical applications. Finally, we implemented more complex data structures using the `nb.jitclass` decorator.

Tools such as PyPy allow us to run Python programs unchanged to obtain significant speed improvements. We demonstrated how to set up PyPy, and we assessed the performance improvements on our particle simulator application.

We also, briefly, described the current ecosystem of the Python compilers and compared them with each other.

In the next chapter, we will learn about concurrency and asynchronous programming. Using these techniques, we will be able to improve the responsiveness and design of applications that spend a lot of time waiting for network and disk resources.

6
Implementing Concurrency

So far, we have explored how to measure and improve the performance of programs by reducing the number of operations performed by the CPU through clever algorithms and more efficient machine code. In this chapter, we will shift our focus to programs where most of the time is spent waiting for resources that are much slower than the CPU, such as persistent storage and network resources.

Asynchronous programming is a programming paradigm that helps to deal with slow and unpredictable resources (such as users) and is widely used to build responsive services and user interfaces. In this chapter, we will show you how to program asynchronously in Python using techniques such as coroutines and reactive programming.

In this chapter, we will cover the following topics:

- The memory hierarchy
- Callbacks
- Futures
- Event loops
- Writing coroutines with `asyncio`
- Converting synchronous code to asynchronous code
- Reactive programming with RxPy
- Working with observables
- Building a memory monitor with RxPY

Asynchronous programming

Asynchronous programming is a way of dealing with slow and unpredictable resources. Rather than waiting idle for resources to become available, asynchronous programs are able to handle multiple resources concurrently and efficiently. Programming in an asynchronous way can be challenging because it is necessary to deal with external requests that can arrive in any order, may take a variable amount of time, or may fail unpredictably. In this section, we will introduce the topic by explaining the main concepts and terminology as well as by giving an idea of how asynchronous programs work.

Waiting for I/O

A modern computer employs different kinds of memory to store data and perform operations. In general, a computer possesses a combination of expensive memory that is capable of operating at fast speeds and cheaper, and more abundant memory that operates at lower speeds and is used to store a larger amount of data.

The memory hierarchy is shown in the following diagram:

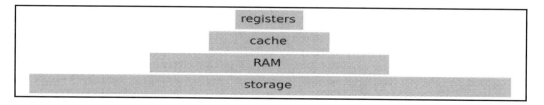

At the top of the memory hierarchy are the CPU registers. Those are integrated in the CPU and are used to store and execute machine instructions. Accessing data in a register generally takes one clock cycle. This means that if the CPU operates at 3 GHz, the time it takes to access one element in a CPU register is in the order of 0.3 nanoseconds.

At the layer just below the **registers**, you can find the CPU cache, which is comprised of multiple levels and is integrated in the processor. The **cache** operates at a slightly slower speed than the **registers** but within the same order of magnitude.

The next item in the hierarchy is the main memory (**RAM**), which holds much more data but is slower than the cache. Fetching an item from memory can take a few hundred clock cycles.

At the bottom layer, you can find persistent storage, such as a rotating disks (HDD) and **Solid State Drives (SSD)**. These devices hold the most data and are orders of magnitude slower than the main memory. An HDD may take a few milliseconds to seek and retrieve an item, while an SSD is substantially faster and takes only a fraction of a millisecond.

To put the relative speed of each memory type into perspective, if you were to have the CPU with a clock speed of about one second, a register access would be equivalent to picking up a pen from the table. A cache access will be equivalent to picking up a book from the shelf. Moving higher in the hierarchy, a RAM access will be equivalent to loading up the laundry (about twenty x slower than the cache). When we move to persistent storage, things are quite a bit different. Retrieving an element from an SSD will be equivalent to doing a four day trip, while retrieving an element from an HDD can take up to six months! The times can stretch even further if we move on to access resources over the network.

From the preceding example, it should be clear that accessing data from storage and other I/O devices is much slower compared to the CPU; therefore, it is very important to handle those resources so that the CPU is never stuck waiting aimlessly. This can be accomplished by carefully designing software capable of managing multiple, ongoing requests at the same time.

Concurrency

Concurrency is a way to implement a system that is able to deal with multiple requests at the same time. The idea is that we can move on and start handling other resources while we wait for a resource to become available. Concurrency works by splitting a task into smaller subtasks that can be executed out of order so that multiple tasks can be partially advanced without waiting for the previous tasks to finish.

As a first example, we will describe how to implement concurrent access to a slow network resource. Let's say we have a web service that takes the square of a number, and the time between our request and the response will be approximately one second. We can implement the `network_request` function that takes a number and returns a dictionary that contains information about the success of the operation and the result. We can simulate such services using the `time.sleep` function, as follows:

```
import time

def network_request(number):
    time.sleep(1.0)
    return {"success": True, "result": number ** 2}
```

We will also write some additional code that performs the request, verifies that the request was successful, and prints the result. In the following code, we define the `fetch_square` function and use it to calculate the square of the number two using a call to `network_request`:

```
def fetch_square(number):
    response = network_request(number)
    if response["success"]:
        print("Result is: {}".format(response["result"]))

fetch_square(2)
# Output:
# Result is:  4
```

Fetching a number from the network will take one second because of the slow network. What if we want to calculate the square of multiple numbers? We can call `fetch_square`, which will start a network request as soon as the previous one is done:

```
fetch_square(2)
fetch_square(3)
fetch_square(4)
# Output:
# Result is:  4
# Result is:  9
# Result is:  16
```

The previous code will take three seconds to run, but it's not the best we can do. Waiting for the previous result to finish is unnecessary as we can technically submit multiple requests at and wait for them parallely.

In the following diagram, the three tasks are represented as boxes. The time spent by the CPU processing and submitting the request is in orange while the waiting times are in blue. You can see how most of the time is spent waiting for the resources while our machine sits idle without doing anything else:

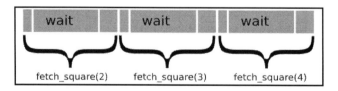

Ideally, we would like to start other new task while we are waiting for the already submitted tasks to finish. In the following figure, you can see that as soon as we submit our request in **fetch_square(2)**, we can start preparing for **fetch_square(3)** and so on. This allows us to reduce the CPU waiting time and to start processing the results as soon as they become available:

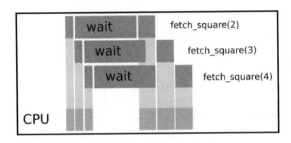

This strategy is made possible by the fact that the three requests are completely independent, and we don't need to wait for the completion of a previous task to start the next one. Also, note how a single CPU can comfortably handle this scenario. While distributing the work on multiple CPUs can further speedup the execution, if the waiting time is large compared to the processing times, the speedup will be minimal.

To implement concurrency, it is necessary to think and code differently; in the following sections, we'll demonstrate techniques and best practices to implement robust concurrent applications.

Callbacks

The code we have seen so far blocks the execution of the program until the resource is available. The call responsible for the waiting is `time.sleep`. To make the code start working on other tasks, we need to find a way to avoid blocking the program flow so that the rest of the program can go on with the other tasks.

One of the simplest ways to accomplish this behavior is through callbacks. The strategy is quite similar to what we do when we request a cab.

Imagine that you are at a restaurant and you've had a few drinks. It's raining outside, and you'd rather not take the bus; therefore, you request a taxi and ask them to call when they're outside so that you can come out, and you don't have to wait in the rain.

What you did in this case is request a taxi (that is, the slow resource) but instead of waiting outside until the taxi arrives, you provide your number and instructions (callback) so that you can come outside when they're ready and go home.

We will now show how this mechanism can work in code. We will compare the blocking code of `time.sleep` with the equivalent non-blocking code of `threading.Timer`.

For this example, we will write a function, `wait_and_print`, that will block the program execution for one second and then print a message:

```
def wait_and_print(msg):
    time.sleep(1.0)
    print(msg)
```

If we want to write the same function in a non-blocking way, we can use the `threading.Timer` class. We can initialize a `threading.Timer` instance by passing the amount of time we want to wait and a callback. A **callback** is simply a function that will be called when the timer expires. Note that we have to also call the `Timer.start` method to activate the timer:

```
import threading

def wait_and_print_async(msg):
    def callback():
        print(msg)

    timer = threading.Timer(1.0, callback)
    timer.start()
```

An important feature of the `wait_and_print_async` function is that none of the statements are blocking the execution flow of the program.

 How is `threading.Timer` capable of waiting without blocking? The strategy used by `threading.Timer` involves starting a new thread that is able to execute code in parallel. If this is confusing, don't worry, we will explore threading and parallel programming in detail in the following chapters.

This technique of registering callbacks for execution in response to certain events is commonly called the *Hollywood principle*. This is because, after an audition for a role at Hollywood, you may be told *"Don't call us, we'll call you"*, meaning that they won't tell you if they chose you for the role immediately, but they'll call you in case they do.

To highlight the difference between the blocking and non-blocking version of `wait_and_print`, we can test and compare the execution of the two versions. In the output comments, the waiting periods are indicated by `<wait...>`:

```
# Syncronous
wait_and_print("First call")
```

```
wait_and_print("Second call")
print("After call")
# Output:
# <wait...>
# First call
# <wait...>
# Second call
# After call
# Async
wait_and_print_async("First call async")
wait_and_print_async("Second call async")
print("After submission")
# Output:
# After submission
# <wait...>
# First call
# Second call
```

The synchronous version behaves in a very familiar way. The code waits for a second, prints First call, waits for another second, and then prints the Second call and After call messages.

In the asynchronous version, wait_and_print_async *submits* (rather than *execute*) those calls and moves on *immediately*. You can see this mechanism in action by acknowledging that the "After submission" message is printed immediately.

With this in mind, we can explore a slightly more complex situation by rewriting our network_request function using callbacks. In the following code, we define the network_request_async function. The biggest difference between network_request_async and its blocking counterpart is that network_request_async *doesn't return anything*. This is because we are merely submitting the request when network_request_async is called, but the value is available only when the request is completed.

If we can't return anything, how do we pass the result of the request? Rather than returning the value, we will pass the result as an argument to the on_done callback.

The rest of the function consists of submitting a callback (called timer_done) to the timer.Timer class that will call on_done when it's ready:

```
def network_request_async(number, on_done):

    def timer_done():
        on_done({"success": True,
                 "result": number ** 2})
```

```
timer = threading.Timer(1.0, timer_done)
timer.start()
```

The usage of `network_request_async` is quite similar to `timer.Timer`; all we have to do is pass the number we want to square and a callback that will receive the result *when it's ready*. This is demonstrated in the following snippet:

```
def on_done(result):
    print(result)

network_request_async(2, on_done)
```

Now, if we submit multiple network requests, we note that the calls get executed concurrently and do not block the code:

```
network_request_async(2, on_done)
network_request_async(3, on_done)
network_request_async(4, on_done)
print("After submission")
```

In order to use `network_request_async` in `fetch_square`, we need to adapt the code to use asynchronous constructs. In the following code, we modify `fetch_square` by defining and passing the `on_done` callback to `network_request_async`:

```
def fetch_square(number):
    def on_done(response):
        if response["success"]:
            print("Result is: {}".format(response["result"]))

    network_request_async(number, on_done)
```

You may have noted that the asynchronous code is significantly more convoluted than its synchronous counterpart. This is due to the fact that we are required to write and pass a callback every time we need to retrieve a certain result, causing the code to become nested and hard to follow.

Futures

Futures are a more convenient pattern that can be used to keep track of the results of asynchronous calls. In the preceding code, we saw that rather than returning values, we accept callbacks and pass the results when they are ready. It is interesting to note that, so far, there is no easy way to track the status of the resource.

A **future** is an abstraction that helps us keep track of the requested resources and that we are waiting to become available. In Python, you can find a future implementation in the `concurrent.futures.Future` class. A `Future` instance can be created by calling its constructor with no arguments:

```
fut = Future()
# Result:
# <Future at 0x7f03e41599e8 state=pending>
```

A future represents a value that is not yet available. You can see that its string representation reports the current status of the result which, in our case, is still pending. In order to make a result available, we can use the `Future.set_result` method:

```
fut.set_result("Hello")
# Result:
# <Future at 0x7f03e41599e8 state=finished returned str>

fut.result()
# Result:
# "Hello"
```

You can see that once we set the result, the `Future` will report that the task is finished and can be accessed using the `Future.result` method. It is also possible to subscribe a callback to a future so that, as soon as the result is available, the callback is executed. To attach a callback, it is sufficient to pass a function to the `Future.add_done_callback` method. When the task completes, the function will be called with the `Future` instance as its first argument and the result can be retrieved using the `Future.result()` method:

```
fut = Future()
fut.add_done_callback(lambda future: print(future.result(),
flush=True))
fut.set_result("Hello")
# Output:
# Hello
```

To get a grasp on how futures can be used in practice, we will adapt the `network_request_async` function to use futures. The idea is that, this time, instead of returning nothing, we return a `Future` that will keep track of the result for us. Note two things:

- We don't need to accept an `on_done callback` as callbacks can be connected later using the `Future.add_done_callback` method. Also, we pass the generic `Future.set_result` method as the callback for `threading.Timer`.

- This time we are able to return a value, thus making the code a bit more similar to the blocking version we saw in the preceding section:

```
from concurrent.futures import Future

def network_request_async(number):
    future = Future()
    result = {"success": True, "result": number ** 2}
    timer = threading.Timer(1.0, lambda: future.set_result(result))
    timer.start()
    return future

fut = network_request_async(2)
```

 Even though we instantiate and manage futures directly in these examples; in practical applications, the futures are handled by frameworks.

If you execute the preceding code, nothing will happen as the code only consists of preparing and returning a `Future` instance. To enable further operation of the future results, we need to use the `Future.add_done_callback` method. In the following code, we adapt the `fetch_square` function to use futures:

```
def fetch_square(number):
    fut = network_request_async(number)

    def on_done_future(future):
        response = future.result()
        if response["success"]:
            print("Result is: {}".format(response["result"]))
    fut.add_done_callback(on_done_future)
```

The code still looks quite similar to the callback version. Futures are a different and slightly more convenient way of working with callbacks. Futures are also advantageous, because they can keep track of the resource status, cancel (unschedule) scheduled tasks, and handle exceptions more naturally.

Event loops

So far, we have implemented parallelism using OS threads. However, in many asynchronous frameworks, the coordination of concurrent tasks is managed by an **event loop**.

The idea behind an event loop is to continuously monitor the status of the various resources (for example, network connections and database queries) and trigger the execution of callbacks when events take place (for example, when a resource is ready or when a timer expires).

Why not just stick to threading?

Events loops are sometimes preferred as every unit of execution never runs at the same time as another and this can simplify dealing with shared variables, data structures, and resources. Read the next chapter for more details about parallel execution and its shortcomings.

As a first example, we will implement a thread-free version of `threading.Timer`. We can define a `Timer` class that will take a timeout and implement the `Timer.done` method that returns `True` if the timer has expired:

```
class Timer:
    def __init__(self, timeout):
        self.timeout = timeout
        self.start = time.time()
    def done(self):
        return time.time() - self.start > self.timeout
```

To determine whether the timer has expired, we can write a loop that continuously checks the timer status by calling the `Timer.done` method. When the timer expires, we can print a message and exit the cycle:

```
timer = Timer(1.0)

while True:
    if timer.done():
        print("Timer is done!")
        break
```

By implementing the timer in this way, the flow of execution is never blocked and we can, in principle, do other work inside the while loop.

Waiting for events to happen by continuously polling using a loop is commonly termed as *busy-waiting*.

Ideally, we would like to attach a custom function that executes when the timer goes off, just like we did in `threading.Timer`. To do this, we can implement a method, `Timer.on_timer_done`, that will accept a callback to be executed when the timer goes off:

```
class Timer:
    # ... previous code
    def on_timer_done(self, callback):
        self.callback = callback
```

Note that `on_timer_done` merely stores a reference to the callback. The entity that monitors the event and executes the callback is the loop. This concept is demonstrated as follows. Rather than using the print function, the loop will call `timer.callback` when appropriate:

```
timer = Timer(1.0)
timer.on_timer_done(lambda: print("Timer is done!"))

while True:
    if timer.done():
        timer.callback()
        break
```

As you can see, an asynchronous framework is starting to take place. All we did outside the loop was define the timer and the callback, while the loop took care of monitoring the timer and executing the associated callback. We can further extend our code by implementing support for multiple timers.

A natural way to implement multiple timers is to add a few `Timer` instances to a list and modify our event loop to periodically check all the timers and dispatch the callbacks when required. In the following code, we define two timers and attach a callback to each of them. Those timers are added to a list, `timers`, that is continuously monitored by our event loop. As soon as a timer is done, we execute the callback and remove the event from the list:

```
timers = []

timer1 = Timer(1.0)
timer1.on_timer_done(lambda: print("First timer is done!"))

timer2 = Timer(2.0)
timer2.on_timer_done(lambda: print("Second timer is done!"))

timers.append(timer1)
timers.append(timer2)

while True:
    for timer in timers:
```

```
        if timer.done():
            timer.callback()
            timers.remove(timer)
    # If no more timers are left, we exit the loop
    if len(timers) == 0:
        break
```

The main restriction of an event loop is, since the flow of execution is managed by a continuously running loop, that it **never uses blocking calls**. If we use any blocking statement (such as `time.sleep`) inside the loop, you can imagine how the event monitoring and callback dispatching will stop until the blocking call is done.

To avoid this, rather than using a blocking call, such as `time.sleep`, we let the event loop detect and execute the callback when the resource is ready. By not blocking the execution flow, the event loop is free to monitor multiple resources in a concurrent way.

The notification for events is usually implemented through operating system calls (such as the `select` Unix tool) that will resume the execution of the program whenever an event is ready (in contrast to busy-waiting).

The Python standard libraries include a very convenient event loop-based concurrency framework, `asyncio`, which will be the topic of the next section.

The asyncio framework

By now, you should have a solid foundation of how concurrency works, and how to use callbacks and futures. We can now move on and learn how to use the `asyncio` package present in the standard library since version 3.4. We will also explore the brand new `async/await` syntax to deal with asynchronous programming in a very natural way.

As a first example, we will see how to retrieve and execute a simple callback using `asyncio`. The `asyncio` loop can be retrieved by calling the `asyncio.get_event_loop()` function. We can schedule a callback for execution using `loop.call_later` that takes a delay in seconds and a callback. We can also use the `loop.stop` method to halt the loop and exit the program. To start processing the scheduled call, it is necessary to start the loop, which can be done using `loop.run_forever`. The following example demonstrates the usage of these basic methods by scheduling a callback that will print a message and halt the loop:

```
    import asyncio
```

```
loop = asyncio.get_event_loop()

def callback():
    print("Hello, asyncio")
    loop.stop()

loop.call_later(1.0, callback)
loop.run_forever()
```

Coroutines

One of the main problems with callbacks is that they require you to break the program execution into small functions that will be invoked when a certain event takes place. As we saw in the earlier sections, callbacks can quickly become cumbersome.

Coroutines are another, perhaps a more natural, way to break up the program execution into chunks. They allow the programmer to write code that resembles synchronous code but will execute asynchronously. You may think of a coroutine as a function that can be stopped and resumed. A basic example of coroutines is generators.

Generators can be defined in Python using the `yield` statement inside a function. In the following example, we implement the `range_generator` function, which produces and returns values from 0 to n. We also add a print statement to log the internal state of the generator:

```
def range_generator(n):
    i = 0
    while i < n:
        print("Generating value {}".format(i))
        yield i
        i += 1
```

When we call the `range_generator` function, the code is not executed immediately. Note that nothing is printed to output when the following snippet is executed. Instead, a *generator object* is returned:

```
generator = range_generator(3)
generator
# Result:
# <generator object range_generator at 0x7f03e418ba40>
```

In order to start pulling values from a generator, it is necessary to use the `next` function:

```
next(generator)
# Output:
# Generating value 0

next(generator)
# Output:
# Generating value 1
```

Note that every time we invoke `next`, the code runs until it encounters the next `yield` statement and it is necessary to issue another `next` statement to resume the generator execution. You can think of a `yield` statement as a breakpoint where we can stop and resume execution (while also maintaining the internal state of the generator). This ability of stopping and resuming execution can be leveraged by the event loop to allow for concurrency.

It is also possible to *inject* (rather than *extract)* values in the generator through the `yield` statement. In the following example, we declare a function parrot that will repeat each message that we send. To allow a generator to receive a value, you can assign yield to a variable (in our case, it is `message = yield`). To insert values in the generator, we can use the `send` method. In the Python world, a generator that can also receive values is called a *generator-based coroutine*:

```
def parrot():
    while True:
        message = yield
        print("Parrot says: {}".format(message))

generator = parrot()
generator.send(None)
generator.send("Hello")
generator.send("World")
```

Note that we also need to issue a `generator.send(None)` before we can start sending messages; this is done to bootstrap the function execution and bring us to the first `yield` statement. Also, note that there is an infinite loop inside `parrot`; if we implement this without using generators, we will get stuck running the loop forever!

With this in mind, you can imagine how an event loop can partially progress several of these generators without blocking the execution of the whole program. You can also imagine how a generator can be advanced only when some resource is ready, therefore eliminating the need for a callback.

It is possible to implement coroutines in `asyncio` using the `yield` statement. However, Python supports the definition of powerful coroutines using a more intuitive syntax since version 3.5.

To define a coroutine with `asyncio`, you can use the `async def` statement:

```
async def hello():
    print("Hello, async!")

coro = hello()
coro
# Output:
# <coroutine object hello at 0x7f314846bd58>
```

As you can see, if we call the `hello` function, the function body is not executed immediately, but a *coroutine object* is returned. The `asyncio` coroutines do not support `next`, but they can be easily run in the `asyncio` event loop using the `run_until_complete` method:

```
loop = asyncio.get_event_loop()
loop.run_until_complete(coro)
```

 Coroutines defined with the `async def` statement are also called *native coroutines*.

The `asyncio` module provides resources (called *awaitables*) that can be requested inside coroutines through the `await` syntax. For example, if we want to wait for a certain time and then execute a statement, we can use the `asyncio.sleep` function:

```
async def wait_and_print(msg):
    await asyncio.sleep(1)
    print("Message: ", msg)
loop.run_until_complete(wait_and_print("Hello"))
```

The result is beautiful, clean code. We are writing perfectly functional asynchronous code without all the ugliness of callbacks!

 You may have noted how `await` provides a breakpoint for the event loop so that, as it wait for the resource, the event loop can move on and concurrently manage other coroutines.

Even better, coroutines are also `awaitable`, and we can use the `await` statement to chain coroutines asynchronously. In the following example, we rewrite the `network_request` function, which we defined earlier, by replacing the call to `time.sleep` with `asyncio.sleep`:

```
async def network_request(number):
    await asyncio.sleep(1.0)
    return {"success": True, "result": number ** 2}
```

We can follow up by reimplementing `fetch_square`. As you can see, we can await `network_request` directly without needing additional futures or callbacks.

```
async def fetch_square(number):
    response = await network_request(number)
    if response["success"]:
        print("Result is: {}".format(response["result"]))
```

The coroutines can be executed individually using `loop.run_until_complete`:

```
loop.run_until_complete(fetch_square(2))
loop.run_until_complete(fetch_square(3))
loop.run_until_complete(fetch_square(4))
```

Running tasks using `run_until_complete` is fine for testing and debugging. However, our program will be started with `loop.run_forever` most of the times, and we will need to submit our tasks while the loop is already running.

`asyncio` provides the `ensure_future` function, which schedules coroutines (as well as futures) for execution. `ensure_future` can be used by simply passing the coroutine we want to schedule. The following code will schedule multiple calls to `fetch_square` that will be executed concurrently:

```
asyncio.ensure_future(fetch_square(2))
asyncio.ensure_future(fetch_square(3))
asyncio.ensure_future(fetch_square(4))

loop.run_forever()
# Hit Ctrl-C to stop the loop
```

As a bonus, when passing a coroutine, the `asyncio.ensure_future` function will return a `Task` instance (which is a subclass of `Future`) so that we can take advantage of the await syntax without having to give up the resource tracking capabilities of regular futures.

Converting blocking code into non-blocking code

While `asyncio` supports connecting to resources in an asynchronous way, it is required to use blocking calls in certain cases. This happens, for example, when third-party APIs exclusively expose blocking calls (for example, many database libraries), but also when executing long-running computations. In this subsection, we will learn how to deal with blocking APIs and make them compatible with `asyncio`.

An effective strategy for dealing with blocking code is to run it in a separate thread. Threads are implemented at the **Operating System (OS)** level and allow parallel execution of blocking code. For this purpose, Python provides the `Executor` interface designed to run tasks in a separate thread and to monitor their progress using futures.

You can initialize a `ThreadPoolExecutor` by importing it from the `concurrent.futures` module. The executor will spawn a collection of threads (called `workers`) that will wait to execute whatever task we throw at them. Once a function is submitted, the executor will take care of dispatching its execution to an available worker thread and keep track of the result. The `max_workers` argument can be used to select the number of threads.

Note that the executor will not destroy a thread once a task is completed. By doing so, it reduces the cost associated with the creation and destruction of threads.

In the following example, we create a `ThreadPoolExecutor` with three workers, and we submit a `wait_and_return` function that will block the program execution for one second and return a message string. We then use the `submit` method to schedule its execution:

```
from concurrent.futures import ThreadPoolExecutor
executor = ThreadPoolExecutor(max_workers=3)

def wait_and_return(msg):
    time.sleep(1)
    return msg

executor.submit(wait_and_return, "Hello. executor")
# Result:
# <Future at 0x7ff616ff6748 state=running>
```

The `executor.submit` method immediately schedules the function and returns a future. It is possible to manage the execution of tasks in `asyncio` using the `loop.run_in_executor` method, which works quite similarly to `executor.submit`:

```
fut = loop.run_in_executor(executor, wait_and_return, "Hello, asyncio
executor")
# <Future pending ...more info...>
```

The `run_in_executor` method will also return an `asyncio.Future` instance that can be awaited from other code, the main difference being that the future will not be run until we start the loop. We can run and obtain the response using `loop.run_until_complete`:

```
loop.run_until_complete(fut)
# Result:
# 'Hello, executor'
```

As a practical example, we can use this technique to implement concurrent fetching of several web pages. To do this, we will import the popular (blocking) `requests` library and run the `requests.get` function in the executor:

```
import requests

async def fetch_urls(urls):
    responses = []
    for url in urls:
        responses.append(await loop.run_in_executor
                            (executor, requests.get, url))
    return responses

loop.run_until_complete(fetch_ruls(['http://www.google.com',
                                    'http://www.example.com',
                                    'http://www.facebook.com']))
# Result
# []
```

This version of `fetch_url` will not block the execution and allow other coroutines in `asyncio` to run; however, it is not optimal as the function will not fetch a URL in parallel. To do this, we can use `asyncio.ensure_future` or employ the `asyncio.gather` convenience function that will submit all the coroutines at once and gather the results as they come. The usage of `asyncio.gather` is demonstrated here:

```
def fetch_urls(urls):
    return asyncio.gather(*[loop.run_in_executor
                            (executor, requests.get, url)
                            for url in urls])
```

The number of URLs you can fetch in parallel with this method will be dependent on the number of worker threads you have. To avoid this limitation, you should use a natively non-blocking library, such as `aiohttp`.

Reactive programming

Reactive programming is a paradigm that aims at building better concurrent systems. Reactive applications are designed to comply with the requirements exemplified by the reactive manifesto:

- **Responsive**: The system responds immediately to the user.
- **Elastic**: The system is capable of handling different levels of load and is able to adapt to accommodate increasing demands.
- **Resilient**: The system deals with failure gracefully. This is achieved by modularity and avoiding having a single point of failure.
- **Message driven**: The system should not block and take advantage of events and messages. A message-driven application helps achieve all the previous requirements.

As you can see, the intent of reactive systems is quite noble, but how exactly does reactive programming work? In this section, we will learn about the principles of reactive programming using the RxPy library.

 The RxPy library is part of ReactiveX (http://reactivex.io/), which is a project that implements reactive programming tools for a large variety of languages.

Observables

As the name implies, the main idea of reactive programming is to *react* to events. In the preceding section, we saw some examples of this idea with callbacks; you subscribe to them and the callback is executed as soon as the event takes place.

In reactive programming, this idea is expanded by thinking of events as streams of data. This can be exemplified by showing examples of such streams in RxPy. A data stream can be created from an iterator using the Observable.from_iterable factory method, as follows:

```
from rx import Observable
obs = Observable.from_iterable(range(4))
```

In order to receive data from obs, we can use the Observable.subscribe method, which will execute the function we pass for each value that the data source emits:

```
obs.subscribe(print)
```

```
# Output:
# 0
# 1
# 2
# 3
```

You may have noted that observables are ordered collections of items just like lists or, more generally, iterators. This is not a coincidence.

> The term observable comes from the combination of observer and iterable. An *observer* is an object that reacts to changes of the variable it observes, while an *iterable* is an object that is capable of producing and keeping track of an iterator.

In Python, iterators are objects that define the __next__ method, and whose elements can be extracted by calling next. An iterator can generally be obtained by a collection using iter; then we can extract elements using next or a for loop. Once an element is consumed from the iterator, we can't go back. We can demonstrate its usage by creating an iterator from a list:

```
collection = list([1, 2, 3, 4, 5])
iterator = iter(collection)

print("Next")
print(next(iterator))
print(next(iterator))

print("For loop")
for i in iterator:
    print(i)

# Output:
# Next
# 1
# 2
# For loop
# 3
# 4
# 5
```

You can see how, every time we call next or we iterate, the iterator produces a value and advances. In a sense, we are *pulling* results from the iterator.

Iterators sound a lot like generators; however, they are more general. In Python, generators are returned by functions that use yield expressions. As we saw, generators support `next`, therefore, they are a special class of iterators.

Now you can appreciate the contrast between an iterator and an observable. An observable *pushes* a stream of data to us whenever it's ready, but that's not everything. An observable is also able to tell us when there is an error and where there is no more data. In fact, it is possible to register further callbacks to the `Observable.subscribe` method. In the following example, we create an observable and register callbacks to be called using `on_next` whenever the next item is available and using the `on_completed` argument when there is no more data:

```
obs = Observable.from_iter(range(4))
obs.subscribe(on_next=lambda x: print(on_next="Next item: {}"),
              on_completed=lambda: print("No more data"))
# Output:
# Next element: 0
# Next element: 1
# Next element: 2
# Next element: 3
# No more data
```

This analogy with the iterator is important because we can use the same techniques that can be used with iterators to handle streams of events.

RxPy provides operators that can be used to create, transform, filter, and group observables. The power of reactive programming lies in the fact that those operations return other observables that can be conveniently chained and composed together. For a quick taste, we will demonstrate the usage of the `take` operator.

Given an observable, `take` will return a new observable that will stop after n items. Its usage is straightforward:

```
obs = Observable.from_iterable(range(100000))
obs2 = obs.take(4)

obs2.subscribe(print)
# Output:
# 0
# 1
# 2
# 3
```

The collection of operations implemented in RxPy is varied and rich, and can be used to build complex applications using these operators as building blocks.

Useful operators

In this subsection, we will explore operators that transform the elements of a source observable in some way. The most prominent member of this family of operators is the familiar map, which emits the elements of the source observable after applying a function to them. For example, we may use map to calculate the square of a sequence of numbers:

```
(Observable.from_iterable(range(4))
            .map(lambda x: x**2)
            .subscribe(print))
# Output:
# 0
# 1
# 4
# 9
```

Operators can be represented with marble diagrams that help us better understand how the operator works, especially when taking into account the fact that elements can be emitted over a region of time. In a marble diagram, a data stream (in our case, an observable) is represented by a solid line. A circle (or other shape) identifies a value emitted by the observable, an **X** symbol represents an error, and a vertical line represents the end of the stream.

In the following figure, we can see the marble diagram of **map**:

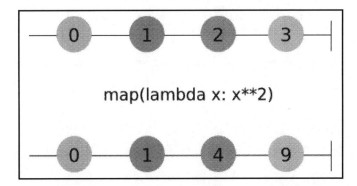

The source observable is placed at the top of the diagram, the transformation is placed in the middle, and the resulting observable is placed at the bottom.

Another example of a transformation is `group_by`, which sorts the items into groups based on a key. The `group_by` operator takes a function that extracts a key when given an element and produces an observable for each key with the elements associated to it.

The `group_by` operation can be expressed more clearly using a marble diagram. In the following figure, you can see how `group_by` emits two observables. Additionally, the items are dynamically sorted into groups *as soon as they are emitted*:

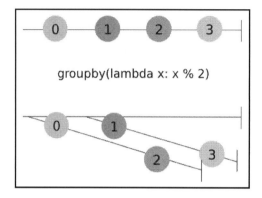

We can further understand how `group_by` works with a simple example. Let's say that we want to group the number according to the fact that they're even or odd. We can implement this using `group_by` by passing the `lambda x: x % 2` expression as a key function, which will return `0` if the number is even and `1` if the number is odd:

```
obs = (Observable.from_range(range(4))
              .group_by(lambda x: x % 2))
```

At this point, if we subscribe and print the content of `obs`, actually two observables are printed:

```
obs.subscribe(print)
# <rx.linq.groupedobservable.GroupedObservable object at
0x7f0fba51f9e8>
# <rx.linq.groupedobservable.GroupedObservable object at
0x7f0fba51fa58>
```

You can determine the group key using the `key` attribute. To extract all the even numbers, we can take the first observable (corresponding to a key equal to 0) and subscribe to it. In the following code, we show how this works:

```
obs.subscribe(lambda x: print("group key: ", x.key))
# Output:
# group key:   0
# group key:   1
obs.take(1).subscribe(lambda x: x.subscribe(print))
# Output:
# 0
# 2
```

With `group_by`, we introduced an observable that emits other observables. This turns out to be quite a common pattern in reactive programming, and there are functions that allow you to combine different observables.

Two useful tools for combining observables are `merge_all` and `concat_all`. Merge takes multiple observables and produces a single observable that contains the element of the two observables in the order they are emitted. This is better illustrated using a marble diagram:

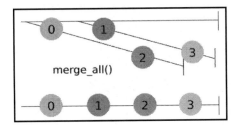

`merge_all` can be compared to a similar operator, `concat_all`, which returns a new observable that emits the elements of all the elements of the first observable, followed by the elements of the second observable and so on. The marble diagram for `concat_all` is presented here:

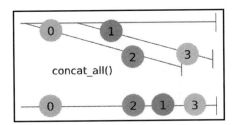

To demonstrate the usage of these two operators, we can apply those operations to the observable of observables returned by `group_by`. In the case of `merge_all`, the items are returned in the same order as they were initially (remember that `group_by` emits elements in the two groups as they come):

```
obs.merge_all().subscribe(print)
# Output
# 0
# 1
# 2
# 3
```

On the other hand, `concat_all` first returns the even elements and then the odd elements as it waits for the first observable to complete, and then starts emitting the elements of the second observable. This is demonstrated in the following snippet. In this specific example, we also applied a function, `make_replay`; this is needed because, by the time the "even" stream is consumed, the elements of the second stream have already been produced and will not be available to `concat_all`. This concept will become much clearer after reading the *Hot and cold observables* section:

```
def make_replay(a):
    result = a.replay(None)
    result.connect()
    return result

obs.map(make_replay).concat_all().subscribe(print)
# Output
# 0
# 2
# 1
# 3
```

This time around, the even numbers are printed first, followed by the odd numbers.

 RxPy also provides the `merge` and `concat` operations that can be used to combine individual observables

Hot and cold observables

In the preceding section, we learned how to create an observable using the `Observable.from_iterable` method. RxPy provides many other tools to create more interesting event sources.

`Observable.interval` takes a time interval in milliseconds, `period`, and will create an observable that emits a value every time the period has passed. The following line of code can be used to define an observable, `obs`, that will emit a number, starting from zero, every second. We use the `take` operator to limit the timer to four events:

```
obs = Observable.interval(1000)
obs.take(4).subscribe(print)
# Output:
# 0
# 1
# 2
# 3
```

A very important fact about `Observable.interval` is that the timer doesn't start until we subscribe. We can observe this by printing both the index and the delay from when the timer starts definition using `time.time()`, as follows:

```
import time

start = time.time()
obs = Observable.interval(1000).map(lambda a:
                                    (a, time.time() - start))

# Let's wait 2 seconds before starting the subscription
time.sleep(2)
obs.take(4).subscribe(print)
# Output:
# (0, 3.003735303878784)
# (1, 4.004871129989624)
# (2, 5.005947589874268)
# (3, 6.00749135017395)
```

As you can see, the first element (corresponding to a 0 index) is produced after three seconds, which means that the timer started when we issue the `subscribe(print)` method.

Observables, such as `Observable.interval`, are called *lazy* because they start producing values only when requested (think of them as vending machines, which won't dispense food unless we press the button). In Rx jargon, these kind of observables are called **cold**. A property of cold observables is that, if we attach two subscribers, the interval timer will be started multiple times. This is quite evident from the following example. Here, we add a new subscription 0.5 seconds after the first, and you can see how the output of the two subscriptions come at different times:

```
start = time.time()
obs = Observable.interval(1000).map(lambda a:
                                    (a, time.time() - start))

# Let's wait 2 seconds before starting the subscription
time.sleep(2)
obs.take(4).subscribe(lambda x: print("First subscriber:
                                      {}".format(x)))
time.sleep(0.5)
obs.take(4).subscribe(lambda x: print("Second subscriber:
                                      {}".format(x)))
# Output:
# First subscriber: (0, 3.0036110877990723)
# Second subscriber: (0, 3.5052847862243652)
# First subscriber: (1, 4.004414081573486)
# Second subscriber: (1, 4.506155252456665)
# First subscriber: (2, 5.005316972732544)
# Second subscriber: (2, 5.506817102432251)
# First subscriber: (3, 6.0062034130096436)
# Second subscriber: (3, 6.508296489715576)
```

Sometimes we may not want this behavior as we may want multiple subscribers to subscribe to the same data source. To make the observable produce the same data, we can delay the data production and ensure that all the subscribers will get the same data using the `publish` method.

Publish will transform our observable into a `ConnectableObservable`, which won't start pushing data immediately, but only when we call the `connect` method. The usage of `publish` and `connect` is demonstrated in the following snippet:

```
start = time.time()
obs = Observable.interval(1000).map(lambda a: (a, time.time() -
start)).publish()
obs.take(4).subscribe(lambda x: print("First subscriber:
                                      {}".format(x)))
obs.connect() # Data production starts here

time.sleep(2)
```

```
obs.take(4).subscribe(lambda x: print("Second subscriber:
                                       {}".format(x)))

# Output:
# First subscriber:  (0, 1.0016899108886719)
# First subscriber:  (1, 2.0027990341186523)
# First subscriber:  (2, 3.003532648086548)
# Second subscriber: (2, 3.003532648086548)
# First subscriber:  (3, 4.004265308380127)
# Second subscriber: (3, 4.004265308380127)
# Second subscriber: (4, 5.005320310592651)
# Second subscriber: (5, 6.005795240402222)
```

In the preceding example, you can see how we first issue `publish`, then we subscribe the first subscriber and, finally, we issue `connect`. When `connect` is issued, the timer will start producing data. The second subscriber joins the party late and, in fact, won't receive the first two messages but will start receiving data from the third and so on. Note how, this time around, the subscribers share the exact same data. This kind of data source, where data is produced independently of the subscribers, is called **hot**.

Similar to `publish`, you can use the `replay` method that will produce the data *from the beginning* for each new subscriber. This is illustrated in the following example that, which is identical to the preceding one except that we replaced `publish` with `replay`:

```
import time

start = time.time()
obs = Observable.interval(1000).map(lambda a: (a, time.time() -
start)).replay(None)
obs.take(4).subscribe(lambda x: print("First subscriber:
                                       {}".format(x)))

obs.connect()

time.sleep(2)
obs.take(4).subscribe(lambda x: print("Second subscriber:
                                       {}".format(x)))

First subscriber: (0, 1.0008857250213623)
First subscriber: (1, 2.0019824504852295)
Second subscriber: (0, 1.0008857250213623)
Second subscriber: (1, 2.0019824504852295)
First subscriber: (2, 3.0030810832977295)
Second subscriber: (2, 3.0030810832977295)
First subscriber: (3, 4.004604816436768)
Second subscriber: (3, 4.004604816436768)
```

You can see how, this time around, even though the second subscriber arrives late to the party, it is still given all the items that have been given out so far.

Another way of creating hot observables is through the `Subject` class. `Subject` is interesting because it's capable of both receiving and pushing data, and thus it can be used to manually *push* items to an observable. Using `Subject` is very intuitive; in the following code, we create a `Subject` and subscribe to it. Later, we push values to it using the `on_next` method; as soon as we do that, the subscriber is called:

```
s = Subject()
s.subscribe(lambda a: print("Subject emitted value: {}".format(x))
s.on_next(1)
# Subject emitted value: 1
s.on_next(2)
# Subject emitted value: 2
```

Note that `Subject` is another example of hot observables.

Building a CPU monitor

Now that we have a grasp on the main reactive programming concepts, we can implement a sample application. In this subsection, we will implement a monitor that will give us real-time information about our CPU usage and is capable of detecting spikes.

The complete code for the CPU monitor can be found in the `cpu_monitor.py` file.

As a first step, let's implement a data source. We will use the `psutil` module that provides a function, `psutil.cpu_percent`, that returns the latest available CPU usage as a percent (and doesn't block):

```
import psutil
psutil.cpu_percent()
# Result: 9.7
```

Since we are developing a monitor, we would like to sample this information over a few time intervals. To accomplish this we can use the familiar `Observable.interval`, followed by `map` just like we did in the previous section. Also, we would like to make this observable *hot* as, for this application, all subscribers should receive a single source of data; to make `Observable.interval` hot, we can use the `publish` and `connect` methods. The full code for the creation of the `cpu_data` observable is as follows

```
cpu_data = (Observable
            .interval(100) # Each 100 milliseconds
```

```
            .map(lambda x: psutil.cpu_percent())
            .publish())
cpu_data.connect()  # Start producing data
```

We can test our monitor by printing a sample of 4 items

```
cpu_data.take(4).subscribe(print)
# Output:
# 12.5
# 5.6
# 4.5
# 9.6
```

Now that our main data source is in place, we can implement a monitor visualization using `matplotlib`. The idea is to create a plot that contains a fixed amount of measurements and, as new data arrives, we include the newest measurement and remove the oldest one. This is commonly referred to as a *moving window* and is better understood with an illustration. In the following figure, our `cpu_data` stream is represented as a list of numbers. The first plot is produced as soon as we have the first four numbers and, each time a new number arrives, we shift the window by one position and update the plot:

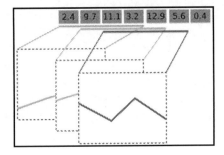

To implement this algorithm, we can write a function, called `monitor_cpu`, that will create and update our plotting window. The function will do the following things:

- Initialize an empty plot and set up the correct plot limits.
- Transform our `cpu_data` observable to return a moving window over the data. This can be accomplished using the `buffer_with_count` operator, which will take the number of points in our window, `npoints`, as parameters and the shift as `1`.
- Subscribe to this new data stream and update the plot with the incoming data.

The complete code for the function is shown here and, as you can see, is extremely compact. Take some time to run the function and play with the parameters:

```python
import numpy as np
from matplotlib import pyplot as plt

def monitor_cpu(npoints):
    lines, = plt.plot([], [])
    plt.xlim(0, npoints)
    plt.ylim(0, 100) # 0 to 100 percent

    cpu_data_window = cpu_data.buffer_with_count(npoints, 1)

    def update_plot(cpu_readings):
        lines.set_xdata(np.arange(npoints))
        lines.set_ydata(np.array(cpu_readings))
        plt.draw()

    cpu_data_window.subscribe(update_plot)

    plt.show()
```

Another feature we may want to develop is, for example, an alert that triggers when the CPU has been high for a certain amount of time as this may indicate that some of the processes in our machine are working very hard. This can be accomplished by combining `buffer_with_count` and `map`. We can take the CPU stream and a window, and then we will test whether all items have a value higher than twenty percent usage (in a quad-core CPU that corresponds to about one processor working at hundred percent) in the map function. If all the points in the window have a higher than twenty percent usage, we display a warning in our plot window.

The implementation of the new observable can be written as follows and will produce an observable that emits `True` if the CPU has high usage, and `False` otherwise:

```python
alertpoints = 4
high_cpu = (cpu_data
            .buffer_with_count(alertpoints, 1)
            .map(lambda readings: all(r > 20 for r in readings)))
```

Now that the `high_cpu` observable is ready, we can create a `matplotlib` label and subscribe to it for updates:

```
label = plt.text(1, 1, "normal")
def update_warning(is_high):
    if is_high:
        label.set_text("high")
    else:
        label.set_text("normal")
high_cpu.subscribe(update_warning)
```

Summary

Asynchronous programming is useful when our code deals with slow and unpredictable resources, such as I/O devices and networks. In this chapter, we explored the fundamental concepts of concurrency and asynchronous programming and how to write concurrent code with the `asyncio` and RxPy libraries.

`asyncio` coroutines are an excellent choice when dealing with multiple, interconnected resources as they greatly simplify the code logic by cleverly avoiding callbacks. Reactive programming is also very good in these situations, but it truly shines when dealing with streams of data that are common in real-time applications and user interfaces.

In the next chapter, we will learn about parallel programming.

7
Parallel Processing

With parallel processing by using multiple cores, you can increase the amount of calculations your program can do in a given time frame without needing a faster processor. The main idea is to divide a problem into independent subunits and use multiple cores to solve those subunits in parallel.

Parallel processing is necessary to tackle large-scale problems. Companies produce massive quantities of data every day that need to be stored in multiple computers and analyzed. Scientists and engineers run parallel code on supercomputers to simulate massive systems.

Parallel processing allows you to take advantage of multicore CPUs as well as GPUs that work extremely well with highly parallel problems. In this chapter, we will cover the following topics:

- A brief introduction to the fundamentals of parallel processing
- Illustrating how to parallelize simple problems with the `multiprocessing` Python library
- Using the simple `ProcessPoolExecutor` interface
- Parallelizing our programs using multithreading with the help of Cython and OpenMP
- Achieving parallelism automatically with Theano and Tensorflow
- Executing code on a GPU with Theano, Tensorflow, and Numba

Introduction to parallel programming

In order to parallelize a program, it is necessary to divide the problem into subunits that can run independently (or almost independently) from each other.

A problem where the subunits are totally independent from each other is called **embarrassingly parallel**. An element-wise operation on an array is a typical example--the operation needs to only know the element it is handling at the moment. Another example is our particle simulator. Since there are no interactions, each particle can evolve independently from the others. Embarrassingly parallel problems are very easy to implement and perform very well on parallel architectures.

Other problems may be divided into subunits but have to share some data to perform their calculations. In those cases, the implementation is less straightforward and can lead to performance issues because of the communication costs.

We will illustrate the concept with an example. Imagine that you have a particle simulator, but this time the particles attract other particles within a certain distance (as shown in the following figure). To parallelize this problem, we divide the simulation box into regions and assign each region to a different processor. If we evolve the system one step at a time, some particles will interact with particles in a neighboring region. To perform the next iteration, communication with the new particle positions of the neighboring region is required.

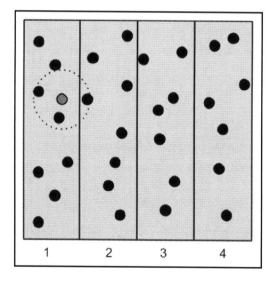

Communication between processes is costly and can seriously hinder the performance of parallel programs. There exist two main ways to handle data communication in parallel programs:

- **Shared memory**
- **Distributed memory**

In shared memory, the subunits have access to the same memory space. The advantage of this approach is that you don't have to explicitly handle the communication as it is sufficient to write or read from the shared memory. However, problems arise when multiple processes try to access and change the same memory location at the same time. Care should be taken to avoid such conflict using synchronization techniques.

In the distributed memory model, each process is completely separated from the others and possesses its own memory space. In this case, communication is handled explicitly between the processes. The communication overhead is typically costlier compared to shared memory as data can potentially travel through a network interface.

One common way to achieve parallelism with the shared memory model is **threads**. Threads are independent subtasks that originate from a process and share resources, such as memory. This concept is further illustrated in the following figure. Threads produce multiple execution context and share the same memory space, while processes provide multiple execution context that possess their own memory space and communication has to be handled explicitly.

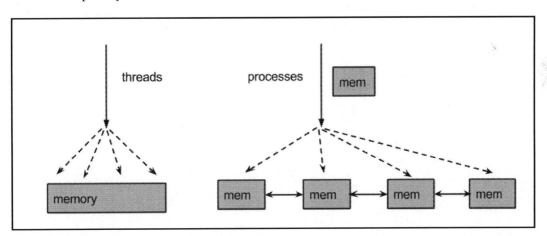

Python can spawn and handle threads, but they can't be used to increase performance; due to the Python interpreter design, only one Python instruction is allowed to run at a time--this mechanism is called **Global Interpreter Lock (GIL)**. What happens is that each time a thread executes a Python statement, the thread acquires a lock and, when the execution is completed, the same lock is released. Since the lock can be acquired only by one thread at a time, other threads are prevented from executing Python statements while some other thread holds the lock.

Even though the GIL prevents parallel execution of Python instructions, threads can still be used to provide concurrency in situations where the lock can be released, such as in time-consuming I/O operations or in C extensions.

 Why not remove the GIL? In past years, many attempts have been made, including the most recent gilectomy experiment. First, removing the GIL is not an easy task and requires modification of most of the Python data structures. Additionally, such fine-grained locking can be costly and may introduce substantial performance loss in single-threaded programs. Despite this, some Python implementations (notable examples are Jython and IronPython) do not use the GIL.

The GIL can be completely sidestepped using processes instead of threads. Processes don't share the same memory area and are independent from each other--each process has its own interpreter. Processes have a few disadvantages: starting up a new process is generally slower than starting a new thread, they consume more memory, and inter-process communication can be slow. On the other hand, processes are still very flexible, and they scale better as they can be distributed on multiple machines.

Graphic processing units

Graphic processing units are special processors designed for computer graphics applications. Those applications usually require processing the geometry of a 3D scene and output an array of pixel to the screen. The operations performed by GPUs involve array and matrix operations on floating point numbers.

GPUs are designed to run this graphics-related operation very efficiently, and they achieve this by adopting a highly parallel architecture. Compared to a CPU, a GPU has many more (thousands) of small processing units. GPUs are intended to produce data at about 60 frames per second, which is much slower than the typical response time of a CPU, which possesses higher clock speeds.

GPUs possess a very different architecture from a standard CPU and are specialized for computing floating point operations. Therefore, to compile programs for GPUs, it is necessary to utilize special programming platforms, such as CUDA and OpenCL.

Compute Unified Device Architecture (CUDA) is a proprietary NVIDIA technology. It provides an API that can be accessed from other languages. CUDA provides the NVCC tool that can be used to compile GPU programs written in a language similar to C (CUDA C) as well as numerous libraries that implement highly optimized mathematical routines.

OpenCL is an open technology with the ability of writing parallel programs that can be compiled for a variety of target devices (CPUs and GPUs of several vendors) and is a good option for non-NVIDIA devices.

GPU programming sounds wonderful on paper. However, don't throw away your CPU yet. GPU programming is tricky and only specific use cases benefit from the GPU architecture. Programmers need to be aware of the costs incurred in memory transfers to and from the main memory and how to implement algorithms to take advantage of the GPU architecture.

Generally, GPUs are great at increasing the amount of operations you can perform per unit of time (also called **throughput**); however, they require more time to prepare the data for processing. In contrast, CPUs are much faster at producing an individual result from scratch (also called **latency**).

For the right problem, GPUs provide extreme (10 to 100 times) speedup. For this reason, they often constitute a very inexpensive (the same speedup will require hundreds of CPUs) solution to improve the performance of numerically intensive applications. We will illustrate how to execute some algorithms on a GPU in the *Automatic Parallelism* section.

Using multiple processes

The standard `multiprocessing` module can be used to quickly parallelize simple tasks by spawning several processes, while avoiding the GIL problem. Its interface is easy to use and includes several utilities to handle task submission and synchronization.

The Process and Pool classes

You can create a process that runs independently by subclassing
`multiprocessing.Process`. You can extend the __init__ method to initialize resources,
and you can write the portion of the code that will be executed in a subprocess by
implementing the `Process.run` method. In the following code, we define a `Process` class
that will wait for one second and print its assigned `id`:

```
import multiprocessing
import time

class Process(multiprocessing.Process):
    def __init__(self, id):
        super(Process, self).__init__()
        self.id = id

    def run(self):
        time.sleep(1)
        print("I'm the process with id: {}".format(self.id))
```

To spawn the process, we have to instantiate the `Process` class and call the
`Process.start` method. Note that you don't directly call `Process.run`; the call to
`Process.start` will create a new process that, in turn, will call the `Process.run` method.
We can add the following lines at the end of the preceding snippet to create and start the
new process:

```
if __name__ == '__main__':
    p = Process(0)
    p.start()
```

The instructions after `Process.start` will be executed immediately without waiting for
the p process to finish. To wait for the task completion, you can use
the `Process.join` method, as follows:

```
if __name__ == '__main__':
    p = Process(0)
    p.start()
    p.join()
```

We can launch four different processes that will run parallely in the same way. In a serial program, the total required time will be four seconds. Since the execution is concurrent, the resulting wallclock time will be of one second. In the following code, we create four processes that will execute concurrently:

```
if __name__ == '__main__':
    processes = Process(1), Process(2), Process(3), Process(4)
    [p.start() for p in processes]
```

Note that the order of the execution for parallel processes is unpredictable and ultimately depends on how the OS schedules their execution. You can verify this behavior by executing the program multiple times; the order will likely be different between runs.

The multiprocessing module exposes a convenient interface that makes it easy to assign and distribute tasks to a set of processes that reside in the multiprocessing.Pool class.

The multiprocessing.Pool class spawns a set of processes--called **workers**--and lets us submit tasks through the apply/apply_async and map/map_async methods.

The Pool.map method applies a function to each element of a list and returns the list of results. Its usage is equivalent to the built-in (serial) map.

To use a parallel map, you should first initialize a multiprocessing.Pool object. It takes the number of workers as its first argument; if not provided, that number will be equal to the number of cores in the system. You can initialize a multiprocessing.Pool object in the following way:

```
pool = multiprocessing.Pool()
pool = multiprocessing.Pool(processes=4)
```

Let's see pool.map in action. If you have a function that computes the square of a number, you can map the function to the list by calling Pool.map and passing the function and the list of inputs as arguments, as follows:

```
def square(x):
    return x * x

inputs = [0, 1, 2, 3, 4]
outputs = pool.map(square, inputs)
```

The `Pool.map_async` function is just like `Pool.map` but returns an `AsyncResult` object instead of the actual result. When we call `Pool.map`, the execution of the main program is stopped until all the workers are finished processing the result. With `map_async`, the `AsyncResult` object is returned immediately without blocking the main program and the calculations are done in the background. We can then retrieve the result using the `AsyncResult.get` method at any time, as shown in the following lines:

```
outputs_async = pool.map_async(square, inputs)
outputs = outputs_async.get()
```

`Pool.apply_async` assigns a task consisting of a single function to one of the workers. It takes the function and its arguments and returns an `AsyncResult` object. We can obtain an effect similar to `map` using `apply_async`, as shown:

```
results_async = [pool.apply_async(square, i) for i in range(100))]
results = [r.get() for r in results_async]
```

The Executor interface

From version 3.2 onward, it is possible to execute Python code in parallel using the `Executor` interface provided in the `concurrent.futures` module. We already saw the `Executor` interface in action in the previous chapter, when we used `ThreadPoolExecutor` to perform multiple tasks concurrently. In this subsection, we'll demonstrate the usage of the `ProcessPoolExecutor` class.

`ProcessPoolExecutor` exposes a very lean interface, at least when compared to the more featureful `multiprocessing.Pool`. A `ProcessPoolExecutor` can be instantiated, similar to `ThreadPoolExecutor`, by passing a number of worker threads using the `max_workers` argument (by default, `max_workers` will be the number of CPU cores available). The main methods available to the `ProcessPoolExecutor` are `submit` and `map`.

The `submit` method will take a function and return a `Future` that will keep track of the execution of the submitted function. The method map works similarly to the `Pool.map` function, except that it returns an iterator rather than a list:

```
from concurrent.futures import ProcessPoolExecutor

executor = ProcessPoolExecutor(max_workers=4)
fut = executor.submit(square, 2)
# Result:
# <Future at 0x7f5b5c030940 state=running>

result = executor.map(square, [0, 1, 2, 3, 4])
```

```
list(result)
# Result:
# [0, 1, 4, 9, 16]
```

To extract the result from one or more `Future` instances, you can use the `concurrent.futures.wait` and `concurrent.futures.as_completed` functions. The `wait` function accepts a list of `future` and will block the execution of the programs until all the futures have completed their execution. The result can then be extracted using the `Future.result` method. The `as_completed` function also accepts a function but will, instead, return an iterator over the results:

```
from concurrent.futures import wait, as_completed

fut1 = executor.submit(square, 2)
fut2 = executor.submit(square, 3)
wait([fut1, fut2])
# Then you can extract the results using fut1.result() and
fut2.result()

results = as_completed([fut1, fut2])
list(results)
# Result:
# [4, 9]
```

Alternatively, you can generate futures using the `asyncio.run_in_executor` function and manipulate the results using all the tools and syntax provided by the `asyncio` libraries so that you can achieve concurrency and parallelism at the same time.

Monte Carlo approximation of pi

As an example, we will implement a canonical, embarrassingly parallel program--the **Monte Carlo approximation of pi**. Imagine that we have a square of size 2 units; its area will be 4 units. Now, we inscribe a circle of 1 unit radius in this square; the area of the circle will be $pi * r^2$. By substituting the value of r in the previous equation, we get that the numerical value for the area of the circle is $pi * (1)^2 = pi$. You can refer to the following figure for a graphical representation.

If we shoot a lot of random points on this figure, some points will fall into the circle, which we'll call **hits,** while the remaining points, **misses,** will be outside the circle. The area of the circle will be proportional to the number of hits, while the area of the square will be proportional to the total number of shots. To get the value of *pi*, it is sufficient to divide the area of the circle (equal to *pi*) by the area of the square (equal to 4):

```
hits/total = area_circle/area_square = pi/4
pi = 4 * hits/total
```

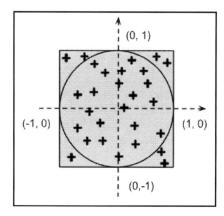

The strategy we will employ in our program will be as follows:

- Generate a lot of uniformly random (*x*, *y*) numbers in the range (**-1, 1**)
- Test whether those numbers lie inside the circle by checking whether $x^{**}2 + y^{**}2 <= 1$

The first step when writing a parallel program is to write a serial version and verify that it works. In a real-world scenario, you also want to leave the parallelization as the last step of your optimization process. First, we need to identify the slow parts, and second, parallelization is time-consuming and gives you *at most* a speedup equal to the number of processors. The implementation of the serial program is as follows:

```
import random

samples = 1000000
hits = 0

for i in range(samples):
    x = random.uniform(-1.0, 1.0)
    y = random.uniform(-1.0, 1.0)

    if x**2 + y**2 <= 1:
```

Chapter 7

```
        hits += 1
    pi = 4.0 * hits/samples
```

The accuracy of our approximation will improve as we increase the number of samples. You can note that each loop iteration is independent from the other--this problem is embarrassingly parallel.

To parallelize this code, we can write a function, called `sample`, that corresponds to a single hit-miss check. If the sample hits the circle, the function will return 1; otherwise, it will return 0. By running `sample` multiple times and summing the results, we'll get the total number of hits. We can run `sample` over multiple processors with `apply_async` and get the results in the following way:

```python
def sample():
    x = random.uniform(-1.0, 1.0)
    y = random.uniform(-1.0, 1.0)

    if x**2 + y**2 <= 1:
        return 1
    else:
        return 0

pool = multiprocessing.Pool()
results_async = [pool.apply_async(sample) for i in range(samples)]
hits = sum(r.get() for r in results_async)
```

We can wrap the two versions in the `pi_serial` and `pi_apply_async` functions (you can find their implementation in the `pi.py` file) and benchmark the execution speed, as follows:

```
$ time python -c 'import pi; pi.pi_serial()'
real    0m0.734s
user    0m0.731s
sys     0m0.004s
$ time python -c 'import pi; pi.pi_apply_async()'
real    1m36.989s
user    1m55.984s
sys     0m50.386
```

As shown in the earlier benchmark, our first parallel version literally cripples our code. The reason is that the time spent doing the actual calculation is small compared to the overhead required to send and distribute the tasks to the workers.

[183]

To solve the issue, we have to make the overhead negligible compared to the calculation time. For example, we can ask each worker to handle more than one sample at a time, thus reducing the task communication overhead. We can write a `sample_multiple` function that processes more than one hit and modifies our parallel version by dividing our problem by 10; more intensive tasks are shown in the following code:

```
def sample_multiple(samples_partial):
    return sum(sample() for i in range(samples_partial))

n_tasks = 10
chunk_size = samples/n_tasks
pool = multiprocessing.Pool()
results_async = [pool.apply_async(sample_multiple, chunk_size)
                 for i in range(n_tasks)]
hits = sum(r.get() for r in results_async)
```

We can wrap this in a function called `pi_apply_async_chunked` and run it as follows:

```
$ time python -c 'import pi; pi.pi_apply_async_chunked()'
real    0m0.325s
user    0m0.816s
sys     0m0.008s
```

The results are much better; we more than doubled the speed of our program. You can also notice that the `user` metric is larger than `real`; the total CPU time is larger than the total time because more than one CPU worked at the same time. If you increase the number of samples, you will note that the ratio of communication to calculation decreases, giving even better speedups.

Everything is nice and simple when dealing with embarrassingly parallel problems. However, sometimes you have to share data between processes.

Synchronization and locks

Even if `multiprocessing` uses processes (with their own independent memory), it lets you define certain variables and arrays as shared memory. You can define a shared variable using `multiprocessing.Value`, passing its data type as a string (`i` integer, `d` double, `f` float, and so on). You can update the content of the variable through the `value` attribute, as shown in the following code snippet:

```
shared_variable = multiprocessing.Value('f')
shared_variable.value = 0
```

When using shared memory, you should be aware of concurrent accesses. Imagine that you have a shared integer variable and each process increments its value multiple times. You will define a process class as follows:

```
class Process(multiprocessing.Process):

    def __init__(self, counter):
        super(Process, self).__init__()
        self.counter - counter

    def run(self):
        for i in range(1000):
            self.counter.value += 1
```

You can initialize the shared variable in the main program and pass it to 4 processes, as shown in the following code:

```
def main():
    counter = multiprocessing.Value('i', lock=True)
    counter.value = 0

    processes = [Process(counter) for i in range(4)]
    [p.start() for p in processes]
    [p.join() for p in processes] # processes are done
    print(counter.value)
```

If you run this program (`shared.py` in the code directory), you will note that the final value of `counter` is not 4000, but it has random values (on my machine, they are between 2000 and 2500). If we assume that the arithmetic is correct, we can conclude that there's a problem with the parallelization.

What happens is that multiple processes are trying to access the same shared variable at the same time. The situation is best explained by looking at the following figure. In a serial execution, the first process reads (the number 0), increments it, and writes the new value (1); the second process reads the new value (1), increments it, and writes it again (2).

In the parallel execution, the two processes read (0), increment it, and write the value (1) at the same time, leading to a wrong answer:

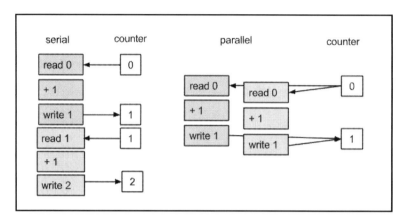

To solve this problem, we need to synchronize the access to this variable so that only one process at a time can access, increment, and write the value on the shared variable. This feature is provided by the multiprocessing.Lock class. A lock can be acquired and released through the acquire method and release, or using the lock as a context manager. Since the lock can be acquired by only one process at a time, this method prevents multiple processes from executing the protected section of code at the same time.

We can define a global lock and use it as a context manager to restrict the access to the counter, as shown in the following code snippet:

```
lock = multiprocessing.Lock()

class Process(multiprocessing.Process):

    def __init__(self, counter):
        super(Process, self).__init__()
        self.counter = counter

    def run(self):
        for i in range(1000):
            with lock: # acquire the lock
                self.counter.value += 1
            # release the lock
```

Synchronization primitives, such as locks, are essential to solve many problems, but they should be kept to a minimum to improve the performance of your program.

 The `multiprocessing` module includes other communication and synchronization tools; you can refer to the official documentation at `http://docs.python.org/3/library/multiprocessing.html` for a complete reference.

Parallel Cython with OpenMP

Cython provides a convenient interface to perform shared-memory parallel processing through **OpenMP**. This lets you write extremely efficient parallel code directly in Cython without having to create a C wrapper.

OpenMP is a specification and an API designed to write multithreaded, parallel programs. The OpenMP specification includes a series of C preprocessor directives to manage threads and provides communication patterns, load balancing, and other synchronization features. Several C/C++ and Fortran compilers (including GCC) implement the OpenMP API.

We can introduce the Cython parallel features with a small example. Cython provides a simple API based on OpenMP in the `cython.parallel` module. The simplest way to achieve parallelism is through `prange`, which is a construct that automatically distributes loop operations in multiple threads.

First of all, we can write the serial version of a program that computes the square of each element of a NumPy array in the `hello_parallel.pyx` file. We define a function, `square_serial`, that takes a buffer as input and populates an output array with the squares of the input array elements; `square_serial` is shown in the following code snippet:

```
import numpy as np

def square_serial(double[:] inp):
    cdef int i, size
    cdef double[:] out
    size = inp.shape[0]
    out_np = np.empty(size, 'double')
    out = out_np

    for i in range(size):
        out[i] = inp[i]*inp[i]

    return out_np
```

Implementing a parallel version of the loop over the array elements involves substituting the range call with prange. There's a caveat--to use prange, it is necessary that the body of the loop is interpreter-free. As already explained, we need to release the GIL and, since interpreter calls generally acquire the GIL, they need to be avoided to make use of threads.

In Cython, you can release the GIL using the nogil context, as follows:

```
with nogil:
    for i in prange(size):
        out[i] = inp[i]*inp[i]
```

Alternatively, you can use the option nogil=True of prange that will automatically wrap the loop body in a nogil block:

```
for i in prange(size, nogil=True):
    out[i] = inp[i]*inp[i]
```

Attempts to call Python code in a prange block will produce an error. Prohibited operations include function calls, objects initialization, and so on. To enable such operations in a prange block (you may want to do so for debugging purposes), you have to re-enable the GIL using the with gil statement:

```
for i in prange(size, nogil=True):
    out[i] = inp[i]*inp[i]
    with gil:
        x = 0 # Python assignment
```

We can now test our code by compiling it as a Python extension module. To enable OpenMP support, it is necessary to change the setup.py file so that it includes the compilation option -fopenmp . This can be achieved by using the distutils.extension.Extension class in distutils and passing it to cythonize. The complete setup.py file is as follows:

```
from distutils.core import setup
from distutils.extension import Extension
from Cython.Build import cythonize

hello_parallel = Extension('hello_parallel',
                           ['hello_parallel.pyx'],
                           extra_compile_args=['-fopenmp'],
                           extra_link_args=['-fopenmp'])

setup(
    name='Hello',
    ext_modules = cythonize(['cevolve.pyx', hello_parallel]),
)
```

Using `prange`, we can easily parallelize the Cython version of our `ParticleSimulator`. The following code contains the `c_evolve` function of the `cevolve.pyx` Cython module that was written in `Chapter 4`, *C Performance with Cython*:

```
def c_evolve(double[:, :] r_i,double[:] ang_speed_i,
             double timestep,int nsteps):

    # cdef declarations

    for i in range(nsteps):
        for j in range(nparticles):
            # loop body
```

First, we will invert the order of the loops so that the outermost loop will be executed in parallel (each iteration is independent from the other). Since the particles don't interact with each other, we can change the order of iteration safely, as shown in the following snippet:

```
for j in range(nparticles):
    for i in range(nsteps):

        # loop body
```

Next, we will replace the `range` call of the outer loop with `prange` and remove calls that acquire the GIL. Since our code was already enhanced with static types, the `nogil` option can be applied safely as follows:

```
for j in prange(nparticles, nogil=True)
```

We can now compare the functions by wrapping them in the benchmark function to assess any performance improvement:

```
In [3]: %timeit benchmark(10000, 'openmp') # Running on 4 processors
1 loops, best of 3: 599 ms per loop
In [4]: %timeit benchmark(10000, 'cython')
1 loops, best of 3: 1.35 s per loop
```

Interestingly, we achieved a 2x speedup by writing a parallel version using `prange`.

Automatic parallelism

As we mentioned earlier, normal Python programs have trouble achieving thread parallelism because of the GIL. So far, we worked around this problem using separate processes; starting a process, however, takes significantly more time and memory than starting a thread.

We also saw that sidestepping the Python environment allowed us to achieve a 2x speedup on an already fast Cython code. This strategy allowed us to achieve lightweight parallelism but required a separate compilation step. In this section, we will further explore this strategy using special libraries that are capable of automatically translating our code into a parallel version for efficient execution.

Examples of packages that implement automatic parallelism are the (by now) familiar JIT compilers `numexpr` and Numba. Other packages have been developed to automatically optimize and parallelize array and matrix-intensive expressions, which are crucial in specific numerical and machine learning applications.

Theano is a project that allows you to define a mathematical expression on arrays (more generally, *tensors*), and compile them to a fast language, such as C or C++. Many of the operations that Theano implements are parallelizable and can run on both CPU and GPU.

Tensorflow is another library that, similar to Theano, is targeted towards expression of array-intensive mathematical expression but, rather than translating the expressions to specialized C code, executes the operations on an efficient C++ engine.

Both Theano and Tensorflow are ideal when the problem at hand can be expressed in a chain of matrix and element-wise operations (such as *neural networks*).

Getting started with Theano

Theano is somewhat similar to a compiler but with the added bonuses of being able to express, manipulate, and optimize mathematical expressions as well as run code on CPU and GPU. Since 2010, Theano has improved release after release and has been adopted by several other Python projects as a way to automatically generate efficient computational models on the fly.

In Theano, you first *define* the function you want to run by specifying variables and transformation using a pure Python API. This specification will then be compiled to machine code for execution.

As a first example, let's examine how to implement a function that computes the square of a number. The input will be represented by a scalar variable, a, and then we will transform it to obtain its square, indicated by a_sq. In the following code, we will use the `T.scalar` function to define the variable and use the normal `**` operator to obtain a new variable:

```
import theano.tensor as T
import theano as th
a = T.scalar('a')
a_sq = a ** 2
```

```
print(a_sq)
# Output:
# Elemwise{pow,no_inplace}.0
```

As you can see, no specific value is computed and the transformation we apply is purely symbolic. In order to use this transformation, we need to generate a function. To compile a function, you can use the `th.function` utility that takes a list of the input variables as its first argument, and the output transformation (in our case `a_sq`) as its second argument:

```
compute_square = th.function([a], a_sq)
```

Theano will take some time and translate the expression to efficient C code and compile it, all in the background! The return value of `th.function` will be a ready-to-use Python function and its usage is demonstrated in the next line of code:

```
compute_square(2)
4.0
```

Unsurprisingly, `compute_square` correctly returns the input value squared. Note, however, that the return type is not an integer (like the input type) but a floating point number. This is because the Theano default variable type is `float64`. you can verify that by inspecting the `dtype` attribute of the `a` variable:

```
a.dtype
# Result:
# float64
```

The Theano behavior is very different compared to what we saw with Numba. Theano doesn't compile generic Python code and, also, doesn't do any type inference; defining Theano functions requires a more precise specification of the types involved.

The real power of Theano comes from its support for array expressions. Defining a one-dimensional vector can be done with the `T.vector` function; the returned variable supports broadcasting operations with the same semantics of NumPy arrays. For instance, we can take two vectors and compute the element-wise sum of their squares, as follows:

```
a = T.vector('a')
b = T.vector('b')
ab_sq = a**2 + b**2
compute_square = th.function([a, b], ab_sq)

compute_square([0, 1, 2], [3, 4, 5])
# Result:
# array([  9.,   17.,   29.])
```

The idea is, again, to use the Theano API as a mini-language to combine various Numpy array expressions will be compiled to efficient machine code.

 One of the selling points of Theano is its ability to perform arithmetic simplifications and automatic gradient calculations. For more information, refer to the official documentation (http://deeplearning. net/software/theano/introduction.html).

To demonstrate Theano functionality on a familiar use case, we can implement our parallel calculation of pi again. Our function will take a collection of two random coordinates as input and return the pi estimate. The input random numbers will be defined as vectors named x and y, and we can test their position inside the circle using standard element-wise operation that we will store in the hit_test variable:

```
x = T.vector('x')
y = T.vector('y')

hit_test = x ** 2 + y ** 2 < 1
```

At this point, we need to count the number of True elements in hit_test, which can be done taking its sum (it will be implicitly cast to integer). To obtain the pi estimate, we finally need to calculate the ratio of hits versus the total number of trials. The calculation is illustrated in the following code block:

```
hits = hit_test.sum()
total = x.shape[0]
pi_est = 4 * hits/total
```

We can benchmark the execution of the Theano implementation using th.function and the timeit module. In our test, we will pass two arrays of size 30,000 and use the timeit.timeit utility to execute the calculate_pi function multiple times:

```
calculate_pi = th.function([x, y], pi_est)

x_val = np.random.uniform(-1, 1, 30000)
y_val = np.random.uniform(-1, 1, 30000)

import timeit
res = timeit.timeit("calculate_pi(x_val, y_val)",
"from __main__ import x_val, y_val, calculate_pi", number=100000)
print(res)
# Output:
# 10.905971487998613
```

The serial execution of this function takes about 10 seconds. Theano is capable of automatically parallelizing the code by implementing element-wise and matrix operations using specialized packages, such as OpenMP and the **Basic Linear Algebra Subprograms (BLAS)** linear algebra routines. Parallel execution can be enabled using configuration options.

In Theano, you can set up configuration options by modifying variables in the theano.config object at import time. For example, you can issue the following commands to enable OpenMP support:

```
import theano
theano.config.openmp = True
theano.config.openmp_elemwise_minsize = 10
```

The parameters relevant to OpenMP are as follows:

- openmp_elemwise_minsize: This is an integer number that represents the minimum size of the arrays where element-wise parallelization should be enabled (the overhead of the parallelization can harm performance for small arrays)
- openmp: This is a Boolean flag that controls the activation of OpenMP compilation (it should be activated by default)

Controlling the number of threads assigned for OpenMP execution can be done by setting the OMP_NUM_THREADS environmental variable before executing the code.

We can now write a simple benchmark to demonstrate the OpenMP usage in practice. In a file test_theano.py, we will put the complete code for the pi estimation example:

```
# File: test_theano.py
import numpy as np
import theano.tensor as T
import theano as th
th.config.openmp_elemwise_minsize = 1000
th.config.openmp = True

x = T.vector('x')
y = T.vector('y')

hit_test = x ** 2 + y ** 2 <= 1
hits = hit_test.sum()
misses = x.shape[0]
pi_est = 4 * hits/misses

calculate_pi = th.function([x, y], pi_est)
```

```
x_val = np.random.uniform(-1, 1, 30000)
y_val = np.random.uniform(-1, 1, 30000)

import timeit
res = timeit.timeit("calculate_pi(x_val, y_val)",
                    "from __main__ import x_val, y_val,
                     calculate_pi", number=100000)
print(res)
```

At this point, we can run the code from the command line and assess the scaling with an increasing number of threads by setting the OMP_NUM_THREADS environment variable:

```
$ OMP_NUM_THREADS=1 python test_theano.py
10.905971487998613
$ OMP_NUM_THREADS=2 python test_theano.py
7.538279129999864
$ OMP_NUM_THREADS=3 python test_theano.py
9.405846934998408
$ OMP_NUM_THREADS=4 python test_theano.py
14.634153957000308
```

Interestingly, there is a small speedup when using two threads, but the performance degrades quickly as we increase their number. This means that for this input size, it is not advantageous to use more than two threads as the price you pay to start new threads and synchronize their shared data is higher than the speedup that you can obtain from the parallel execution.

Achieving good parallel performance can be tricky as it will depend on the specific operations and how they access the underlying data. As a general rule, measuring the performance of a parallel program is crucial and obtaining substantial speedups is a work of trial and error.

As an example, we can see that the parallel performance quickly degrades using a slightly different code. In our hit test, we used the sum method directly and relied on the explicit casting of the hit_tests Boolean array. If we make the cast explicit, Theano will generate a slightly different code that benefits less from multiple threads. We can modify the test_theano.py file to verify this effect:

```
# Older version
# hits = hit_test.sum()
hits = hit_test.astype('int32').sum()
```

If we rerun our benchmark, we see that the number of threads does not affect the running time significantly. Despite that, the timings improved considerably as compared to the original version:

```
$ OMP_NUM_THREADS=1 python test_theano.py
5.822126664999814
$ OMP_NUM_THREADS=2 python test_theano.py
5.697357518001809
$ OMP_NUM_THREADS=3 python test_theano.py
5.636914656002773
$ OMP_NUM_THREADS=4 python test_theano.py
5.764030176000233
```

Profiling Theano

Given the importance of measuring and analyzing performance, Theano provides powerful and informative profiling tools. To generate profiling data, the only modification needed is the addition of the profile=True option to th.function:

```
calculate_pi = th.function([x, y], pi_est, profile=True)
```

The profiler will collect data as the function is being run (for example, through timeit or direct invocation). The profiling summary can be printed to output by issuing the summary command, as follows:

```
calculate_pi.profile.summary()
```

To generate profiling data, we can rerun our script after adding the profile=True option (for this experiment, we will set the OMP_NUM_THREADS environmental variable to 1). Also, we will revert our script to the version that performed the casting of hit_tests implicitly.

You can also set up profiling globally using the config.profile option.

The output printed by `calculate_pi.profile.summary()` is quite long and informative. A part of it is reported in the next block of text. The output is comprised of three sections that refer to timings sorted by `Class`, `Ops`, and `Apply`. In our example, we are concerned with `Ops`, which roughly maps to the functions used in the Theano compiled code. As you can see, roughly 80% of the time is spent in taking the element-wise square and sum of the two numbers, while the rest of the time is spent calculating the sum:

```
Function profiling
==================
   Message: test_theano.py:15

... other output
Time in 100000 calls to Function.__call__: 1.015549e+01s
... other output

Class
---
<% time> <sum %> <apply time> <time per call> <type> <#call> <#apply>
<Class name>
.... timing info by class

Ops
---
<% time> <sum %> <apply time> <time per call> <type> <#call> <#apply> <Op
name>
  80.0%    80.0%        6.722s        6.72e-05s    C      100000          1
Elemwise{Composite{LT((sqr(i0) + sqr(i1)), i2)}}
  19.4%    99.4%        1.634s        1.63e-05s    C      100000          1
Sum{acc_dtype=int64}
   0.3%    99.8%        0.027s        2.66e-07s    C      100000          1
Elemwise{Composite{((i0 * i1) / i2)}}
   0.2%   100.0%        0.020s        2.03e-07s    C      100000          1
Shape_i{0}
   ... (remaining 0 Ops account for   0.00%(0.00s) of the runtime)

Apply
------
<% time> <sum %> <apply time> <time per call> <#call> <id> <Apply name>
... timing info by apply
```

This information is consistent with what was found in our first benchmark. The code went from about 11 seconds to roughly 8 seconds when two threads were used. From these numbers, we can analyze how the time was spent.

Out of these 11 seconds, 80% of the time (about 8.8 seconds) was spent doing element-wise operations. This means that, in perfectly parallel conditions, the increase in speed by adding two threads will be 4.4 seconds. In this scenario, the theoretical execution time will be 6.6 seconds. Considering that we obtained a timing of about 8 seconds, it looks like there is some extra overhead (1.4 seconds) for the thread usage.

Tensorflow

Tensorflow is another library designed for fast numerical calculations and automatic parallelism. It was released as an open source project by Google in 2015. Tensorflow works by building mathematical expressions similar to Theano, except that the computation is not compiled to machine code but is executed on an external engine written in C++. Tensorflow supports execution and deployment of parallel codes on one or more CPUs and GPUs.

The usage of Tensorflow is quite similar to that of Theano. To create a variable in Tensorflow, you can use the `tf.placeholder` function that takes a data type as input:

```
import tensorflow as tf

a = tf.placeholder('float64')
```

Tensorflow mathematical expressions can be expressed quite similarly to Theano, except for a few different naming conventions as well as a more restricted support for the NumPy semantics.

Tensorflow doesn't compile functions to C and then machine code like Theano, but serializes the defined mathematical functions (the data structure containing variables and transformations is called **computation graph**) and executes them on specific devices. The configuration of devices and context can be done using the `tf.Session` object.

Once the desired expression is defined, a `tf.Session` needs to be initialized and can be used to execute computation graphs using the `Session.run` method. In the following example, we demonstrate the usage of the Tensorflow API to implement a simple element-wise sum of squares:

```
a = tf.placeholder('float64')
b = tf.placeholder('float64')
ab_sq = a**2 + b**2

with tf.Session() as session:
    result = session.run(ab_sq, feed_dict={a: [0, 1, 2],
                                            b: [3, 4, 5]})
```

```
        print(result)
    # Output:
    # array([  9.,   17.,   29.])
```

Parallelism in Tensorflow is achieved automatically by its smart execution engine, and it generally works well without much fiddling. However, note that it is mostly suited for deep learning workloads that involve the definition of complex functions that use a lot of matrix multiplications and calculate their gradient.

We can now replicate the estimation of the pi example using Tensorflow capabilities and benchmark its execution speed and parallelism against the Theano implementation. What we will do is this:

- Define our x and y variables and perform a hit test using broadcasted operations.
- Calculate the sum of `hit_tests` using the `tf.reduce_sum` function.
- Initialize a `Session` object with the `inter_op_parallelism_threads` and `intra_op_parallelism_threads` configuration options. These options control the number of threads used for different classes of parallel operations. Note that the first `Session` created with such options sets the number of threads for the whole script (even future `Session` instances).

We can now write a script name, `test_tensorflow.py`, containing the following code. Note that the number of threads is passed as the first argument of the script (`sys.argv[1]`):

```
import tensorflow as tf
import numpy as np
import time
import sys

NUM_THREADS = int(sys.argv[1])
samples = 30000

print('Num threads', NUM_THREADS)
x_data = np.random.uniform(-1, 1, samples)
y_data = np.random.uniform(-1, 1, samples)

x = tf.placeholder('float64', name='x')
y = tf.placeholder('float64', name='y')

hit_tests = x ** 2 + y ** 2 <= 1.0
hits = tf.reduce_sum(tf.cast(hit_tests, 'int32'))

with tf.Session
    (config=tf.ConfigProto
```

```
    (inter_op_parallelism_threads=NUM_THREADS,
     intra_op_parallelism_threads=NUM_THREADS)) as sess:
start = time.time()
for i in range(10000):
    sess.run(hits, {x: x_data, y: y_data})
print(time.time() - start)
```

If we run the script multiple times with different values of NUM_THREADS, we see that the performance is quite similar to Theano and that the speedup increased by parallelization is quite modest:

```
$ python test_tensorflow.py 1
13.059704780578613
$ python test_tensorflow.py 2
11.938535928726196
$ python test_tensorflow.py 3
12.783955574035645
$ python test_tensorflow.py 4
12.158143043518066
```

The main advantage of using software packages such as Tensorflow and Theano is the support for parallel matrix operations that are commonly used in machine learning algorithms. This is very effective because those operations can achieve impressive performance gains on GPU hardware that is designed to perform these operations with high throughput.

Running code on a GPU

In this subsection, we will demonstrate the usage of a GPU with Theano and Tensorflow. As an example, we will benchmark the execution of a very simple matrix multiplication on the GPU and compare it to its running time on a CPU.

 The code in this subsection requires the possession of a GPU. For learning purposes, it is possible to use the Amazon EC2 service (https://aws.amazon.com/ec2) to request a GPU-enabled instance.

The following code performs a simple matrix multiplication using Theano. We use the T.matrix function to initialize a two-dimensional array, and then we use the T.dot method to perform the matrix multiplication:

```
from theano import function, config
import theano.tensor as T
import numpy as np
```

```
import time

N = 5000

A_data = np.random.rand(N, N).astype('float32')
B_data = np.random.rand(N, N).astype('float32')

A = T.matrix('A')
B = T.matrix('B')

f = function([A, B], T.dot(A, B))

start = time.time()
f(A_data, B_data)

print("Matrix multiply ({}) took {} seconds".format(N, time.time() -
start))
    print('Device used:', config.device)
```

It is possible to ask Theano to execute this code on a GPU by setting the
config.device=gpu option. For added convenience, we can set up the configuration
value from the command line using the THEANO_FLAGS environmental variable, shown as
follows. After copying the previous code in the test_theano_matmul.py file, we can
benchmark the execution time by issuing the following command:

```
$ THEANO_FLAGS=device=gpu python test_theano_gpu.py
Matrix multiply (5000) took 0.4182612895965576 seconds
Device used: gpu
```

We can analogously run the same code on the CPU using the device=cpu configuration
option:

```
$ THEANO_FLAGS=device=cpu python test_theano.py
Matrix multiply (5000) took 2.9623231887817383 seconds
Device used: cpu
```

As you can see, the GPU is 7.2 times faster than the CPU version for this example!

For comparison, we may benchmark equivalent code using Tensorflow. The
implementation of a Tensorflow version is reported in the next code snippet. The main
differences with the Theano version are as follows:

- The usage of the tf.device config manager that serves to specify the target
  device (/cpu:0 or /gpu:0)

- The matrix multiplication is performed using the `tf.matmul` operator:

```
import tensorflow as tf
import time
import numpy as np
N = 5000

A_data = np.random.rand(N, N)
B_data = np.random.rand(N, N)

# Creates a graph.

with tf.device('/gpu:0'):
    A = tf.placeholder('float32')
    B = tf.placeholder('float32')

    C = tf.matmul(A, B)

with tf.Session() as sess:
    start = time.time()
    sess.run(C, {A: A_data, B: B_data})
    print('Matrix multiply ({}) took: {}'.format(N, time.time() -
start))
```

If we run the `test_tensorflow_matmul.py` script with the appropriate `tf.device` option, we obtain the following timings:

```
# Ran with tf.device('/gpu:0')
Matrix multiply (5000) took: 1.417285680770874

# Ran with tf.device('/cpu:0')
Matrix multiply (5000) took: 2.9646761417388916
```

As you can see, the performance gain is substantial (but not as good as the Theano version) in this simple case.

Another way to achieve automatic GPU computation is the now familiar Numba. With Numba, it is possible to compile Python code to programs that can be run on a GPU. This flexibility allows for advanced GPU programming as well as more simplified interfaces. In particular, Numba makes extremely easy-to-write, GPU-ready, generalized universal functions.

In the next example, we will demonstrate how to write a universal function that applies an exponential function on two numbers and sums the results. As we already saw in Chapter 5, *Exploring Compilers* this can be accomplished using the nb.vectorize function (we'll also specify the cpu target explicitly):

```
import numba as nb
import math
@nb.vectorize(target='cpu')
def expon_cpu(x, y):
    return math.exp(x) + math.exp(y)
```

The expon_cpu universal function can be compiled for the GPU device using the target='cuda' option. Also, note that it is necessary to specify the input types for CUDA universal functions. The implementation of expon_gpu is as follows:

```
@nb.vectorize(['float32(float32, float32)'], target='cuda')
def expon_gpu(x, y):
    return math.exp(x) + math.exp(y)
```

We can now benchmark the execution of the two functions by applying the functions on two arrays of size 1,000,000. Also, note that we execute the function before measuring the timings to trigger the Numba just-in-time compilation:

```
import numpy as np
import time

N = 1000000
niter = 100

a = np.random.rand(N).astype('float32')
b = np.random.rand(N).astype('float32')

# Trigger compilation
expon_cpu(a, b)
expon_gpu(a, b)

# Timing
start = time.time()
for i in range(niter):
    expon_cpu(a, b)
print("CPU:", time.time() - start)

start = time.time()
for i in range(niter):
    expon_gpu(a, b)
print("GPU:", time.time() - start)
# Output:
```

```
# CPU: 2.4762887954711914
# GPU: 0.8668839931488037
```

Thanks to the GPU execution, we were able to achieve a 3x speedup over the CPU version. Note that transferring data on the GPU is quite expensive; therefore, GPU execution becomes advantageous only for very large arrays.

Summary

Parallel processing is an effective way to improve performance on large datasets. Embarrassingly parallel problems are excellent candidates for parallel execution that can be easily implemented to achieve good performance scaling.

In this chapter, we illustrated the basics of parallel programming in Python. We learned how to circumvent Python threading limitation by spawning processes using the tools available in the Python standard library. We also explored how to implement a multithreaded program using Cython and OpenMP.

For more complex problems, we learned how to use the Theano, Tensorflow, and Numba packages to automatically compile array-intensive expressions for parallel execution on CPU and GPU devices.

In the next chapter, we will learn how to write and execute parallel programs on multiple processors and machines using libraries such as dask and PySpark.

8
Advanced Introduction to Concurrent and Parallel Programming

This chapter will provide an overview of what concurrent programming is (in contrast to sequential programming). We will briefly discuss the differences between a program that can be made concurrent and one that cannot. We will go over the history of concurrent engineering and programming, and we will provide a number of examples of how concurrent programming is used in the present day. Finally, we will give a brief introduction to the approach that will be taken in this book, including an outline of the chapter structure and detailed instructions for how to download the code and create a working Python environment.

The following topics will be covered in this chapter:

- The concept of concurrency
- Why some programs cannot be made concurrent, and how to differentiate them from programs that can
- The history of concurrency in computer science: how it is used in the industry today, and what can be expected in the future
- The specific topics that will be covered in each section/chapter of the book
- How to set up a Python environment, and how to check out/download code from GitHub

Technical requirements

Check out the following video to see the Code in Action: http://bit.ly/2TAMAeR

What is concurrency?

It is estimated that the amount of data that needs to be processed by computer programs doubles every two years. The **International Data Corporation (IDC)**, for example, estimates that, by 2020, there will be 5,200 GB of data for every person on earth. With this staggering volume of data come insatiable demands for computing power, and, while numerous computing techniques are being developed and utilized every day, concurrent programming remains one of the most prominent ways to effectively and accurately process data.

While some might be intimidated when the word concurrency appears, the notion behind it is quite intuitive, and it is very common, even in a non-programming context. However, this is not to say that concurrent programs are as simple as sequential ones; they are indeed more difficult to write and understand. Yet, once a correct and effective concurrent structure is achieved, significant improvement in execution time will follow, as you will see later on.

Concurrent versus sequential

Perhaps the most obvious way to understand concurrent programming is to compare it to sequential programming. While a sequential program is in one place at a time, in a concurrent program, different components are in independent, or semi-independent, states. This means that components in different states can be executed independently, and therefore at the same time (as the execution of one component does not depend on the result of another). The following diagram illustrates the basic differences between these two types:

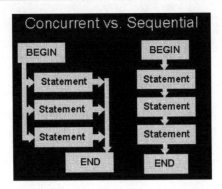

Difference between concurrent and sequential programs

One immediate advantage of concurrency is an improvement in execution time. Again, since some tasks are independent and can therefore be completed at the same time, less time is required for the computer to execute the whole program.

Example 1 – checking whether a non-negative number is prime

Let's consider a quick example. Suppose that we have a simple function that checks whether a non-negative number is prime, as follows:

```python
# Chapter08/example1.py

from math import sqrt

def is_prime(x):
    if x < 2:
    return False

if x == 2:
    return True

if x % 2 == 0:
    return False

limit = int(sqrt(x)) + 1
    for i in range(3, limit, 2):
        if x % i == 0:
            return False

return True
```

Also, suppose that we have a list of significantly large integers (10^{13} to $10^{13} + 500$), and we want to check whether each of them is prime by using the preceding function:

```
input = [i for i in range(10 ** 13, 10 ** 13 + 500)]
```

A sequential approach would be to simply pass one number after another to the `is_prime()` function, as follows:

```
# Chapter08/example1.py

from timeit import default_timer as timer

# sequential
start = timer()
result = []
for i in input:
    if is_prime(i):
        result.append(i)
print('Result 1:', result)
print('Took: %.2f seconds.' % (timer() - start))
```

Copy the code or download it from the GitHub repository and run it (using the `python example1.py` command). The first section of your output will be something similar to the following:

```
> python example1.py
Result 1: [10000000000037, 10000000000051, 10000000000099, 10000000000129,
10000000000183, 10000000000259, 10000000000267, 10000000000273,
10000000000279, 10000000000283, 10000000000313, 10000000000343,
10000000000391, 10000000000411, 10000000000433, 10000000000453]
Took: 3.41 seconds.
```

You can see that the program took around 3.41 seconds to process all of the numbers; we will come back to this number soon. For now, it will also be beneficial for us to check how hard the computer was working while running the program. Open an Activity Monitor application in your operating system, and run the Python script again; the following screenshot shows my results:

System:	6.63%	CPU LOAD	Threads:	1439
User:	10.46%		Processes:	371
Idle:	82.91%			

Activity Monitor showing computer performance

Evidently, the computer was not working too hard, as it was nearly 83% idle.

Now, let's see if concurrency can actually help us to improve our program. The `is_prime()` function contains a lot of heavy computation, and therefore it is a good candidate for concurrent programming. Since the process of passing one number to the `is_prime()` function is independent from passing another, we could potentially apply concurrency to our program, as follows:

```
# Chapter08/example1.py

# concurrent
start = timer()
result = []
with concurrent.futures.ProcessPoolExecutor(max_workers=20) as executor:
    futures = [executor.submit(is_prime, i) for i in input]

    for i, future in enumerate(concurrent.futures.as_completed(futures)):
        if future.result():
            result.append(input[i])

print('Result 2:', result)
print('Took: %.2f seconds.' % (timer() - start))
```

Roughly speaking, we are splitting the tasks into different, smaller chunks, and running them at the same time. Don't worry about the specifics of the code for now, as we will discuss this use of a pool of processes in greater detail later on.

When I executed the function, the execution time was noticeably better, and the computer also used more of its resources, being only 37% idle:

```
> python example1.py
Result 2: [10000000000183, 10000000000037, 10000000000129, 10000000000273,
10000000000259, 10000000000343, 10000000000051, 10000000000267,
10000000000279, 10000000000099, 10000000000283, 10000000000313,
10000000000391, 10000000000433, 10000000000411, 10000000000453]
Took: 2.33 seconds
```

The output of the Activity Monitor application will look something like the following:

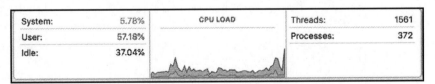

Activity Monitor showing computer performance

Concurrent versus parallel

At this point, if you have had some experience in parallel programming, you might be wondering whether concurrency is any different from parallelism. The key difference between concurrent and parallel programming is that, while in parallel programs there are a number of processing flows (mainly CPUs and cores) working independently all at once, there might be different processing flows (mostly threads) accessing and using **a shared resource** at the same time in concurrent programs.

Since this shared resource can be read and overwritten by any of the different processing flows, some form of coordination is required at times, when the tasks that need to be executed are not entirely independent from one another. In other words, it is important for some tasks to be executed after the others, to ensure that the programs will produce the correct results.

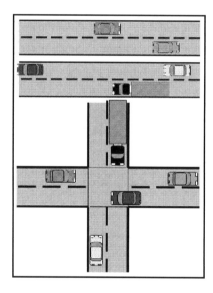

Difference between concurrency and parallelism

The preceding figure illustrates the difference between concurrency and parallelism: while in the upper section, parallel activities (in this case, cars) that do not interact with each other can run at the same time, in the lower section, some tasks have to wait for others to finish before they can be executed.

We will look at more examples of these distinctions later on.

A quick metaphor

Concurrency is a quite difficult concept to fully grasp immediately, so let's consider a quick metaphor, in order to make concurrency and its differences from parallelism easier to understand.

Although some neuroscientists might disagree, let's briefly assume that different parts of the human brain are responsible for performing separate, exclusive body part actions and activities. For example, the left hemisphere of the brain controls the right side of the body, and hence, the right hand (and vice versa); or, one part of the brain might be responsible for writing, while another solely processes speaking.

Now, let's consider the first example, specifically. If you want to move your left hand, the right side of your brain (and only the right side) has to process that command to move, which means that the left side of your brain is *free* to process other information. So, it is possible to move and use the left and right hands at the same time, in order to do different things. Similarly, it is possible to be writing *and* talking at the same time.

That is parallelism: where different processes don't interact with, and are independent of, each other. Remember that concurrency is not quite like parallelism. Even though there are instances where processes are executed together, concurrency also involves sharing the same resources. If parallelism is similar to using your left and right hands for independent tasks at the same time, concurrency can be associated with juggling, where the two hands perform different tasks simultaneously, but they also interact with the same object (in this case, the juggling balls), and some form of coordination between the two hands is therefore required.

Not everything should be made concurrent

Not all programs are created equal: some can be made parallel or concurrent relatively easily, while others are **inherently sequential,** and thus cannot be executed concurrently, or in parallel. An extreme example of the former is **embarrassingly parallel** programs, which can be divided into different parallel tasks, between which there is little or no dependency or need for communication.

Embarrassingly parallel

A common example of an embarrassingly parallel program is the 3D video rendering handled by a graphics processing unit, where each frame or pixel can be processed with no interdependency. Password cracking is another embarrassingly parallel task that can easily be distributed on CPU cores. In a later chapter, we will tackle a number of similar problems, including image processing and web scraping, which can be made concurrent/parallel intuitively, resulting in significantly improved execution times.

Inherently sequential

In opposition to embarrassingly parallel tasks, the execution of some tasks depends heavily on the results of others. In other words, those tasks are not independent, and thus, cannot be made parallel or concurrent. Furthermore, if we were to try to implement concurrency into those programs, it could cost us more execution time to produce the same results. Let's go back to our prime-checking example from earlier; the following is the output that we saw:

```
> python example1.py
Result 1: [10000000000037, 10000000000051, 10000000000099, 10000000000129,
10000000000183, 10000000000259, 10000000000267, 10000000000273,
10000000000279, 10000000000283, 10000000000313, 10000000000343,
10000000000391, 10000000000411, 10000000000433, 10000000000453]
Took: 3.41 seconds.
Result 2: [10000000000183, 10000000000037, 10000000000129, 10000000000273,
10000000000259, 10000000000343, 10000000000051, 10000000000267,
10000000000279, 10000000000099, 10000000000283, 10000000000313,
10000000000391, 10000000000433, 10000000000411, 10000000000453]
Took: 2.33 seconds.
```

Pay close attention, and you will see that the two results from the two methods are not identical; the primes in the second result list are **out of order**. (Recall that, in the second method, to apply concurrency we specified splitting the tasks into different groups to be executed simultaneously, and the order of the results we obtained is the order in which each task finished being executed.) This is a direct result of using concurrency in our second method: we split the tasks to be executed by the program into different groups, and our program processed the tasks in these groups at the same time.

Since tasks across different groups were executed simultaneously, there were tasks that were behind other tasks in the input list, and yet were executed before those other tasks. For example, the number `10000000000183` was behind the number `10000000000129` in our input list, but was processed prior to, and therefore in front of, the number `10000000000129` in our output list. In fact, if you execute the program again and again, the second result will vary in almost every run.

Evidently, this situation is not desirable if the result we'd like to obtain needs to be in the order of the input we originally had. Of course, in this example, we can simply modify the result by using some form of sorting, but it will cost us extra execution time in the end, which might make it even more expensive than the original sequential approach.

A concept that is commonly used to illustrate the innate sequentiality of some tasks is pregnancy: the number of women will never reduce the length of pregnancy. As opposed to parallel or concurrent tasks, where an increase in the number of processing entities will improve the execution time, adding more processors in inherently sequential tasks will not. Famous examples of inherent sequentiality include iterative algorithms: Newton's method, iterative solutions to the three-body problem, or iterative numerical approximation methods.

Example 2 – inherently sequential tasks

Let us consider a quick example:

Computing $f^{1000}(3)$, with $f(x) = x^2 - x + 1$, and $f^{n+1}(x) = f(f^n(x))$.

With complicated functions like f (where it is relatively difficult to find a general form of $f^n(x)$), the only obviously reasonable way to compute $f^{1000}(3)$ or similar values is to iteratively compute $f^2(3) = f(f(3))$, $f^3(3) = f(f^2(3))$, ... , $f^{999}(3) = f(f^{998}(3))$, and, finally, $f^{1000}(3) = f(f^{999}(3))$.

Since it will take significant time to actually compute $f^{1000}(3)$, even when using a computer, we will only consider $f^{20}(3)$ in our code (my laptop actually started heating up after $f^{25}(3)$):

```
# Chapter08/example2.py

def f(x):
    return x * x - x + 1

# sequential
def f(x):
    return x * x - x + 1

start = timer()
```

```
result = 3
for i in range(20):
    result = f(result)

print('Result is very large. Only printing the last 5 digits:', result %
100000)
print('Sequential took: %.2f seconds.' % (timer() - start))
```

Run it (or use `python example2.py`); the following code shows the output I received:

```
> python example2.py
Result is very large. Only printing the last 5 digits: 35443
Sequential took: 0.10 seconds.
```

Now, if we were to attempt to apply concurrency to this script, the only possible way would be through a `for` loop. One solution might be as follows:

```
# Chapter08/example2.py

# concurrent
def concurrent_f(x):
    global result
    result = f(result)

result = 3

with concurrent.futures.ThreadPoolExecutor(max_workers=20) as exector:
    futures = [exector.submit(concurrent_f, i) for i in range(20)]

    _ = concurrent.futures.as_completed(futures)

print('Result is very large. Only printing the last 5 digits:', result %
100000)
print('Concurrent took: %.2f seconds.' % (timer() - start))
```

The output I received is shown as follows:

```
> python example2.py
Result is very large. Only printing the last 5 digits: 35443
Concurrent took: 0.19 seconds.
```

Even though both methods produced the same result, the concurrent method took almost twice as long as the sequential method. This is due to the fact that every time a new thread (from `ThreadPoolExecutor`) was spawned, the function `conconcurrent_f()`, inside that thread, needed to wait for the variable `result` to be processed by the previous thread completely, and the program as a whole was thus executed in a sequential manner, nonetheless.

So, while there was no actual concurrency involved in the second method, the overhead cost of spawning new threads contributed to the significantly worse execution time. This is one example of inherently sequential tasks, where concurrency or parallelism should not be applied to attempt an improvement in execution time.

I/O bound

Another way to think about sequentiality is the concept (in computer science) of a condition called I/O bound, in which the time it takes to complete a computation is mainly determined by the time spent waiting for **input/output (I/O)** operations to be completed. This condition arises when the rate at which data is requested is slower than the rate at which it is consumed, or, in short, more time is spent requesting data than processing it.

In an I/O bound state, the CPU must stall its operation, waiting for data to be processed. This means that, even if the CPU gets faster at processing data, processes tend to not increase in speed in proportion to the increased CPU speed, since they get more I/O-bound. With faster computation speed being the primary goal of new computer and processor designs, I/O bound states are becoming undesirable, yet more and more common, in programs.

As you have seen, there are a number of situations in which the application of concurrent programming results in decreased processing speed, and they should thus be avoided. It is therefore important for us to not see concurrency as a golden ticket that can produce unconditionally better execution times, and to understand the differences between the structures of programs that benefit from concurrency and programs that do not.

The history, present, and future of concurrency

In the following sub-topics, we will discuss the past, present, and future of concurrency.

The field of concurrent programming has enjoyed significant popularity since the early days of computer science. In this section, we will discuss how concurrent programming started and evolved throughout its history, its current usage in the industry, and some predictions regarding how concurrency will be used in the future.

The history of concurrency

The concept of concurrency has been around for quite some time. The idea developed from early work on railroads and telegraphy in the nineteenth and early twentieth centuries, and some terms have even survived to this day (such as **semaphore**, which indicates a variable that controls access to a shared resource in concurrent programs). Concurrency was first applied to address the question of how to handle multiple trains on the same railroad system, in order to avoid collisions and maximize efficiency, and how to handle multiple transmissions over a given set of wires in early telegraphy.

A significant portion of the theoretical groundwork for concurrent programming was actually laid in the 1960s. The early algorithmic language ALGOL 68, which was first developed in 1959, includes features that support concurrent programming. The academic study of concurrency officially started with a seminal paper in 1965 from Edsger Dijkstra, who was a pioneer in computer science, best known for the path-finding algorithm that was named after him.

That seminal paper is considered the first paper in the field of concurrent programming, in which Dijkstra identified and solved the mutual exclusion problem. Mutual exclusion, which is a property of concurrency control that prevents race conditions (which we will discuss later on), went on to become one of the most discussed topics in concurrency.

Yet, there was no considerable interest after that. From around 1970 to early 2000, processors were said to double in executing speed every 18 months. During this period, programmers did not need to concern themselves with concurrent programming, as all they had to do to have their programs run faster was wait. However, in the early 2000s, a paradigm shift in the processor business took place; instead of making increasingly big and fast processors for computers, manufacturers started focusing on smaller, slower processors, which were put together in groups. This was when computers started to have multicore processors.

Nowadays, an average computer has more than one core. So, if a programmer writes all of their programs to be non-concurrent in any way, they will find that their programs utilize only one core or one thread to process data, while the rest of the CPU sits idle, doing nothing (as we saw in the *Example 1 – Checking whether a non-negative number is prime* section). This is one reason for the recent push in concurrent programming.

Another reason for the increasing popularity of concurrency is the growing field of graphical, multimedia, and web-based application development, in which the application of concurrency is widely used to solve complex and meaningful problems. For example, concurrency is a major player in web development: each new request made by a user typically comes in as its own process (this is called multiprocessing; see `Chapter 13`, *Working with Processes in Python*) or asynchronously coordinated with other requests (this is called asynchronous programming; see `Chapter 16`, *Introduction to Asynchronous Programming*); if any of those requests need to access a shared resource (a database, for example) where data can be changed, concurrency should be taken into consideration.

The present

Considering the present day, where an explosive growth the internet and data sharing happens every second, concurrency is more important than ever. The current use of concurrent programming emphasizes correctness, performance, and robustness.

Some concurrent systems, such as operating systems or database management systems, are generally designed to operate indefinitely, including automatic recovery from failure, and not terminate unexpectedly. As mentioned previously, concurrent systems use shared resources, and thus they require some form of **semaphore** in their implementation, to control and coordinate access to those resources.

Concurrent programming is quite ubiquitous in the field of software development. Following are a few examples where concurrency is present:

- Concurrency plays an important role in most common programming languages: C++, C#, Erlang, Go, Java, Julia, JavaScript, Perl, Python, Ruby, Scala, and so on.
- Again, since almost every computer today has more than one core in its CPU, desktop applications need to be able to take advantage of that computing power, in order to provide truly well-designed software.

Multicore processors used in MacBook Pro computers

- The iPhone 4S, which was released in 2011, has a dual-core CPU, so mobile development also has to stay connected to concurrent applications.
- As for video games, two of the biggest players on the current market are the Xbox 360, which is a multi-CPU system, and Sony's PS3, which is essentially a multicore system.
- Even the current iteration of the $35 Raspberry Pi is built around a quad-core system.
- It is estimated that on average, Google processes over 40,000 search queries every second, which equates to over 3.5 billion searches per day, and 1.2 trillion searches per year, worldwide. Apart from having massive machines with incredible processing power, concurrency is the best way to handle that amount of data requests.

A large percentage of today's data and applications are stored in the cloud. Since computing instances on the cloud are relatively small in size, almost every web application is therefore forced to be concurrent, processing different small jobs simultaneously. As it gains more customers and has to process more requests, a well-designed web application can simply utilize more servers while keeping the same logic; this corresponds to the property of robustness that we mentioned earlier.

Even in the increasingly popular fields of artificial intelligence and data science, major advances have been made, in part due to the availability of high-end graphics cards (GPUs), which are used as parallel computing engines. In every notable competition on the biggest data science website (https://www.kaggle.com/), almost all prize-winning solutions feature some form of GPU usage during the training process. With the sheer amount of data that big data models have to comb through, concurrency provides an effective solution. Some AI algorithms are even designed to break their input data down into smaller portions and process them independently, which is a perfect opportunity to apply concurrency in order to achieve better model-training time.

The future

In this day and age, computer/internet users expect instant output, no matter what applications they are using, and developers often find themselves struggling with the problem of providing better speed for their applications. In terms of usage, concurrency will continue to be one of the main players in the field of programming, providing unique and innovative solutions to those problems. As mentioned earlier, whether it be video game design, mobile apps, desktop software, or web development, concurrency is, and will be, omnipresent in the near future.

Given the need for concurrency support in applications, some might argue that concurrent programming will also become more standard in academia. Even though specific topics in concurrency and parallelism are being covered in computer science courses, in-depth, complex subjects on concurrent programming (both theoretical and applied subjects) will be implemented in undergraduate and graduate courses, to better prepare students for the industry, where concurrency is being used every day. Computer science courses on building concurrent systems, studying data flows, and analyzing concurrent and parallel structures will only be the beginning.

Others might have a more skeptical view of the future of concurrent programming. Some say that concurrency is really about dependency analysis: a sub-field of compiler theory that analyzes execution-order constraints between statements/instructions, and determines whether it is safe for a program to **reorder** or **parallelize** its statements. Furthermore, since only a very small number of programmers truly understand concurrency and all of its intricacies, there will be a push for compilers, along with support from the operating system, to take on the responsibility of actually implementing concurrency into the programs they compile on their own.

Specifically, in the future programmers will not have to concern themselves with the concepts and problems of concurrent programming, nor should they. An algorithm implemented on the compiler-level should look at the program being compiled, analyze the statements and instructions, produce a dependency graph to determine the optimal order of execution for those statements and instructions, and apply concurrency/parallelism where it is appropriate and efficient. In short, the combination of the low number of programmers understanding and being able to effectively work with concurrent systems and the possibility of automating the design of concurrency will lead to a decrease in interest in concurrent programming.

In the end, only time will tell what the future holds for concurrent programming. We programmers can only look at how concurrency is currently being used in the real world, and determine whether it is worth learning or not: which, as we have seen in this case, it is. Furthermore, even though there are strong connections between designing concurrent programs and dependency analysis, I personally see concurrent programming as a more intricate and involved process, which might be very difficult to achieve through automation.

Concurrent programming is indeed extremely complicated and very hard to get right, but that also means the knowledge gained through the process will be beneficial and useful to any programmer, and I see that as a good enough reason to learn about concurrency. The ability to analyze the problems of program speedup, restructure your programs into different independent tasks, and coordinate those tasks to use the same resources, are the main skills that programmers build while working with concurrency, and knowledge of these topics will help them with other programming problems, as well.

A brief overview of mastering concurrency in Python

Python is one of the most popular programming languages out there, and for good reason. The language comes with numerous libraries and frameworks that facilitate high-performance computing, whether it be software development, web development, data analysis, or machine learning. Yet, there have been discussions among developers criticizing Python, which often revolve around the **Global Interpreter Lock (GIL)** and the difficulty of implementing concurrent and parallel programs that it leads to.

While concurrency and parallelism do behave differently in Python than in other common programming languages, it is still possible for programmers to implement Python programs that run concurrently or in parallel, and achieve significant speedup for their programs.

This book will serve as a comprehensive introduction to various advanced concepts in concurrent engineering and programming in Python and will also provide a detailed overview of how concurrency and parallelism are being used in real-world applications. It is a perfect blend of theoretical analyses and practical examples, which will give you a full understanding of the theories and techniques regarding concurrent programming in Python.

This book will be divided into six main sections. It will start with the idea behind concurrency and concurrent programming—the history, how it is being used in the industry today, and finally, a mathematical analysis of the speedup that concurrency can potentially provide. Additionally, the last section in this chapter (which is our next section) will cover instructions for how to follow the coding examples in this book, including setting up a Python environment on your own computer, downloading/cloning the code included in this book from GitHub, and running each example from your computer.

The next three sections will cover three of the main implementation approaches in concurrent programming: threads, processes, and asynchronous I/O, respectively. These sections will include theoretical concepts and principles for each of these approaches, the syntax and various functionalities that the Python language provides to support them, discussions of best practices for their advanced usage, and hands-on projects that directly apply these concepts to solve real-world problems.

Section five will introduce readers to some of the most common problems that engineers and programmers face in concurrent programming: deadlock, starvation, and race conditions. Readers will learn about the theoretical foundations and causes for each problem, analyze and replicate each of them in Python, and finally implement potential solutions. The last chapter in this section will discuss the aforementioned GIL, which is specific to the Python language. It will cover the GIL's integral role in the Python ecosystem, some challenges that the GIL poses for concurrent programming, and how to implement effective workarounds.

Throughout this book, you will be building essential skills for working with concurrent programs, just through following the discussions, the example code, and the hands-on projects. You will understand the fundamentals of the most important concepts in concurrent programming, how to implement them in Python programs, and how to apply that knowledge to advanced applications. You will have a unique combination of extensive theoretical knowledge regarding concurrency, and practical know-how of the various applications of concurrency in the Python language.

Why Python?

As mentioned previously, one of the difficulties that developers face while working with concurrency in the Python programming language (specifically, CPython—a reference implementation of Python written in C) is its GIL. The GIL is a mutex that protects access to Python objects, preventing multiple threads from executing Python byte codes at once. This lock is necessary mainly because CPython's memory management is not thread-safe. CPython uses reference counting to implement its memory management. This results in the fact that multiple threads can access and execute Python code simultaneously; this situation is undesirable, as it can cause an incorrect handling of data, and we say that this type of memory management is not thread-safe. To address this problem, the GIL is, as the name suggests, a lock that allows only one thread to access Python code and objects. However, this also means that, to implement multithreading programs in CPython, developers need to be aware of the GIL and work around it. That is why many have problems with implementing concurrent systems in Python.

So, why use Python for concurrency at all? Even though the GIL prevents multithreaded CPython programs from taking full advantage of multiprocessor systems in certain situations, most blocking or long-running operations, such as I/O, image processing, and NumPy number crunching, happen outside the GIL. Therefore, the GIL only becomes a potential bottleneck for multithreaded programs that spend significant time inside the GIL. As you will see in future chapters, multithreading is only a form of concurrent programming, and, while the GIL poses some challenges for multithreaded CPython programs that allow more than one thread to access shared resources, other forms of concurrent programming do not have this problem. For example, multiprocessing applications that do not share any common resources among processes, such as I/O, image processing, or NumPy number crunching, can work seamlessly with the GIL. We will discuss the GIL and its place in the Python ecosystem in greater depth in `Chapter 22`, *The Global Interpret Lock*.

Aside from that, Python has been gaining increasing popularity from the programming community. Due to its user-friendly syntax and overall readability, more and more people have found it relatively straightforward to use Python in their development, whether it is beginners learning a new programming language, intermediate users looking for the advanced functionalities of Python, or experienced programmers using Python to solve complex problems. It is estimated that the development of Python code can be up to 10 times faster than C/C++ code.

The large number of developers using Python has resulted in a strong, ever-growing support community. Libraries and packages in Python are being developed and released every day, tackling different problems and technologies. Currently, the Python language supports an incredibly wide range of programming—namely, software development, desktop GUIs, video game design, web and internet development, and scientific and numeric computing. In recent years, Python has also been growing as one of the top tools in data science, big data, and machine learning, competing with the long-time player in the field, R.

The sheer number of development tools available in Python has encouraged more developers to start programming with Python, making Python even more popular and easy to use; I call this *the vicious circle of Python*. David Robinson, chief data scientist at DataCamp, wrote a blog (`https://stackoverflow.blog/2017/09/06/incredible-growth-python/`) about the incredible growth of Python, and called it the most popular programming language.

However, Python is slow, or at least slower than other popular programming languages. This is due to the fact that Python is a dynamically typed, interpreted language, where values are stored not in dense buffers, but in scattered objects. This is a direct result of Python's readability and user-friendliness. Luckily, there are various options regarding how to make your Python program run faster, and concurrency is one of the most complex of them; that is what we are going to master throughout this book.

Setting up your Python environment

Before we move any further, let's go through a number of specifications regarding how to set up the necessary tools that you will be using throughout this book. In particular, we will discuss the process of obtaining a Python distribution for your system and an appropriate development environment, as well as how to download the code used in the examples included in the chapters of this book.

General setup

Let's look at the process of obtaining a Python distribution for your system and an appropriate development environment:

- Any developer can obtain their own Python distribution from `https://www.python.org/downloads/`.
- Even though both Python 2 and Python 3 are being supported and maintained, throughout this book we will be using Python 3.
- The choice of an **integrated development environment** (IDE) is flexible for this book. Although it is technically possible to develop Python applications using a minimal text editor, such as Notepad or TextEdit, it is usually much easier to read and write code with IDEs designed specifically for Python. These include IDLE (`https://docs.python.org/3/library/idle.html`), PyCharm (`https://www.jetbrains.com/pycharm/`), Sublime Text (`https://www.sublimetext.com/`), and Atom (`https://atom.io/`).

Summary

You have now been introduced to the concept of concurrent and parallel programming. It is about designing and structuring programming commands and instructions, so that different sections of the program can be executed in an efficient order, while sharing the same resources. Since time is saved when some commands and instructions are executed at the same time, concurrent programming provides significant improvements in program execution time, as compared to traditional sequential programming.

However, various factors need to be taken into consideration while designing a concurrent program. While there are specific tasks that can easily be broken down into independent sections that can be executed in parallel (embarrassingly parallel tasks), others require different forms of coordination between the program commands, so that shared resources are used correctly and efficiently. There are also inherently sequential tasks, in which no concurrency and parallelism can be applied to achieve program speedup. You should know the fundamental differences between these tasks, so that you can design your concurrent programs appropriately.

Recently, there was a paradigm shift that facilitated the implementation of concurrency into most aspects of the programming world. Now, concurrency can be found almost everywhere: desktop and mobile applications, video games, web and internet development, AI, and so on. Concurrency is still growing, and it is expected to keep growing in the future. It is therefore crucial for any experienced programmer to understand concurrency and its relevant concepts, and to know how to integrate those concepts into their applications.

Python, on the other hand, is one of the most (if not the most) popular programming languages. It provides powerful options in most sub-fields of programming. The combination of concurrency and Python is therefore one of the topics most worth learning and mastering in programming.

In the next chapter, on Amdahl's Law, we will discuss how significant the improvements in speedup that concurrency provides for our programs are. We will analyze the formula for Amdahl's Law, discussing its implications and considering Python examples.

Questions

- What is the idea behind concurrency, and why is it useful?
- What are the differences between concurrent programming and sequential programming?
- What are the differences between concurrent programming and parallel programming?
- Can every program be made concurrent or parallel?
- What are embarrassingly parallel tasks?
- What are inherently sequential tasks?
- What does I/O bound mean?
- How is concurrent processing currently being used in the real world?

Further reading

For more information you can refer to the following links:

- *Python Parallel Programming Cookbook*, by Giancarlo Zaccone, Packt Publishing Ltd, 2015
- *Learning Concurrency in Python: Build highly efficient, robust, and concurrent applications* (2017), by Forbes, Elliot
- "The historical roots of concurrent engineering fundamentals." *IEEE Transactions on Engineering Management* 44.1 (1997): 67-78, by Robert P. Smith
- *Programming language pragmatics*, Morgan Kaufmann, 2000, by Michael Lee Scott

9
Amdahl's Law

Often used in discussions revolving around concurrent programs, Amdahl's Law explains the theoretical speedup of the execution of a program that can be expected when using concurrency. In this chapter, we will discuss the concept of Amdahl's Law, and we will analyze its formula, which estimates the potential speedup of a program and replicates it in Python code. This chapter will also briefly cover the relationship between Amdahl's Law and the law of diminishing returns.

The following topics will be covered in this chapter:

- Amdahl's Law
- Amdahl's Law: its formula and interpretation
- The relationship between Amdahl's Law and the law of diminishing returns
- Simulation in Python, and the practical applications of Amdahl's Law

Technical requirements

The following is a list of prerequisites for this chapter:

- Ensure that you have Python 3 installed on your computer
- Download the GitHub repository at `https://github.com/PacktPublishing/MasteringPython`
- During this chapter, we will be working with the subfolder named `Chapter09`
- Check out the following video to see the Code in Action: `http://bit.ly/2DWaOeQ`

Amdahl's Law

How do you find a balance between parallelizing a sequential program (by increasing the number of processors) and optimizing the execution speed of the sequential program itself? For example, which is the better option: Having four processors running a given program for 40% of its execution, or using only two processors executing the same program, but for twice as long? This type of trade-off, which is commonly found in concurrent programming, can be strategically analyzed and answered by applying Amdahl's Law.

Additionally, while concurrency and parallelism can be a powerful tool that provides significant improvements in program execution time, they are not a silver bullet that can speed up any non-sequential architecture infinitely and unconditionally. It is therefore important for developers and programmers to know and understand the limits of the speed improvements that concurrency and parallelism offer to their programs, and Amdahl's Law addresses those concerns.

Terminology

Amdahl's Law provides a mathematical formula that calculates the potential improvement in speed of a concurrent program by increasing its resources (specifically, the number of available processors). Before we can get into the theory behind Amdahl's Law, first, we must clarify some terminology, as follows:

- Amdahl's Law solely discusses the potential speedup in latency resulting from executing a task in **parallel**. While concurrency is not directly discussed here, the results from Amdahl's Law concerning parallelism will nonetheless give us an estimation regarding concurrent programs.
- The **speed** of a program denotes the time it takes for the program to execute in full. This can be measured in any increment of time.
- **Speedup** is the time that measures the benefit of executing a computation in parallel. It is defined as the time it takes a program to execute in serial (with one processor), divided by the time it takes to execute in parallel (with multiple processors). The formula for speedup is as follows:

$$S = \frac{T(1)}{T(j)}$$

In the preceding formula, $T(j)$ is the time it takes to execute the program when using j processors.

Formula and interpretation

Before we get into the formula for Amdahl's Law and its implications, let's explore the concept of speedup, through some brief analysis. Let's assume that there are N workers working on a given job that is fully parallelizable—that is, the job can be perfectly divided into N equal sections. This means that N workers working together to complete the job will only take $1/N$ of the time it takes one worker to complete the same job.

However, most computer programs are not 100% parallelizable: some parts of a program might be inherently sequential, while others are broken up into parallel tasks.

The formula for Amdahl's Law

Now, let B denote the fraction of the program that is strictly serial, and consider the following:

- $B * T(1)$ is the time it takes to execute the parts of the program that are inherently sequential.
- $T(1) - B * T(1) = (1 - B) * T(1)$ is the time it takes to execute the parts of the program that are parallelizable, with one processor:
    - Then, $(1 - B) * T(1) / N$ is the time it takes to execute these parts with N processors
- So, $B * T(1) + (1 - B) * T(1) / N$ is the total time it takes to execute the whole program with N processors.

Coming back to the formula for the speedup quantity, we have the following:

$$S = \frac{T(1)}{T(j)} = \frac{T(1)}{B.T(1) + \frac{(1-B).T(1)}{j}} = \frac{1}{B + \frac{1-B}{j}}$$

This formula is actually a form of Amdahl's Law, used to estimate the speedup in a parallel program.

A quick example

Let's assume that we have a computer program, and the following applies to it:

- 40% of it is subject to parallelism, so B = 1 - 40% = 0.6
- Its parallelizable parts will be processed by four processors, so j = 4

Amdahl's Law states that the overall speedup of applying the improvement will be as follows:

$$S = \frac{1}{B + \frac{1-B}{j}} = \frac{1}{0.6 + \frac{1-0.6}{4}} = \frac{10}{7} \approx 1.43$$

Implications

The following is a quote from Gene Amdahl, in 1967:

> *"For over a decade prophets have voiced the contention that the organization of a single computer has reached its limits and that truly significantly advances can be made only by interconnection of a multiplicity of computers in such a manner as to permit cooperative solution... The nature of this overhead (in parallelism) appears to be sequential so that it is unlikely to be amenable to parallel processing techniques. Overhead alone would then place an upper limit on throughput of five to seven times the sequential processing rate, even if the housekeeping were done in a separate processor... At any point in time it is difficult to foresee how the previous bottlenecks in a sequential computer will be effectively overcome."*

Through the quote, Amdahl indicated that whatever concurrent and parallel techniques are implemented in a program, the sequential nature of the overhead portion required in the program always sets an upper boundary on how much speedup the program will gain. This is one of the implications that Amdahl's Law further suggests. Consider the following example:

$$\frac{1-B}{j} > \frac{1-B}{j+1} \implies \frac{1}{B + \frac{1-B}{j}} < \frac{1}{B + \frac{1-B}{j+1}} \implies S_j < S_{j+1}$$

S_n denotes the speedup gained from n processors

This shows that, as the number of resources (specifically, the number of available processors) increases, the speedup of the execution of the whole task also increases. However, this does not mean that we should always implement concurrency and parallelism with as many system processors as possible, to achieve the highest performance. In fact, from the formula, we can also gather that the speedup achieved from incrementing the number of processors decreases. In other words, as we add more processors for our concurrent program, we will obtain less and less improvement in execution time.

Furthermore, as mentioned previously, another implication that Amdahl's Law suggests concerns the upper limit of the execution time improvement:

$$\begin{cases} S \le \frac{1}{B} \\ \lim_{j \to \infty} S = \frac{1}{B} \end{cases}$$

$\frac{1}{B}$ is the cap of how much improvement concurrency and parallelism can offer your program. This is to say that, no matter how many available resources your system has, it is impossible to obtain a speedup larger than $\frac{1}{B}$ through concurrency, and this limit is dictated by the sequential overhead portion of the program (B is the fraction of the program that is strictly serial).

Amdahl's Law's relationship to the law of diminishing returns

Amdahl's Law is often conflated with the law of diminishing returns, which is a rather popular concept in economics. However, the law of diminishing returns is only a special case of applying Amdahl's Law, depending on the order of improvement. If the order of separate tasks in the program is chosen to be improved in an **optimal** way, a monotonically decreasing improvement in execution time will be observed, demonstrating diminishing returns. An optimal method indicates first applying those improvements that will result in the greatest speedups, and leaving those improvements yielding smaller speedups for later.

Now, if we were to reverse this sequence for choosing resources, in which we improve less optimal components of our program before more optimal components, the speedup achieved through the improvement would increase throughout the process. Furthermore, it is actually more beneficial for us to implement system improvements in this **reverse-optimal** order in reality, as the more optimal components are usually more complex, and take more time to improve.

Another similarity between Amdahl's Law and the law of diminishing returns concerns the improvement in speedup obtained through adding more processors to a system. Specifically, as a new processor is added to the system to process a fixed-size task, it will offer less usable computation power than the previous processor. As we discussed in the last section, the improvement in this situation strictly decreases as the number of processors increases, and the total throughout approaches the upper boundary of *1/B*.

It is important to note that this analysis does not take into account other potential bottlenecks, such as memory bandwidth and I/O bandwidth. In fact, if these resources do not scale with the number of processors, then simply adding processors results in even lower returns.

How to simulate in Python

In this section, we will look at the results of Amdahl's Law through a Python program. Still considering the task of determining whether an integer is a prime number, as discussed in *Chapter 8, Advanced Introduction to Concurrent and Parallel Programming,* we will see what actual speedup is achieved through concurrency. If you already have the code for the book downloaded from the GitHub page, we are looking at the Chapter09/example1.py file.

As a refresher, the function that checks for prime numbers is as follows:

```
# Chapter09/example1.py

from math import sqrt

def is_prime(x):
    if x < 2:
        return False

    if x == 2:
        return x

    if x % 2 == 0:
        return False

    limit = int(sqrt(x)) + 1
    for i in range(3, limit, 2):
        if x % i == 0:
            return False

    return x
```

The next part of the code is a function that takes in an integer that indicates the number of processors (workers) that we will be utilizing to concurrently solve the problem (in this case, it is used to determine which numbers in a list are prime numbers):

```
# Chapter09/example1.py

import concurrent.futures

from timeit import default_timer as timer

def concurrent_solve(n_workers):
    print('Number of workers: %i.' % n_workers)

    start = timer()
    result = []

    with concurrent.futures.ProcessPoolExecutor(
      max_workers=n_workers) as executor:

        futures = [executor.submit(is_prime, i) for i in input]
        completed_futures = concurrent.futures.as_completed(futures)

        sub_start = timer()

        for i, future in enumerate(completed_futures):
            if future.result():
                result.append(future.result())

        sub_duration = timer() - sub_start

    duration = timer() - start
    print('Sub took: %.4f seconds.' % sub_duration)
    print('Took: %.4f seconds.' % duration)
```

Notice that the variables `sub_start` and `sub_duration` measure the portion of the task that is being solved concurrently, which, in our earlier analysis, is denoted as *1 - B*. As for the input, we will be looking at numbers between 10^{13} and $10^{13} + 1000$:

```
input = [i for i in range(10 ** 13, 10 ** 13 + 1000)]
```

Lastly, we will be looping from one to the maximum number of processors available in our system, and we will pass that number to the preceding `concurrent_solve()` function. As a quick tip, to obtain the number of available processors from your computer, call `multiprocessing.cpu_count()`, as follows:

```
for n_workers in range(1, multiprocessing.cpu_count() + 1):
    concurrent_solve(n_workers)
    print('_' * 20)
```

You can run the whole program by entering the command `python example1.py`. Since my laptop has four cores, the following is my output after running the program:

```
Number of workers: 1.
Sub took: 7.5721 seconds.
Took: 7.6659 seconds.

_____

Number of workers: 2.
Sub took: 4.0410 seconds.
Took: 4.1153 seconds.

_____

Number of workers: 3.
Sub took: 3.8949 seconds.
Took: 4.0063 seconds.

_____

Number of workers: 4.
Sub took: 3.9285 seconds.
Took: 4.0545 seconds.

_____
```

A few things to note are as follows:

- First, in each iteration, the subsection of the task was almost as long as the whole program. In other words, the concurrent computation formed the majority of the program during each iteration. This is quite understandable, since there is hardly any other heavy computation in the program, aside from prime checking.
- Secondly, and arguably more interestingly, we can see that, while considerable improvements were gained after increasing the number of processors from 1 to 2 (`7.6659 seconds` to `4.1153 seconds`), hardly any speedup was achieved during the third iteration. It took longer during the forth iteration than the third, but this was most likely overhead processing. This is consistent with our earlier discussions regarding the similarity between Amdahl's Law and the law of diminishing returns, when considering the number of processors.

- We can also refer to a speedup curve to visualize this phenomenon. A speedup curve is simply a graph with the *x* axis showing the number of processors, compared to the *y* axis showing the speedup achieved. In a perfect scenario, where $S = j$ (that is, the speedup achieved is equal to the number of processors used), the speedup curve would be a straight, 45-degree line. Amdahl's Law shows that the speedup curve produced by any program will remain below that line, and will begin to flatten out as efficiency reduced. In the preceding program, this was during the transition from two to three processors:

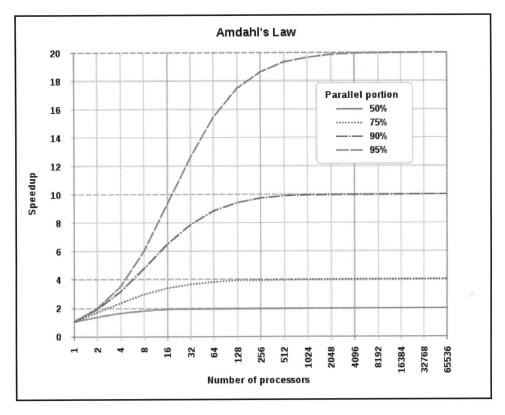

Speedup curves with different parallel portions

Practical applications of Amdahl's Law

As we have discussed, by analyzing the sequential and parallelizable portion of a given program or system with Amdahl's Law, we can determine, or at least estimate, the upper limit of any potential improvements in speed resulting from parallel computing. Upon obtaining this estimation, we can then make an informed decision on whether an improved execution time is worth an increase in processing power.

From our examples, we can see that Amdahl's Law is applied when you have a concurrent program that is a mixture of both sequentially and executed-in-parallels instructions. By performing analysis using Amdahl's Law, we can determine the speedup through each incrementation of the number of cores available to perform the execution, as well as how close that incrementation is to helping the program achieve the best possible speedup from parallelization.

Now, let's come back to the initial problem that we raised at the beginning of the chapter: the trade-off between an increase in the number of processors versus an increase in how long parallelism can be applied. Let's suppose that you are in charge of developing a concurrent program that currently has 40 percent of its instructions parallelizable. This means that multiple processors can be running simultaneously for 40 percent of the program execution. Now you have been tasked with increasing the speed of this program by implementing either of the following two choices:

- Having four processors implemented to execute the program instructions
- Having two processors implemented, in addition to increasing the parallelizable portion of the program to 80 percent

How can we analytically compare these two choices, in order to determine the one that will produce the best speed for our program? Luckily, Amdahl's Law can assist us during this process:

- For the first option, the speedup that can be obtained is as follows:

$$S = \frac{1}{B + \frac{1-B}{j}} = \frac{1}{1 - 0.4 + \frac{0.4}{4}} = \frac{10}{7} \approx 1.43$$

- For the second option, the speedup is as follows:

$$S = \frac{1}{B + \frac{1-B}{j}} = \frac{1}{1 - 0.8 + \frac{0.8}{2}} = \frac{10}{6} \approx 1.67$$

As you can see, the second option (which has fewer processors than the first) is actually the better choice to speed up our specific program. This is another example of Amdahl's Law, illustrating that sometimes simply increasing the number of available processors is, in fact, undesirable in terms of improving the speed of a program. Similar trade-offs, with potentially different specifications, can also be analyzed this way.

As a final note, it is important for us to know that, while Amdahl's Law offers an estimation of potential speedup in an unambiguous way, the law itself makes a number of underlying assumptions and does not take into account some potentially important factors, such as the overhead of parallelism or the speed of memory. For this reason, the formula of Amdahl's Law simplifies various considerations that might be common in practice.

So, how should programmers of concurrent programs think about and use Amdahl's Law? We should keep in mind that the results of Amdahl's Law are simply estimates that can provide us with an idea about where, and by how much, we can further optimize a concurrent system, specifically by increasing the number of available processors. In the end, only actual measurements can precisely answer our questions about how much speedup our concurrent programs will achieve in practice. With that said, Amdahl's Law can still help us to effectively identify good theoretical strategies for improving computing speed using concurrency and parallelism.

Summary

Amdahl's Law offers us a method to estimate the potential speedup in execution time of a task that we can expect from a system when its resources are improved. It illustrates that, as the resources of the system are improved, so is the execution time. However, the differential speedup when incrementing the resources strictly decreases, and the throughput speedup is limited by the sequential overhead of its program.

You also saw that in specific situations (namely, when only the number of processors increases), Amdahl's Law resembles the law of diminishing returns. Specifically, as the number of processors increases, the efficiency gained through the improvement decreases, and the speedup curve flattens out.

Lastly, this chapter showed that improvement through concurrency and parallelism is not always desirable, and detailed specifications are needed for an effective and efficient concurrent program.

With more knowledge of the extent to which concurrency can help to speed up our programs, we will now start to discuss the specific tools that Python provides to implement concurrency. Specifically, we will consider one of the main players in concurrent programming, threads, in the next chapter, including their application in Python programming.

Questions

- What is Amdahl's Law? What problem does Amdahl's Law try to solve?
- Explain the formula of Amdahl's Law, along with its components.
- According to Amdahl's Law, will speedup increase indefinitely as the resources of the system improve?
- What is the relationship between Amdahl's Law and the law of diminishing returns?

Further reading

For more information you can refer to the following links:

- *Amdahl's Law* (`https://home.wlu.edu/~whaleyt/classes/parallel/topics/amdahl.html`), by Aaron Michalove
- *Uses and abuses of Amdahl's Law*, Journal of Computing Sciences in Colleges 17.2 (2001): 288-293, S. Krishnaprasad
- *Learning Concurrency in Python: Build highly efficient, robust, and concurrent applications* (2017), Elliot Forbes

Working with Threads in Python

10

In *Chapter 08*, *Advanced Introduction to Concurrent and Parallel Programming*, you saw an example of threads being used in concurrent and parallel programming. In this chapter, you will be introduced to the formal definition of a thread, as well as the `threading` module in Python. We will cover a number of ways to work with threads in a Python program, including activities such as creating new threads, synchronizing threads, and working with multithreaded priority queues, via specific examples. We will also discuss the concept of a lock in thread synchronization, and we will implement a lock-based multithreaded application, in order to better understand the benefits of thread synchronization.

The following topics will be covered in this chapter:

- The concept of a thread in the context of concurrent programming in computer science
- The basic API of the `threading` module in Python
- How to create a new thread via the `threading` module
- The concept of a lock and how to use different locking mechanisms to synchronize threads
- The concept of a queue in the context of concurrent programming, and how to use the `Queue` module to work with queue objects in Python

Technical requirements

The following is a list of prerequisites for this chapter:

- Ensure that you have Python 3 installed on your computer
- Download the GitHub repository
  at `https://github.com/PacktPublishing/AdvancedPythonProgramming`
- During this chapter, we will be working with the subfolder titled `Chapter10`
- Check out the following video to see the Code in Action: `http://bit.ly/2SeD2oz`

The concept of a thread

In the field of computer science, a **thread of execution** is the smallest unit of programming commands (code) that a scheduler (usually as part of an operating system) can process and manage. Depending on the operating system, the implementation of threads and processes (which we will cover in future chapters) varies, but a thread is typically an element (a component) of a process.

Threads versus processes

More than one thread can be implemented within the same process, most often executing concurrently and accessing/sharing the same resources, such as memory; separate processes do not do this. Threads in the same process share the latter's instructions (its code) and context (the values that its variables reference at any given moment).

The key difference between the two concepts is that a thread is typically a component of a process. Therefore, one process can include multiple threads, which can be executing simultaneously. Threads also usually allow for shared resources, such as memory and data, while it is fairly rare for processes to do so. In short, a thread is an independent component of computation that is similar to a process, but the threads within a process can share the address space, and hence the data, of that process:

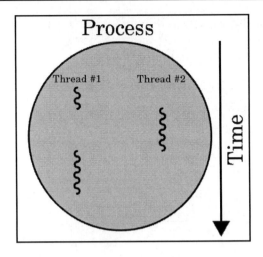

A process with two threads of execution running on one processor

Threads were reportedly first used for a variable number of tasks in OS/360 multiprogramming, which is a discontinued batch processing system that was developed by IBM in 1967. At the time, threads were called tasks by the developers, while the term thread became popular later on and has been attributed to Victor A. Vyssotsky, a mathematician and computer scientist who was the founding director of Digital's Cambridge Research Lab.

Multithreading

In computer science, single-threading is similar to traditional sequential processing, executing a single command at any given time. On the other hand, **multithreading** implements more than one thread to exist and execute in a single process, simultaneously. By allowing multiple threads to access shared resources/contexts and be executed independently, this programming technique can help applications to gain speed in the execution of independent tasks.

Multithreading can primarily be achieved in two ways. In single-processor systems, multithreading is typically implemented via **time slicing**, a technique that allows the CPU to switch between different software running on different threads. In time slicing, the CPU switches its execution so quickly and so often that users usually perceive that the software is running in parallel (for example, when you open two different software at the same time on a single-processor computer):

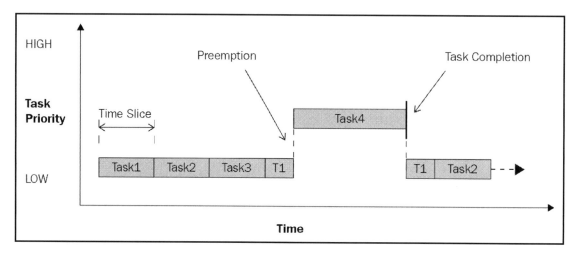

An example of a time slicing technique called round-robin scheduling

As opposed to single-processor systems, systems with multiple processors or cores can easily implement multithreading, by executing each thread in a separate process or core, simultaneously. Additionally, time slicing is an option, as these multiprocess or multicore systems can have only one processor/core to switch between tasks—although this is generally not a good practice.

Multithreaded applications have a number of advantages, as compared to traditional sequential applications; some of them are listed as follows:

- **Faster execution time**: One of the main advantages of concurrency through multithreading is the speedup that is achieved. Separate threads in the same program can be executed concurrently or in parallel, if they are sufficiently independent of one another.

- **Responsiveness**: A single-threaded program can only process one piece of input at a time; therefore, if the main execution thread blocks on a long-running task (that is, a piece of input that requires heavy computation and processing), the whole program will not be able to continue with other input, and hence, it will appear to be frozen. By using separate threads to perform computation and remain running to take in different user input simultaneously, a multithreaded program can provide better responsiveness.
- **Efficiency in resource consumption**: As we mentioned previously, multiple threads within the same process can share and access the same resources. Consequently, multithreaded programs can serve and process many client requests for data concurrently, using significantly fewer resources than would be needed when using single-threaded or multiprocess programs. This also leads to quicker communication between threads.

That being said, multithreaded programs also have their disadvantages, as follows:

- **Crashes**: Even though a process can contain multiple threads, a single illegal operation within one thread can negatively affect the processing of all of the other threads in the process, and can crash the entire program as a result.
- **Synchronization**: Even though sharing the same resources can be an advantage over traditional sequential programming or multiprocessing programs, careful consideration is also needed for the shared resources. Usually, threads must be coordinated in a deliberate and systematic manner, so that shared data is computed and manipulated correctly. Unintuitive problems that can be caused by careless thread coordination include deadlocks, livelocks, and race conditions, all of which will be discussed in future chapters.

An example in Python

To illustrate the concept of running multiple threads in the same process, let's look at a quick example in Python. If you have already downloaded the code for this book from the GitHub page, go ahead and navigate to the Chapter10 folder. Let's take a look at the Chapter10/my_thread.py file, as follows:

```
# Chapter10/my_thread.py

import threading
import time


class MyThread(threading.Thread):
    def __init__(self, name, delay):
```

```
            threading.Thread.__init__(self)
            self.name = name
            self.delay = delay

        def run(self):
            print('Starting thread %s.' % self.name)
            thread_count_down(self.name, self.delay)
            print('Finished thread %s.' % self.name)

    def thread_count_down(name, delay):
        counter = 5

        while counter:
            time.sleep(delay)
            print('Thread %s counting down: %i...' % (name, counter))
            counter -= 1
```

In this file, we are using the threading module from Python as the foundation of the MyThread class. Each object of this class has a name and delay parameter. The function run(), which is called as soon as a new thread is initialized and started, prints out a starting message, and, in turn, calls the thread_count_down() function. This function counts down from the number 5 to the number 0, while sleeping between iterations for a number of seconds, specified by the delay parameter.

The point of this example is to show the concurrent nature of running more than one thread in the same program (or process) by starting more than one object of the MyThread class at the same time. We know that, as soon as each thread is started, a time-based countdown for that thread will also start. In a traditional sequential program, separate countdowns will be executed separately, in order (that is, a new countdown will not start until the current one finishes). As you will see, the separate countdowns for separate threads are executed concurrently.

Let's look at the Chapter10/example1.py file, as follows:

```
# Chapter10/example1.py

from my_thread import MyThread


thread1 = MyThread('A', 0.5)
thread2 = MyThread('B', 0.5)

thread1.start()
thread2.start()

thread1.join()
```

```
thread2.join()
```

```
print('Finished.')
```

Here, we are initializing and starting two threads together, each of which has 0.5 seconds as its delay parameter. Run the script using your Python interpreter. You should get the following output:

```
> python example1.py
Starting thread A.
Starting thread B.
Thread A counting down: 5...
Thread B counting down: 5...
Thread B counting down: 4...
Thread A counting down: 4...
Thread B counting down: 3...
Thread A counting down: 3...
Thread B counting down: 2...
Thread A counting down: 2...
Thread B counting down: 1...
Thread A counting down: 1...
Finished thread B.
Finished thread A.
Finished.
```

Just as we expected, the output tells us that the two countdowns for the threads were executed concurrently; instead of finishing the first thread's countdown and then starting the second thread's countdown, the program ran the two countdowns at almost the same time. Without including some overhead and miscellaneous declarations, this threading technique allows almost double improvement in speed for the preceding program.

There is one additional thing that should be taken note of in the preceding output. After the first countdown for number 5, we can see that the countdown of thread B actually got ahead of thread A in execution, even though we know that thread A was initialized and started before thread B. This change actually allowed thread B to finish before thread A. This phenomenon is a direct result of concurrency via multithreading; since the two threads were initialized and started almost simultaneously, it was quite likely for one thread to get ahead of the other in execution.

If you were to execute this script many times, it would be quite likely for you to get varying output, in terms of the order of execution and the completion of the countdowns. The following are two pieces of output that I obtained by executing the script again and again. The first output shows a uniform and unchanging order of execution and completion, in which the two countdowns were executed hand in hand. The second shows a case in which thread A was executed significantly faster than thread B; it even finished before thread B counted to number 1. This variation of output further illustrates the fact that the threads were treated and executed by Python equally.

The following code shows one possible output of the program:

```
> python example1.py
Starting thread A.
Starting thread B.
Thread A counting down: 5...
Thread B counting down: 5...
Thread A counting down: 4...
Thread B counting down: 4...
Thread A counting down: 3...
Thread B counting down: 3...
Thread A counting down: 2...
Thread B counting down: 2...
Thread A counting down: 1...
Thread B counting down: 1...
Finished thread A.
Finished thread B.
Finished.
```

The following is another possible output:

```
> python example1.py
Starting thread A.
Starting thread B.
Thread A counting down: 5...
Thread B counting down: 5...
Thread A counting down: 4...
Thread B counting down: 4...
Thread A counting down: 3...
Thread B counting down: 3...
Thread A counting down: 2...
Thread B counting down: 2...
Thread A counting down: 1...
Finished thread A.
Thread B counting down: 1...
Finished thread B.
Finished.
```

An overview of the threading module

There are a lot of choices when it comes to implementing multithreaded programs in Python. One of the most common ways to work with threads in Python is through the `threading` module. Before we dive into the module's usage and its syntax, first, let's explore the `thread` model, which was previously the main thread-based development module in Python.

The thread module in Python 2

Before the `threading` module became popular, the primary thread-based development module was `thread`. If you are using an older version of Python 2, it is possible to use the module as it is. However, according to the module documentation page, the `thread` module was, in fact, renamed `_thread` in Python 3.

For readers that have been working with the `thread` module to build multithreaded applications and are looking to port their code from Python 2 to Python 3, the 2to3 tool might be a solution. The 2to3 tool handles most of the detectable incompatibilities between the different versions of Python, while parsing the source and traversing the source tree to convert Python 2.x code into Python 3.x code. Another trick to achieve the conversion is to change the import code from `import thread` to `import _thread as thread` in your Python programs.

The main feature of the `thread` module is its fast and sufficient method of creating new threads to execute functions: the `thread.start_new_thread()` function. Aside from this, the module only supports a number of low-level ways to work with multithreaded primitives and share their global data space. Additionally, simple lock objects (for example, mutexes and semaphores) are provided for synchronization purposes.

The threading module in Python 3

The old `thread` module has been considered deprecated by Python developers for a long time, mainly because of its rather low-level functions and limited usage. The `threading` module, on the other hand, is built on top of the `thread` module, providing easier ways to work with threads through powerful, higher-level APIs. Python users have actually been encouraged to utilize the new `threading` module over the `thread` module in their programs.

Additionally, the `thread` module considers each thread a function; when the `thread.start_new_thread()` is called, it actually takes in a separate function as its main argument, in order to spawn a new thread. However, the `threading` module is designed to be user-friendly for those that come from the object-oriented software development paradigm, treating each thread that is created as an object.

In addition to all of the functionality for working with threads that the `thread` module provides, the `threading` module supports a number of extra methods, as follows:

- `threading.activeCount()`: This function returns the number of currently active thread objects in the program
- `threading.currentThread()`: This function returns the number of thread objects in the current thread control from the caller
- `threading.enumerate()`: This function returns a list of all of the currently active thread objects in the program

Following the object-oriented software development paradigm, the `threading` module also provides a `Thread` class that supports the object-oriented implementation of threads. The following methods are supported in this class:

- `run()`: This method is executed when a new thread is initialized and started
- `start()`: This method starts the initialized calling thread object by calling the `run()` method
- `join()`: This method waits for the calling thread object to terminate before continuing to execute the rest of the program
- `isAlive()`: This method returns a Boolean value, indicating whether the calling thread object is currently executing
- `getName()`: This method returns the name of the calling thread object
- `setName()`: This method sets the name of the calling thread object

Creating a new thread in Python

Having provided an overview of the `threading` module and its differences from the old `thread` module, in this section, we will explore a number of examples of creating new threads by using these tools in Python. As mentioned previously, the `threading` module is most likely the most common way of working with threads in Python. Specific situations require use of the `thread` module and maybe other tools, as well, and it is important for us to be able to differentiate those situations.

Starting a thread with the thread module

In the `thread` module, new threads are created to execute functions concurrently. As we have mentioned, the way to do this is by using the `thread.start_new_thread()` function:

```
thread.start_new_thread(function, args[, kwargs])
```

When this function is called, a new thread is spawned to execute the function specified by the parameters, and the identifier of the thread is returned when the function finishes its execution. The `function` parameter is the name of the function to be executed, and the `args` parameter list (which has to be a list or a tuple) includes the arguments to be passed to the specified function. The optional `kwargs` argument, on the other hand, includes a separate dictionary of additional keyword arguments. When the `thread.start_new_thread()` function returns, the thread also terminates silently.

Let's look at an example of using the `thread` module in a Python program. If you have already downloaded the code for this book from the GitHub page, go ahead and navigate to the `Chapter10` folder and the `Chapter10/example2.py` file. In this example, we will look at the `is_prime()` function that we have also used in previous chapters:

```python
# Chapter10/example2.py

from math import sqrt

def is_prime(x):
    if x < 2:
        print('%i is not a prime number.' % x)

    elif x == 2:
        print('%i is a prime number.' % x)

    elif x % 2 == 0:
        print('%i is not a prime number.' % x)

    else:
        limit = int(sqrt(x)) + 1
        for i in range(3, limit, 2):
            if x % i == 0:
                print('%i is not a prime number.' % x)

        print('%i is a prime number.' % x)
```

You may have noticed that there is quite a difference in the way this is_prime(x) function returns the result of its computation; instead of returning true or false, to indicate whether the x parameter is a prime number, this is_prime() function directly prints out that result. As you saw earlier, the thread.start_new_thread() function executes the parameter function through spawning a new thread, but it actually returns the thread's identifier. Printing out the result inside of the is_prime() function is a workaround for accessing the result of that function through the thread module.

In the main part of our program, we will loop through a list of potential candidates for prime numbers, and we will call the thread.start_new_thread() function on the is_prime() function and each number in that list, as follows:

```
# Chapter10/example2.py

import _thread as thread

my_input = [2, 193, 323, 1327, 433785907]

for x in my_input:
    thread.start_new_thread(is_prime, (x, ))
```

You will notice that, in the Chapter10/example2.py file, there is a line of code to take in the user's input at the end:

```
a = input('Type something to quit: \n')
```

For now, let's comment out this last line. Then, when we execute the whole Python program, it will be observed that the program terminates without printing out any output; in other words, the program terminates before the threads can finish executing. This is due to the fact that, when a new thread is spawned through the thread.start_new_thread() function to process a number in our input list, the program continues to loop through the next input number while the newly created thread executes.

So, by the time the Python interpreter reaches the end of the program, if any thread has not finished executing (in our case, it is all of the threads), that thread will be ignored and terminated, and no output will be printed out. However, once in a while, one of the output is 2 is a prime number. which will be printed out before the program terminates, because the thread processing the number 2 is able to finish executing prior to that point.

The last line of code is another workaround for the `thread` module—this time, to address the preceding problem. This line prevents the program from exiting until the user presses any key on their keyboard, at which time the program will quit. The strategy is to wait for the program to finish executing all of the threads (that is, to finish processing all of the numbers in our input list). Uncomment the last line and execute the file, and your output should be similar to the following:

```
> python example2.py
Type something to quit:
2 is a prime number.
193 is a prime number.
1327 is a prime number.
323 is not a prime number.
433785907 is a prime number.
```

As you can see, the `Type something to quit:` line, which corresponds to the last line of code in our program, was printed out before the output from the `is_prime()` function; this is consistent with the fact that that line is executed before any of the other threads finish executing, most of the time. I say most of the time because, when the thread that is processing the first input (the number 2) finishes executing before the Python interpreter reaches the last line, the output of the program would be something similar to the following:

```
> python example2.py
2 is a prime number.
Type something to quit:
193 is a prime number.
323 is not a prime number.
1327 is a prime number.
433785907 is a prime number.
```

Starting a thread with the threading module

You now know how to start a thread with the `thread` module, and you know about its limited and low-level use of threading and the need for considerably unintuitive workarounds when working with it. In this subsection, we will explore the preferred `threading` module and its advantages over the `thread` module, with regard to the implementation of multithreaded programs in Python.

To create and customize a new thread using the `threading` module, there are specific steps that need to be followed:

1. Define a subclass of the `threading.Thread` class in your program
2. Override the default `__init__(self [,args])` method inside of the subclass, in order to add custom arguments for the class
3. Override the default `run(self [,args])` method inside of the subclass, in order to customize the behavior of the thread class when a new thread is initialized and started

You actually saw an example of this in the first example of this chapter. As a refresher, the following is what we have to use to customize a `threading.Thread` subclass, in order to perform a five-step countdown, with a customizable delay between each step:

```python
# Chapter10/my_thread.py

import threading
import time


class MyThread(threading.Thread):
    def __init__(self, name, delay):
        threading.Thread.__init__(self)
        self.name = name
        self.delay = delay

    def run(self):
        print('Starting thread %s.' % self.name)
        thread_count_down(self.name, self.delay)
        print('Finished thread %s.' % self.name)

def thread_count_down(name, delay):
    counter = 5

    while counter:
        time.sleep(delay)
        print('Thread %s counting down: %i...' % (name, counter))
        counter -= 1
```

In our next example, we will look at the problem of determining whether a specific number is a prime number. This time, we will be implementing a multithreaded Python program through the `threading` module. Navigate to the `Chapter10` folder and the `example3.py` file. Let's first focus on the `MyThread` class, as follows:

```
# Chapter10/example3.py

import threading

class MyThread(threading.Thread):
    def __init__(self, x):
        threading.Thread.__init__(self)
        self.x = x

    def run(self):
        print('Starting processing %i...' % x)
        is_prime(self.x)
```

Each instance of the `MyThread` class will have a parameter called x, specifying the prime number candidate to be processed. As you can see, when an instance of the class is initialized and started (that is, in the `run(self)` function), the `is_prime()` function, which is the same prime-checking function that we used in the previous example, on the x parameter, before that a message is also printed out by the `run()` function to specify the beginning of the processing.

In our main program, we still have the same list of input for prime-checking. We will be going through each number in that list, spawning and running a new instance of the `MyThread` class with that number, and appending that `MyThread` instance to a separate list. This list of created threads is necessary because, after that, we will have to call the `join()` method on all of those threads, which ensures that all of the threads have finished executing successfully:

```
my_input = [2, 193, 323, 1327, 433785907]

threads = []

for x in my_input:
    temp_thread = MyThread(x)
    temp_thread.start()

    threads.append(temp_thread)

for thread in threads:
    thread.join()

print('Finished.')
```

Notice that, unlike when we used the `thread` module, this time, we do not have to invent a workaround to make sure that all of the threads have finished executing successfully. Again, this is done by the `join()` method provided by the `threading` module. This is only one example of the many advantages of using the more powerful, higher-level API of the `threading` module, rather than using the `thread` module.

Synchronizing threads

As you saw in the previous examples, the `threading` module has many advantages over its predecessor, the `thread` module, in terms of functionality and high-level API calls. Even though some recommend that experienced Python developers know how to implement multithreaded applications using both of these modules, you will most likely be using the `threading` module to work with threads in Python. In this section, we will look at using the `threading` module in thread synchronization.

The concept of thread synchronization

Before we jump into an actual Python example, let's explore the concept of synchronization in computer science. As you saw in previous chapters, sometimes, it is undesirable to have all portions of a program execute in a parallel manner. In fact, in most contemporary concurrent programs, there are sequential portions and concurrent portions of the code; furthermore, even inside of a concurrent portion, some form of coordination between different threads/processes is also required.

Thread/process synchronization is a concept in computer science that specifies various mechanisms to ensure that no more than one concurrent thread/process can process and execute a particular program portion at a time; this portion is known as the **critical section**, and we will discuss it in further detail when we consider common problems in concurrent programming in *Chapter 20*, *Starvation*, and *Chapter 21*, *Race Conditions*.

In a given program, when a thread is accessing/executing the critical section of the program, the other threads have to wait until that thread finishes executing. The typical goal of thread synchronization is to avoid any potential data discrepancies when multiple threads access their shared resources; allowing only one thread to execute the critical section of the program at a time guarantees that no data conflicts occur in multithreaded applications.

The threading.Lock class

One of the most common ways to apply thread synchronization is through the implementation of a locking mechanism. In our `threading` module, the `threading.Lock` class provides a simple and intuitive approach to creating and working with locks. Its main usage includes the following methods:

- `threading.Lock()`: This method initializes and returns a new lock object.
- `acquire(blocking)`: When this method is called, all of the threads will run synchronously (that is, only one thread can execute the critical section at a time):
    - The optional argument `blocking` allows us to specify whether the current thread should wait to acquire the lock
    - When `blocking = 0`, the current thread does not wait for the lock and simply returns `0` if the lock cannot be acquired by the thread, or `1` otherwise
    - When `blocking = 1`, the current thread blocks and waits for the lock to be released and acquires it afterwards
- `release()`: When this method is called, the lock is released.

An example in Python

Let's consider a specific example. In this example, we will be looking at the `Chapter10/example4.py` file. We will go back to the thread example of counting down from five to one, which we looked at at the beginning of this chapter; take a moment to look back if you do not remember the problem. In this example, we will be tweaking the `MyThread` class, as follows:

```
# Chapter10/example4.py

import threading
import time

class MyThread(threading.Thread):
    def __init__(self, name, delay):
        threading.Thread.__init__(self)
        self.name = name
        self.delay = delay

    def run(self):
        print('Starting thread %s.' % self.name)
        thread_lock.acquire()
```

```
        thread_count_down(self.name, self.delay)
        thread_lock.release()
        print('Finished thread %s.' % self.name)

def thread_count_down(name, delay):
    counter = 5

    while counter:
        time.sleep(delay)
        print('Thread %s counting down: %i...' % (name, counter))
        counter -= 1
```

As opposed to the first example of this chapter, in this example, the MyThread class utilizes a lock object (whose variable is named thread_lock) inside of its run() function. Specifically, the lock object is acquired right before the thread_count_down() function is called (that is, when the countdown begins), and the lock object is released right after its ends. Theoretically, this specification will alter the behavior of the threads that we saw in the first example; instead of executing the countdown simultaneously, the program will now execute the threads separately, and the countdowns will take place one after the other.

Finally, we will initialize the thread_lock variable as well as run two separate instances of the MyThread class:

```
thread_lock = threading.Lock()

thread1 = MyThread('A', 0.5)
thread2 = MyThread('B', 0.5)

thread1.start()
thread2.start()

thread1.join()
thread2.join()


print('Finished.')
```

The output will be as follows:

```
> python example4.py
Starting thread A.
Starting thread B.
Thread A counting down: 5...
Thread A counting down: 4...
Thread A counting down: 3...
Thread A counting down: 2...
Thread A counting down: 1...
```

```
Finished thread A.
Thread B counting down: 5...
Thread B counting down: 4...
Thread B counting down: 3...
Thread B counting down: 2...
Thread B counting down: 1...
Finished thread B.
Finished.
```

Multithreaded priority queue

A computer science concept that is widely used in both non-concurrent and concurrent programming is queuing. A **queue** is an abstract data structure that is a collection of different elements maintained in a specific order; these elements can be the other objects in a program.

A connection between real-life and programmatic queues

Queues are an intuitive concept that can easily be related to our everyday life, such as when you stand in line to board a plane at the airport. In an actual line of people, you will see the following:

- People typically enter at one end of the line and exit from the other end
- If person A enters the line before person B, person A will also leave the line before person B (unless person B has more priority)
- Once everyone has boarded the plane, there will be no one left in the line. In other words, the line will be empty

In computer science, a queue works in a considerably similar way:

- Elements can be added to the end of the queue; this task is called **enqueue**.
- Elements can also be removed from the beginning of the queue; this task is called **dequeue**.

- In a **First In First Out (FIFO)** queue, the elements that are added first will be removed first (hence, the name FIFO). This is contrary to another common data structure in computer science, called **stack**, in which the last element that is added will be removed first. This is known as **Last In First Out (LIFO)**.
- If all of the elements inside of a queue have been removed, the queue will be empty and there will be no way to remove further elements from the queue. Similarly, if a queue is at the maximum capacity of the number of elements it can hold, there is no way to add any other elements to the queue:

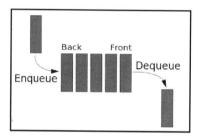

A visualization of the queue data structure

The queue module

The queue module in Python provides a simple implementation of the queue data structure. Each queue in the queue.Queue class can hold a specific amount of element, and can have the following methods as its high-level API:

- get(): This method returns the next element of the calling queue object and removes it from the queue object
- put(): This method adds a new element to the calling queue object
- qsize(): This method returns the number of current elements in the calling queue object (that is, its size)
- empty(): This method returns a Boolean, indicating whether the calling queue object is empty
- full(): This method returns a Boolean, indicating whether the calling queue object is full

Queuing in concurrent programming

The concept of a queue is even more prevalent in the sub-field of concurrent programming, especially when we need to implement a fixed number of threads in our program to interact with a varying number of shared resources.

In the previous examples, we have learned to assign a specific task to a new thread. This means that the number of tasks that need to be processed will dictate the number of threads our program should spawn. (For example, in our `Chapter10/example3.py` file, we had five numbers as our input and we therefore created five threads—each took one input number and processed it.)

Sometimes it is undesirable to have as many threads as the tasks we have to process. Say we have a large number of tasks to be processed, then it will be quite inefficient to spawn the same large number of threads and have each thread execute only one task. It could be more beneficial to have a fixed number of threads (commonly known as a thread pool) that would work through the tasks in a cooperative manner.

Here is when the concept of a queue comes in. We can design a structure in which the pool of threads will not hold any information regarding the tasks they should each execute, instead the tasks are stored in a queue (in other words task queue), and the items in the queue will be fed to individual members of the thread pool. As a given task is completed by a member of the thread pool, if the task queue still contains elements to be processed, then the next element in the queue will be sent to the thread that just became available.

This diagram further illustrates this setup:

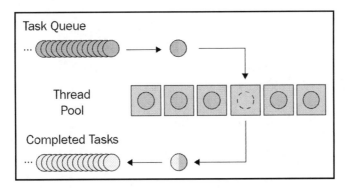

Queuing in threading

Let's consider a quick example in Python, in order to illustrate this point. Navigate to the `Chapter10/example5.py` file. In this example, we will be considering the problem of printing out all of the positive factors of an element in a given list of positive integers. We are still looking at the previous `MyThread` class, but with some adjustments:

```python
# Chapter10/example5.py
import queue
import threading
import time


class MyThread(threading.Thread):
    def __init__(self, name):
        threading.Thread.__init__(self)
        self.name = name

    def run(self):
        print('Starting thread %s.' % self.name)
        process_queue()
        print('Exiting thread %s.' % self.name)

def process_queue():
    while True:
        try:
            x = my_queue.get(block=False)
        except queue.Empty:
            return
        else:
            print_factors(x)

        time.sleep(1)

def print_factors(x):
    result_string = 'Positive factors of %i are: ' % x
    for i in range(1, x + 1):
        if x % i == 0:
            result_string += str(i) + ' '
    result_string += '\n' + '_' * 20

    print(result_string)


# setting up variables
input_ = [1, 10, 4, 3]

# filling the queue
my_queue = queue.Queue()
```

```
for x in input_:
    my_queue.put(x)


# initializing and starting 3 threads
thread1 = MyThread('A')
thread2 = MyThread('B')
thread3 = MyThread('C')

thread1.start()
thread2.start()
thread3.start()

# joining all 3 threads
thread1.join()
thread2.join()
thread3.join()

print('Done.')
```

There is a lot going on, so let's break the program down into smaller pieces. First, let's look at our key function, as follows:

```
# Chapter10/example5.py

def print_factors(x):
    result_string = 'Positive factors of %i are: ' % x
    for i in range(1, x + 1):
        if x % i == 0:
            result_string += str(i) + ' '
    result_string += '\n' + '_' * 20

    print(result_string)
```

This function takes in an argument, x then iterates through all positive numbers between 1 and itself, to check whether a number is a factor of x. It finally prints out a formatted message that contains all of the information that it cumulates through the loop.

In our new `MyThread` class, when a new instance is initialized and started, the `process_queue()` function will be called. This function will first attempt to obtain the next element of the queue object that the `my_queue` variable holds in a non-blocking manner by calling the `get(block=False)` method. If a `queue.Empty` exception occurs (which indicates that the queue currently holds no value), then we will end the execution of the function. Otherwise we simply pass that element we just obtained to the `print_factors()` function.

```
# Chapter10/example5.py

def process_queue():
    while True:
        try:
            x = my_queue.get(block=False)
        except queue.Empty:
            return
        else:
            print_factors(x)

        time.sleep(1)
```

The `my_queue` variable is defined in our main function as a `Queue` object from the `queue` module that contains the elements in the `input_` list:

```
# setting up variables
input_ = [1, 10, 4, 3]

# filling the queue
my_queue = queue.Queue(4)
for x in input_:
    my_queue.put(x)
```

For the rest of the main program, we simply initiate and run three separate threads until all of them finish their respective execution. Here we choose to create only three threads to simulate the design that we discussed earlier—a fixed number of threads processing a queue of input whose number of elements can change independently:

```
# initializing and starting 3 threads
thread1 = MyThread('A')
thread2 = MyThread('B')
thread3 = MyThread('C')

thread1.start()
thread2.start()
thread3.start()
```

```
# joining all 3 threads
thread1.join()
thread2.join()
thread3.join()

print('Done.')
```

Run the program and you will see the following output:

```
> python example5.py
Starting thread A.
Starting thread B.
Starting thread C.
Positive factors of 1 are: 1
_____
Positive factors of 10 are: 1 2 5 10
_____
Positive factors of 4 are: 1 2 4
_____
Positive factors of 3 are: 1 3
_____
Exiting thread C.
Exiting thread A.
Exiting thread B.
Done.
```

In this example, we have implemented the structure that we discussed earlier: a task queue that holds all the tasks to be executed and a thread pool (threads A, B, and C) that interacts with the queue to process its elements individually.

Multithreaded priority queue

The elements in a queue are processed in the order that they were added to the queue; in other words, the first element that is added leaves the queue first (FIFO). Even though this abstract data structure simulates real life in many situations, depending on the application and its purposes, sometimes, we need to redefine/change the order of the elements dynamically. This is where the concept of priority queuing comes in handy.

The **priority queue** abstract data structure is similar to the queue (and even the aforementioned stack) data structure, but each of the elements in a priority queue, as the name suggests, has a priority associated with it; in other words, when an element is added to a priority queue, its priority needs to be specified. Unlike in regular queues, the dequeuing principle of a priority queue relies on the priority of the elements: the elements with higher priorities are processed before those with lower priorities.

The concept of a priority queue is used in a variety of different applications—namely, bandwidth management, Dijkstra's algorithm, best-first search algorithms, and so on. Each of these applications typically uses a definite scoring system/function to determine the priority of its elements. For example, in bandwidth management, prioritized traffic, such as real-time streaming, is processed with the least delay and the least likelihood of being rejected. In best-search algorithms that are used to find the shortest path between two given nodes of a graph, a priority queue is implemented to keep track of unexplored routes; the routes with shorter estimated path lengths are given higher priorities in the queue.

Summary

A thread of execution is the smallest unit of programming commands. In computer science, multithreaded applications allow for multiple threads to exist within the same process simultaneously, in order to implement concurrency and parallelism. Multithreading provides a variety of advantages, in execution time, responsiveness, and the efficiency of resource consumption.

The `threading` module in Python 3, which is commonly considered superior to the old `thread` module, provides an efficient, powerful, and high-level API to work with threads while implementing multithreaded applications in Python, including options to spawn new threads dynamically and synchronize threads through different locking mechanisms.

Queuing and priority queuing are important data structures in the field of computer science, and they are essential concepts in concurrent and parallel programming. They allow for multithreaded applications to efficiently execute and complete their threads in an accurate manner, ensuring that the shared resources are processed in a specific and dynamic order.

In the next chapter, we will discuss a more advanced function of Python, the `with` statement, and how it complements the use of multithreaded programming in Python.

Questions

- What is a thread? What are the core differences between a thread and a process?
- What are the API options provided by the `thread` module in Python?
- What are the API options provided by the `threading` module in Python?
- What are the processes of creating new threads via the `thread` and `threading` modules?
- What is the idea behind thread synchronization using locks?
- What is the process of implementing thread synchronization using locks in Python?
- What is the idea behind the queue data structure?
- What is the main application of queuing in concurrent programming?
- What are the core differences between a regular queue and a priority queue?

Further reading

For more information you can refer to the following links:

- *Python Parallel Programming Cookbook*, Giancarlo Zaccone, Packt Publishing Ltd, 2015
- "Learning Concurrency in Python: Build highly efficient, robust, and concurrent applications", Elliot Forbes (2017)
- *Real-time concepts for embedded systems*, Qing Li and Caroline Yao, CRC Press, 2003

11
Using the with Statement in Threads

The `with` statement in Python sometimes causes confusion for novice and experienced Python programmers alike. This chapter explains in depth the idea behind the `with` statement as a context manager and its usage in concurrent and parallel programming, specifically regarding the use of locks while synchronizing threads. This chapter also provides specific examples of how the `with` statement is most commonly used.

The following topics will be covered in this chapter:

- The concept of context management and the options that the `with` statement provides as a context manager, specifically in concurrent and parallel programming
- The syntax of the `with` statement and how to use it effectively and efficiently
- The different ways of using the `with` statement in concurrent programming

Technical requirements

The following is a list of prerequisites for this chapter:

- Python 3 must be installed on your computer
- Download the GitHub repository at
  `https://github.com/PacktPublishing/AdvancedPythonProgramming`
- During this chapter, we will be working with the subfolder named `Chapter11`
- Check out the following video to see the Code in Action: `http://bit.ly/2DSGLEZ`

Context management

The new `with` statement was first introduced in Python 2.5 and has been in use for quite some time. However, there still seems to be confusion regarding its usage, even for experienced Python programmers. The `with` statement is most commonly used as a context manager that properly manages resources, which is essential in concurrent and parallel programming, where resources are shared across different entities in the concurrent or parallel application.

Starting from managing files

As an experienced Python user, you have probably seen the `with` statement being used to open and read external files inside Python programs. Looking at this problem at a lower level, the operation of opening an external file in Python will consume a resource—in this case, a file descriptor—and your operating system will set a limit on this resource. This means that there is an upper limit on how many files a single process running on your system can open simultaneously.

Let's consider a quick example to illustrate this point further. Let's take a look at the `Chapter11/example1.py` file, as shown in the following code:

```
# Chapter11/example1.py

n_files = 10
files = []

for i in range(n_files):
    files.append(open('output1/sample%i.txt' % i, 'w'))
```

This quick program simply creates 10 text files inside the `output1` folder: `sample0.txt`, `sample1.txt`, ..., `sample9.txt`. What might be of more interest to us is the fact that the files were opened inside the `for` loop but were not closed—this is a bad practice in programming that we will discuss later. Now, let's say we wanted to reassign the `n_files` variable to a large number—say 10,000—as shown in the following code:

```
# Chapter11/example1.py

n_files = 10000
files = []

# method 1
for i in range(n_files):
    files.append(open('output1/sample%i.txt' % i, 'w'))
```

We would get an error similar to the following:

```
> python example1.py
Traceback (most recent call last):
  File "example1.py", line 7, in <module>
OSError: [Errno 24] Too many open files: 'output1/sample253.txt'
```

Looking closely at the error message, we can see that my laptop can only handle 253 opened files simultaneously (as a side note, if you are working on a UNIX-like system, running `ulimit -n` will give you the number of files that your system can handle). More generally, this situation arose from what is known as **file descriptor leakage**. When Python opens a file inside a program, that opened file is essentially represented by an integer. This integer acts as a reference point that the program can use in order to have access to that file, while not giving the program complete control over the underlying file itself.

By opening too many files at the same time, our program assigned too many file descriptors to manage the open files, hence the error message. File descriptor leakage can lead to a number of difficult problems—especially in concurrent and parallel programming—namely, unauthorized I/O operations on open files. The solution to this is to simply close opened files in a coordinated manner. Let's look at our `Chapter11/example1.py` file in the second method. In the `for` loop, we would do the following:

```python
# Chapter11/example1.py

n_files = 1000
files = []

# method 2
for i in range(n_files):
    f = open('output1/sample%i.txt' % i, 'w')
    files.append(f)
    f.close()
```

The with statement as a context manager

In real-life applications, it is rather easy to mismanage opened files in your programs by forgetting to close them; it can sometimes also be the case that it is impossible to tell whether the program has finished processing a file, and we programmers will therefore be unable to make a decision as to when to put the statement to close the files appropriately. This situation is even more common in concurrent and parallel programming, where the order of execution between different elements changes frequently.

One possible solution to this problem that is also common in other programming languages is to use a `try...except...finally` block every time we want to interact with an external file. This solution still requires the same level of management and significant overhead and does not provide a good improvement in the ease and readability of our programs either. This is when the `with` statement of Python comes into play.

The `with` statement gives us a simple way of ensuring that all opened files are properly managed and cleaned up when the program finishes using them. The most notable advantage of using the `with` statement comes from the fact that, even if the code is successfully executed or it returns an error, the `with` statement always handles and manages the opened files appropriately via context. For example, let's look at our `Chapter11/example1.py` file in more detail:

```
# Chapter11/example1.py

n_files = 254
files = []

# method 3
for i in range(n_files):
    with open('output1/sample%i.txt' % i, 'w') as f:
        files.append(f)
```

While this method accomplishes the same job as the second method we saw earlier, it additionally provides a cleaner and more readable way to manage the opened files that our program interacts with. More specifically, the `with` statement helps us indicate the scope of certain variables—in this case, the variables that point to the opened files—and hence, their context.

For example, in the third method in the preceding code, the `f` variable indicates the current opened file within the `with` block at each iteration of the `for` loop, and as soon as our program exits that `with` block (which is outside the scope of that `f` variable), there is no longer any other way to access it. This architecture guarantees that all cleanup associated with a file descriptor happens appropriately. The `with` statement is hence called a context manager.

The syntax of the with statement

The syntax of the `with` statement can be intuitive and straightforward. With the purpose of wrapping the execution of a block with methods defined by a context manager, it consists of the following simple form:

```
with [expression] (as [target]):
    [code]
```

Note that the `as [target]` part of the `with` statement is actually not required, as we will see later on. Additionally, the `with` statement can also handle more than one item on the same line. Specifically, the context managers created are treated as if multiple `with` statements were nested inside one another. For example, look at the following code:

```
with [expression1] as [target1], [expression2] as [target2]:
    [code]
```

This is interpreted as follows:

```
with [expression1] as [target1]:
    with [expression2] as [target2]:
        [code]
```

The with statement in concurrent programming

Obviously, opening and closing external files does not resemble concurrency very much. However, we mentioned earlier that the `with` statement, as a context manager, is not only used to manage file descriptors, but most resources in general. And if you actually found managing lock objects from the `threading.Lock()` class similar to managing external files while going through *Chapter 9, Amdahl's Law*, then this is where the comparison between the two comes in handy.

As a refresher, locks are mechanisms in concurrent and parallel programming that are typically used to synchronize threads in a multithreaded application (that is, to prevent more than one thread from accessing the critical session simultaneously). However, as we will discuss again in *Chapter 20, Starvation*, locks are also a common source of **deadlock**, during which a thread **acquires** a lock but never **releases** it because of an unhandled occurrence, thereby stopping the entire program.

Example of deadlock handling

Let's look at a quick example in Python. Let's a take look at the `Chapter11/example2.py` file, as shown in the following code:

```
# Chapter11/example2.py

from threading import Lock

my_lock = Lock()

def get_data_from_file_v1(filename):
    my_lock.acquire()

    with open(filename, 'r') as f:
        data.append(f.read())

    my_lock.release()

data = []

try:
    get_data_from_file('output2/sample0.txt')
except FileNotFoundError:
    print('Encountered an exception...')

my_lock.acquire()
print('Lock can still be acquired.')
```

In this example, we have a `get_data_from_file_v1()` function that takes in the path to an external file, reads the data from it, and appends that data to a predeclared list called `data`. Inside this function, a lock object called `my_lock`, which is also predeclared prior to the function being called, is acquired and released as the parameter file is read before and after, respectively.

In the main program, we will try to call `get_data_from_file_v1()` on a nonexistent file, which is one of the most common errors in programming. At the end of the program, we also acquire the lock object again. The point is to see whether our programming could handle the error of reading a nonexistent file appropriately and gracefully with just the `try...except` block that we have.

After running the script, you will notice that our program will print out the error message specified in the `try...except` block, `Encountered an exception...`, which is expected, since the file could not be found. However, the program will also fail to execute the rest of the code; it will never get to the last line of code—`print('Lock acquired.')`—and will hang forever (or until you hit *Ctrl + C* to force-quit the program).

This is a deadlock situation, which, again, occurs when `my_lock` is acquired inside the `get_data_from_file_v1()` function, but since our program encountered an error before executing `my_lock.release()`, the lock was never released. This in turn caused the `my_lock.acquire()` line at the end of the program to hang, as the lock could not be acquired in any way. Our program hence could not reach its last line of code, `print('Lock acquired.')`.

This problem, however, could be handled with a `with` statement easily and effortlessly. In the `example2.py` file, simply comment out the line calling `get_data_from_file_v1()` and uncomment the line calling `get_data_from_file_v2()`, and you will have the following:

```
# Chapter11/example2.py

from threading import Lock

my_lock = Lock()

def get_data_from_file_v2(filename):
    with my_lock, open(filename, 'r') as f:
        data.append(f.read())

data = []

try:
    get_data_from_file_v2('output2/sample0.txt')
except:
    print('Encountered an exception...')

my_lock.acquire()
print('Lock acquired.')
```

In the `get_data_from_file_v2()` function, we have the equivalent of a pair of nested `with` statements, as follows:

```
with my_lock:
    with open(filename, 'r') as f:
        data.append(f.read())
```

Since `Lock` objects are context managers, simply using `with my_lock:` would ensure that the lock object is acquired and released appropriately, even if an exception is encountered inside the block. After running the script, you will have the following output:

```
> python example2.py
Encountered an exception...
Lock acquired.
```

We can see that, this time, our program was able to acquire the lock and reach the end of the script gracefully and without errors.

Summary

The `with` statement in Python offers an intuitive and convenient way to manage resources while ensuring that errors and exceptions are handled correctly. This ability to manage resources is even more important in concurrent and parallel programming, where various resources are shared and utilized across different entities—specifically, by using the `with` statement with `threading.Lock` objects that are used to synchronize different threads in a multithreaded application.

Aside from better error handling and guaranteed cleanup tasks, the `with` statement also provides extra readability from your programs, which is one of the strongest features that Python offers its developers.

In the next chapter, we will be discussing one of the most popular uses of Python at the moment: web-scraping applications. We will look at the concept and the basic idea behind web scraping, the tools that Python provides to support web scraping, and how concurrency will significantly help your web-scraping applications.

Questions

- What is a file descriptor and in what ways can it be handled in Python?
- What problem arises when file descriptors are not handled carefully?
- What is a lock and in what ways can it be handled in Python?
- What problem arises when locks are not handled carefully?
- What is the idea behind context managers?
- What options does the `with` statement in Python provide in terms of context management?

Further reading

For more information, you can refer to the following links:

- *Python Parallel Programming Cookbook,* by Zaccone and Giancarlo, published by Packt, 2015
- *Improve Your Python: the with Statement and Context Managers,* Jeff **Knupp** (`https:/ /jeffknupp.com/blog/2016/03/07/improve-your-python-the-with-statement- and-context-managers/`)
- *Compound statements,* Python Software Foundation (`https://docs.python.org/ 3/reference/compound_stmts.html`)

12
Concurrent Web Requests

This chapter will focus on the application of concurrency in making web requests. Intuitively, making requests to a web page to collect information about it is independent to applying the same task to another web page. Concurrency, specifically threading in this case, therefore can be a powerful tool that provides a significant speedup in this process. In this chapter, we will learn the fundamentals of web requests and how to interact with websites using Python. We will also see how concurrency can help us make multiple requests in an efficient way. Finally, we will look at a number of good practices in web requests.

In this chapter, we will cover the following concepts:

- The basics of web requests
- The requests module
- Concurrent web requests
- The problem of timeout
- Good practices in making web requests

Technical requirements

The following is a list of prerequisites for this chapter:

- Python 3 must be installed on your computer
- Download the GitHub repository at
  `https://github.com/PacktPublishing/AdvancedPythonProgramming`
- During this chapter, we will be working with the subfolder named `Chapter12`
- Check out the following video to see the Code in Action: `http://bit.ly/2Fy1ZcS`

The basics of web requests

The worldwide capacity to generate data is estimated to double in size every two years. Even though there is an interdisciplinary field known as data science that is entirely dedicated to the study of data, almost every programming task in software development also has something to do with collecting and analyzing data. A significant part of this is, of course, data collection. However, the data that we need for our applications is sometimes not stored nicely and cleanly in a database—sometimes, we need to collect the data we need from web pages.

For example, web scraping is a data extraction method that automatically makes requests to web pages and downloads specific information. Web scraping allows us to comb through numerous websites and collect any data we need in a systematic and consistent manner—the collected data can be analyzed later on by our applications or simply saved on our computers in various formats. An example of this would be Google, which programs and runs numerous web scrapers of its own to find and index web pages for the search engine.

The Python language itself provides a number of good options for applications of this kind. In this chapter, we will mainly work with the `requests` module to make client-side web requests from our Python programs. However, before we look into this module in more detail, we need to understand some web terminology in order to be able to effectively design our applications.

HTML

Hypertext Markup Language (HTML) is the standard and most common markup language for developing web pages and web applications. An HTML file is simply a plaintext file with the `.html` file extension. In an HTML document, texts are surrounded and delimited by tags, written in angle brackets: `<p>`, `<img>`, `<i>`, and so on. These tags typically consist of pairs—an opening tag and a closing tag—indicating the styling or the nature of the data included inside.

It is also possible to include other forms of media in HTML code, such as images or videos. There are also numerous other tags that are used in common HTML documents. Some specify a group of elements that share some common characteristics, such as `<id></id>` and `<class></class>`.

The following is an example of HTML code:

```html
<div class="topNavTop">
    <p>Welcome to Chilli restaurant</p>
    <div class="topNavRight">
        <img src="assets/top-nav/icon-phone.png">
        <p>416-455-3221</p>
        <img src="assets/top-nav/icon-email.png">
        <p>info@company.com</p>
        <img src="assets/top-nav/icon-magnifying-glass.png">
    </div>
</div>
<div class="topNavBottom">
    <img src="assets/chilli-logo.png">
    <div class="topNavRightBottom">
        <a href="index.html">HOME</a>
        <a href="menu.html">MENU</a>
        <a href="events.html">EVENTS</a>
        <a href="#contact">CONTACT</a>
    </div>
</div>
```

Sample HTML code

Fortunately, detailed knowledge on what each HTML tag accomplishes is not required for us to be able to make effective web requests. As we will see later on in this chapter, the more essential part of making web requests is the ability to interact with web pages efficiently.

HTTP requests

In a typical communication process on the web, HTML texts are the data that is to be saved and/or further processed. This data needs to be first collected from web pages, but how can we go about doing that? Most of the communication is done via the internet—more specifically, the World Wide Web—and this utilizes the **Hypertext Transfer Protocol (HTTP)**. In HTTP, request methods are used to convey the information of what data is being requested and should be sent back from a server.

For example, when you type packtpub.com in your browser, the browser sends a request method via HTTP to the Packt website's main server asking for data from the website. Now, if both your internet connection and Packt's server are working well, then your browser will receive a response back from the server, as shown in the following diagram. This response will be in the form of an HTML document, which will be interpreted by your browser, and your browser will display the corresponding HTML output to the screen.

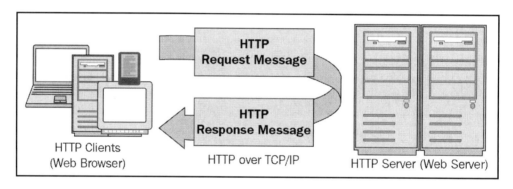

Diagram of HTTP communication

Generally, request methods are defined as verbs that indicate the desired action to be performed while the HTTP client (web browsers) and the server communicate with each other: GET, HEAD, POST, PUT, DELETE, and so on. Of these methods, GET and POST are two of the most common request methods used in web-scraping applications; their function is described in the following list:

- The GET method makes a request for a specific data from the server. This method only retrieves data and has no other effect on the server and its databases.
- The POST method sends data in a specific form that is accepted by the server. This data could be, for example, a message to a bulletin board, mailing list, or a newsgroup; information to be submitted to a web form; or an item to be added to a database.

All general-purpose HTTP servers that we commonly see on the internet are actually required to implement at least the GET (and HEAD) method, while the POST method is considered optional.

HTTP status code

It is not always the case that, when a web request is made and sent to a web server, the server will process the request and return the requested data without fail. Sometimes, the server might be completely down or already busy interacting with other clients and therefore unresponsive to a new request; sometimes, the client itself makes bad requests to a server (for example, incorrectly formatted or malicious requests).

As a way to categorize these problems as well as provide the most information as possible during the communication resulting from a web request, HTTP requires servers to respond to each request from its clients an **HTTP response status code**. A status code is typically a three-digit number that indicates the specific characteristics of the response that the server sends back to a client.

There are in total five large categories of HTTP response status codes, indicated by the first digit of the code. They are as follows:

- **1xx (informational status code)**: The request was received and the server is processing it. For example, 100 means the request header has been received and the server is waiting for the request body; 102 indicates that the request is currently being processed (this is used for large requests and to prevent clients from timing out).
- **2xx (successful status code)**: The request was successfully received, understood, and processed by the server. For example, 200 means the request was successfully fulfilled; 202 indicates that the request has been accepted for processing, but the processing itself is not complete.
- **3xx (redirectional status code)**: Additional actions need to be taken so that the request can be successfully processed. For example, 300 means that there are multiple options regarding how the response from the server should be processed (for example, giving the client multiple video format options when a video file is to be downloaded); 301 indicates that the server has been moved permanently and all requests should be directed to another address (provided in the response from the server).

- **4xx (error status code for the client)**: The request was incorrectly formatted by the client and could not be processed. For example, 400 means that the client sent in a bad request (for example, syntax error or the size of the request is too large); 404 (arguably the most well-known status code) indicates that the request method is not supported by the server.
- **5xx (error status code for the server)**: The request, although valid, could not be processed by the server. For example, 500 means there is an internal server error in which an unexpected condition was encountered; 504 (Gateway Timeout) means that the server, which was acting as a gateway or a proxy, did not receive a response from the final server in time.

A lot more can be said about these status codes, but it is already sufficient for us to keep in mind the big five categories previously mentioned when making web requests from Python. If you would like to find more specific information about the above or other status codes, the **Internet Assigned Numbers Authority (IANA)** maintains the official registry of HTTP status codes.

The requests module

The `requests` module allows its users to make and send HTTP request methods. In the applications that we will be considering, it is mainly used to make contact with the server of the web pages we want to extract data from and obtain the response for the server.

 According to the official documentation of the module, the use of Python 3 is **highly recommended** over Python 2 for `requests`.

To install the module on your computer, run the following:

```
pip install requests
```

You should use this code if you are using `pip` as your package manager. If, however, you are using Anaconda instead, simply use the following:

```
conda install requests
```

These commands should install `requests` and any other required dependencies (`idna`, `certifi`, `urllib3`, and so on) for you if your system does not have those already. After this, run `import requests` in a Python interpreter to confirm that the module has been installed successfully.

Making a request in Python

Let's look at an example usage of the module. If you already have the code for this book downloaded from the GitHub page, go ahead and navigate to the `Chapter12` folder. Let's take a look at the `example1.py` file, as shown in the following code:

```
# Chapter12/example1.py

import requests

url = 'http://www.google.com'

res = requests.get(url)

print(res.status_code)
print(res.headers)

with open('google.html', 'w') as f:
    f.write(res.text)

print('Done.')
```

In this example, we are using the `requests` module to download the HTML code of the web page, `www.google.com`. The `requests.get()` method sends a `GET` request method to `url` and we store the response to the `res` variable. After checking the status and headers of the response by printing them out, we create a file called `google.html` and write the HTML code, which is stored in the response text, to the file.

After running the programming (assuming that your internet is working and the Google server is not down), you should get the following output:

```
200
{'Date': 'Sat, 17 Nov 2018 23:08:58 GMT', 'Expires': '-1', 'Cache-Control':
'private, max-age=0', 'Content-Type': 'text/html; charset=ISO-8859-1',
'P3P': 'CP="This is not a P3P policy! See g.co/p3phelp for more info."',
'X-XSS-Protection': '1; mode=block', 'X-Frame-Options': 'SAMEORIGIN',
'Content-Encoding': 'gzip', 'Server': 'gws', 'Content-Length': '4958',
'Set-Cookie': '1P_JAR=2018-11-17-23; expires=Mon, 17-Dec-2018 23:08:58 GMT;
path=/; domain=.google.com, NID=146=NHT7fic3mjBO_vdiFB3-
gqnFPyGN1EGxyMkkNPnFMEVsqjGJ8S0EwrivDBWBgUS7hCPZGHbosLE4uxz31shnr3X4adRpe7u
ICEiK8qh3Asu6LH_bIKSLWStAp8gMK1f9_GnQO_JKQoMvG-
OLrT_fwV0hwTR5r2UVYsUJ6xHtX2s; expires=Sun, 19-May-2019 23:08:58 GMT;
path=/; domain=.google.com; HttpOnly'}
Done.
```

The response had a `200` status code, which we know means that the request has been successfully completed. The header of the response, stored in `res.headers`, additionally contains further specific information regarding the response. For example, we can see the date and time the request was made or that the content of the response is text and HTML and the total length of the content is `4958`.

The complete data sent from the server was also written to the `google.html` file. When you open the file in a text editor, you will be able to see the HTML code of the web page that we have downloaded using requests. On the other hand, if you use a web browser to open the file, you will see how **most** of the information from the original web page is now being displayed through a downloaded offline file.

For example, the following is how Google Chrome on my system interprets the HTML file:

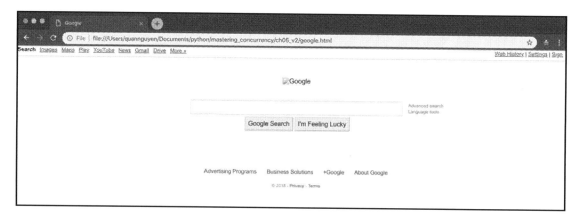

Downloaded HTML opened offline

There is other information that is stored on the server that web pages of that server make reference to. This means that not all of the information that an online web page provides can be downloaded via a `GET` request, and this is why offline HTML code sometimes fails to contain all of the information available on the online web page that it was downloaded from. (For example, the downloaded HTML code in the preceding screenshot does not display the Google icon correctly.)

Running a ping test

With the basic knowledge of HTTP requests and the `requests` module in Python in mind, we will go through the rest of this chapter with a central problem: running a ping test. A ping test is a process in which you test the communication between your system and specific web servers, simply by making a request to each of the servers in question. By considering the HTTP response status code (potentially) returned by the server, the test is used to evaluate either the internet connection of your own system or the availability of the servers.

Ping tests are quite common among web administrators, who usually have to manage a large number of websites simultaneously. Ping tests are a good tool to quickly identify pages that are unexpectedly unresponsive or down. There are many tools that provide you with powerful options in ping tests and, in this chapter, we will be designing a ping test application that can concurrently send multiple web requests at the same time.

To simulate different HTTP response status codes to be sent back to our program, we will be using `httpstat.us`, a website that can generate various status codes and is commonly used to test how applications that make web requests can handle varying response. Specifically, to use a request that will return a 200 status code in a program, we can simply make a request to `httpstat.us/200` and the same applies for other status codes. In our ping test program, we will have a list of `httpstat.us` URLs with different status codes.

Let's now a take look at the `Chapter12/example2.py` file, as shown in the following code:

```
# Chapter12/example2.py

import requests

def ping(url):
    res = requests.get(url)
    print(f'{url}: {res.text}')

urls = [
    'http://httpstat.us/200',
    'http://httpstat.us/400',
    'http://httpstat.us/404',
    'http://httpstat.us/408',
    'http://httpstat.us/500',
    'http://httpstat.us/524'
]
```

```
for url in urls:
    ping(url)

print('Done.')
```

In this program, the `ping()` function takes in a URL and attempts to make a GET request to the site. It will then print out the content of the response returned by the server. In our main program, we have a list of different status codes that we mentioned earlier, each of which we will go through and call the `ping()` function on.

The final output after running the preceding example should be as follows:

```
http://httpstat.us/200:  200 OK
http://httpstat.us/400:  400 Bad Request
http://httpstat.us/404:  404 Not Found
http://httpstat.us/408:  408 Request Timeout
http://httpstat.us/500:  500 Internal Server Error
http://httpstat.us/524:  524 A timeout occurred
Done.
```

We see that our ping test program was able to obtain corresponding responses from the server.

Concurrent web requests

In the context of concurrent programming, we can see that the process of making a request to a web server and obtaining the returned response is independent from the same procedure for a different web server. This is to say that we could apply concurrency and parallelism to our ping test application to speed up our execution.

In the concurrent ping test applications that we are designing, multiple HTTP requests will be made to the server simultaneously and corresponding responses will be sent back to our program, as shown in the following figure. As discussed before, concurrency and parallelism have significant applications in web development, and most servers nowadays have the ability to handle a large amount of requests at the same time:

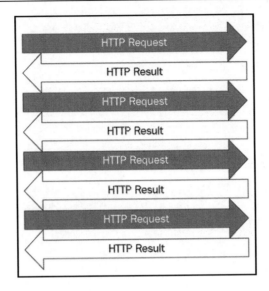

Parallel HTTP requests

Spawning multiple threads

To apply concurrency, we simply use the `threading` module that we have been discussing to create separate threads to handle different web requests. Let's take a look at the `Chapter12/example3.py` file, as shown in the following code:

```
# Chapter12/example3.py

import threading
import requests
import time

def ping(url):
    res = requests.get(url)
    print(f'{url}: {res.text}')

urls = [
    'http://httpstat.us/200',
    'http://httpstat.us/400',
    'http://httpstat.us/404',
    'http://httpstat.us/408',
    'http://httpstat.us/500',
    'http://httpstat.us/524'
]
```

```
start = time.time()
for url in urls:
    ping(url)
print(f'Sequential: {time.time() - start : .2f} seconds')

print()

start = time.time()
threads = []
for url in urls:
    thread = threading.Thread(target=ping, args=(url,))
    threads.append(thread)
    thread.start()
for thread in threads:
    thread.join()

print(f'Threading: {time.time() - start : .2f} seconds')
```

In this example, we are including the sequential logic from the previous example to process our URL list, so that we can compare the improvement in speed when we apply threading to our ping test program. We are also creating a thread to ping each of the URLs in our URL list using the threading module; these threads will be executing independently from each other. Time taken to process the URLs sequentially and concurrently are also tracked using methods from the time module.

Run the program and your output should be similar to the following:

```
http://httpstat.us/200: 200 OK
http://httpstat.us/400: 400 Bad Request
http://httpstat.us/404: 404 Not Found
http://httpstat.us/408: 408 Request Timeout
http://httpstat.us/500: 500 Internal Server Error
http://httpstat.us/524: 524 A timeout occurred
Sequential: 0.82 seconds

http://httpstat.us/404: 404 Not Found
http://httpstat.us/200: 200 OK
http://httpstat.us/400: 400 Bad Request
http://httpstat.us/500: 500 Internal Server Error
http://httpstat.us/524: 524 A timeout occurred
http://httpstat.us/408: 408 Request Timeout
Threading: 0.14 seconds
```

While the specific time that the sequential logic and threading logic take to process all the URLs might be different from system to system, there should still be a clear distinction between the two. Specifically, here we can see that the threading logic was almost six times faster than the sequential logic (which corresponds to the fact that we had six threads processing six URLs in parallel). There is no doubt, then, that concurrency can provide significant speedup for our ping test application specifically and for the process of making web requests in general.

Refactoring request logic

The current version of our ping test application works as intended, but we can improve its readability by refactoring the logic where we make web requests into a thread class. Consider the `Chapter12/example4.py` file, specifically the `MyThread` class:

```
# Chapter12/example4.py

import threading
import requests

class MyThread(threading.Thread):
    def __init__(self, url):
        threading.Thread.__init__(self)
        self.url = url
        self.result = None

    def run(self):
        res = requests.get(self.url)
        self.result = f'{self.url}: {res.text}'
```

In this example, `MyThread` inherits from the `threading.Thread` class and contains two additional attributes: `url` and `result`. The `url` attribute holds the URL that the thread instance should process, and the response returned from the web server to that thread will be written to the `result` attribute (in the `run()` function).

Outside of this class, we now can simply loop through the URL list, and create and manage the threads accordingly while not having to worry about the request logic in the main program:

```
urls = [
    'http://httpstat.us/200',
    'http://httpstat.us/400',
    'http://httpstat.us/404',
    'http://httpstat.us/408',
    'http://httpstat.us/500',
```

```
        'http://httpstat.us/524'
]

start = time.time()

threads = [MyThread(url) for url in urls]
for thread in threads:
    thread.start()
for thread in threads:
    thread.join()
for thread in threads:
    print(thread.result)

print(f'Took {time.time() - start : .2f} seconds')

print('Done.')
```

Note that we are now storing the responses in the `result` attribute of the `MyThread` class, instead of directly printing them out as in the old `ping()` function from the previous examples. This means that, after making sure that all threads have finished, we will need to loop through the threads one more time and print out those responses.

Refactoring the request logic should not greatly affect the performance of our current program; we are keeping track of the execution speed to see if this is actually the case. Execute the program and you will obtain the output similar to the following:

```
http://httpstat.us/200: 200 OK
http://httpstat.us/400: 400 Bad Request
http://httpstat.us/404: 404 Not Found
http://httpstat.us/408: 408 Request Timeout
http://httpstat.us/500: 500 Internal Server Error
http://httpstat.us/524: 524 A timeout occurred
Took 0.14 seconds
Done.
```

Just as we expected, we are still achieving a significant speedup from the sequential version of the program with this refactored request logic. Again, our main program is now more readable, and further adjustments of the request logic (as we will see in the next section) can simply be directed to the `MyThread` class, without affecting the rest of the program.

The problem of timeout

In this section, we will explore a potential improvement to be made to our ping test application: timeout handling. Timeouts typically occur when the server takes an unusually long time to process a specific request, and the connection between the server and its client is terminated.

In the context of a ping test application, we will be implementing a customized threshold for the timeout. Recall that a ping test is used to determine whether specific servers are still responsive, so we can specify in our program that, if a request takes more than our timeout threshold for the server to response, we will categorize that specific server with a timeout.

Support from httpstat.us and simulation in Python

In addition to different options for status codes, the `httpstat.us` website additionally provides a way to simulate a delay in its response when we send in requests. Specifically, we can customize the delay time (in milliseconds) with a query argument in our GET request. For example, `httpstat.us/200?sleep=5000` will return a response after five seconds of delay.

Now, let us see how a delay like this would affect the execution of our program. Consider the `Chapter12/example5.py` file, which contains the current request logic of our ping test application but has a different URL list:

```
# Chapter12/example5.py

import threading
import requests

class MyThread(threading.Thread):
    def __init__(self, url):
        threading.Thread.__init__(self)
        self.url = url
        self.result = None

    def run(self):
        res = requests.get(self.url)
        self.result = f'{self.url}: {res.text}'

urls = [
    'http://httpstat.us/200',
    'http://httpstat.us/200?sleep=20000',
```

```
        'http://httpstat.us/400'
    ]

    threads = [MyThread(url) for url in urls]
    for thread in threads:
        thread.start()
    for thread in threads:
        thread.join()
    for thread in threads:
        print(thread.result)

    print('Done.')
```

Here we have a URL that will take around 20 seconds to return a response. Considering that we will block the main program until all threads finish their execution (with the `join()` method), our program will most likely appear to be hanging for 20 seconds before any response is printed out.

Run the program to experience this for yourself. A 20 second delay will occur (which will make the execution take significantly longer to finish) and we will obtain the following output:

```
http://httpstat.us/200: 200 OK
http://httpstat.us/200?sleep=20000: 200 OK
http://httpstat.us/400: 400 Bad Request
Took 22.60 seconds
Done.
```

Timeout specifications

An efficient ping test application should not be waiting for responses from its websites for a long time; it should have a set threshold for timeout that, if a server fails to return a response under that threshold, the application will deem that server non-responsive. We therefore need to implement a way to keep track of how much time has passed since a request is sent to a server. We will do this by counting down from the timeout threshold and, once that threshold is passed, all responses (whether returned or not yet returned) will be printed out.

Additionally, we will also be keeping track of how many requests are still pending and have not had their responses returned. We will be using the isAlive() method from the threading.Thread class to indirectly determine whether a response has been returned for a specific request: if, at one point, the thread processing a specific request is alive, we can conclude that that specific request is still pending.

Navigate to the Chapter12/example6.py file and consider the process_requests() function first:

```
# Chapter05/example6.py

import time

UPDATE_INTERVAL = 0.01

def process_requests(threads, timeout=5):
    def alive_count():
        alive = [1 if thread.isAlive() else 0 for thread in threads]
        return sum(alive)

    while alive_count() > 0 and timeout > 0:
        timeout -= UPDATE_INTERVAL
        time.sleep(UPDATE_INTERVAL)
    for thread in threads:
        print(thread.result)
```

The function takes in a list of threads that we have been using to make web requests in the previous examples, as well as an optional argument specifying the timeout threshold. Inside this function, we have an inner function, alive_count(), which returns the count of the threads that are still alive at the time of the function call.

In the process_requests() function, as long as there are threads that are currently alive and processing requests, we will allow the threads to continue with their execution (this is done in the while loop with the double condition). The UPDATE_INTERVAL variable, as you can see, specifies how often we check for this condition. If either condition fails (if there are no alive threads left or if the threshold timeout is passed), then we will proceed with printing out the responses (even if some might have not been returned).

Let's turn our attention to the new MyThread class:

```
# Chapter12/example6.py

import threading
import requests

class MyThread(threading.Thread):
```

```
    def __init__(self, url):
        threading.Thread.__init__(self)
        self.url = url
        self.result = f'{self.url}: Custom timeout'

    def run(self):
        res = requests.get(self.url)
        self.result = f'{self.url}: {res.text}'
```

This class is almost identical to the one we considered in the previous example, except that the initial value for the `result` attribute is a message indicating a timeout. In the case that we discussed earlier where the timeout threshold specified in the `process_requests()` function is passed, this initial value will be used when the responses are printed out.

Finally, let's consider our main program:

```
# Chapter12/example6.py

urls = [
    'http://httpstat.us/200',
    'http://httpstat.us/200?sleep=4000',
    'http://httpstat.us/200?sleep=20000',
    'http://httpstat.us/400'
]

start = time.time()

threads = [MyThread(url) for url in urls]
for thread in threads:
    thread.setDaemon(True)
    thread.start()
process_requests(threads)

print(f'Took {time.time() - start : .2f} seconds')

print('Done.')
```

Here, in our URL list, we have a request that would take 4 seconds and another that would take 20 seconds, aside from the ones that would respond immediately. As the timeout threshold that we are using is 5 seconds, theoretically we should be able to see that the 4-second-delay request will successfully obtain a response, while the 20-second-delay one will not.

There is another point to be made about this program: daemon threads. In the `process_requests()` function, if the timeout threshold is passed while there is still at least one thread processing, then the function will proceed to print out the `result` attribute of each thread:

```
while alive_count() > 0 and timeout > 0:
    timeout -= UPDATE_INTERVAL
    time.sleep(UPDATE_INTERVAL)
for thread in threads:
    print(thread.result)
```

This means that we do not block our program until all of the threads have finished their execution by using the `join()` function, and the program therefore can simply move forward if the timeout threshold is reached. However, this means that the threads themselves do not terminate at this point. The 20-second-delay request, specifically, will still most likely be running after our program exits out of the `process_requests()` function.

If the thread processing this request is not a daemon thread (as we know, daemon threads execute in the background and never terminate), it will block the main program from finishing until the thread itself finishes. By making this thread, and any other thread, a daemon thread, we allow the main program to finish as soon as it executes the last line of its instructions, even if there are threads still running.

Let us see this program in action. Execute the code and your output should be similar to the following:

```
http://httpstat.us/200: 200 OK
http://httpstat.us/200?sleep=4000: 200 OK
http://httpstat.us/200?sleep=20000: Custom timeout
http://httpstat.us/400: 400 Bad Request
Took 5.70 seconds
Done.
```

As you can see, it took around 5 seconds for our program to finish this time. This is because it spent 5 seconds waiting for the threads that were still running and, as soon as the 5-second threshold was passed, the program printed out the results. Here we see that the result from the 20-second-delay request was simply the default value of the `result` attribute of the `MyThread` class, while the rest of the requests were able to obtain the correct response from the server (including the 4-second-delay request, since it had enough time to obtain the response).

If you would like to see the effect of non-daemon threads that we discussed earlier, simply comment out the corresponding line of code in our main program, as follows:

```
threads = [MyThread(url) for url in urls]
for thread in threads:
    #thread.setDaemon(True)
    thread.start()
process_requests(threads)
```

You will see that the main program will hang for around 20 seconds, as the non-daemon thread processing the 20-second-delay request is still running, before being able to finish its execution (even though the output produced will be identical).

Good practices in making web requests

There are a few aspects of making concurrent web requests that require careful consideration and implementation. In this section, we will be going over those aspects and some of the best practices that you should use when developing your applications.

Consider the terms of service and data-collecting policies

Unauthorized data collection has been the topic of discussion in the technology world for the past few years, and it will continue to be for a long time—and for good reason too. It is therefore extremely important for developers who are making automated web requests in their applications to look for websites' policies on data collecting. You can find these policies in their terms of service or similar documents. When in doubt, it is generally a good rule of thumb to contact the website directly to ask for more details.

Error handling

Error is something that no one can easily avoid in the field of programming, and this is especially true in making web requests. Errors in these programs can include making bad requests (invalid requests or even bad internet connections), mishandling downloaded HTML code, or unsuccessfully parsing HTML code. It is therefore important to make use of try...except blocks and other error-handling tools in Python to avoid crashing your application. Avoiding crashes is especially important if your code/applications are used in production and larger applications.

Specifically in concurrent web scraping, it might be possible for some threads to collect data successfully, while others fail. By implementing error-handling functionalities in multithreaded parts of your program, you can make sure that a failed thread will not be able to crash the entirety of your program and ensure that successful threads can still return their results.

However, it is important to note that blind error-catching is still undesirable. This term indicates the practice where we have a large `try...expect` block in our program that will catch any and all errors that occur in the program execution, and no further information regarding the errors can be obtained; this practice might also be known as error swallowing. It's highly recommended to have specific error handling code in a program, so that not only appropriate actions can be taken with regards to that specific error, but other errors that have not been taken into account might also reveal themselves.

Update your program regularly

It is quite common for websites to change their request-handling logic as well as their displayed data regularly. If a program that makes requests to a website has considerably inflexible logic to interact with the server of the website (for example, structuring its requests in a specific format, only handling one kind of response), then if and when the website alters the way it handles its client requests, the program will most likely stop functioning correctly. This situation happens frequently with web scraping programs that look for data in specific HTML tags; when the HTML tags are changed, these programs will fail to find their data.

This practice is implemented to prevent automated data collecting programs from functioning. The only way to keep using a website that recently changed its request-handling logic is to analyze the updated protocols and alter our programs accordingly.

Avoid making a large number of requests

Each time one of the programs that we have been discussing runs, it makes HTTP requests to a server that manages the site that you'd like to extract data from. This process happens significantly more frequently and over a shorter amount of time in a concurrent program, where multiple requests are being submitted to that server.

As mentioned before, servers nowadays have the ability to handle multiple requests simultaneously with ease. However, to avoid having to overwork and overconsume resources, servers are also designed to stop answering requests that come in too frequently. Websites of big tech companies, such as Amazon or Twitter, look for large amounts of automated requests that are made from the same IP address and implement different response protocols; some requests might be delayed, some might be refused a response, or the IP address might even be banned from making further requests for a specific amount of time.

Interestingly, making repeated, heavy-duty requests to servers is actually a form of hacking a website. In **Denial of Service (DoS)** and **Distributed Denial of Service (DDoS)** attacks, a very large number of requests are made at the same time to the server, flooding the bandwidth of the targeted server with traffic, and as a result, normal, nonmalicious requests from other clients are denied because the servers are busy processing the concurrent requests, as illustrated in the following diagram:

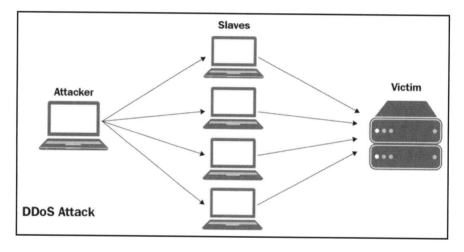

A of a DDoS attack

It is therefore important to space out the concurrent requests that your application makes to a server so that the application would not be considered an attacker and be potentially banned or treated as a malicious client. This could be as simple as limiting the maximum number of threads/requests that can be implemented at a time in your program or pausing the threading for a specific amount of time (for example, using the `time.sleep()` function) before making a request to the server.

Summary

In this chapter, we have learned about the basics of HTML and web requests. The two most common web requests are GET and POST requests. There are five main categories for HTTP response status code, each indicating a different concept regarding the communication between the server and its client. By considering the status codes received from different websites, we can write a ping test application that effectively checks for the responsiveness of those websites.

Concurrency can be applied to the problem of making multiple web requests simultaneously via threading to provide a significant improvement in application speed. However, it is important to keep in mind a number of considerations when make concurrent web requests.

In the next chapter, we will start discussing another major player in concurrent programming: processes. We will be considering the concept of and the basic idea behind a process, and the options that Python provides for us to work with processes.

Questions

- What is HTML?
- What are HTTP requests?
- What are HTTP response status codes?
- How does the requests module help with making web requests?
- What is a ping test and how is one typically designed?
- Why is concurrency applicable in making web requests?
- What are the considerations that need to be made while developing applications that make concurrent web requests?

Further reading

For more information, you can refer to the following links:

- *Automate the boring stuff with Python: practical programming for total beginners*, Al. Sweigart, No Starch Press, 2015
- *Web Scraping with Python*, Richard Lawson, Packt Publishing Ltd, 2015
- *Instant Web Scraping with Java*, Ryan Mitchell, Packt Publishing Ltd, 2013

13
Working with Processes in Python

This chapter is the first of three chapters on using concurrency through multiprocessing programming in Python. We have seen various examples of processes being used in concurrent and parallel programming. In this chapter, you will be introduced to the formal definition of a process, as well as the `multiprocessing` module in Python. This chapter will go through some of the most common ways of working with processes using the API of the `multiprocessing` module, such as the `Process` class, the `Pool` class, and interprocess communication tools such as the `Queue` class. This chapter will also look at the key differences between multithreading and multiprocessing in concurrent programming.

The following topics will be covered in this chapter:

- The concept of a process in the context of concurrent programming in computer science
- The basic API of the `multiprocessing` module in Python
- How to interact with processes and the advanced functionalities that the `multiprocessing` module provides
- How the `multiprocessing` module supports interprocess communication
- The key differences between multiprocessing and multithreading in concurrent programming

Technical requirements

The following is a list of prerequisites for this chapter:

- Install Python 3 on your computer
- Download the GitHub repository at `https://github.com/PacktPublishing/AdvancedPythonProgramming`
- Ensure that you can access the subfolder named `Chapter13`
- Check out the following video to see the Code in Action: `http://bit.ly/2BtwlJw`

The concept of a process

In the field of computer science, a **process of execution** is an instance of a specific computer program or software that is being executed by the operating system. A process contains both the program code and its current activities and interactions with other entities. Depending on the operating system, the implementation of a process can be made up of multiple threads of execution that can execute instructions concurrently or in parallel.

It is important to note that a process is not equivalent to a computer program. While a program is simply a static collection of instructions (program code), a process is instead the actual execution of those instructions. This also means that the same program could be run concurrently by spawning multiple processes. These processes execute the same code from the parent program.

For example, the internet browser Google Chrome usually manages a process called **Google Chrome Helper** for its main program in order to facilitate web browsing and other processes, to assist with various purposes. An easy way to see what different processes your system is running and managing involves using **Task Manager** for Windows, **Activity Monitor** for iOS, and **System Monitor** for Linux operating systems.

The following is a screenshot of my **Activity Monitor**. Multiple processes with the name **Google Chrome Helper** can be seen in the list. The **PID** column (which stands for **process ID**) reports the unique ID that each process has:

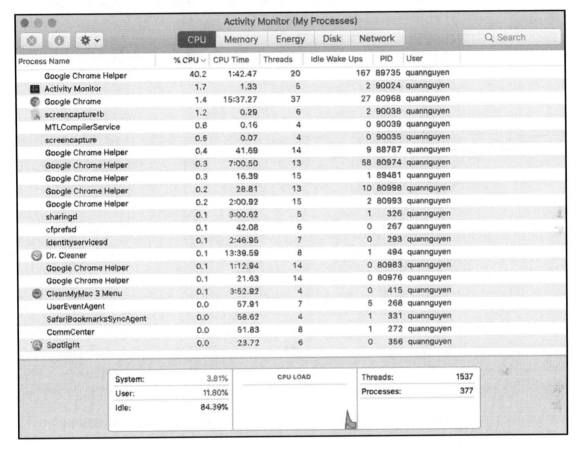

Process Name	% CPU ⌄	CPU Time	Threads	Idle Wake Ups	PID	User
Google Chrome Helper	40.2	1:42.47	20	167	89735	quannguyen
Activity Monitor	1.7	1.33	5	2	90024	quannguyen
Google Chrome	1.4	15:37.27	37	27	80968	quannguyen
screencapturetb	1.2	0.29	6	2	90038	quannguyen
MTLCompilerService	0.6	0.16	4	0	90039	quannguyen
screencapture	0.5	0.07	4	0	90035	quannguyen
Google Chrome Helper	0.4	41.69	14	9	88787	quannguyen
Google Chrome Helper	0.3	7:00.50	13	58	80974	quannguyen
Google Chrome Helper	0.3	16.39	15	1	89481	quannguyen
Google Chrome Helper	0.2	28.81	13	10	80998	quannguyen
Google Chrome Helper	0.2	2:00.92	15	2	80993	quannguyen
sharingd	0.1	3:00.62	5	1	326	quannguyen
cfprefsd	0.1	42.08	6	0	267	quannguyen
identityservicesd	0.1	2:46.95	7	0	293	quannguyen
Dr. Cleaner	0.1	13:39.59	8	1	494	quannguyen
Google Chrome Helper	0.1	1:12.94	14	0	80983	quannguyen
Google Chrome Helper	0.1	21.63	14	0	80976	quannguyen
CleanMyMac 3 Menu	0.1	3:52.92	4	0	415	quannguyen
UserEventAgent	0.0	57.91	7	5	268	quannguyen
SafariBookmarksSyncAgent	0.0	58.62	4	1	331	quannguyen
CommCenter	0.0	51.83	8	1	272	quannguyen
Spotlight	0.0	23.72	6	0	356	quannguyen

System:	3.81%	CPU LOAD	Threads:	1537
User:	11.80%		Processes:	377
Idle:	84.39%			

Sample list of processes

Processes versus threads

One of the most common mistakes that programmers make when developing concurrent and parallel applications is to confuse the structure and functionalities of processes and threads. As we have seen from `Chapter 10`, *Working with Threads in Python*, a thread is the smallest unit of programming code, and is typically a component of a process. Furthermore, more than one thread can be implemented within the same process to access and share memory or other resources, while different processes do not interact in this way. This relationship is shown in the following diagram:

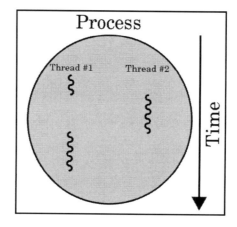

Diagram of two threads executing in one process

Since a process is a larger programming unit than a thread, it is also more complicated and consists of more programming components. A process, therefore, also requires more resources, while a thread does not and is sometimes called a lightweight process. In a typical computer system process, there are a number of main resources, as shown in the following list:

- An image (or copy) of the code being executed from the parent program.
- Memory associated with an instance of a program. This might include executable code, input and output for that specific process, a call stack to manage program-specific events, or a heap that contains generated computation data and is currently being used by the process during runtime.
- Descriptors for the resources allocated to that specific process by the operating system. We have seen an example of these—file descriptors—in `Chapter 11`, *Using the with Statement in Threads*.

- Security components of a specific process, namely the owner of the process and its permissions and allowed operations.
- The processor state, also known as the process context. The context data of a process is often located in processor registers, the memory used by the process, or in control registers used by the operating system to manage the process.

Because each process has a state dedicated to it, processes hold more state information than threads; multiple threads within a process in turn share process states, memory, and other various resources. For similar reasons, processes only interact with each other through system-facilitated interprocess communication methods, while threads can communicate with one another easily through shared resources.

Additionally, context-switching—the act of saving the state data of a process or a thread to interrupt the execution of a task and resume it at a later time—takes more time between different processes than between different threads within the same process. However, while we have seen that communication between threads requires careful memory synchronization to ensure correct data handling, since there is less communication between separate processes, little or no memory synchronization is needed for processes.

Multiprocessing

A common concept in computer science is multitasking. When multitasking, an operating system simply switches between different processes at high speed to give the appearance that these processes are being executed simultaneously, even though it is usually the case that only one process is executing on one single **central processing unit (CPU)** at any given time. In contrast, multiprocessing is the method of using more than one CPU to execute a task.

While there are a number of different uses of the term multiprocessing, in the context of concurrency and parallelism multiprocessing refers to the execution of multiple concurrent processes in an operating system, in which each process is executed on a separate CPU, as opposed to a single process being executed at any given time. By the nature of processes, an operating system needs to have two or more CPUs in order to be able to implement multiprocessing tasks, as it needs to support many processors at the same time and allocate tasks between them appropriately.

This relationship is shown in the following diagram:

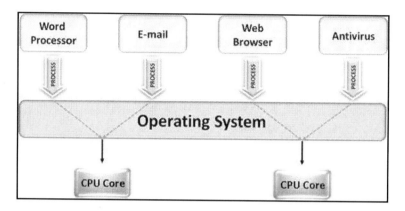

Example diagram of multiprocessing using two CPU cores

We have seen in `Chapter 10`, *Working with Threads in Python*, that multithreading shares a somewhat similar definition to multiprocessing. Multithreading means that only one processor is utilized, and the system switches between tasks within that processor (also known as **time slicing**), while multiprocessing generally denotes the actual concurrent/parallel execution of multiple processes using multiple processors.

Multiprocessing applications have enjoyed significant popularity in the field of concurrent and parallel programming. Some reasons for this are listed as follows:

- **Faster execution time**: As we know, when done correctly concurrency always provides additional speedups for your programs, provided that some parts of them can be executed independently.
- **Synchronization free**: Given the fact that separate processes do not share resources among themselves in a multiprocessing application, developers rarely need to spend their time coordinating the sharing and synchronization of these resources, unlike multithreaded applications, where efforts need to be made to make sure that data is being manipulated correctly.
- **Safety from crashes**: As processes are independent from each other in terms of both computing procedures and input/output, the failure of one process will not affect the execution of another in a multiprocessing program, if handled correctly. This implies that programmers could afford to spawn a larger number of processes (that their system can still handle) and the chance of crashing the entire application would not increase.

With that being said, there are also noteworthy disadvantages to using multiprocessing that we should consider, as shown in the following list:

- **Multiple processors are needed**: Again, multiprocessing requires the operating system to have more than one CPU. Even though multiple processors are fairly common for computer systems nowadays, if yours does not have more than one, then the implementation of multiprocessing will not be possible.
- **Processing time and space**: As mentioned before, there are many complex components involved in implementing a process and its resources. It therefore takes significant computing time and power to spawn and manage processes in comparison to doing the same with threads.

Introductory example in Python

To illustrate the concept of running multiple processes on one operating system, let's look at a quick example in Python. Let's take a look at the `Chapter13/example1.py` file, as shown in the following code:

```
# Chapter13/example1.py

from multiprocessing import Process
import time


def count_down(name, delay):
    print('Process %s starting...' % name)

    counter = 5

    while counter:
        time.sleep(delay)
        print('Process %s counting down: %i...' % (name, counter))
        counter -= 1

    print('Process %s exiting...' % name)


if __name__ == '__main__':
    process1 = Process(target=count_down, args=('A', 0.5))
    process2 = Process(target=count_down, args=('B', 0.5))

    process1.start()
    process2.start()
```

```
        process1.join()
        process2.join()

        print('Done.')
```

In this file, we are going back to the counting-down example that we saw in *Chapter 10, Working with Threads in Python*, while we look at the concept of a thread. Our `count_down()` function takes in a string as a process identifier and a delay time range. It will then count down from 5 to 1 while sleeping between iterations for a number of seconds specified by the `delay` parameter. The function also prints out a message with the process identifier at each iteration.

As we saw in *Chapter 10, Working with Threads in Python*, the point of this counting-down example is to show the concurrent nature of running separate tasks at the same time, this time through different processes by using the `Process` class from the `multiprocessing` module. In our main program, we initialize two processes at the same time to implement two separate time-based countdowns simultaneously. Similar to how two separate threads would do this, our two processes will carry out their own countdowns concurrently.

After running the Python script, your output should be similar to the following:

```
> python example1.py
Process A starting...
Process B starting...
Process B counting down: 5...
Process A counting down: 5...
Process B counting down: 4...
Process A counting down: 4...
Process B counting down: 3...
Process A counting down: 3...
Process B counting down: 2...
Process A counting down: 2...
Process A counting down: 1...
Process B counting down: 1...
Process A exiting...
Process B exiting...
Done.
```

Just as we expected, the output tells us that the two countdowns from the separate processes were executed concurrently; instead of finishing the first process' countdown and then starting the second's, the program ran the two countdowns at almost the same time. Even though processes are more expensive and contain more overhead than threads, multiprocessing also allows double the improvement in terms of speed for programs such as the preceding one.

Remember that in multithreading we saw a phenomenon in which the order of the printed output changed between different runs of the program. Specifically, sometimes process B would get ahead of process A during the countdown and finish before process A, even though it was initialized later. This is, again, a direct result of implementing and starting two processes that execute the same function at almost the same time. By executing the script many times, you will see that it is quite likely for you to obtain changing output in terms of the order of the counting and the completion of the countdowns.

An overview of the multiprocessing module

The multiprocessing module is one of the most commonly used implementations of multiprocessing programming in Python. It offers methods to spawn and interact with processes using an API similar to the threading module (as we saw with the start() and join() methods in the preceding example). According to its documentation website, the module allows both local and remote concurrency and effectively avoids the **global interpreter lock (GIL)** in Python (which we will discuss in more detail later in *Chapter 22, The Global Interpreter Lock*) by using subprocesses instead of threads.

The process class

In the multiprocessing module, processes are typically spawned and managed through the Process class. Each Process object represents an activity that executes in a separate process. Conveniently, the Process class has equivalent methods and APIs that can be found in the threading.Thread class.

Specifically, utilizing an object-oriented programming approach, the Process class from multiprocessing provides the following resources:

- run(): This method is executed when a new process is initialized and started
- start(): This method starts the initialized calling Process object by calling the run() method
- join(): This method waits for the calling Process object to terminate before continuing with the execution of the rest of the program

- `isAlive()`: This method returns a Boolean value indicating whether the calling `Process` object is currently executing
- `name`: This attribute contains the name of the calling `Process` object
- `pid`: This attribute contains the process ID of the calling `Process` object
- `terminate()`: This method terminates the calling `Process` object

As you can see from our previous example, while initializing a `Process` object, we can pass parameters to a function and execute it in a separate process by specifying the `target` (for the target function) and `args` (for target function arguments) parameters. Note that one could also override the default `Process()` constructor and implement one's own `run()` function.

As it is a major player in the `multiprocessing` module and in concurrency in Python in general, we will look at the `Process` class again in the next section.

The Pool class

In the `multiprocessing` module, the `Pool` class is mainly used to implement a pool of processes, each of which will carry out tasks submitted to a `Pool` object. Generally, the `Pool` class is more convenient than the `Process` class, especially if the results returned from your concurrent application should be ordered.

Specifically, we have seen that the order of completion for different items in a list is considerably likely to change when put through a function concurrently as the program runs over and over again. This leads to difficulty when reordering the outputs of the program with respect to the order of the inputs that produced them. One possible solution to this is to create tuples of processes and their outputs, and to sort them by process ID.

This problem is addressed by the `Pool` class: the `Pool.map()` and `Pool.apply()` methods follow the convention of Python's traditional `map()` and `apply()` methods, ensuring that the returned values are ordered in the same way that the input is. These methods, however, block the main program until a process has finished processing. The `Pool` class, therefore, also has the `map_async()` and `apply_async()` functions to better assist concurrency and parallelism.

Determining the current process, waiting, and terminating processes

The `Process` class provides a number of ways to easily interact with processes in a concurrent program. In this section, we will explore the options of managing different processes by determining the current process, waiting, and terminating processes.

Determining the current process

Working with processes is at times considerably difficult, and significant debugging is therefore required. One of the methods of debugging a multiprocessing program is to identify the processes that encounter errors. As a refresher, in the previous countdown example we passed a `name` parameter to the `count_down()` function to determine where each process is during the countdown.

This is, however, unnecessary as each `Process` object has a `name` parameter (with a default value) that can be changed. Naming processes is a better way to keep track of running processes than passing an identifier to the target function itself (as we did earlier), especially in applications with different types of processes running at the same time. One powerful functionality that the `multiprocessing` module provides is the `current_process()` method, which will return the `Process` object that is currently running at any point of a program. This is another way to keep track of running processes effectively and effortlessly.

Let's look at this in more detail using an example. Navigate to the `Chapter13/example2.py` file, as shown in the following code:

```
# Chapter13/example2.py

from multiprocessing import Process, current_process
import time


def f1():
    pname = current_process().name
    print('Starting process %s...' % pname)
    time.sleep(2)
    print('Exiting process %s...' % pname)

def f2():
    pname = current_process().name
    print('Starting process %s...' % pname)
    time.sleep(4)
```

```
      print('Exiting process %s...' % pname)


if __name__ == '__main__':
    p1 = Process(name='Worker 1', target=f1)
    p2 = Process(name='Worker 2', target=f2)
    p3 = Process(target=f1)

    p1.start()
    p2.start()
    p3.start()

    p1.join()
    p2.join()
    p3.join()
```

In this example, we have two dummy functions, f1() and f2(), each of which prints out the name of the process that executes the function before and after sleeping for a specified period of time. In our main program, we initialize three separate processes. The first two we name Worker 1 and Worker 2 respectively, and the last we purposefully leave blank to give it the default value of its name (that is, 'Process-3'). After running the script, you should have an output similar to the following:

```
> python example2.py
Starting process Worker 1...
Starting process Worker 2...
Starting process Process-3...
Exiting process Worker 1...
Exiting process Process-3...
Exiting process Worker 2...
```

We can see that the current_process() successfully helped us access the correct process that ran each function, and the third process was assigned the name Process-3 by default. Another way to keep track of the running processes in your program is to look at the individual process IDs using the os module. Let's take a look at a modified example in the Chapter13/example3.py file, as shown in the following code:

```
# Chapter13/example3.py

from multiprocessing import Process, current_process
import time
import os


def print_info(title):
    print(title)
```

```
    if hasattr(os, 'getppid'):
        print('Parent process ID: %s.' % str(os.getppid()))

    print('Current Process ID: %s.\n' % str(os.getpid()))

def f():
    print_info('Function f')

    pname = current_process().name
    print('Starting process %s...' % pname)
    time.sleep(1)
    print('Exiting process %s...' % pname)


if __name__ == '__main__':
    print_info('Main program')

    p = Process(target=f)
    p.start()
    p.join()

    print('Done.')
```

Our main focus for this example is the `print_info()` function, which uses the `os.getpid()` and `os.getppid()` functions to identify the current process using its process ID. Specifically, `os.getpid()` returns the process ID of the current process, and `os.getppid()` (which is only available on Unix systems) returns the ID of the parent process. The following is my input after running the script:

```
> python example3.py
Main program
Parent process ID: 14806.
Current Process ID: 29010.

Function f
Parent process ID: 29010.
Current Process ID: 29012.

Starting process Process-1...
Exiting process Process-1...
Done.
```

The process IDs might vary from system to system, but their relative relationship should be the same. Specifically for my output, we can see that, while the ID for the main Python program was 29010, the ID of its parent process was 14806. Using **Activity Monitor**, I crosschecked this ID and connected it to my Terminal and Bash profile, which makes sense since I ran this Python script from my Terminal. You can see the displayed results from Activity Monitor in the following screenshot:

Process Name	% CPU	CPU Time	Threads	Idle Wake Ups	PID ∧	User
Terminal	0.0	41.16	6	0	14803	quannguyen
MTLCompilerService	0.0	0.13	2	0	14804	quannguyen
bash	0.0	0.39	1	0	14806	quannguyen

Screenshot of Activity Monitor being used to crosscheck PIDs

In addition to the main Python program, we also called `print_info()` inside the `f()` function, whose process ID was 29012. We can also see that the parent process of the process running the `f()` function is actually our main process, whose ID was 29010.

Waiting for processes

Oftentimes, we'd like to wait for all of our concurrent processes to finish executing before moving to a new section of the program. As mentioned before, the `Process` class from the `multiprocessing` module provides the `join()` method in order to implement a way to wait until a process has completed its task and exits.

However, sometimes developers want to implement processes that run in the background and do not block the main program from exiting. This specification is commonly used when there is no easy way for the main program to tell whether it is appropriate to interrupt the process at any given time, or when exiting the main program without completing the worker does not affect the end result.

These processes are called **daemon processes**. The `Process` class also provides an easy option to specify whether a process is a daemon through the `daemon` attribute, which takes a Boolean value. The default value for the `daemon` attribute is `False`, so setting it to `True` will turn a given process into a daemon. Let's look at this in more detail using an example in the `Chapter13/example4.py` file, as shown in the following code:

```
# Chapter13/example4.py

from multiprocessing import Process, current_process
import time
```

```
def f1():
    p = current_process()
    print('Starting process %s, ID %s...' % (p.name, p.pid))
    time.sleep(4)
    print('Exiting process %s, ID %s...' % (p.name, p.pid))

def f2():
    p = current_process()
    print('Starting process %s, ID %s...' % (p.name, p.pid))
    time.sleep(2)
    print('Exiting process %s, ID %s...' % (p.name, p.pid))


if __name__ == '__main__':
    p1 = Process(name='Worker 1', target=f1)
    p1.daemon = True
    p2 = Process(name='Worker 2', target=f2)

    p1.start()
    time.sleep(1)
    p2.start()
```

In this example, we have a long-running function (represented by f1(), which has a sleep period of 4 seconds) and a faster function (represented by f2(), which has a sleep period of only 2 seconds). We also have two separate processes, as shown in the following list:

- The p1 process, which is a daemon process assigned to run f1()
- The p2 process, which is a regular process assigned to run f2()

In our main program, we start both processes without calling the join() method on either of them at the end of the program. Since p1 is a long-running process, it will most likely not finish executing before p2 (which is the faster process of the two) finishes. We also know that p1 is a daemon process, so our program should exit before it finishes executing. After running the Python script, your output should be similar to the following code:

```
> python example4.py
Starting process Worker 1, ID 33784...
Starting process Worker 2, ID 33788...
Exiting process Worker 2, ID 33788...
```

Again, even though the process IDs might be different when you yourself run the script, the general format of the output should be the same. As we can see, the output is consistent with what we discussed: both p1 and p2 processes were initialized and started by our main program, and the program terminated after the nondaemon process exited without waiting for the daemon process to finish.

The ability to terminate the main program without having to wait for specific tasks that the daemon is processing is indeed extremely useful. However, sometimes we might want to wait for daemon processes for a specified amount of time before exiting; this way, if the specifications of the program allow some waiting time for the process' execution, we could complete some potential daemon processes instead of terminating all of them prematurely.

The combination of daemon processes and the `join()` method from the `multiprocessing` module can help us implement this architecture, especially given that, while the `join()` method blocks the program execution indefinitely (or at least until the task finishes), it is also possible to pass a timeout argument to specify the number of seconds to wait for the process before exiting. Let's consider a modified version of the previous example in `Chapter13/example5.py`. With the same `f1()` and `f2()` functions, in the following script, we are changing the way we handle the daemon process in the main program:

```
# Chapter13/example5.py

if __name__ == '__main__':
    p1 = Process(name='Worker 1', target=f1)
    p1.daemon = True
    p2 = Process(name='Worker 2', target=f2)

    p1.start()
    time.sleep(1)
    p2.start()

    p1.join(1)
    print('Whether Worker 1 is still alive:', p1.is_alive())
    p2.join()
```

Instead of terminating without waiting for the daemon process, in this example, we are calling the `join()` method on both processes: we allow one second for p1 to finish while we block the main program until p2 finishes. If p1 has not finished executing after that one second, the main program simply continues executing the rest of the program and exits, at which time we will see that p1—or `Worker 1`—is still alive. After running the Python script, your output should be similar to the following:

```
> python example5.py
Starting process Worker 1, ID 36027...
Starting process Worker 2, ID 36030...
Whether Worker 1 is still alive: True
Exiting process Worker 2, ID 36030...
```

We see that p1 was indeed still alive by the time the program moved on after waiting for it for one second.

Terminating processes

The `terminate()` method from the `multiprocessing.Process` class offers a way to quickly terminate a process. When the method is called, exit handlers, finally causes, or similar resources that are specified in the `Process` class or an overridden class will not be executed. However, descendant processes of the terminated process will not be terminated. These processes are known as **orphaned processes**.

Although terminating processes is sometimes frowned upon, it is sometimes necessary because some processes interact with interprocess-communication resources, such as locks, semaphores, pipes, or queues, and forcibly stopping those processes is likely to cause those resources to become corrupted or unavailable to other processes. If, however, the processes in your program never interact with the aforementioned resources, the `terminate()` method is considerably useful, especially if a process appears to be unresponsive or deadlocked.

One thing to note when using the `terminate()` method is that, even though the `Process` object is effectively killed after calling the method, it is important that you call `join()` on the object as well. Since the `alive` status of `Process` objects is sometimes not immediately updated after the `terminate()` method, this practice gives the background system an opportunity to implement the update itself to reflect the termination of the processes.

Interprocess communication

While locks are one of the most common synchronization primitives that are used for communication among threads, pipes and queues are the main way of communicating between different processes. Specifically, they provide message-passing options to facilitate communication between processes—pipes for connections between two processes and queues for multiple producers and consumers.

In this section, we will be exploring the usage of queues, specifically the `Queue` class from the `multiprocessing` module. The implementation of the `Queue` class is, in fact, both thread-and process-safe, and we have already seen the use of queues in *Chapter 10, Working with Threads in Python*. All pickleable objects in Python can be passed through a `Queue` object; in this section, we will be using queues to pass messages back and forth between processes.

Using a message queue for interprocess communication is preferred over having shared resources since, if certain processes mishandle and corrupt shared memory and resources while those resources are being shared, then there will be numerous undesirable and unpredictable consequences. If, however, a process failed to handle its message correctly, other items in the queue will remain intact. The following diagram represents the differences in architecture between using a message queue and shared resources (specifically memory) for interprocess communication:

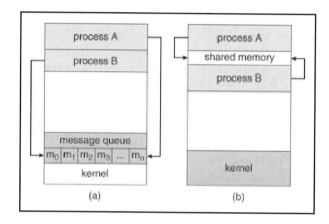

The architecture involved in using a message queue and shared resources for interprocess communication

Message passing for a single worker

Before we dive into the example code in Python, first we need to discuss specifically how we use a `Queue` object in our multiprocessing application. Let's say that we have a `worker` class that performs heavy computations and does not require significant resource sharing and communication. Yet these worker instances still need to be able to receive information from time to time during their execution.

This is where the use of a queue comes in: when we put all the workers in a queue. At the same time, we will also have a number of initialized processes, each of which will go through that queue and process one worker. If a process has finished executing a worker and there are still other workers in the queue, it will move on to another worker and execute it. Looking back at the earlier diagram, we can see that there are two separate processes that keep picking up and executing messages from a queue.

From a `Queue` object, we will be using two main methods, as shown in the following list:

- `get()`: This method returns the next item in the calling `Queue` object
- `put()`: This method adds the parameter passed to it as an additional item to the calling `Queue` object

Let's look at an example script showing the use of a queue in Python. Navigate to and open the `Chapter13/example6.py` file, as shown in the following code:

```
# Chapter13/example6.py

import multiprocessing

class MyWorker():
    def __init__(self, x):
        self.x = x

    def process(self):
        pname = multiprocessing.current_process().name
        print('Starting process %s for number %i...' % (pname, self.x))

def work(q):
    worker = q.get()
    worker.process()

if __name__ == '__main__':
    my_queue = multiprocessing.Queue()

    p = multiprocessing.Process(target=work, args=(my_queue,))
    p.start()

    my_queue.put(MyWorker(10))

    my_queue.close()
    my_queue.join_thread()
    p.join()

    print('Done.')
```

In this script, we have a `MyWorker` class that takes in a number x parameter and performs a computation from it (for now, it will only print out the number). In our main function, we initialize a `Queue` object from the `multiprocessing` module and add a `MyWorker` object with the number 10 in it. We also have the `work()` function, which upon being called will get the first item from the queue and process it. Finally, we have a process whose task is to call the `work()` function.

The structure is designed to pass a message—in this case, a `MyWorker` object—to one single process. The main program then waits for the process to finish executing. After running the script, your output should be similar to the following:

```
> python example6.py
Starting process Process-1 for number 10...
Done.
```

Message passing between several workers

As mentioned earlier, our goal is to have a structure where there are several processes constantly executing workers from a queue, and if a process finishes executing one worker, then it will pick up another. To do this, we will be utilizing a subclass of `Queue` called `JoinableQueue`, which will provide the additional `task_done()` and `join()` methods, as described in the following list:

- `task_done()`: This method tells the program that the calling `JoinableQueue` object is complete
- `join()`: This method blocks until all items in the calling `JoinableQueue` object have been processed

Now the goal here, again, is to have a `JoinableQueue` object holding all the tasks that are to be executed—we will call this the task queue—and a number of processes. As long as there are items (messages) in the task queue, the processes will take their turn to execute those items. We will also have a `Queue` object to store all the results returned from the processes—we will call this the result queue.

Navigate to the `Chapter13/example7.py` file and take a look at the `Consumer` class and the `Task` class, as shown in the following code:

```
# Chapter13/example7.py

from math import sqrt
import multiprocessing

class Consumer(multiprocessing.Process):

    def __init__(self, task_queue, result_queue):
        multiprocessing.Process.__init__(self)
        self.task_queue = task_queue
        self.result_queue = result_queue

    def run(self):
```

```
            pname = self.name

            while not self.task_queue.empty():

                temp_task = self.task_queue.get()

                print('%s processing task: %s' % (pname, temp_task))

                answer = temp_task.process()
                self.task_queue.task_done()
                self.result_queue.put(answer)

class Task():
    def __init__(self, x):
        self.x = x

    def process(self):
        if self.x < 2:
            return '%i is not a prime number.' % self.x

        if self.x == 2:
            return '%i is a prime number.' % self.x

        if self.x % 2 == 0:
            return '%i is not a prime number.' % self.x

        limit = int(sqrt(self.x)) + 1
        for i in range(3, limit, 2):
            if self.x % i == 0:
                    return '%i is not a prime number.' % self.x

        return '%i is a prime number.' % self.x

    def __str__(self):
        return 'Checking if %i is a prime or not.' % self.x
```

The `Consumer` class, which is an overridden subclass of the `multiprocessing.Process` class, is our processor logic, which takes in a task queue and a result queue. When started, each `Consumer` object will get the next item in its task queue, execute it, and finally call `task_done()` and put the returned result to its result queue. Each item in the task queue is in turn represented by the `Task` class, whose main functionality is to prime-check its `x` parameter. As one instance of the `Consumer` class interacts with one instance of the `Task` class, it will also print out a help message for us to easily keep track of which consumer is executing which task.

Let's move on and consider our main program, as shown in the following code:

```
# Chapter13/example7.py

if __name__ == '__main__':
    tasks = multiprocessing.JoinableQueue()
    results = multiprocessing.Queue()

    # spawning consumers with respect to the
    # number cores available in the system
    n_consumers = multiprocessing.cpu_count()
    print('Spawning %i consumers...' % n_consumers)
    consumers = [Consumer(tasks, results) for i in range(n_consumers)]
    for consumer in consumers:
        consumer.start()

    # enqueueing jobs
    my_input = [2, 36, 101, 193, 323, 513, 1327, 100000, 9999999,
433785907]
    for item in my_input:
        tasks.put(Task(item))

    tasks.join()

    for i in range(len(my_input)):
        temp_result = results.get()
        print('Result:', temp_result)

    print('Done.')
```

As we said earlier, we create a task queue and a result queue in our main program. We also create a list of `Consumer` objects and start all of them; the number of processes created corresponds to the number of CPUs available in our system. Next, from a list of inputs that requires heavy computation from the `Task` class, we initialize a `Task` object with each input and put them all in the task queue. At this point our processes—our `Consumer` objects—will start executing these tasks.

Finally, at the end of our main program, we call `join()` on our task queue to ensure that all items have been executed and print out the result by looping through our result queue. After running the script, your output should be similar to the following:

```
> python example7.py
Spawning 4 consumers...
Consumer-3 processing task: Checking if 2 is a prime or not.
Consumer-2 processing task: Checking if 36 is a prime or not.
Consumer-3 processing task: Checking if 101 is a prime or not.
Consumer-2 processing task: Checking if 193 is a prime or not.
```

```
Consumer-3 processing task: Checking if 323 is a prime or not.
Consumer-2 processing task: Checking if 1327 is a prime or not.
Consumer-3 processing task: Checking if 100000 is a prime or not.
Consumer-4 processing task: Checking if 513 is a prime or not.
Consumer-3 processing task: Checking if 9999999 is a prime or not.
Consumer-2 processing task: Checking if 433785907 is a prime or not.
Result: 2 is a prime number.
Result: 36 is not a prime number.
Result: 193 is a prime number.
Result: 101 is a prime number.
Result: 323 is not a prime number.
Result: 1327 is a prime number.
Result: 100000 is not a prime number.
Result: 9999999 is not a prime number.
Result: 513 is not a prime number.
Result: 433785907 is a prime number.
Done.
```

Everything seems to be working, but if we look closely at the messages our processes have printed out, we will notice that most of the tasks were executed by either `Consumer-2` or `Consumer-3`, and that `Consumer-4` executed only one task while `Consumer-1` failed to execute any. What happened here?

Essentially, when one of our consumers—let's say `Consumer-3`—finished executing a task, it tried to look for another task to execute immediately after. Most of the time, it would get priority over other consumers, since it was already being run by the main program. So while `Consumer-2` and `Consumer-3` were constantly finishing their tasks' executions and picking up other tasks to execute, `Consumer-4` was only able to "squeeze" itself in once, and `Consumer-1` failed to do this altogether.

When running the script over and over again, you will notice a similar trend: only one or two consumers executed most of the tasks, while others failed to do this. This situation is undesirable for us, since the program is not utilizing all of the available processes that were created at the beginning of the program.

To address this issue, a technique has been developed, to stop consumers from immediately taking the next item from the task queue, called **poison pill**. The idea is that, after setting up the real tasks in the task queue, we also add in dummy tasks that contain "stop" values and that will have the current consumer hold and allow other consumers to get the next item in the task queue first; hence the name "poison pill."

To implement this technique, we need to add in our `tasks` value in the main program's special objects, one per consumer. Additionally, in our `Consumer` class, the implementation of the logic to handle these special objects is also required. Let's take a look at the `example8.py` file (a modified version of the previous example, containing the implementation of the poison pill technique), specifically in the `Consumer` class and the main program, as shown in the following code:

```
# Chapter13/example8.py

class Consumer(multiprocessing.Process):

    def __init__(self, task_queue, result_queue):
        multiprocessing.Process.__init__(self)
        self.task_queue = task_queue
        self.result_queue = result_queue

    def run(self):
        pname = self.name

        while True:
            temp_task = self.task_queue.get()

            if temp_task is None:
                print('Exiting %s...' % pname)
                self.task_queue.task_done()
                break

            print('%s processing task: %s' % (pname, temp_task))

            answer = temp_task.process()
            self.task_queue.task_done()
            self.result_queue.put(answer)

class Task():
    def __init__(self, x):
        self.x = x

    def process(self):
        if self.x < 2:
            return '%i is not a prime number.' % self.x

        if self.x == 2:
            return '%i is a prime number.' % self.x

        if self.x % 2 == 0:
            return '%i is not a prime number.' % self.x
```

```
        limit = int(sqrt(self.x)) + 1
        for i in range(3, limit, 2):
            if self.x % i == 0:
                return '%i is not a prime number.' % self.x

        return '%i is a prime number.' % self.x

    def __str__(self):
        return 'Checking if %i is a prime or not.' % self.x

if __name__ == '__main__':

    tasks = multiprocessing.JoinableQueue()
    results = multiprocessing.Queue()

    # spawning consumers with respect to the
    # number cores available in the system
    n_consumers = multiprocessing.cpu_count()
    print('Spawning %i consumers...' % n_consumers)
    consumers = [Consumer(tasks, results) for i in range(n_consumers)]
    for consumer in consumers:
        consumer.start()

    # enqueueing jobs
    my_input = [2, 36, 101, 193, 323, 513, 1327, 100000, 9999999,
433785907]
    for item in my_input:
        tasks.put(Task(item))

    for i in range(n_consumers):
        tasks.put(None)

    tasks.join()

    for i in range(len(my_input)):
        temp_result = results.get()
        print('Result:', temp_result)

    print('Done.')
```

The `Task` class remains the same as our previous example. We can see that our poison pill is the `None` value: in the main program, we add in `None` values of a number equal to the number of consumers we have spawned to the task queue; in the `Consumer` class, if the current task to be executed holds the value `None`, then the class object will print out a message indicating the poison pill, call `task_done()`, and exit.

Run the script; your output should be similar to the following:

```
> python example8.py
Spawning 4 consumers...
Consumer-1 processing task: Checking if 2 is a prime or not.
Consumer-2 processing task: Checking if 36 is a prime or not.
Consumer-3 processing task: Checking if 101 is a prime or not.
Consumer-4 processing task: Checking if 193 is a prime or not.
Consumer-1 processing task: Checking if 323 is a prime or not.
Consumer-2 processing task: Checking if 513 is a prime or not.
Consumer-3 processing task: Checking if 1327 is a prime or not.
Consumer-1 processing task: Checking if 100000 is a prime or not.
Consumer-2 processing task: Checking if 9999999 is a prime or not.
Consumer-3 processing task: Checking if 433785907 is a prime or not.
Exiting Consumer-1...
Exiting Consumer-2...
Exiting Consumer-4...
Exiting Consumer-3...
Result: 2 is a prime number.
Result: 36 is not a prime number.
Result: 323 is not a prime number.
Result: 101 is a prime number.
Result: 513 is not a prime number.
Result: 1327 is a prime number.
Result: 100000 is not a prime number.
Result: 9999999 is not a prime number.
Result: 193 is a prime number.
Result: 433785907 is a prime number.
Done.
```

This time, as well as seeing the poison pill messages being printed out, the output also shows a significantly better distribution in terms of which consumer executed which task.

Summary

In the field of computer science, a process is an instance of a specific computer program or software that is being executed by the operating system. A process contains both the program code and its current activities and interactions with other entities. More than one thread can be implemented within the same process to access and share memory or other resources, while different processes do not interact in this way.

In the context of concurrency and parallelism, multiprocessing refers to the execution of multiple concurrent processes from an operating system, in which each process is executed on a separate CPU, as opposed to a single process being executed at any given time. The `multiprocessing` module in Python provides a powerful and flexible API to spawn and manage processes for a multiprocessing application. It also allows complex techniques for interprocess communication via the `Queue` class.

In the next chapter, we will be discussing a more advanced function of Python—reduction operations—and how it is supported in multiprocessing programming.

Questions

- What is a process? What are the core differences between a process and a thread?
- What is multiprocessing? What are the core differences between multiprocessing and multithreading?
- What are the API options provided by the `multiprocessing` module?
- What are the core differences between the `Process` class and the `Pool` class from the `multiprocessing` module?
- What are the options to determine the current process in a Python program?
- What are daemon processes? What are their purposes in terms of waiting for processes in a multiprocessing program?
- How do you terminate a process? Why is it sometimes acceptable to terminate processes?
- What is one of the ways to facilitate interprocess communication in Python?

Further reading

For more information, you can refer to the following links:

- *Python Parallel Programming Cookbook,* by Giancarlo Zaccone, Packt Publishing Ltd (2015).
- "Learning Concurrency in Python: Build highly efficient, robust, and concurrent applications", Elliot Forbes (2017).
- Python Module of The Week. "Communication Between Processes" (pymotw.com/2/multiprocessing/communication.html). This contains functions that you can use to identify the current process.

14
Reduction Operators in Processes

The concept of reduction operators—in which many or all elements of an array are reduced into one single result—is closely associated with concurrent and parallel programming. Specifically, because of the associative and communicative nature of the operators, concurrency and parallelism can be applied to greatly improve their execution time.

This chapter discusses the theoretical concurrent approach to designing and writing a reduction operator from the perspective of programmers and developers. From here, this chapter also makes connections to similar problems that can be solved using concurrency in similar ways.

The following topics will be covered in this chapter:

- The concept of a reduction operator in computer science
- The communicative and associative properties of reduction operators, and therefore the reason why concurrency can be applied
- How to identify problems that are equivalent to a reduction operator and how to apply concurrent programming in such cases

Technical requirements

The following is a list of prerequisites for this chapter:

- You must have Python 3 installed on your computer
- Download the GitHub repository from `https://github.com/PacktPublishing/AdvancedPythonProgramming`
- During this chapter, we will be working with the subfolder titled `Chapter14`
- Check out the following video to see the Code in Action: `http://bit.ly/2TD5odl`

The concept of reduction operators

As experienced programmers, you have undoubtedly encountered situations where you need to calculate the sum or the product of all the numbers in an array, or compute the result of applying the AND operator to all Boolean elements of an array to see whether there is any false value in that array. These are called **reduction operators**, which take a set or an array of elements and perform some form of computation to return only one single result.

Properties of a reduction operator

Not every mathematical or computer science operator is a reduction operator. In fact, even if an operator is capable of reducing an array of elements into one single value, there is no guarantee that it is a reduction operator. An operator is a reduction operator if it satisfies the following conditions:

- The operator can reduce an array of elements into one scalar value
- The end result (the scalar value) must be obtained through creating and computing partial tasks

The first condition is indicative of the phrase "reduction operators", as all elements of the input array have to be combined and reduced into one single value. However, the second condition is, essentially, in terms of concurrency and parallelism. It requires the computation of any reduction operator to be able to be divided into smaller partial computations.

First, let's consider one of the most common reduction operators: addition. For example, consider the input array [1, 4, 8, 3, 2, 5]—the sum of the elements in this array is as follows:

```
  1 + 4 + 8 + 3 + 2 + 5
= (((((1 + 4) + 8) + 3) + 2) + 5
= ((((5 + 8) + 3) + 2) + 5
= (((13 + 3) + 2) + 5
= ((16 + 2) + 5
= 18 + 5
= 23
```

In the preceding computation, we reduced the numbers in our array into their sum, 23, in a sequential order. In other words, we went through each and every element of the array from the beginning to the end and added the current sum. Now, we know that addition is a commutative and associative operator, which means: $a + b = b + a$ and $(a + b) + c = a + (b + c)$.

Therefore, we can perform the preceding computation in a more efficient way by breaking the summation into smaller summations:

```
1 + 4 + 8 + 3 + 2 + 5
= ((1 + 4) + (8 + 3)) + (2 + 5)
= (5 + 11) + 7
= 16 + 7
= 23
```

This technique is at the heart of applying concurrency and parallelism (specifically multiprocessing) to a reduction operator. By breaking the whole task into smaller subtasks, multiple processes can perform those small computations simultaneously, and the system as a whole can arrive at the result much more quickly.

For the same reason, the communicative and associative properties are considered to be equivalent to the requirements for a reduction operator that we discussed earlier. In other words, the operator $\circ$ is a reduction operator that's communicative and associative. Specifically the following:

- Communicative: $a \circ b = b \circ a$
- Associative: $(a \circ b) \circ c = a \circ (b \circ c)$

Here a, b, and c are elements of input arrays.

So, if an operator is a reduction operator, it has to be communicative and associative, and therefore has the ability to break down a big task into smaller, more manageable subtasks, which can be computed in a more efficient way using multiprocessing.

Examples and non-examples

So far, we have seen that addition is one example of a reduction operator. To perform addition as a reduction operator, we first divide the elements from our input array into groups of two, each of which is one of our subtasks. We then perform addition on each group, take the added result from each group, and divide them into groups of two again.

This process continues until we arrive at one single number. This process follows a model called binary tree reduction, which utilizes groups of two to form the subtasks:

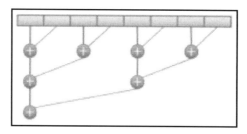

Diagram of binary tree reduction for addition

In the preceding example with the array [1, 4, 8, 3, 2, 5], after dividing the numbers into three different groups of two numbers (1 and 4, 8 and 3, 2 and 5), we used three separate processes to add the pairs of numbers together. We then obtained the array [5, 11, 7], which we used for one process to obtain [16, 7], and again another process to finally obtain 23. So, with three CPUs or more, an addition operator of six elements can be done in $\log_2 6 = 3$ steps instead of five steps in sequential addition.

Other common examples of reduction operators are multiplication and logical AND. For example, reducing the same array of numbers [1, 4, 8, 3, 2, 5] using multiplication as a reduction operator would be done as follows:

```
1 x 4 x 8 x 3 x 2 x 5
= ((1 x 4) x (8 x 3)) x (2 x 5)
= (4 x 24) x 10
= 96 x 10
= 960
```

To reduce an array of Boolean values, for example (True, False, False, True), using the logical AND operator, we could do the following:

```
True AND False AND False AND True
= (True AND False) AND (False AND True)
= False AND False
= False
```

A non-example of reduction operators is the power function, as changing the order of computation would change the final result (that is, the function is not communicative). For example, reducing the array `[2, 1, 2]` sequentially would give us the following:

```
2 ^ 1 ^ 2 = 2 ^ (1 ^ 2) = 2 ^ 1 = 2
```

And if we were to change the order of operation as follows:

```
(2 ^ 1) ^ 2 = 2 ^ 2 = 4
```

We would obtain a different value. Therefore, the power function is not a reduction operation.

Example implementation in Python

As we mentioned previously, due to their communicative and associative properties, reduction operators can have their partial tasks created and processed independently, and this is where concurrency can be applied. To truly understand how a reduction operator utilizes concurrency, let's try implementing a concurrent, multiprocessing reduction operator from scratch—specifically the add operator.

Similar to what we saw in the previous chapter, in this example, we will be using a task queue and a result queue to facilitate our interprocess communication. Specifically, the program will store all of the numbers in the input array in the task queue as individual tasks. As each of our consumers (individual processes) executes, it will call `get()` on the task queue **twice** to obtain two task numbers (except for some edge cases where there is no or only one number left in the task queue), add them together, and put the result in the result queue.

Similar to adding pairs of numbers together, like we did in the previous section, after our processes iterate through the tasks queue one time and put the added pairs of task numbers in the result queue, the number of elements in the input array will have been reduced by half. For example, an input array of `[1, 4, 8, 3, 2, 5]` will become `[5, 11, 7]`.

Now, our program will assign the new task queue to be the result queue (so, in this example, `[5, 11, 7]` is now the new task queue), and our processes will continue going through it and adding pairs of numbers together to generate a new result queue, which will become the next task queue. This process repeats itself until the result queue only contains one element, since we know that that single number is the sum of the numbers in the original input array.

The following diagram shows the changes in the task queue and the result queue in each iteration of processing the input array `[1, 4, 8, 3, 2, 5]`; the process stops when the result queue contains only one number (`23`):

```
┌─────────────────────────────────────────────────────────────────────┐
│ Iteration 1                                                           │
│ Task queue:                                                           │
│ ┌──────────┬──────────┬──────────┬──────────┬──────────┬──────────┐  │
│ │ 1        │ 4        │ 8        │ 3        │ 2        │ 5        │  │
│ └──────────┴──────────┴──────────┴──────────┴──────────┴──────────┘  │
│ Result queue:                                                         │
│ ┌──────────┬──────────┬──────────┐                                   │
│ │ 5        │ 11       │ 7        │                                   │
│ └──────────┴──────────┴──────────┘                                   │
│                                                                       │
│ Iteration 2                                                           │
│ Task queue:                                                           │
│ ┌──────────┬──────────┬──────────┐                                   │
│ │ 5        │ 11       │ 7        │                                   │
│ └──────────┴──────────┴──────────┘                                   │
│ Result queue:                                                         │
│ ┌──────────┬──────────┐                                              │
│ │ 16       │ 7        │                                              │
│ └──────────┴──────────┘                                              │
│                                                                       │
│ Iteration 3                                                           │
│ Task queue:                                                           │
│ ┌──────────┬──────────┐                                              │
│ │ 16       │ 7        │                                              │
│ └──────────┴──────────┘                                              │
│ Result queue:                                                         │
│ ┌──────────┐                                                         │
│ │ 23       │                                                         │
│ └──────────┘                                                         │
└─────────────────────────────────────────────────────────────────────┘
```

Sample diagram of the multiprocessing add operator

Let's take a look at the `ReductionConsumer` class in the `Chapter14/example1.py` file:

```python
# Chapter14/example1.py

class ReductionConsumer(multiprocessing.Process):

    def __init__(self, task_queue, result_queue):
        multiprocessing.Process.__init__(self)
        self.task_queue = task_queue
        self.result_queue = result_queue

    def run(self):
        pname = self.name
        print('Using process %s...' % pname)

        while True:
            num1 = self.task_queue.get()
```

```
        if num1 is None:
            print('Exiting process %s.' % pname)
            self.task_queue.task_done()
            break

        self.task_queue.task_done()
        num2 = self.task_queue.get()
        if num2 is None:
            print('Reaching the end with process %s and number
                    %i.' % (pname, num1))
            self.task_queue.task_done()
            self.result_queue.put(num1)
            break

        print('Running process %s on numbers %i and %i.' % (
                pname, num1, num2))
        self.task_queue.task_done()
        self.result_queue.put(num1 + num2)
```

We implement the `ReductionConsumer` class by overriding the
`multiprocessing.Process` class. This consumer class takes in a task queue and a result
queue when initialized, and handles the consumer process logic of the program, which calls
`get()` twice on the task queue to obtain two numbers from the queue, and adds their sum
to the result queue.

While doing this, the `ReductionConsumer` class also handles cases where there is no or
only one number left in the task queue (that is, when either the `num1` or `num2` variable is
`None`, which, as we know from the previous chapter, is what we use to indicate a poison
pill).

Additionally, recall that the `JoinableQueue` class of the `multiprocessing` module is
used to implement our task queues, and that it requires the `task_done()` function to be
called after each time the `get()` function is called, otherwise the subsequent `join()`
function that we will call on the task queue later will block indefinitely. So, in the case
where the consumer process calls `get()` two times, it is important to call `task_done()` on
the current task queue twice, and when we only call `get()` once (when the first number is a
poison pill), then we should call `task_done()` only once. This is one of the more complex
considerations while working with multiprocessing programs that facilitate interprocess
communication.

To process and coordinate different consumer processes as well as manipulate the task queue and the result queue after each iteration, we have a separate function called `reduce_sum()`:

```
def reduce_sum(array):
    tasks = multiprocessing.JoinableQueue()
    results = multiprocessing.JoinableQueue()
    result_size = len(array)

    n_consumers = multiprocessing.cpu_count()

    for item in array:
        results.put(item)

    while result_size > 1:
        tasks = results
        results = multiprocessing.JoinableQueue()

        consumers = [ReductionConsumer(tasks, results)
                        for i in range(n_consumers)]
        for consumer in consumers:
            consumer.start()

        for i in range(n_consumers):
            tasks.put(None)

        tasks.join()
        result_size = result_size // 2 + (result_size % 2)
        #print('-' * 40)

    return results.get()
```

This function takes in a Python list of numbers to compute the sum of its elements. Aside from a task queue and a result queue, the function also keeps track of another variable called `result_size`, which indicates the number of elements in the current result queue.

After initializing its base variables, the function spawns its consumer processes to reduce the current task queue inside a while loop. As we discussed previously, in each iteration of the while loop, the elements in the task queue are added together pairwise, and the added results are stored in the result queue. After that, the task queue will take over the elements of that result queue, and add additional None values to the queue to implement the poison pill technique.

In each iteration, a new empty result queue is also initialized as a `JoinableQueue` object—this is different from the `multiprocessing.Queue` class that we used for our result queue in the previous chapter, since we will be assigning `tasks = results` at the beginning of the next iteration, and the task queue needs to be a `JoinableQueue` object.

We also update the value of `result_size` at the end of each iteration through `result_size = result_size // 2 + (result_size % 2)`. It is important to note here that while the `qsize()` method from the `JoinableQueue` class is a potential method to keep track of the length of its object (that is, the number of elements in a `JoinableQueue` object), this method is usually considered to be unreliable for various reasons—it is not even implemented in Unix operating systems.

Since we can easily predict how the number of remaining numbers from our input array will change after each iteration (it is halved if it is an even number, otherwise it is halved by integer division, and then `1` is added to that result), we can keep track of that number using a separate variable called `result_size`.

As for our main program for this example, we simply pass a Python list to the `reduce_sum()` function. Here, we are adding numbers from 0 to 19:

```
my_array = [i for i in range(20)]

result = reduce_sum(my_array)
print('Final result: %i.' % result)
```

After running the script, your output should be similar to the following:

```
> python example1.py
Using process ReductionConsumer-1...
Running process ReductionConsumer-1 on numbers 0 and 1.
Using process ReductionConsumer-2...
Running process ReductionConsumer-2 on numbers 2 and 3.
Using process ReductionConsumer-3...

[...Truncated for readability..]

Exiting process ReductionConsumer-17.
Exiting process ReductionConsumer-18.
Exiting process ReductionConsumer-19.
Using process ReductionConsumer-20...
Exiting process ReductionConsumer-20.
Final result: 190.
```

Real-life applications of concurrent reduction operators

The communicative and associative nature of the way reduction operators process their data enables the subtasks of an operator to be processed independently, and is thus highly connected to concurrency and parallelism. Consequently, various topics in concurrent programming could be related to reduction operators, and by applying the same principles of reduction operators, problems regarding those topics could be made more intuitive and efficient.

As we have seen, add and multiply operators are reduction operators. More generally, number-crunching problems that usually involve communicative and associative operators are prime candidates for applying concurrency and parallelism. This is actually a true case for the famous, and arguably one of the most used modules in Python—NumPy, whose code is implemented to be as parallelizable as possible.

Furthermore, applying the logic operators AND, OR, or XOR to an array of Boolean values works the same way as reduction operators. Some real-world applications for concurrent bitwise reduction operators include the following:

- Finite state machines, which commonly take advantage of logic operators while processing logic gates. Finite state machines can be found in both hardware structures and software designs.
- Communication across sockets/ports, which typically involves parity and stop bits to check for data errors, or flow control algorithms. These techniques utilize logic values of individual bytes to process information through the use of logic operators.
- Compression and encryption techniques, which heavily depend on bitwise algorithms.

Summary

Careful considerations need to be made while implementing multiprocessing reduction operators in Python, especially if the program utilizes task queues and result queues to facilitate communication across the consumer processes.

The operations of various real-world problems resemble reduction operators, and the use of concurrency and parallelism for these problems could greatly improve efficiency and thus productivity of the programs processing them. It is therefore important to be able to identify these problems, and relate back to the concept of reduction operators to implement their solutions.

In the next chapter, we will be discussing a specific real-world application for multiprocessing programs in Python: image processing. We will be going over the basic ideas behind image processing and how concurrency—specifically multiprocessing—could be applied to image-processing applications.

Questions

- What is a reduction operator? What conditions must be satisfied so that an operator can be a reduction one?
- What properties do reduction operators have that are equivalent to the required conditions?
- What is the connection between reduction operators and concurrent programming?
- What are some of the considerations that must be made while working with multiprocessing programs that facilitate interprocess communication in Python?
- What are some real-life applications of concurrent reduction operators?

Further reading

For more information, you can refer to the following links:

- *Python Parallel Programming Cookbook*, Giancarlo Zaccone, Packt Publishing Ltd, 2015
- *Learning Concurrency in Python: Build highly efficient, robust, and concurrent applications.*, Elliot Forbes (2017)
- *Parallel Programming in OpenMP*, Morgan Kaufmann, Chandra, Rohit (2001)
- *Fundamentals of Parallel Multicore Architecture*, Yan Solihin (2016), CRC Press

15
Concurrent Image Processing

This chapter analyzes the process of processing and manipulating images through concurrent programming, especially multiprocessing. Since images are processed independently of one another, concurrent programming can provide image processing with a significant speedup. This chapter discusses the basics behind image processing techniques, illustrates the improvements that concurrent programming provides, and finally, goes over some of the best practices used in image processing applications.

The following topics will be covered in this chapter:

- The idea behind image processing and a number of basic techniques in image processing
- How to apply concurrency to image processing, and how to analyze the improvements it provides
- Best practices in concurrent image processing

Technical requirements

Following is a list of prerequisites for this chapter:

- You must have Python 3 installed on your computer
- You must have OpenCV and NumPy installed for your Python 3 distribution
- Download the GitHub repository from `https://github.com/PacktPublishing/AdvancedPythonProgramming`
- During this chapter, we will be working with the subfolder named `Chapter15`
- Check out the following video to see the Code in Action: `http://bit.ly/2R8ydN8`

Image processing fundamentals

Digital/computational image processing (which we will refer to simply as image processing from this point forward) has become so popular in the modern era that it exists in numerous aspects in our everyday life. Image processing and manipulation is involved when you take a picture with your camera or phone using different filters, or when advanced image editing software such as Adobe Photoshop is used, or even when you simply edit images using Microsoft Paint.

Many of the techniques and algorithms used in image processing were developed in the early 1960s for various purposes such as medical imaging, satellite image analysis, character recognition, and so on. However, these image processing techniques required significant computing power, and the fact that the available computer equipment at the time was unable to accommodate the need for fast number-crunching slowed down the use of image processing.

Fast-forwarding to the future, where powerful computers with fast, multicore processors were developed, image processing techniques consequently became much more accessible, and research on image processing increased significantly. Nowadays, numerous image processing applications are being actively developed and studied, including pattern recognition, classification, feature extraction, and so on. Specific image processing techniques, which take advantage of concurrent and parallel programming and would otherwise be extremely computationally time-consuming, include Hidden Markov models, independent component analysis, and even up-and-coming neural network models:

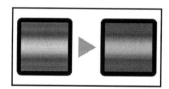

One sample use of image processing: grayscaling

Python as an image processing tool

As we have stated multiple times throughout this book, the Python programming language is on its way to becoming the most popular programming language. This is especially true in the field of computational image processing, which, most of the time, requires fast prototyping and designing, and significant automation capabilities.

As we will find out in the following section, digital images are represented in two-dimensional and three-dimensional matrices so that computers can process them easily. Consequently, most of the time, digital image processing involves matrix calculation. Multiple Python libraries and modules not only provide efficient matrix calculation options, but also interact seamlessly with other libraries that handle image reading/writing.

As we already know, automating tasks and making them concurrent are both Python's strong suit. This makes Python the prime candidate to implement your image processing applications. For this chapter, we will be working with two main Python libraries: **OpenCV** (which stands for **Open Source Computer Vision**), which is a library that provides image processing and computer vision options in C++, Java, and Python, and NumPy, which, as we know, is one of the most popular Python modules and performs efficient and parallelizable number-crunching calculations.

Installing OpenCV and NumPy

To install NumPy for your Python distribution using the `pip` package manager, run the following command:

```
pip install numpy
```

If, however, you are using Anaconda/Miniconda to manage your packages, run the following command:

```
conda install numpy
```

Installing OpenCV might be more complicated, depending on your operating system. The easiest option is to have Anaconda handle the installation process by following this guide (`https://anaconda.org/conda-forge/opencv`) after installing Anaconda (`https://www.anaconda.com/download/`) as your main Python package manager. If, however, you are not using Anaconda, the main option for installing OpenCV is to follow its official documentation guide, which can be found at `https://docs.opencv.org/master/df/d65/tutorial_table_of_content_introduction.html`. After successfully installing OpenCV, open a Python interpreter and try importing the library, as follows:

```
>>> import cv2
>>> print(cv2.__version__)
3.1.0
```

We import OpenCV using the name `cv2`, which is the library alias of OpenCV in Python. The success message indicates the version of my OpenCV library that has been downloaded (3.1.0).

Computer image basics

Before we jump into processing and manipulating digital image files, we first need to discuss the fundamentals of those files, and how computers interpret data from them. Specifically, we need to understand how data regarding the colors and coordinates of individual pixels in an image file is represented, and how to extract it using Python.

RGB values

RGB values are the basics of how colors are represented digitally. Standing for **Red**, **Green**, and **Blue**, **RGB** values are constructed from the fact that all colors can be generated from a specific combination of red, green, and blue. An RGB value therefore is a tuple of three integer numbers, each of which ranges from 0 (which indicates no color at all) to 255 (which indicates the deepest shade of that specific color).

For example, the color red corresponds to the tuple (255, 0, 0); in the tuple, there is only the highest value for red and no value for the other colors, so the whole tuple represents the pure color red. Similarly, blue is represented by (0, 0, 255), and green is represented by (0, 255, 0). The color yellow is the result of mixing equal amounts of red and green, and is therefore represented by (255, 255, 0) (the maximum amount of red and green, with no blue). White, which is the combination of all three colors, is (255, 255, 255), while black, which is the opposite of white and therefore lacks all colors, is represented by (0, 0, 0).

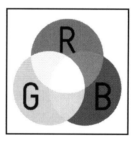

RGB values basics

Pixels and image files

So, an RGB value indicates a specific color, but how do we connect this to a computer image? If we were to view an image on our computer and try to zoom in as much as we can, we would observe that as we zoom in deeper and deeper, the image will start breaking apart into increasingly discernible colored squares—these squares are called pixels, which are the smallest units of color on a computer display or in a digital image:

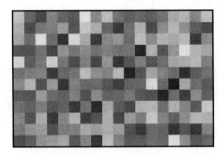

Examples of pixels in digital images

A set of different pixels arranged in a tabular format (rows and columns of pixels) makes up a computer image. Each pixel, in turn, is an RGB value; in other words, a pixel is a tuple of three integers. This means that a computer image is simply a two-dimensional array of tuples, whose sides correspond to the size of the image. For example, a 128 x 128 image has 128 rows and 128 columns of RGB tuples for its data.

Coordinates inside an image

Similar to indexing for two-dimensional arrays, the coordinate for a digital image pixel is a pair of two integers, representing the x- and y-coordinates of that pixel; the x-coordinate indicates the pixel's location along the horizontal axis starting from the left, and the y-coordinate indicates the pixel's location along the vertical axis starting from the top.

Here, we can see how heavy computational number-crunching processes are typically involved when it comes to image processing, as each image is a matrix of integer tuples. This also suggests that, with the help of the NumPy library and concurrent programming, we can implement significant improvements in execution time for Python image processing applications.

Following the convention of indexing two-dimensional arrays in NumPy, the location of a pixel is still a pair of integers, but the first number indicates the index of the row containing the pixel, which corresponds to the *y*-coordinate, and similarly, the second number indicates the *x*-coordinate of the pixel.

OpenCV API

There are a surprising number of methods to read in, perform image processing, and display a digital image file in Python. However, OpenCV provides some of the easiest and most intuitive APIs to do this. One important thing to note regarding OpenCV is that it actually inverts RGB values to BGR values when interpreting its images, so instead of red, green, and blue in order, the tuples in an image matrix will represent blue, green, and red, in that order.

Let's look at an example of interacting with OpenCV in Python. Let's a take look at the `Chapter15/example1.py` file:

```
# Chapter15/example1.py

import cv2

im = cv2.imread('input/ship.jpg')
cv2.imshow('Test', im)
cv2.waitKey(0) # press any key to move forward here

print(im)
print('Type:', type(im))
print('Shape:', im.shape)
print('Top-left pixel:', im[0, 0])

print('Done.')
```

There are a few methods from OpenCV that have been used in this script that we need to discuss:

- `cv2.imread()`: This method takes in a path to an image file (common file extensions include `.jpeg`, `.jpg`, `.png`, and so on) and returns an image object, which, as we will see later, is represented by a NumPy array.
- `cv2.imshow()`: This method takes in a string and an image object and displays it in a separate window. The title of the window is specified by the passed-in string. The method should always be followed by the `cv2.waitKey()` method.

- `cv2.waitKey()`: This method takes in a number and blocks the program for a corresponding number of milliseconds, unless the number 0 is passed in, in which case it will block indefinitely until the user presses a key on their keyboard. This method should always follow the `cv2.imshow()` method.

After calling `cv2.imshow()` on the `ship.jpg` file inside the input subfolder so that it's displayed from the Python interpreter, the program will stop until a key is pressed, at which point it will execute the rest of the program. If run successfully, the script will display the following image:

You should also obtain the following output for the rest of the main program after pressing any key to close the displayed picture:

```
> python example1.py
[[[199 136 86]
  [199 136 86]
  [199 136 86]
  ...,
  [198 140 81]
  [197 139 80]
  [201 143 84]]
```

```
[...Truncated for readability...]

 [[ 56 23 4]
  [ 59 26 7]
  [ 60 27 7]
  ...,
  [ 79 43 7]
  [ 80 44 8]
  [ 75 39 3]]]
Type: <class 'numpy.ndarray'>
Shape: (1118, 1577, 3)
Top-left pixel: [199 136 86]
Done.
```

The output confirms a few of the things that we discussed earlier:

- First, when printing out the image object returned from the `cv2.imread()` function, we obtained a matrix of numbers.
- Using the `type()` method from Python, we found out that the class of this matrix is indeed a NumPy array: `numpy.ndarray`.
- Calling the `shape` attribute of the array, we can see that the image is a three-dimensional matrix of the shape (`1118`, `1577`, `3`), which corresponds to a table with `1118` rows and `1577` columns, each element of which is a pixel (three-number tuple). The numbers for the rows and columns also correspond to the size of the image.
- Focusing on the top-left pixel in the matrix (the first pixel in the first row, that is, `im[0, 0]`), we obtained the BGR value of (`199`, `136`, `86`)—`199` blue, `136` green, and `86` red. By looking up this BGR value through any online converter, we can see that this is a light blue that corresponds to the sky, which is the upper part of the image.

Image processing techniques

We have already seen some Python APIs that are provided by OpenCV to read in data from image files. Before we can use OpenCV to perform various image processing tasks, let's discuss the theoretical foundation for a number of techniques that are commonly used in image processing.

Grayscaling

We saw an example of grayscaling earlier in this chapter. Arguably one of the most used image processing techniques, grayscaling is the process of reducing the dimensionality of the image pixel matrix by only considering the intensity information of each pixel, which is represented by the amount of light available.

As a result, pixels of grayscale images no longer hold three-dimensional information (red, green, and blue), and only one-dimensional black-and-white data. These images are exclusively composed of shades of gray, with black indicating the weakest light intensity and white indicating the strongest.

Grayscaling serves a number of important purposes in image processing. Firstly, as mentioned, it reduces the dimensionality of the image pixel matrix by mapping traditional three-dimensional color data to one-dimensional gray data. So, instead of having to analyze and process three layers of color data, image processing programs only have to do one third of the job with grayscale images. Additionally, by only representing colors using one spectrum, important patterns in the image are more likely to be recognized with just black and white data.

There are multiple algorithms for converting color to grayscale: colorimetric conversion, luma coding, single channel, and so on. Luckily, we do not have to implement one ourselves, as the OpenCV library provides a one-line method to convert normal images to grayscale ones. Still using the image of a ship from the last example, let's look at the `Chapter15/example2.py` file:

```python
# Chapter15/example2.py

import cv2

im = cv2.imread('input/ship.jpg')
gray_im = cv2.cvtColor(im, cv2.COLOR_BGR2GRAY)

cv2.imshow('Grayscale', gray_im)
cv2.waitKey(0) # press any key to move forward here

print(gray_im)
print('Type:', type(gray_im))
print('Shape:', gray_im.shape)
cv2.imwrite('output/gray_ship.jpg', gray_im)

print('Done.')
```

In this example, we are using the `cvtColor()` method from OpenCV to convert our original image to a grayscale one. After running this script, the following image should be displayed on your computer:

Output from Grayscaling

Pressing any key to unblock your program, you should obtain the following output:

```
> python example2.py
[[128 128 128 ..., 129 128 132]
 [125 125 125 ..., 129 128 130]
 [124 125 125 ..., 129 129 130]
 ...,
 [ 20 21 20 ..., 38 39 37]
 [ 19 22 21 ..., 41 42 37]
 [ 21 24 25 ..., 36 37 32]]
Type: <class 'numpy.ndarray'>
Shape: (1118, 1577)
Done.
```

We can see that the structure of our grayscale image object is different from what we saw with our original image object. Even though it is still represented by a NumPy array, it is now a two-dimensional array of integers, each of which ranges from 0 (for black) to 255 (for white). The table of pixels, however, still consists of `1118` rows and `1577` columns.

In this example, we also used the `cv2.imwrite()` method, which saves the image object to your local computer. The grayscale image can therefore be found in the output subfolder of this chapter's folder, as specified in our code.

Thresholding

Another important technique in image processing is thresholding. With the goal of categorizing each pixel in a digital image into different groups (also known as image segmentation), thresholding provides a quick and intuitive way to create binary images (with just black and white pixels).

The idea behind thresholding is to replace each pixel in an image with a white pixel if the pixel's intensity is greater than a previously specified threshold, and with a black pixel if the pixel's intensity is less than that threshold. Similar to the goal of grayscaling, thresholding amplifies the differences between high- and low-intensity pixels, and from that important features and patterns in an image can be recognized and extracted.

Recall that grayscaling converts a fully colored image to a version that only has different shades of gray; in this case, each pixel has a value of an integer ranging from 0 to 255. From a grayscale image, thresholding can convert it to a fully black-and-white one, each pixel of which is now only either 0 (black) or 255 (white). So, after performing thresholding on an image, each pixel of that image can only hold two possible values, also significantly reducing the complexity of our image data.

The key to an effective thresholding process is therefore finding an appropriate threshold so that the pixels in an image are segmented in a way that allows separate regions in the image to become more obvious. The most simple form of thresholding is to use a constant threshold to process all pixels throughout a whole image. Let's consider an example of this method in the `Chapter15/example3.py` file:

```
# Chapter15/example3.py

import cv2

im = cv2.imread('input/ship.jpg')
gray_im = cv2.cvtColor(im, cv2.COLOR_BGR2GRAY)

ret, custom_thresh_im = cv2.threshold(gray_im, 127, 255, cv2.THRESH_BINARY)
```

```
cv2.imwrite('output/custom_thresh_ship.jpg', custom_thresh_im)

print('Done.')
```

In this example, after converting the image of a ship that we have been using to grayscale, we call the `threshold(src, thresh, maxval, type)` function from OpenCV, which takes in the following arguments:

- `src`: This argument takes in the input/source image.
- `thresh`: The constant threshold to be used throughout the image. Here, we are using `127`, as it is simply the middle point between 0 and 255.
- `maxval`: Pixels whose original values are greater than the constant threshold will take this value after the thresholding process. We pass in 255 to specify that those pixels should be completely white.
- `type`: This value indicates the thresholding type used by OpenCV. We are performing a simple binary thresholding, so we pass in `cv2.THRESH_BINARY`.

After running the script, you should be able to find the following image in the output with the name `custom_thresh_ship.jpg`:

Output from simple thresholding

We can see that with a simple threshold (127), we have obtained an image that highlights separate regions of the image: the sky, the ship, and the sea. However, there are a number of problems that this method of simple thresholding poses, the most common of which is finding the appropriate constant threshold. Since different images have different color tones, lighting conditions, and so on, it is undesirable to use a static value across different images as their threshold.

This issue is addressed by adaptive thresholding methods, which calculate the dynamic thresholds for small regions of an image. This process allows the threshold to adjust according to the input image, and not depend solely on a static value. Let's consider two examples of these adaptive thresholding methods, namely Adaptive Mean Thresholding and Adaptive Gaussian Thresholding. Navigate to the Chapter15/example4.py file:

```
# Chapter15/example4.py

import cv2

im = cv2.imread('input/ship.jpg')
im = cv2.cvtColor(im, cv2.COLOR_BGR2GRAY)

mean_thresh_im = cv2.adaptiveThreshold(im, 255, cv2.ADAPTIVE_THRESH_MEAN_C,
cv2.THRESH_BINARY, 11, 2)
cv2.imwrite('output/mean_thresh_ship.jpg', mean_thresh_im)

gauss_thresh_im = cv2.adaptiveThreshold(im, 255,
cv2.ADAPTIVE_THRESH_GAUSSIAN_C, cv2.THRESH_BINARY, 11, 2)
cv2.imwrite('output/gauss_thresh_ship.jpg', gauss_thresh_im)

print('Done.')
```

Similar to what we did with the cv2.threshold() method earlier, here, we again convert the original image to its grayscale version, and then we pass it to the adaptiveThreshold() method from OpenCV. This method takes in similar arguments to the cv2.threshold() method, except that, instead of taking in a constant to be the threshold, it takes in an argument for the adaptive method. We used cv2.ADAPTIVE_THRESH_MEAN_C and cv2.ADAPTIVE_THRESH_GAUSSIAN_C, respectively.

The second to last argument specifies the size of the window to perform thresholding; this number has to be an odd positive integer. Specifically, we used 11 in our example, so for each pixel in the image, the algorithm will consider the neighboring pixels (in an 11 x 11 square surrounding the original pixel). The last argument specifies the adjustment to make for each pixel in the final output. These two arguments, again, help localize the threshold for different regions of the image, thus making the thresholding process more dynamic and, as the name suggests, adaptive.

After running the script, you should be able to find the following images as output with the names `mean_thresh_ship.jpg` and `gauss_thresh_ship.jpg`. The output for `mean_thresh_ship.jpg` is as follows:

Output from mean thresholding

The output for `gauss_thresh_ship.jpg` is as follows:

Output from Gaussian thresholding

We can see that with adaptive thresholding, details in specific regions will be thresholded and highlighted in the final output image. These techniques are useful when we need to recognize small details in an image, while simple thresholding is useful when we only want to extract big regions of an image.

Applying concurrency to image processing

We have talked a lot about the basics of image processing and some common image processing techniques. We also know why image processing is a heavy number-crunching task, and that concurrent and parallel programming can be applied to speed up independent processing tasks. In this section, we will be looking at a specific example on how to implement a concurrent image processing application that can handle a large number of input images.

First, head to the current folder for this chapter's code. Inside the `input` folder, there is a subfolder called `large_input`, which contains 400 images that we will be using for this example. These pictures are different regions in our original ship image, which have been cropped from it using the array-indexing and -slicing options that NumPy provides to slice OpenCV image objects. If you are curious as to how these images were generated, check out the `Chapter15/generate_input.py` file.

Our goal in this section is to implement a program that can concurrently process these images using thresholding. To do this, let's look at the `example5.py` file:

```
from multiprocessing import Pool
import cv2

import sys
from timeit import default_timer as timer


THRESH_METHOD = cv2.ADAPTIVE_THRESH_GAUSSIAN_C
INPUT_PATH = 'input/large_input/'
OUTPUT_PATH = 'output/large_output/'

n = 20
names = ['ship_%i_%i.jpg' % (i, j) for i in range(n) for j in range(n)]


def process_threshold(im, output_name, thresh_method):
    gray_im = cv2.cvtColor(im, cv2.COLOR_BGR2GRAY)
    thresh_im = cv2.adaptiveThreshold(gray_im, 255, thresh_method,
            cv2.THRESH_BINARY, 11, 2)

    cv2.imwrite(OUTPUT_PATH + output_name, thresh_im)


if __name__ == '__main__':

    for n_processes in range(1, 7):
```

```
                  start = timer()

                  with Pool(n_processes) as p:
                      p.starmap(process_threshold, [(
                          cv2.imread(INPUT_PATH + name),
                          name,
                          THRESH_METHOD
                      ) for name in names])

                  print('Took %.4f seconds with %i process(es).
                      ' % (timer() - start, n_processes))

          print('Done.')
```

In this example, we are using the `Pool` class from the `multiprocessing` module to manage our processes. As a refresher, a `Pool` object supplies convenient options to map a sequence of inputs to separate processes using the `Pool.map()` method. We are using the `Pool.starmap()` method in our example, however, to pass multiple arguments to the target function.

At the beginning of our program, we make a number of house-keeping assignments: the thresholding method to perform adaptive thresholding when processing the images, paths for the input and output folders, and the names of the images to process. The `process_threshold()` function is what we use to actually process the images; which takes in an image object, the name for the processed version of the image, and which thresholding method to use. Again, this is why we need to use the `Pool.starmap()` method instead of the traditional `Pool.map()` method.

In the main program, to demonstrate the differences between sequential and multiprocessing image processing, we want to run our program with different numbers of processes, specifically from one single process to six different processes. In each iteration of the `for` loop, we initialize a `Pool` object and map the necessary arguments of each image to the `process_threshold()` function, while keeping track of how much time it takes to process and save all of the images.

After running the script, the processed images can be found in the `output/large_output/` subfolder in our current chapter's folder. You should obtain an output similar to the following:

```
> python example5.py
Took 0.6590 seconds with 1 process(es).
Took 0.3190 seconds with 2 process(es).
Took 0.3227 seconds with 3 process(es).
Took 0.3360 seconds with 4 process(es).
Took 0.3338 seconds with 5 process(es).
```

```
Took 0.3319 seconds with 6 process(es).
Done.
```

We can see a big difference in execution time when we go from one single process to two separate processes. However, there is negligible or even negative speedup after going from two to higher numbers of processes. Generally, this is because of the heavy overhead, which is the product of implementing a large number of separate processes, in comparison to a relatively low number of inputs. Even though we are not implementing this comparison in the interest of simplicity, with an increased number of inputs we would see better improvements from a high number of working processes.

So far, we have seen that concurrent programming could provide a significant speedup for image processing applications. However, if we take a look at our preceding program, we can see that there are additional adjustments that we can make to improve the execution time even further. Specifically, in our preceding program, we are reading in images in a sequential way by using list comprehension in the following line:

```
with Pool(n_processes) as p:
    p.starmap(process_threshold, [(
        cv2.imread(INPUT_PATH + name),
        name,
        THRESH_METHOD
    ) for name in names])
```

Theoretically, if we were to make the process of reading in different image files concurrent, we could also gain additional speedup with our program. This is especially true in an image processing application that deals with large input files, where significant time is spent on waiting for input to be read. With that in mind, let's consider the following example, in which we will implement concurrent input/output processing. Navigate to the example6.py file:

```
from multiprocessing import Pool
import cv2

import sys
from functools import partial
from timeit import default_timer as timer


THRESH_METHOD = cv2.ADAPTIVE_THRESH_GAUSSIAN_C
INPUT_PATH = 'input/large_input/'
OUTPUT_PATH = 'output/large_output/'

n = 20
names = ['ship_%i_%i.jpg' % (i, j) for i in range(n) for j in range(n)]
```

```
def process_threshold(name, thresh_method):
    im = cv2.imread(INPUT_PATH + name)
    gray_im = cv2.cvtColor(im, cv2.COLOR_BGR2GRAY)
    thresh_im = cv2.adaptiveThreshold(gray_im, 255, thresh_method,
cv2.THRESH_BINARY, 11, 2)

    cv2.imwrite(OUTPUT_PATH + name, thresh_im)


if __name__ == '__main__':

    for n_processes in range(1, 7):
        start = timer()

        with Pool(n_processes) as p:
            p.map(partial(process_threshold, thresh_method=THRESH_METHOD),
names)

        print('Took %.4f seconds with %i process(es).' % (timer() - start,
n_processes))
    print('Done.')
```

The structure of this program is similar to that of the previous one. However, instead of preparing the necessary images to be processed and other relevant input information, we implement them inside the `process_threshold()` function, which now only takes the name of the input image and handles reading the image itself.

As a side note, we are using Python's built-in `functools.partial()` method in our main program to pass in a partial argument (hence the name), specifically `thresh_method`, to the `process_threshold()` function, as this argument is fixed across all images and processes. More information about this tool can be found at `https://docs.python.org/3/library/functools.html`.

After running the script, you should obtain an output similar to the following:

```
> python example6.py
Took 0.5300 seconds with 1 process(es).
Took 0.4133 seconds with 2 process(es).
Took 0.2154 seconds with 3 process(es).
Took 0.2147 seconds with 4 process(es).
Took 0.2213 seconds with 5 process(es).
Took 0.2329 seconds with 6 process(es).
Done.
```

Compared to our last output, this implementation of the application indeed gives us a significantly better execution time.

Good concurrent image processing practices

Up until this point, you have most likely realized that image processing is quite an involved process, and implementing concurrent and parallel programming in an image processing application can add more complexity to our work. There are, however, good practices that will guide us in the right direction while developing our image processing applications. The following section discusses some of the most common practices that we should keep in mind.

Choosing the correct way (out of many)

We have hinted at this practice briefly when we learned about thresholding. How an image processing application handles and processes its image data heavily depends on the problems it is supposed to solve, and what kind of data will be fed to it. Therefore, there is significant variability when it comes to choosing specific parameters when processing your image.

For example, as we have seen earlier, there are various ways to threshold an image, and each will result in very different output: if you want to focus on only the large, distinct regions of an image, simple constant thresholding will prove to be more beneficial than adaptive thresholding; if, however, you want to highlight small changes in the details of an image, adaptive thresholding will be significantly better.

Let's consider another example, in which we will see how tuning a specific parameter for an image processing function results in better output. In this example, we are using a simple Haar Cascade model to detect faces in images. We will not go too deeply into how the model handles and processes its data, since it is already built into OpenCV; again, we are only using this model on a high level, changing its parameters to obtain different results.

Navigate to the `example7.py` file in this chapter's folder. The script is designed to detect faces in the `obama1.jpeg` and `obama2.jpg` images in our input folder:

```
import cv2

face_cascade =
cv2.CascadeClassifier('input/haarcascade_frontalface_default.xml')

for filename in ['obama1.jpeg', 'obama2.jpg']:
    im = cv2.imread('input/' + filename)
    gray_im = cv2.cvtColor(im, cv2.COLOR_BGR2GRAY)
```

```
faces = face_cascade.detectMultiScale(im)

for (x, y, w, h) in faces:
    cv2.rectangle(im, (x, y), (x + w, y + h), (0, 255, 0), 2)

cv2.imshow('%i face(s) found' % len(faces), im)
cv2.waitKey(0)

print('Done.')
```

First, the program loads the pretrained Haar Cascade model from the input folder using the cv2.CascadeClassifier class. For each input image, the script converts it to grayscale and feeds it to the pretrained model. The script then draws a green rectangle around each face found in the image, and finally displays it in a separate window.

Run the program, and you will see the following image with the title 5 face(s) found:

Correct face detection

It looks like our program is working well so far. Press any key to continue, and you should see the following image with the title `7 face(s) found`:

Incorrect face detection

Now, our program is mistaking some other objects as actual faces, resulting in two false-positives. The reason behind this involves how the pretrained model was created. Specifically, the Haar Cascade model used a training dataset with images of specific (pixel) sizes, and when an input image contains faces of different sizes—which is common when it is a group picture with some people being close to the camera, while others are far away—is fed into this model, it will cause false-positives in the output.

The `scaleFactor` parameter in the `detectMultiScale` method of the `cv2.CascadeClassifier` class addresses this issue. This parameter will scale down different areas of the input image before trying to predict whether those areas contain a face or not—doing this negates the potential difference in face sizes. To implement this, change the line where we pass the input images to the model to the following to specify the `scaleFactor` parameter as `1.2`:

```
faces = face_cascade.detectMultiScale(im, scaleFactor=1.2)
```

Run the program, and you will see that this time our application is able to correctly detect all of the faces in our input images without making any false-positives.

From this example, we can see that it is important to know about the potential challenges that the input images will pose to your image processing application in execution, and to try different methods or parameters within one method of processing to achieve the best results.

Spawning an appropriate number of processes

One point we noticed in our example for concurrent image processing is that the task of spawning processes takes a considerable amount of time. Due to this, if the number of processes available to analyze the data is too high in comparison to the amount of input, the improvement in execution time received from increasing the number of working processes will diminish and sometimes even become negative.

However, there is no concrete way to tell whether a specific number of separate processes is appropriate for a program unless we also take into account its input images. For example, if the input images are relatively large files, and it takes a significant amount of time for the program to load them from storage, having a larger number of processes might be beneficial; when some processes are waiting for their images to load, others can proceed to perform processing on theirs. In other words, having a larger number of processes will allow for some overlapping between loading and processing time, which will result in better speedup.

In short, it is important to test out different processes that are available for your image processing application to see what the optimal number for scalability is.

Processing input/output concurrently

We saw that loading input images in a sequential way might have a negative effect on the execution time of an image processing application, as opposed to allowing separate processes to load their own inputs. This is specifically true if the image files are significantly large, as the loading time in separate processes might overlap with the loading/processing time in other processes. The same is applicable for writing output images to files.

Summary

Image processing is the task of analyzing and manipulating digital image files to create new versions of the images or to extract important data from them. These digital images are represented by tables of pixels, which are RGB values, or in essence, tuples of numbers. Therefore, digital images are simply multidimensional matrices of numbers, which results in the fact that image processing tasks typically come down to heavy number-crunching.

Since images can be analyzed and processed independently from each other in an image processing application, concurrent and parallel programming – specifically multiprocessing – provides a way to achieve significant improvements in execution time for the application. Additionally, there are a number of good practices to follow while implementing your own concurrent image processing program.

So far in this book, we have covered the main two forms of concurrent programming: multithreading and multiprocessing. In the next chapter, we will be moving on to the topic of asynchronous I/O, which is also one of the key elements of concurrency and parallelism.

Questions

- What is an image processing task?
- What is the smallest unit of digital imaging? How is it represented in computers?
- What is grayscaling? What purpose does this technique serve?
- What is thresholding? What purpose does this technique serve?
- Why should image processing be made concurrent?
- What are some good practices for concurrent image processing?

Further reading

For more information, you can refer to the following links:

- Automate the Boring Stuff with Python: Practical Programming for Total Beginners, Al Sweigart, No Starch Press, 2015
- *Learning Image Processing with OpenCV*, Garcia, Gloria Bueno, et al, Packt Publishing Ltd, 2015
- A Computational Introduction to Digital Image Processing, Alasdair McAndrew, Chapman and Hall/CRC, 2015
- Howse, J., P. Joshi, and M. Beyeler. OpenCV: *Computer Vision Projects with Python.* Packt Publishing Ltd, 2016

16
Introduction to Asynchronous Programming

In this chapter, we will introduce readers to the formal definition of asynchronous programming. We will be discussing the basic idea behind asynchronous processing, the differences between asynchronous programming and other programming models that we have seen, and the reason why asynchronous programming is such a major factor in concurrency.

The following topics will be covered in this chapter:

- The concept of asynchronous programming
- The key differences between asynchronous programming and other programming models

Technical requirements

The following is a list of prerequisites for this chapter:

- You must have Python 3 installed on your computer
- Download the GitHub repository from `https://github.com/PacktPublishing/AdvancedPythonProgramming`
- During this chapter, we will be working with the subfolder titled `Chapter16`, so make sure that you have it at the ready
- Check out the following video to see the Code in Action: `http://bit.ly/2DF700L`

A quick analogy

Asynchronous programming is a model of programming that focuses on coordinating different tasks in an application. Its goal is to ensure that the application finishes executing those tasks in the smallest amount of time possible. From this perspective, asynchronous programming is about switching from one task to another when it is appropriate to create overlapping between waiting and processing time, and from there, shorten the total time taken to finish the whole program.

To understand the underlying idea of asynchronous programming, let's consider a quick, real-life analogy. Imagine a scenario in which you are cooking a three-course meal that contains the following:

- An appetizer that will take 2 minutes of preparation and 3 minutes of cooking/waiting
- A main course that will take 5 minutes of preparation and 10 minutes of cooking/waiting
- A dessert that will take 3 minutes of preparation and 5 minutes of cooking/waiting

Now, considering the order in which the courses finish cooking, your goal is to determine a way to produce the three courses that will take the least amount of time. For example, if we are cooking the courses in a sequential way, we will finish the appetizer first, which will take 5 minutes, then we will move on to the main course, which will take 15 minutes, and then finally the dessert, which will take 8 minutes, respectively. In total, the whole meal will take 28 minutes to finish.

The key to finding a quicker way to go about this is to **overlap** the cooking/waiting time of one course with the preparation time of another. Since you will not be occupied while waiting for the food that has already been prepared for cooking, this time could be saved by preparing the food for another dish. For example, improvements could be achieved through the following steps:

- Preparing the appetizer: 2 minutes.
- Preparing the main course while waiting for the appetizer to cook: 5 minutes. The appetizer will have finished during this step.
- Preparing and cooking the dessert while waiting for the main course to cook: 8 minutes. The dessert will have finished during this step, and the main course will have 2 minutes of cooking remaining.
- Waiting for the main course to finish cooking: 2 minutes. The main course will have cooking finished during this step.

By overlapping the time, we have saved a significant amount of time cooking the three meals, which now takes only 17 minutes in total, compared to 28 minutes if we had done this in the sequential way. However, there is obviously more than one way to decide which dish we should start first, and which dish should be cooked second and last. Another variation of the cooking order could be as follows:

- Preparing the main course: 5 minutes.
- Preparing the appetizer while waiting for the main course to cook: 2 minutes. The main course will have 8 minutes of cooking left.
- Preparing the dessert while waiting for the appetizer and the main course to cook: 3 minutes. The appetizer will have finished during this step, and the main course will have 5 minutes of cooking left.
- Waiting for the main course and the dessert to finish cooking: 5 minutes. Both the main course and the dessert will have finished during this step.

This time, it only takes 15 minutes in total to produce the whole meal. As we can see, different variations of the cooking order might result in a different total cooking time. Finding the best order to execute and switch between tasks in a program is the main idea behind asynchronous programming: instead of executing all of the instructions of that program in a sequential way, we coordinate those instructions so that we can create overlapped waiting and processing times and finally achieve a better execution time.

Asynchronous versus other programming models

Asynchronous programming is one of the major concepts in concurrency specifically, and in programming in general. However, it is quite a complex concept that can be considerably challenging for us to sometimes differentiate it from other programming models. In this section, we will be comparing asynchronous programming with synchronous programming and other concurrent programming models that we have seen (that is, threading and multiprocessing).

Asynchronous versus synchronous programming

Again, asynchronous programming is fundamentally different from synchronous programming because of its task-switching nature. In synchronous programming, the instructions of a program are executed sequentially: a task has to have finished executing before the next task in the program starts processing. With asynchronous programming, if the current task takes significant time to finish, you have the option to specify a time during the task at which the execution is switched to another task. As we have observed, doing this would result in potential improvements in the execution time of the whole program.

One common example of asynchronous programming is the interaction between a server and a client during an HTTP request. If HTTP requests were synchronous, clients would have to wait after making a request until receiving the response from the server. Imagine a scenario in which your browser would hang every time you go to a new link or start playing a video until the actual data returns from the server. This would be extremely inconvenient and inefficient for HTTP communication.

A better approach is asynchronous communication, where the client is free to continue working, and when data from the requests made returns from the server is when the client will be notified and proceed to process that data. Asynchronous programming is so common in web development that a whole programming model called **AJAX** (short for **Asynchronous JavaScript and XML**) is now used in almost every website. Additionally, if you have used common libraries in JavaScript such as jQuery or Node.js, chances are you have worked with, or at least heard the term **callback**, which simply means a function that can be passed to another function to execute later in the future. Switching back and forth between the execution of functions is the main idea of asynchronous programming.

The following diagram further illustrates the difference between synchronous and asynchronous client-server communication:

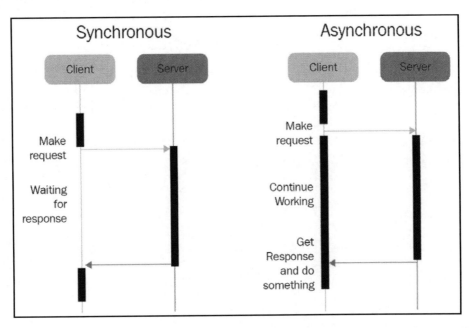

Differences between synchronous and asynchronous HTTP requests

Asynchronous programming is, of course, not limited to HTTP requests. Tasks that involve general network communication, software data processing, interaction with databases, and so on all take advantage of asynchronous programming. Contrary to synchronous programming, asynchronous programming provides responsiveness for users by preventing the program from hanging while waiting for data. Therefore, it is a great tool to implement in programs that deal with a large amount of data.

Asynchronous versus threading and multiprocessing

While providing somewhat similar benefits to those that threading and multiprocessing provide, asynchronous programming is fundamentally different from these two programming models, especially in the Python programming language.

As we know, in multiprocessing, multiple copies of our main program—together with its instructions and variables—are created and executed independently across different cores. Threads, which are also known as lightweight processes, operate on the same basis: although the code is not executed in separate cores, independent portions of the code that are executed in separate threads do not interact with one another either.

Asynchronous programming, on the other hand, keeps all of the instructions of a program in the same thread and process. The main idea behind asynchronous programming is to have a single executor to switch from one task to another if it is more efficient (in terms of execution time) to simply wait for the first task while processing the second. This means that asynchronous programming will not take advantage of the multiple cores that a system might have.

An example in Python

While we will go into more depth regarding how asynchronous programming can be implemented in Python and the main tools we will be using, including the `asyncio` module, let's consider how asynchronous programming can improve the execution time of our Python programs.

Let's take a look at the `Chapter16/example1.py` file:

```python
# Chapter16/example1.py

from math import sqrt

def is_prime(x):
    print('Processing %i...' % x)

    if x < 2:
        print('%i is not a prime number.' % x)

    elif x == 2:
        print('%i is a prime number.' % x)

    elif x % 2 == 0:
        print('%i is not a prime number.' % x)

    else:
        limit = int(sqrt(x)) + 1
        for i in range(3, limit, 2):
            if x % i == 0:
                print('%i is not a prime number.' % x)
                return
```

```
        print('%i is a prime number.' % x)

if __name__ == '__main__':

    is_prime(9637529763296797)
    is_prime(427920331)
    is_prime(157)
```

Here, we have our familiar prime-checking `is_prime()` function, which takes in an integer and prints out a message indicating whether that input is a prime number or not. In our main program, we call `is_prime()` on three different numbers. We are also keeping track of how much time it takes for our program to process all three numbers.

Once you execute the script, your output should be similar to the following:

```
> python example1.py
Processing 9637529763296797...
9637529763296797 is a prime number.
Processing 427920331...
427920331 is a prime number.
Processing 157...
157 is a prime number.
```

You have probably noticed that the program took quite some time to process the first input. Because of the way the `is_prime()` function is implemented, if the input of the prime number is large, then it takes `is_prime()` longer to process it. So, since we have a large prime number as the first input, our Python program will hang for a significant amount of time before printing out the output. This typically creates a non-responsive feel for our program, which is not desirable in both software engineering and web development.

To improve the responsiveness of the program, we will take advantage of the `asyncio` module, which has been implemented in the `Chapter16/example2.py` file:

```
# Chapter16/example2.py

from math import sqrt

import asyncio

async def is_prime(x):
    print('Processing %i...' % x)

    if x < 2:
        print('%i is not a prime number.' % x)

    elif x == 2:
```

```
            print('%i is a prime number.' % x)

        elif x % 2 == 0:
            print('%i is not a prime number.' % x)

        else:
            limit = int(sqrt(x)) + 1
            for i in range(3, limit, 2):
                if x % i == 0:
                    print('%i is not a prime number.' % x)
                    return
                elif i % 100000 == 1:
                    #print('Here!')
                    await asyncio.sleep(0)

            print('%i is a prime number.' % x)

async def main():

    task1 = loop.create_task(is_prime(9637529763296797))
    task2 = loop.create_task(is_prime(427920331))
    task3 = loop.create_task(is_prime(157))

    await asyncio.wait([task1, task2, task3])

if __name__ == '__main__':
    try:
        loop = asyncio.get_event_loop()
        loop.run_until_complete(main())
    except Exception as e:
        print('There was a problem:')
        print(str(e))
    finally:
        loop.close()
```

We will go into the details of this code in the next chapter. For now, simply run the script, and you will see an improvement in responsiveness in the printed output:

```
> python example2.py
Processing 9637529763296797...
Processing 427920331...
427920331 is a prime number.
Processing 157...
157 is a prime number.
9637529763296797 is a prime number.
```

Specifically, while `9637529763296797` (our largest input) was being processed, the program decided to switch to the next inputs. Therefore, the results for `427920331` and `157` were returned before it, hence improving the responsiveness of the program.

Summary

Asynchronous programming is a programming model that is based on task coordination through task switching. It is different from traditional sequential (or synchronous) programming since it creates an overlap between processing and waiting time, which provides potential improvements in speed. Asynchronous programming is also different from threading and multiprocessing, as it only takes place within one single thread in one single process.

Asynchronous programming is mostly used to improve the responsiveness of a program. When a large input takes a significant amount of time to process, the sequential version of a program will appear to be hanging, while the asynchronous program will move to other less heavy tasks. This allows small inputs to finish executing first and help the program to be more responsive.

In the next chapter, we will learn about the main structure of an asynchronous program and look into the `asyncio` module and its functionalities in more detail.

Questions

- What is the idea behind asynchronous programming?
- How is asynchronous programming different from synchronous programming?
- How is asynchronous programming different from threading and multiprocessing?

Further reading

For more information, you can refer to the following links:

- *Parallel Programming with Python,* by Jan Palach, Packt Publishing Ltd, 2014
- *Python Parallel Programming Cookbook,* by Giancarlo Zaccone, Packt Publishing Ltd, 2015
- *RabbitMQ Cookbook,* by Sigismondo Boschi and Gabriele Santomaggio, Packt Publishing Ltd, 2013

17
Implementing Asynchronous Programming in Python

This chapter will introduce you to the `asyncio` module in Python. It will cover the idea behind this new concurrency module, which utilizes event loops and coroutines and provides an API that is as readable as synchronous code. In this chapter, we will also discuss the implementation of asynchronous programming, in addition to threading and multiprocessing through the `concurrent.futures` module. During this process, we will cover the application of asynchronous programming via the most common uses of `asyncio`, including asynchronous input/output and avoiding blocking tasks.

The following topics will be covered in this chapter:

- The fundamental elements of implementing asynchronous programming using `asyncio`
- The framework for asynchronous programming provided by `asyncio`
- The `concurrent.futures` module and its usage, in respect to `asyncio`

Technical requirements

The following is the list a prerequisites for this chapter:

- Ensure that you have Python 3 installed on your computer
- Download the GitHub repository at `https://github.com/PacktPublishing/AdvancedPythonProgramming`
- During this chapter, we will be working with the subfolder titled `Chapter17`
- Check out the following video to see the Code in Action: `http://bit.ly/2TAtTrA`

The asyncio module

As you saw in the previous chapter, the `asyncio` module provides an easy way to convert a sequential program to an asynchronous one. In this section, we will be discussing the general structure of an asynchronous program, and subsequently, how to implement the conversion from a sequential to an asynchronous program in Python.

Coroutines, event loops, and futures

There are a few common elements that most asynchronous programs have, and coroutines, event loops, and futures are three of those elements. They are defined as follows:

- **Event loops** are the main coordinators of tasks in an asynchronous program. An event loop keeps track of all of the tasks that are to be run asynchronously, and decides which of those tasks should be executed at a given moment. In other words, event loops handle the task switching aspect (or the execution flow) of asynchronous programming.
- **Coroutines** are a special type of function that wrap around specific tasks, so that they can be executed asynchronously. A coroutine is required in order to specify where in the function the task switching should take place; in other words, they specify when the function should give back the flow of execution to the event loop. The tasks for coroutines are typically either stored in a task queue or created inside the event loop.
- **Futures** are placeholders for the results returned from coroutines. These future objects are created as soon as coroutines are initiated in the event loop, so futures can represent actual results, pending results (if the coroutines have not finished executing), or even an exception (if that is what the coroutine will return).

An event loop, coroutines, and their corresponding futures, are the core elements of an asynchronous programming process. First, the event loop is started and interacts with its task queue, in order to obtain the first task. The coroutine for this task and its corresponding future are then created. When a task switching has to take place inside of that coroutine, the coroutine suspends, and the next coroutine is called; all data and the context from the first coroutine are also saved.

Now, if that coroutine is blocking (for example, input/output processing or sleeping), the flow of execution is released back to the event loop, which will move on to the next item in the task queue. The event loop will initiate the last item in the task queue before it switches back to the first coroutine, and will proceed the execution from where it was last suspended.

As each task finishes executing, it will be dequeued from the task queue, its coroutine will be terminated, and the corresponding future will register the returned result from the coroutine. This process will go on until all tasks in the task queue are completely executed. The following diagram further illustrates the general structure of the asynchronous process described earlier:

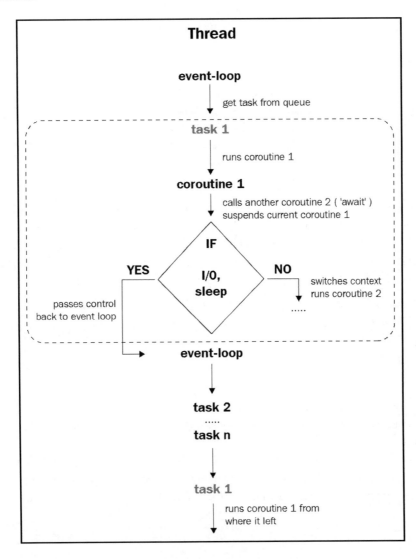

Asynchronous programming process

Asyncio API

With the general structure of an asynchronous program in mind, let's consider the specific APIs that the `asyncio` module and Python provide for the implementation of asynchronous programs. The first foundation for this API is the `async` and `await` keywords that were added to Python 3.5. These keywords are used to specify the main elements of an asynchronous program to Python.

Specifically, `async` is typically put in front of the `def` keyword when a function is declared. A function with the `async` keyword in front of it will be interpreted by Python as a coroutine. As we discussed, inside of each coroutine, there has to be a specification regarding when the task switching events will take place. The `await` keyword is then used to specify where and when, exactly, to give back the flow of execution to the event loop; this is typically done through waiting for another coroutine to produce a result (`await coroutine`) or through helper functions from the `asyncio` module, such as the `asyncio.sleep()` and `asyncio.wait()` functions.

It is important to note that the `async` and `await` keywords are actually provided by Python and are not managed by the `asyncio` module. This means that asynchronous programming can actually be implemented without `asyncio`, but, as you will see, `asyncio` provides a framework and infrastructure to streamline this process, and is therefore the primary tool in Python for the implementation of asynchronous programming.

Specifically, the most commonly used API from the `asyncio` module is event-loop-managing functionalities. With `asyncio`, you can start to manipulate your tasks and event loop with intuitive and easy function calls, without extensive boilerplate code. These include the following:

- `asyncio.get_event_loop()`: This method returns the event loop for the current context, which is an `AbstractEventLoop` object. Most of the time, we do not need to worry about this class, as the `asyncio` module already provides a high-level API to manage our event loops.
- `AbstractEventLoop.create_task()`: This method is to be called by an event loop. It adds its input to the current task queue of the calling event loop; the input is typically a coroutine (that is, a function with the `async` keyword).

- `AbstractEventLoop.run_until_complete()`: This method is also to be called by an event loop. It takes in the main coroutine of an asynchronous program and executes it until the corresponding future of the coroutine is returned. While the method initiates the event loop execution, it also blocks all subsequent code following it, until all futures are complete.
- `AbstractEventLoop.run_forever()`: This method is somewhat similar to `AbstractEventLoop.run_until_complete()`, except for the fact that, as suggested by the method name, the calling event loop will run forever, unless the `AbstractEventLoop.stop()` method is called. So, instead of exiting, the loop will continue to run, even upon obtaining the returned futures.
- `AbstractEventLoop.stop()`: This method causes the calling event loop to stop executing and exit at the nearest appropriate opportunity, without causing the whole program to crash.

Aside from these methods, we use a number of non-blocking functions to facilitate the task switching event. These include the following:

- `asyncio.sleep()`: While in itself a coroutine, this function creates an additional coroutine that completes after a given time (specified by the input, in seconds). It is typically used as `asyncio.sleep(0)`, to cause an immediate task switching event.
- `asyncio.wait()`: This function is also a coroutine, and hence, it can be used to switch tasks. It takes in a sequence (usually a list) of futures and waits for them to complete their execution.

The asyncio framework in action

As you have seen, `asyncio` provides a simple and intuitive way to implement the framework of an asynchronous program with Python's asynchronous programming keywords. With that, let's consider the process of applying the framework provided to a synchronous application in Python, and convert it to an asynchronous one.

Asynchronously counting down

Let's take a look at the `Chapter17/example1.py` file, as follows:

```python
# Chapter17/example1.py

import time

def count_down(name, delay):
    indents = (ord(name) - ord('A')) * '\t'

    n = 3
    while n:
        time.sleep(delay)

        duration = time.perf_counter() - start
        print('-' * 40)
        print('%.4f \t%s%s = %i' % (duration, indents, name, n))

        n -= 1

start = time.perf_counter()

count_down('A', 1)
count_down('B', 0.8)
count_down('C', 0.5)

print('-' * 40)
print('Done.')
```

The goal of this example is to illustrate the asynchronous nature of overlapping the processing and waiting time of independent tasks. To do this, we will be analyzing a countdown function (`count_down()`) that takes in a string and a delay time. It will then count down from three to one, in seconds, while printing out the time elapsed from the beginning of the function's execution and the input string (with the current countdown number).

In our main program, we will call the `count_down()` function on the letters A, B, and C, with different delay times. After running the script, your output should be similar to the following:

```
> python example1.py
----------------------------------------
1.0006 A = 3
----------------------------------------
2.0041 A = 2
----------------------------------------
```

```
3.0055 A = 1
-----------------------------------------
3.8065          B = 3
-----------------------------------------
4.6070          B = 2
-----------------------------------------
5.4075          B = 1
-----------------------------------------
5.9081                    C = 3
-----------------------------------------
6.4105                    C = 2
-----------------------------------------
6.9107                    C = 1
-----------------------------------------
Done.
```

The numbers at the beginning of the lines indicate the total numbers of seconds elapsed from the beginning of the program. You can see that the program counted down for letter A first, with one-second intervals, and it moved on to letter B, with 0.8-second intervals, and finally, to letter C, with 0.5-second intervals. This is a purely sequential, synchronous program, since there is no overlapping between processing and waiting time. Additionally, it took approximately 6.9 seconds to run the program, which is the sum of the counting down time of all three letters:

```
1 second x 3 (for A) + 0.8 seconds x 3 (for B) + 0.5 seconds x 3 (for C) =
6.9 seconds
```

Keeping the idea behind asynchronous programming in mind, we can see that it is actually possible for us to convert this program to an asynchronous one. Specifically, let's suppose that during the first second of the program, while we are waiting to count down the letter A, we can switch tasks to move to other letters. In fact, we will implement this setup for all of the letters inside the count_down() function (in other words, we will turn count_down() into a coroutine).

Theoretically, now that all counting down tasks are coroutines in an asynchronous program, we should achieve better execution time and responsiveness for our program. Since all three tasks are processed independently, the countdown messages should be printed out of order (jumping between different letters), and the asynchronous program should only take about the same time as the largest task takes (that is, three seconds for letter A).

But first, let's make our program asynchronous. To do this, we first need to make `count_down()` into a coroutine and specify a point inside the function to be a task switching event. In other words, we will add the keyword `async` in front of the function, and, instead of the `time.sleep()` function, we will be using the `asyncio.sleep()` function along with the `await` keyword; the rest of the function should remain the same. Our `count_down()` coroutine should now be as follows:

```
# Chapter17/example2.py

async def count_down(name, delay):
    indents = (ord(name) - ord('A')) * '\t'

    n = 3
    while n:
        await asyncio.sleep(delay)

        duration = time.perf_counter() - start
        print('-' * 40)
        print('%.4f \t%s%s = %i' % (duration, indents, name, n))

        n -= 1
```

As for our main program, we will need to initialize and manage an event loop. Specifically, we will create an empty event loop with the `asyncio.get_event_loop()` method, add all of the three counting down tasks into the task queue with `AbstractEventLoop.create_task()`, and, finally, start running the event loop with `AbstractEventLoop.run_until_complete()`. Our main program should look like the following:

```
# Chapter17/example2.py

loop = asyncio.get_event_loop()
tasks = [
    loop.create_task(count_down('A', 1)),
    loop.create_task(count_down('B', 0.8)),
    loop.create_task(count_down('C', 0.5))
]

start = time.perf_counter()
loop.run_until_complete(asyncio.wait(tasks))

print('-' * 40)
print('Done.')
```

The complete script can also be found in the code repository of the book, inside the `Chapter17` subfolder, named `example2.py`. After running the script, your output should look similar to the following:

```
> python example2.py
-----------------------------------------
0.5029                    C = 3
-----------------------------------------
0.8008          B = 3
-----------------------------------------
1.0049 A = 3
-----------------------------------------
1.0050                    C = 2
-----------------------------------------
1.5070                    C = 1
-----------------------------------------
1.6011          B = 2
-----------------------------------------
2.0090 A = 2
-----------------------------------------
2.4068          B = 1
-----------------------------------------
3.0147 A = 1
-----------------------------------------
Done.
```

Now, you can see how having an asynchronous program can improve the execution time and responsiveness of our programs. Instead of executing individual tasks sequentially, our program now switches between different countdowns and overlaps their processing/waiting times. This, as we discussed, results in different letters being printed out in between each other, or simultaneously.

At the beginning of the program, instead of waiting for the whole first second to print out the first message A = 3, the program switches to the next task in the task queue (in this case, it is waiting for 0.8 seconds for the letter B). This process continues until 0.5 seconds have passed and C = 3 is printed out, and 0.3 seconds later (at the time 0.8 seconds), B = 3 is printed out. This all happens before A = 3 is printed out.

This task-switching property of our asynchronous program makes it significantly more responsive. Instead of hanging for one second before the first message is printed, the program now only takes 0.5 seconds (the shortest waiting period) to print out its first message. As for the execution time, you can see that this time, it only takes three seconds, in total, to execute the whole program (instead of 6.9 seconds). This corresponds to what we speculated: that the execution time would be right around the time it takes to execute the largest task.

A note about blocking functions

As you have seen, we have to replace our original `time.sleep()` function with its equivalent from the `asyncio` module. This is because `time.sleep()` is, by nature, a blocking function, which means that it cannot be used to implement a task switching event. To test this, in our `Chapter17/example2.py` file (our asynchronous program), we will replace the following line of code:

```
await asyncio.sleep(delay)
```

The preceding code will be replaced with the following code:

```
time.sleep(delay)
```

After running this new script, your output will simply be the same as that of our original sequential, synchronous program. So, replacing `await asyncio.sleep()` with `time.sleep()` actually converts our program back to synchronous, ignoring the event loop that we implemented. What happened was, when our program proceeded to that line inside of the `count_down()` function, `time.sleep()` actually blocked and prevented the release of the execution flow, essentially rendering the whole program synchronous once again. Revert `time.sleep()` back to `await asyncio.sleep()` to fix this problem.

The following diagram illustrates an example of the difference in execution time between blocking and non-blocking file handling:

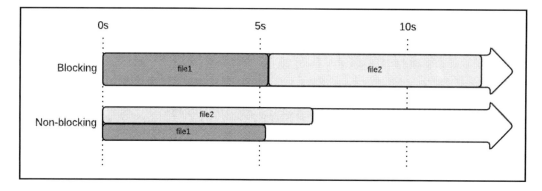

Blocking versus non-blocking

This phenomenon raises an interesting issue: if a heavy, long-running task is blocking, then it is literally impossible to implement asynchronous programming with that task as a coroutine. So, if we really wanted to achieve what a blocking function returns in an asynchronous application, we would need to implement another version of that blocking function, which could be made into a coroutine and allow for task switching events to take place at at least one point inside the function.

Luckily, after implementing `asyncio` as one of the official features of Python, Python core developers have been on working to produce the coroutine version of the most commonly used Python blocking functions. This means that if you ever find blocking functions that prevent your program from being truly asynchronous, you will most likely be able to find the coroutine versions of those functions to implement in your program.

However, the fact that there are asynchronous versions of traditionally blocking functions in Python with potentially different APIs means that you will need to familiarize yourself with those APIs from separate functions. Another way to handle blocking functions without having to implement their coroutine versions is to use an executor to run the functions in separate threads or separate processes, to avoid blocking the thread of the main event loop.

Asynchronous prime-checking

Moving on from our starting counting-down example, let's reconsider the example from the previous chapter. As a refresher, the following is the code for the synchronous version of the program:

```
# Chapter16/example1.py

from math import sqrt

def is_prime(x):
    print('Processing %i...' % x)

    if x < 2:
        print('%i is not a prime number.' % x)

    elif x == 2:
        print('%i is a prime number.' % x)

    elif x % 2 == 0:
        print('%i is not a prime number.' % x)

    else:
        limit = int(sqrt(x)) + 1
```

```
            for i in range(3, limit, 2):
                if x % i == 0:
                    print('%i is not a prime number.' % x)
                    return

            print('%i is a prime number.' % x)

    if __name__ == '__main__':

        is_prime(9637529763296797)
        is_prime(427920331)
        is_prime(157)
```

As we discussed in the last chapter, here, we have a simple prime-checking function, `is_prime(x)`, that prints out messages indicating whether the input integer that it takes in, x, is a prime number. In our main program, we call `is_prime()` on three prime numbers, in an order of decreasing magnitude sequentially. This setup again creates a significant period of time during which the program appears to be hanging while processing the large input, resulting in a low responsiveness for the program.

The output produced by the program will look similar to the following:

```
Processing 9637529763296797...
9637529763296797 is a prime number.
Processing 427920331...
427920331 is a prime number.
Processing 157...
157 is a prime number.
```

To implement asynchronous programming for this script, first, we will have to create our first main component: the event loop. To do this, instead of using the '__main__' scope, we will convert it to a separate function. This function and our `is_prime()` prime-checking function will be the coroutines in our final asynchronous program.

Now, we need to convert both the `is_prime()` and `main()` functions into coroutines; again, this means putting the `async` keyword in front of the `def` keyword, and the `await` keyword inside each function, to specify the task-switching event. For `main()`, we simply implement that event while waiting for the task queue by using `aysncio.wait()`, as follows:

```
# Chapter16/example2.py

async def main():

    task1 = loop.create_task(is_prime(9637529763296797))
    task2 = loop.create_task(is_prime(427920331))
```

```
    task3 = loop.create_task(is_prime(157))

    await asyncio.wait([task1, task2, task3])
```

Things are more complicated in the `is_prime()` function, as there is no clear point during which the execution flow should be released back to the event loop, like in our previous counting-down example. Recall that the goal of asynchronous programming is to achieve a better execution time and responsiveness, and to implement this, the task-switching event should take place during a heavy, long-running task. This requirement, however, is dependent on the specifics of your program—particularly, the coroutine, the task queue of the program, and the individual tasks in the queue.

For example, the task queue of our program consists of three numbers: `9637529763296797`, `427920331`, and `157`; in order, we can consider them as a large task, a medium task, and a small task. To improve responsiveness, we would like to switch tasks during the large task, and not during the small task. This setup will allow the medium and small tasks to be started, processed, and maybe finished during the execution of the large task, even if the large task is in front in the task queue of the program.

Then, we will consider our `is_prime()` coroutine. After checking for some specific edge cases, it iterates in a `for` loop through every odd number under the square root of the input integer and tests for the divisibility of the input with regards to the current odd number in question. Inside this long-running `for` loop, then, is the perfect place to switch tasks—that is, to release the execution flow back to the event loop.

However, we still need to decide at which specific points in the `for` loop to implement the task-switching event. Again, taking into account the individual tasks in the task queue, we are looking for a point that is fairly common in the large task, not so common in the medium task, and non-existent in the small task. I have decided that this point is every 1,00,000-number period, which does satisfy our requirements, and I have used the `await asyncio.sleep(0)` command to facilitate the task-switching event, as follows:

```
# Chapter16/example2.py

from math import sqrt
import asyncio

async def is_prime(x):
    print('Processing %i...' % x)

    if x < 2:
        print('%i is not a prime number.' % x)

    elif x == 2:
```

```
        print('%i is a prime number.' % x)

    elif x % 2 == 0:
        print('%i is not a prime number.' % x)

    else:
        limit = int(sqrt(x)) + 1
        for i in range(3, limit, 2):
            if x % i == 0:
                print('%i is not a prime number.' % x)
                return
            elif i % 100000 == 1:
                await asyncio.sleep(0)

    print('%i is a prime number.' % x)
```

Finally, in our main program (not to be confused with the `main()` coroutine), we create our event loop and use it to run our `main()` coroutine, until it completes its execution:

```
try:
    loop = asyncio.get_event_loop()
    loop.run_until_complete(main())
except Exception as e:
    print('There was a problem:')
    print(str(e))
finally:
    loop.close()
```

As you saw in the previous chapter, better responsiveness was achieved through this asynchronous version of the script. Specifically, instead of appearing like it is hanging while processing the first large task, our program now prints out output messages for the other, smaller tasks, before it finishes executing the large task. Our end result will look similar to the following:

```
Processing 9637529763296797...
Processing 427920331...
427920331 is a prime number.
Processing 157...
157 is a prime number.
9637529763296797 is a prime number.
```

Improvements from Python 3.7

As of 2018, Python 3.7 has just come out, with several major new features, such as data classes, guaranteed ordered dictionaries, better timing precision, and so on. Asynchronous programming and the `asyncio` module received a number of important improvements.

First of all, `async` and `await` are now officially reserved keywords in Python. While we have been calling them keywords, Python did not, in fact, treat these words as reserved keywords, up until now. This means that neither `async` nor `await` can be used to name variables or functions in a Python program. If you are using Python 3.7, fire up a Python interpreter and try to use these keywords for variable or function names, and you should receive the following error message:

```
>>> def async():
  File "<stdin>", line 1
    def async():
            ^
SyntaxError: invalid syntax
>>> await = 0
  File "<stdin>", line 1
    await = 0
          ^
SyntaxError: invalid syntax
```

A major improvement in Python 3.7 comes with the `asyncio` module. Specifically, you might have noticed from our previous examples that the main program typically contains a fair amount of boilerplate code to initiate and run the event loop, which most likely remains the same in all asynchronous programs:

```
loop = asyncio.get_event_loop()
asyncio.run_until_complete(main())
```

With `main()` being a coroutine in our program, `asyncio` allows us to simply run it in an event loop by using the `asyncio.run()` method. This eliminates significant boilerplate code in Python asynchronous programming.

So, we can convert the preceding code to a more simplified version in Python 3.7, as follows:

```
asyncio.run(main())
```

There are other improvements regarding asynchronous programming, in both performance and ease in usage, that were implemented in Python 3.7; however, we will not be discussing them in this book.

Inherently blocking tasks

In the first example in this chapter, you saw that asynchronous programming can provide our Python programs with better execution time, but that is not always the case. Asynchronous programming alone can only provide improvements in speed if all processing tasks are non-blocking. However, similar to the comparison between concurrency and inherent sequentiality in programming tasks, some computing tasks in Python are inherently blocking, and therefore, they cannot be taken advantage of by asynchronous programming.

This means that if your asynchronous programming has inherently blocking tasks in some coroutines, the program will not gain any additional improvement in speed from the asynchronous architecture. While task-switching events still take place in those programs, which will improve the responsiveness of the programs, no instructions will be overlapping each other, and no additional speed will thus be gained. In fact, since there is considerable overhead regarding the implementation of asynchronous programming in Python, our programs might even take longer to finish their execution than the original, synchronous programs.

For example, let's look at a comparison in speed between the two versions of our prime-checking program. Since the primary processing portion of the program is the `is_prime()` coroutine, which solely consists of number crunching, we know that this coroutine contains blocking tasks. So, the asynchronous version is, in fact, expected to run more slowly than the synchronous version.

Navigate to the `Chapter17` subfolder of the code repository and take a look at the files `example3.py` and `example4.py`. These files contain the same code for the synchronous and asynchronous prime-checking programs that we have been seeing, but with the addition that we are also tracking how much time it takes to run the respective programs. The following is my output after running `example3.py`, the synchronous version of the program:

```
> python example3.py
Processing 9637529763296797...
9637529763296797 is a prime number.
Processing 427920331...
427920331 is a prime number.
Processing 157...
157 is a prime number.
Took 5.60 seconds.
```

The following code shows my output when running `example4.py`, the asynchronous program:

```
> python example4.py
Processing 9637529763296797...
Processing 427920331...
427920331 is a prime number.
Processing 157...
157 is a prime number.
9637529763296797 is a prime number.
Took 7.89 seconds.
```

While the output that you receive might be different in the specific times it took to run either program, it should be the case that, as we discussed, the asynchronous program actually took longer to run than the synchronous (sequential) one. Again, this is because the number crunching tasks inside our `is_prime()` coroutine are blocking, and, instead of overlapping these tasks in order to gain additional speed, our asynchronous program simply switched between these tasks in its execution. In this case, only responsiveness is achieved through asynchronous programming.

However, this does not mean that if your program contains blocking functions, asynchronous programming is out of the question. As mentioned previously, all execution in an asynchronous program, if not specified otherwise, occurs entirely in the same thread and process, and blocking CPU-bound tasks can thus prevent program instructions from overlapping each other. However, this is not the case if the tasks are distributed to separate threads/processes. In other words, threading and multiprocessing can help asynchronous programs with blocking instructions to achieve better execution time.

concurrent.futures as a solution for blocking tasks

In this section, we will be considering another way to implement threading/multiprocessing: the `concurrent.futures` module, which is designed to be a high-level interface for implementing asynchronous tasks. Specifically, the `concurrent.futures` module works seamlessly with the `asyncio` module, and, in addition, it provides an abstract class called `Executor`, which contains the skeleton of the two main classes that implement asynchronous threading and multiprocessing, respectively (as suggested by their names): `ThreadPoolExecutor` and `ProcessPoolExecutor`.

Changes in the framework

Before we jump into the API from `concurrent.futures`, let's discuss the theoretical basics of asynchronous threading/multiprocessing, and how it plays into the framework of the asynchronous programming that `asyncio` provides.

As a reminder, we have three major elements in our ecosystem of asynchronous programming: the event loop, the coroutines, and their corresponding futures. We still need the event loop while utilizing threading/multiprocessing, to coordinate the tasks and handle their returned results (futures), so these elements typically remain consistent with single-threaded asynchronous programming.

As for the coroutines, since the idea of combining asynchronous programming with threading and multiprocessing involves avoiding blocking tasks in the coroutines by executing them in separate threads and processes, the coroutines do not necessarily have to be interpreted as actual coroutines by Python anymore. Instead, they can simply be traditional Python functions.

One new element that we will need to implement is the executor that facilitates threading or multiprocessing; this can be an instance of the `ThreadPoolExecutor` class or the `ProcessPoolExecutor` class. Now, every time we add a task to our task queue in the event loop, we will also need to reference this executor, so that separate tasks will be executed in separated threads/processes. This is done through the `AbstractEventLoop.run_in_executor()` method, which takes in an executor, a coroutine (though, again, it does not have to be an actual coroutine), and arguments for the coroutines to be executed in separate threads/processes. We will see an example of this API in the next section.

Examples in Python

Let's look at a specific implementation of the `concurrent.futures` module. Recall that in this chapter's first example (the counting down example), the blocking `time.sleep()` function prevented our asynchronous program from becoming truly asynchronous, and had to be replaced with its non-blocking version, `asyncio.sleep()`. Now, we are executing the individual countdowns in separate threads or processes, which means that the blocking `time.sleep()` function will not pose any problems in terms of executing our program asynchronously.

Navigate to the `Chapter17/example5.py` file, as follows:

```python
# Chapter17/example5.py

from concurrent.futures import ThreadPoolExecutor
import asyncio
import time

def count_down(name, delay):
    indents = (ord(name) - ord('A')) * '\t'

    n = 3
    while n:
        time.sleep(delay)

        duration = time.perf_counter() - start
        print('-' * 40)
        print('%.4f \t%s%s = %i' % (duration, indents, name, n))

        n -= 1

async def main():
    futures = [loop.run_in_executor(
        executor,
        count_down,
        *args
    ) for args in [('A', 1), ('B', 0.8), ('C', 0.5)]]

    await asyncio.gather(*futures)

    print('-' * 40)
    print('Done.')

start = time.perf_counter()
executor = ThreadPoolExecutor(max_workers=3)
loop = asyncio.get_event_loop()
loop.run_until_complete(main())
```

Notice that `count_down()` is declared as a typical, non-coroutine Python function. In `main()`, which remains a coroutine, we declare our task queue for the event loop. Again, we are using the `run_in_executor()` method during this process, instead of the `create_task()` method that is used in single-threaded asynchronous programming. In our main program, we also need to initiate an executor, which, in this case, is an instance of the `ThreadPoolExecutor` class from the `concurrent.futures` module.

The decision between using threading and multiprocessing is, as we discussed in previous chapters, dependent on the nature of the program. Here, we need to share the `start` variable (holding the time at which the program starts to execute) among separate coroutines, so that they can perform the act of counting down; so, threading is chosen over multiprocessing.

After running the script, your output should be similar to the following:

```
> python example5.py
-----------------------------------------
0.5033                  C = 3
-----------------------------------------
0.8052          B = 3
-----------------------------------------
1.0052 A = 3
-----------------------------------------
1.0079                  C = 2
-----------------------------------------
1.5103                  C = 1
-----------------------------------------
1.6064          B = 2
-----------------------------------------
2.0093 A = 2
-----------------------------------------
2.4072          B = 1
-----------------------------------------
3.0143 A = 1
-----------------------------------------
Done.
```

This output is identical to the one that we obtained from the asynchronous program with pure `asyncio` support. So, even with a blocking processing function, we were able to make the execution of our program asynchronous, with threading implemented by the `concurrent.futures` module.

Let's now apply the same concept to our prime-checking problem. We are first converting our `is_prime()` coroutine to its original, non-coroutine form, and executing it in separate processes again (which are more desirable than threads, as the `is_prime()` function is an intensive number-crunching task). An additional benefit of using the original version of `is_prime()` is that we will not have to perform a check of the task-switching condition that we have in our single-threaded asynchronous program:

```
elif i % 100000 == 1:
    await asyncio.sleep(0)
```

This will provide us with a significant speedup, as well. Let's take a look at the
`Chapter17/example6.py` file, as follows:

```python
# Chapter17/example6.py

from math import sqrt
import asyncio
from concurrent.futures import ProcessPoolExecutor
from timeit import default_timer as timer

#async def is_prime(x):
def is_prime(x):
    print('Processing %i...' % x)

    if x < 2:
        print('%i is not a prime number.' % x)

    elif x == 2:
        print('%i is a prime number.' % x)

    elif x % 2 == 0:
        print('%i is not a prime number.' % x)

    else:
        limit = int(sqrt(x)) + 1
        for i in range(3, limit, 2):
            if x % i == 0:
                print('%i is not a prime number.' % x)
                return

        print('%i is a prime number.' % x)

async def main():

    task1 = loop.run_in_executor(executor, is_prime, 9637529763296797)
    task2 = loop.run_in_executor(executor, is_prime, 427920331)
    task3 = loop.run_in_executor(executor, is_prime, 157)

    await asyncio.gather(*[task1, task2, task3])

if __name__ == '__main__':
    try:
        start = timer()

        executor = ProcessPoolExecutor(max_workers=3)
        loop = asyncio.get_event_loop()
        loop.run_until_complete(main())
```

```
        print('Took %.2f seconds.' % (timer() - start))

    except Exception as e:
        print('There was a problem:')
        print(str(e))

    finally:
        loop.close()
```

After running the script, I obtained the following output:

```
> python example6.py
Processing 9637529763296797...
Processing 427920331...
Processing 157...
157 is a prime number.
427920331 is a prime number.
9637529763296797 is a prime number.
Took 5.26 seconds.
```

Again, your execution time will most likely be different from mine, although the comparison between this and the other two versions of our prime-checking program should always be consistent: the original, synchronous version takes less time than the single-threaded asynchronous version, but more than the multiprocessing asynchronous version. In other words, by combining multiprocessing with asynchronous programming, we get the best of both worlds: the consistent responsiveness from asynchronous programming, and the improvement in speed from multiprocessing.

Summary

In this chapter, you learned about asynchronous programming, which is a model of programming that takes advantage of coordinating computing tasks to overlap the waiting and processing times. There are three main components to an asynchronous program: the event loop, the coroutines, and the futures. The event loop is in charge of scheduling and managing coroutines using its task queue. Coroutines are computing tasks that are to be executed asynchronously; each coroutine has to specify inside of its function exactly where it will give the execution flow back to the event loop (that is, the task-switching event). Futures are placeholder objects that contain the results obtained from the coroutines.

The `asyncio` module, together with the Python keywords `async` and `await`, provides an easy-to-use API and an intuitive framework to implement asynchronous programs; additionally, this framework makes the asynchronous code just as readable as synchronous code, which is generally quite rare in asynchronous programming. However, we cannot apply single-threaded asynchronous programming on blocking computing tasks with the `asyncio` module alone. The solution to this is the `concurrent.futures` module, which provides a high-level API to implement asynchronous threading and multiprocessing, and can be used in addition to the `asyncio` module.

In the next chapter, we will be discussing one of the most common applications of asynchronous programming, **Transmission Control Protocol (TCP)**, as a means of server-client communication. You will learn about the basics of the concept, how it takes advantage of asynchronous programming, and how to implement it in Python.

Questions

- What is asynchronous programming? What advantages does it provide?
- What are the main elements in an asynchronous program? How do they interact with each other?
- What are the `async` and `await` keywords? What purposes do they serve?
- What options does the `asyncio` module provide, in terms of the implementation of asynchronous programming?
- What are the improvements in regards to asynchronous programming provided in Python 3.7?
- What are blocking functions? Why do they pose a problem for traditional asynchronous programming?
- How does `concurrent.futures` provide a solution to blocking functions for asynchronous programming? What options does it provide?

Further reading

For more information, you can refer to the following links:

- Zaccone, Giancarlo. *Python Parallel Programming Cookbook*. Packt Publishing Ltd, 2015
- *A guide to asynchronous programming in Python with asyncio* (`medium.freecodecamp.org/a-guide-to-asynchronous-programming-in-python-with-asyncio`), Mariia Yakimova
- *AsyncIO for the Working Python Developer* (`hackernoon.com/asyncio-for-the-working-python-developer`), Yeray Diaz
- Python Documentation. Tasks and coroutines. `docs.python.org/3/library/asyncio`
- *Modern Concurrency*, (`speakerdeck.com/pybay/2017-luciano-ramalho-modern-concurrency`), PyBay 2017

18
Building Communication Channels with asyncio

Communication channels are a big part of applied concurrency in the field of computer science. In this chapter, we will cover the fundamental theories of transports, which are classes provided by the `asyncio` module in order to abstract various forms of communication channels. We will also cover an implementation of a simple echoing server-client logic in Python, in order to further illustrate the use of `asyncio` and concurrency in communication systems. The code for this example will serve as the foundation for an advanced example that will appear later in this book.

The following topics will be covered in this chapter:

- The fundamentals of communication channels and applying asynchronous programming to them
- How to build an asynchronous server in Python by using `asyncio` and `aiohttp`
- How to make requests to multiple servers asynchronously and handle asynchronous file reading and writing

Technical requirements

The following is a list of prerequisites for this chapter:

- Ensure that you have Python 3 installed on your computer
- Ensure that you have Telnet installed on your computer
- Ensure that you have the Python module `aiohttp` installed with your Python 3 distribution
- Download the GitHub repository at `https://github.com/PacktPublishing/AdvancedPythonProgramming`
- In this chapter, we will be working with the subfolder named `Chapter18`
- Check out the following video to see the Code in Action: `http://bit.ly/2FMwKL8`

The ecosystem of communication channels

Communication channels are used to denote both the physical wiring connection between different systems and the logical communication of data that facilitates computer networks. In this chapter, we will only be concerned with the latter, as it is a problem that is related to computing and is more germane to the idea of asynchronous programming. In this section, we will be discussing the general structure of a communication channel, and two specific elements in that structure that are particularly relevant to asynchronous programming.

Communication protocol layers

Most data transmission processes that are done through communication channels are facilitated in the form of the **Open Systems Interconnection** (**OSI**) model protocol layers. The OSI model lays out the major layers and topics in an intersystem communication process.

The following diagram shows the general structure of an OSI model:

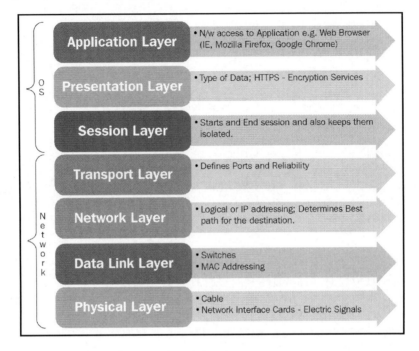

OSI model structure

As indicated in the preceding diagram, there are seven main layers of communication in a data transmission process, with varying degrees of computing level. We will not be going into the details of the purposes and specific functions of each layer, but it is still important that you understand the general ideas behind the media and host layers.

The three bottom layers contain fairly low-level operations that interact with the underlying process of the communication channel. The operations in the physical and data link layers include coding schemes, access schemes, low-level error detection and correction, bit synchronization, and so on. These operations are used to implement and specify the logic of processing and preparing data before transferring it. The network layer, on the other hand, handles forwarding packets of data from one system (for example, the server) to another (for example, the client) in a computer network, via determining the address of the recipient and which path of data transfer to take.

On the other hand, the top layers deal with high-level data communication and manipulation. Among these layers, we will be focusing on the transport layer, as it is directly utilized by the `asyncio` module in implementing communication channels. This layer is often viewed as the conceptual transition between the media layers and the host layers (for example, the client and the server), responsible for sending data along end-to-end connections between different systems. Additionally, because packets of data (prepared by the network layer) might be lost or corrupted during transmission processes due to network errors, the transport layer is also in charge of detecting these errors via methods in error detection code.

The other host layers implement mechanisms for handling, interpreting, and providing the data sent from another system. After receiving data from the transport layer, the session layer handles the authentication, authorization, and session restoration processes. The presentation layer then translates the same data and reorganizes it into an interpretable representation. Finally, the application layer displays that data in user-friendly formats.

Asynchronous programming for communication channels

Given the nature of asynchronous programming, it is no surprise that the programming model can provide functionalities that complement the process of facilitating communication channels efficiently. Using the topic of HTTP communication as an example, the server can asynchronously handle multiple clients at the same time; while it is waiting for a specific client to make an HTTP request, it can switch to another client and process that client's request. Similarly, if a client needs to make HTTP requests to multiple servers, and has to wait for large responses from some servers, it can process the more lightweight responses, which have already been processed and were sent back to the client first. The following diagram shows an example of how servers and clients interact with each other asynchronously in HTTP requests:

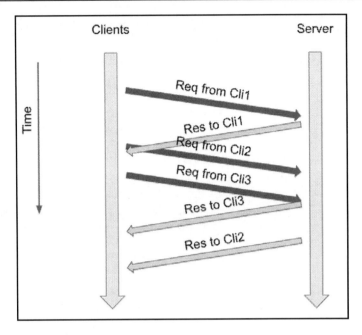

Asynchronous, interleaved HTTP requests

Transports and protocols in asyncio

The `asyncio` module provides a number of different transport classes. In essence, these classes are the implementations of the functionalities of the transport layer that were discussed in the preceding section. You already know that the transport layer plays an integral role in communication channels; the transport classes, therefore, give `asyncio` (and consequently, the developers) more control over the process of implementing our own communication channels.

The `asyncio` module combines the abstract of transports with the implementation of an asynchronous program. Specifically, even though transports are the central elements of communication channels, in order to utilize the transport classes and other relevant communication channel tools, we need to initiate and call an event loop, which is an instance of the `asyncio.AbstractEventLoop` class. The event loop itself will then create the transports and manage the low-level communication procedures.

It is important to note that a `transport` object in an established communication channel in `asyncio` is always associated with an instance of the `asyncio.Protocol` class. As the name suggests, the `Protocol` class specifies the underlying protocols that the communication channels use; for each connection made with another system, a new protocol object from this class will be created. While working closely with a `transport` object, a protocol object can call various methods from the `transport` object; this is the point where we can implement the specific inner workings of a communication channel.

For this reason, generally we need to focus on the implementation of an `asyncio.Protocol` subclass and its methods while building a connection channel. In other words, we use `asyncio.Protocol` as a parent class to derive a subclass that meets the needs of our communication channel. To do this, we overwrite the following methods from the `asyncio.Protocol` base class in our own custom protocol subclass:

- `Protocol.connection_made(transport)`: This method is automatically called whenever a connection from another system is made. The `transport` argument holds the `transport` object that is associated with the connection. Again, each `transport` needs to be paired with a protocol; we generally store this `transport` object as an attribute of this specific protocol object in the `connection_made()` method.
- `Protocol.data_received(data)`: This method is automatically called whenever the one system that we are connected to sends its data. Note that the `data` argument, which holds the sent information, is usually represented in bytes, so the `encode()` function of Python should be used before `data` is processed further.

Next, let us consider the important methods from the transport classes from `asyncio`. All transport classes inherit from a parent transport class, called `asyncio.BaseTransport`, for which we have the following common methods:

- `BaseTransport.get_extra_info()`: This method returns, as the name suggests, additional channel-specific information for the calling `transport` object. The result can include information regarding the socket, the pipe, and the subprocess associated with that transport. Later in this chapter, we will be calling `BaseTransport.get_extra_info('peername')`, in order to obtain the remote address from which the transport traveled.

- `BaseTransport.close()`: This method is used to close the calling `transport` object, after which the connections between different systems will be stopped. The corresponding protocol of the transport will automatically call its `connection_lost()` method.

Out of the many implementations of transport classes, we will focus on the `asyncio.WriteTransport` class, which again inherits the methods from the `BaseTransport` class, and additionally implements other methods that are used to facilitate write-only transport functionalities. Here, we will be using the `WriteTransport.write()` method, which will write the data that we would like to send to the other system that we communicate with via the `transport` object. As a part of the `asyncio` module, this method is not a blocking function; instead, it buffers and sends out the written data in an asynchronous way.

The big picture of asyncio's server client

You have learned that asynchronous programming, and `asyncio` specifically, can drastically improve the execution of your communication channels. You have also seen the specific methods that you will need to use when implementing an asynchronous communication channel. Before we dive into a working example in Python, let us briefly discuss the big picture of what we are trying to accomplish – or, in other words, the general structure of our program.

As mentioned earlier, we need to implement a subclass of `asyncio.Protocol` to specify the underlying organization of our communication channel. Again, there is an event loop at the heart of each asynchronous program, so we also need to create a server outside of the context of the protocol class, and initiate that server inside of the event loop of our program. This process will set up the asynchronous architecture of our entire server, and can be done via the `asyncio.create_server()` method, which we will look at in our upcoming example.

Finally, we will run the event loop of our asynchronous program forever by using the `AbstractEventLoop.run_forever()` method. Similar to an actual, real-life server, we would like to keep our sever running until it encounters a problem, in which case we will close the server gracefully. The following diagram illustrates this whole process:

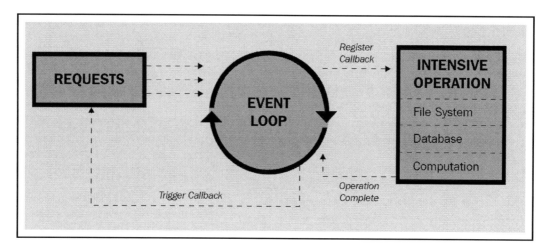

Asynchronous program structure in communication channels

Python example

Now, let us look at a specific Python example that implements a server that facilitates asynchronous communication. Download the code for this book from the GitHub page (https://github.com/PacktPublishing/Mastering-Concurrency-in-Python), and navigate to the Chapter18 folder.

Starting a server

In the Chapter18/example1.py file, let's look at the EchoServerClientProtocol class, as follows:

```
# Chapter18/example1.py

import asyncio

class EchoServerClientProtocol(asyncio.Protocol):
    def connection_made(self, transport):
        peername = transport.get_extra_info('peername')
```

```
        print('Connection from {}'.format(peername))
        self.transport = transport

    def data_received(self, data):
        message = data.decode()
        print('Data received: {!r}'.format(message))
```

Here, our `EchoServerClientProtocol` class is a subclass of `asyncio.Protocol`. As we discussed earlier, inside of this class, we need to implement the `connection_made(transport)` and `data_received(data)` methods. In the `connection_made()` method, we simply obtain the address of the connected system via the `get_extra_info()` method (with the `'peername'` argument), print a message out with that information, and finally store the `transport` object in an attribute of the class. In order to print out a similar message in the `data_received()` method, again we use the `decode()` method to obtain a string object from byte data.

Let us move on to the main program of our script, as follows:

```
# Chapter18/example1.py

loop = asyncio.get_event_loop()
coro = loop.create_server(EchoServerClientProtocol, '127.0.0.1', 8888)
server = loop.run_until_complete(coro)

# Serve requests until Ctrl+C is pressed
print('Serving on {}'.format(server.sockets[0].getsockname()))
try:
    loop.run_forever()
except KeyboardInterrupt:
    pass

# Close the server
server.close()
loop.run_until_complete(server.wait_closed())
loop.close()
```

We are using the familiar `asyncio.get_event_loop()` function to create an event loop for our asynchronous program. Then, we create a server for our communication by having that event loop call the `create_server()` method; this method takes in a subclass from the `asyncio.Protocol` class, an address for our server (in this case, it is our local host: `127.0.0.1`), and finally, a port for that address (typically, `8888`).

Note that this method does not create the server itself; it only initiates the process of creating the server asynchronously, and returns a coroutine that will finish the process. For this reason, we need to store the returned coroutine from the method in a variable (`coro`, in our case) and have our event loop run that coroutine. After printing out a message using the `sockets` attribute of our server object, we will run the event loop forever, in order to keep the server running, except for the case of a `KeyboardInterrupt` exception being invoked.

Finally, at the end of our program, we will handle the house cleaning portion of the script, which is closing the server gracefully. This is typically done by having the server object call the `close()` method (to initiate the closing process of the server) and using the event loop to run the `wait_closed()` method on the server object, to make sure that the server is properly closed. Finally, we close the event loop.

Installing Telnet

Before we can run our sample Python program, we have to install the Telnet program, in order to correctly simulate a connection channel between a client and a server. Telnet is a program that provides Terminal commands that facilitate protocols for bidirectional, interactive, text-oriented communication. If you already have Telnet working on your computer, simply skip to the next section; otherwise, find the information appropriate to your system in this section.

In Windows systems, Telnet is already installed, but might not be enabled. To enable it, you can either utilize the **Turn Windows features on or off** window and make sure that the **Telnet Client** box is checked, or run the following command:

```
dism /online /Enable-Feature /FeatureName:TelnetClient
```

Linux systems typically come with Telnet preinstalled, so if you own a Linux system, simply move on to the next section.

In macOS systems, it is possible that Telnet has already been installed on your computer. If not, you will need to do it via the package management software Homebrew, as follows:

```
brew install telnet
```

Note that macOS systems do have a preinstalled alternative to Telnet, called Netcat. If you do not want Telnet installed on your macOS computer, simply use the `nc` command instead of `telnet` in the following examples, and you will achieve the same effect.

Simulating a connection channel

There are multiple steps to running the following server example. First, we need to run the script to start the server, from which you will obtain the following output:

```
> python example1.py
Serving on ('127.0.0.1', 8888)
```

Notice that the program will run until you invoke the *Ctrl + C* key combination. With the program still running in one Terminal (this is our server Terminal), open another Terminal and connect to the server (127.0.0.1) at the specified port (8888); this will server as our client Terminal:

```
telnet 127.0.0.1 8888
```

Now, you will see some changes in both the server and the client Terminals. Most likely, your client Terminal will have the following output:

```
> telnet 127.0.0.1 8888
Trying 127.0.0.1...
Connected to localhost.
```

This is from the interface of the Telnet program, which indicates that we have successfully connected to our local server. The more interesting output is on our server Terminal, and it will be similar to the following:

```
> python example1.py
Serving on ('127.0.0.1', 8888)
Connection from ('127.0.0.1', 60332)
```

Recall that this is an information message that we implemented in our `EchoServerClientProtocol` class—specifically in the `connection_made()` method. Again, as a connection between the server and a new client is made, this method will be called automatically, in order to initiate the communication. From the output message, we know that the client is making their requests from port 60332 of server 127.0.0.1 (which is the same as the running server, since they are both local).

Another feature that we implemented in the `EchoServerClientProtocol` class was in the `data_received()` method. Specifically, we print the decoded data that is sent from the client. To simulate this type of communication, simply type a message in your client Terminal and press the *Return* (*Enter*, for Windows) key. You will not see any changes in the client Terminal output, but the server Terminal should print out a message, as specified in the `data_received()` method of our protocol class.

For example, the following is my server Terminal output when I send the message Hello, World! from my client Terminal:

```
> python example1.py
Serving on ('127.0.0.1', 8888)
Connection from ('127.0.0.1', 60332)
Data received: 'Hello, World!\r\n'
```

The \r and \n characters are simply the return characters included in the message string. With our current protocol, you can send multiple messages to the server, and can even have multiple clients send messages to the server. To implement this, simply open another Terminal and connect to the local server again. You will see from your server Terminal that a different client (from a different port) has made a connection to the server, while the original communication of our server with the old client is still being maintained. This is another result achieved from asynchronous programming, allowing multiple clients to communicate with the same server seamlessly, without using threading or multiprocessing.

Sending messages back to clients

So, in our current example, we are able to have our asynchronous server receive, read, and process messages from clients. However, in order for our communication channel to be useful, we would also like to send messages from the server to the clients. In this section, we will update our server to an echo server, which, by definition, will send any and all data that it receives from a specific client back to the client.

To do this, we will be using the write() method from the asyncio.WriteTransport class. Examine the Chapter18/example2.py file, in the data_received() method of the EchoServerClientProtocol class, as follows:

```python
# Chapter18/example2.py

import asyncio

class EchoServerClientProtocol(asyncio.Protocol):
    def connection_made(self, transport):
        peername = transport.get_extra_info('peername')
        print('Connection from {}'.format(peername))
        self.transport = transport

    def data_received(self, data):
        message = data.decode()
        print('Data received: {!r}'.format(message))

        self.transport.write(('Echoed back: {}'.format(message)).encode())
```

```
loop = asyncio.get_event_loop()
coro = loop.create_server(EchoServerClientProtocol, '127.0.0.1', 8888)
server = loop.run_until_complete(coro)

# Serve requests until Ctrl+C is pressed
print('Serving on {}'.format(server.sockets[0].getsockname()))
try:
    loop.run_forever()
except KeyboardInterrupt:
    pass

# Close the server
server.close()
loop.run_until_complete(server.wait_closed())
loop.close()
```

After receiving the data from the `transport` object and printing it out, we write a corresponding message to the `transport` object, which will go back to the original client. By running the `Chapter18/example2.py` script and simulating the same communication that we implemented in the last example with Telnet or Netcat, you will see that after typing a message in the client Terminal, the client receives an echoed message from the server. The following is my output after initiating the communication channel and typing in the `Hello, World!` message:

```
> telnet 127.0.0.1 8888
Trying 127.0.0.1...
Connected to localhost.
Hello, World!
Echoed back: Hello, World!
```

In essence, this example illustrates the capability of a bidirectional communication channel that we can implement through a custom `asyncio.Protocol` class. While running a server, we can obtain data sent from various clients connected to the server, process the data, and finally send the desired result back to the appropriate clients.

Closing the transports

Occasionally, we will want to forcefully close a transport in a communication channel. For example, even with asynchronous programming and other forms of concurrency, it is possible for your server to be overwhelmed with constant communications from multiple clients. On the other hand, it is undesirable to have the server completely handle some of the sent requests and plainly reject the rest of the requests as soon as the server is at its maximum capacity.

So, instead of keeping the communication open for each and every client connected to the server, we can specify in our protocol that each connection should be closed after a successful communication. We will do this by using the `BaseTransport.close()` method to forcefully close the calling `transport` object, which will stop the connection between the server and that specific client. Again, we are modifying the `data_received()` method of the `EchoServerClientProtocol` class in `Chapter18/example3.py`, as follows:

```
# Chapter18/example3.py

import asyncio

class EchoServerClientProtocol(asyncio.Protocol):
    def connection_made(self, transport):
        peername = transport.get_extra_info('peername')
        print('Connection from {}'.format(peername))
        self.transport = transport

    def data_received(self, data):
        message = data.decode()
        print('Data received: {!r}'.format(message))

        self.transport.write(('Echoed back: {}'.format(message)).encode())

        print('Close the client socket')
        self.transport.close()

loop = asyncio.get_event_loop()
coro = loop.create_server(EchoServerClientProtocol, '127.0.0.1', 8888)
server = loop.run_until_complete(coro)

# Serve requests until Ctrl+C is pressed
print('Serving on {}'.format(server.sockets[0].getsockname()))
try:
    loop.run_forever()
except KeyboardInterrupt:
    pass

# Close the server
server.close()
loop.run_until_complete(server.wait_closed())
loop.close()
```

Run the script, try to connect to the specified server, and type in some messages, in order to see the changes that we implemented. With our current setup, after a client connects and sends a message to the server, it will receive an echoed message back, and its connection with the server will be closed. The following is the output (again, from the interface of the Telnet program) that I obtained after simulating this process with our current implementation of the protocol:

```
> telnet 127.0.0.1 8888
Trying 127.0.0.1...
Connected to localhost.
Hello, World!
Echoed back: Hello, World!
Connection closed by foreign host.
```

Client-side communication with aiohttp

In previous sections, we covered examples of implementing asynchronous communication channels with the asyncio module, mostly from the perspective of the server side of the communication process. In other words, we have been considering handling and processing requests sent from external systems. This, however, is only one side of the equation, and we also have the client side of communication to explore. In this section, we will discuss applying asynchronous programming to make requests to servers.

As you have most likely guessed, the end goal of this process is to efficiently collect data from external systems by asynchronously making requests to those systems. We will be revisiting the concept of web scraping, which is the process of automating HTTP requests to various websites and extracting specific information from their HTML source code. If you have not read Chapter 12, *Concurrent Web Requests*, I highly recommend going through it before proceeding with this section, as that chapter covers the foundational ideas of web scraping, and other relevant, important concepts.

In this section, you will also be introduced to another module that supports asynchronous programming options: aiohttp (which stands for **Asynchronous I/O HTTP**). This module provides high-level functionalities that streamline HTTP communication procedures, and it also works seamlessly with the asyncio module, in order to facilitate asynchronous programming.

Installing aiohttp and aiofiles

The `aiohttp` module does not come preinstalled with your Python distribution; however, similarly to other packages, you can easily install the module by using the `pip` or `conda` commands. We will also be installing another module, `aiofiles`, which facilitates asynchronous file-writing. If you use `pip` as your package manager, simply run the following commands:

```
pip install aiohttp
pip install aiofiles
```

If you'd like to use Anaconda, run the following commands:

```
conda install aiohttp
conda install aiofiles
```

As always, to confirm that you have successfully installed a package, open your Python interpreter and try to import the module. In this case, run the following code:

```
>>> import aiohttp
>>> import aiofiles
```

There will be no error messages if the package has been successfully installed.

Fetching a website's HTML code

First, let's look at how to make a request and obtain the HTML source code from a single website with `aiohttp`. Note that even with only one task (a website), our application remains asynchronous, and the structure of an asynchronous program still needs to be implemented. Now, navigate to the `Chapter11/example4.py` file, as follows:

```
# Chapter18/example4.py

import aiohttp
import asyncio

async def get_html(session, url):
    async with session.get(url, ssl=False) as res:
        return await res.text()

async def main():
    async with aiohttp.ClientSession() as session:
        html = await get_html(session, 'http://packtpub.com')
        print(html)
```

```
loop = asyncio.get_event_loop()
loop.run_until_complete(main())
```

Let's consider the `main()` coroutine first. We are initiating an instance from the `aiohttp.ClientSession` class within a context manager; note that we are also placing the `async` keyword in front of this declaration, since the whole context block itself will also be treated as a coroutine. Inside of this block, we are calling and waiting for the `get_html()` coroutine to process and return.

Turning our attention to the `get_html()` coroutine, we can see that it takes in a session object and a URL for the website that we want to extract the HTML source code from. Inside of this function, we make another context manager asynchronous, which is used to make a `GET` request and store the response from the server to the `res` variable. Finally, we return the HTML source code stored in the response; since the response is an object returned from the `aiohttp.ClientSession` class, its methods are asynchronous functions, and therefore we need to specify the `await` keyword when we call the `text()` function.

As you run the program, the entire HTML source code of Packt's website will be printed out. For example, the following is a portion of my output:

HTML source code from aiohttp

Writing files asynchronously

Most of the time, we would like to collect data by making requests to multiple websites, and simply printing out the response HTML code is inappropriate (for many reasons); instead, we'd like to write the returned HTML code to output files. In essence, this process is asynchronous downloading, which is also implemented in the underlying architecture of popular download managers. To do this, we will use the aiofiles module, in combination with aiohttp and asyncio.

Navigate to the Chapter18/example5.py file. First, we will look at the download_html() coroutine, as follows:

```
# Chapter18/example5.py

async def download_html(session, url):
    async with session.get(url, ssl=False) as res:
        filename = f'output/{os.path.basename(url)}.html'

        async with aiofiles.open(filename, 'wb') as f:
            while True:
                chunk = await res.content.read(1024)
                if not chunk:
                    break
                await f.write(chunk)

        return await res.release()
```

This is an updated version of the get_html() coroutine from the last example. Instead of using an aiohttp.ClientSession instance to make a GET request and print out the returned HTML code, now we write the HTML code to the file using the aiofiles module. For example, to facilitate asynchronous file writing, we use the asynchronous open() function from aiofiles to read in a file in a context manager. Furthermore, we read the returned HTML in chunks, asynchronously, using the read() function for the content attribute of the response object; this means that after reading 1024 bytes of the current response, the execution flow will be released back to the event loop, and the task-switching event will take place.

The `main()` coroutine and the main program of this example remain relatively the same as those in our last example:

```
async def main(url):
    async with aiohttp.ClientSession() as session:
        await download_html(session, url)

urls = [
    'http://packtpub.com',
    'http://python.org',
    'http://docs.python.org/3/library/asyncio',
    'http://aiohttp.readthedocs.io',
    'http://google.com'
]

loop = asyncio.get_event_loop()
loop.run_until_complete(
    asyncio.gather(*(main(url) for url in urls))
)
```

The `main()` coroutine takes in a URL and passes it to the `download_html()` coroutine, along with an `aiohttp.ClientSession` instance. Finally, in our main program, we create an event loop and pass each item in a specified list of URLs to the `main()` coroutine. After running the program, your output should look similar to the following, although the time it takes to run the program might vary:

```
> python3 example5.py
Took 0.72 seconds.
```

Additionally, a subfolder named `output` (inside of the `Chapter18` folder) will be filled with the downloaded HTML code from each website in our list of URLs. Again, these files were created and written asynchronously, via the functionalities of the `aiofiles` module, which we discussed earlier. As you can see, to compare the speed of this program and its corresponding synchronous version, we are also keeping track of the time it takes to run the entire program.

Now, head to the `Chapter18/example6.py` file. This script contains the code of the synchronous version of our current program. Specifically, it makes HTTP GET requests to individual websites in order, and the process of file writing is also implemented sequentially. This script produced the following output:

```
> python3 example6.py
Took 1.47 seconds.
```

While it achieved the same results (downloading the HTML code and writing it to files), our sequential program took significantly more time than its asynchronous counterpart.

Summary

There are seven main layers of communication in a data transmission process, with varying degrees of computing level. The media layers contain fairly low-level operations that interact with the underlying process of the communication channel, while the host layers deals with high-level data communication and manipulation. Of the seven, the transport layer is often viewed as the conceptual transition between the media layers and the host layers, responsible for sending data along end-to-end connections between different systems. Asynchronous programming can provide functionalities that complement the process of efficiently facilitating communication channels.

Server-wise, the `asyncio` module combines the abstract of transports with the implementation of an asynchronous program. Specifically, via its `BaseTransport` and `BaseProtocol` classes, `asyncio` provides different ways to customize the underlying architecture of a communication channel. Together with the `aiohttp` module, `asyncio` offers efficiency and flexibility regarding client-side communication processes. The `aiofiles` module, which can work in conjunction with the other two asynchronous programming modules, can also help to facilitate asynchronous file reading and writing.

We have now explored three of the biggest, most important topics in concurrent programming: threading, multiprocessing, and asynchronous programming. We have shown how each of them can be applied to various programming problems and provide significant improvements in speed. In the next chapter of this book, we will start to discuss problems that concurrent programming commonly poses to developers and programmers, starting with deadlocks.

Questions

- What is a communication channel? What is its connection to asynchronous programming?
- What are the two main parts of the OSI model protocol layers? What purposes do each of them serve?
- What is the transport layer? Why is it crucial to communication channels?
- How does `asyncio` facilitate the implementation of server-side communication channels?
- How does `asyncio` facilitate the implementation of client-side communication channels?
- What is `aiofiles`?

Further reading

For more information, you can refer to the following links:

- *IoT Systems and Communication Channels* (`bridgera.com/iot-communication-channels/`), by Bridgera
- *Automate the boring stuff with Python: practical programming for total beginners*, No Starch Press, Al. Sweigart
- *Transports and protocols* (`docs.python.org/3/library/asyncio-protocol`), Python documentation

19
Deadlocks

Deadlocks, one of the most common concurrency problems, will be the first problem that we analyze in this book. In this chapter, we will discuss the theoretical causes of deadlocks in concurrent programming. We will cover a classical synchronization problem in concurrency, called the Dining Philosophers problem, as a real-life example of deadlock. We will also illustrate an actual implementation of deadlock in Python. We will discuss several methods to address the problem. This chapter will also cover the concept of livelock, which is relevant to deadlock and is a relatively common problem in concurrent programming.

The following topics will be covered in this chapter:

- The idea behind deadlock, and how to simulate it in Python
- Common solutions to deadlock, and how to implement them in Python
- The concept of livelock, and its connection to deadlock

Technical requirements

The following is a list of prerequisites for this chapter:

- Ensure that you have Python 3 installed on your computer
- Download the GitHub repository at `https://github.com/PacktPublishing/AdvancedPythonProgramming`
- In this chapter, we will be working with the subfolder titled `Chapter19`
- Check out the following video to see the Code in Action: `http://bit.ly/2r2WKaU`

The concept of deadlock

In the field of computer science, deadlock refers to a specific situation in concurrent programming, in which no progress can be made and the program becomes locked in its current state. In most cases, this phenomenon is caused by a lack of, or mishandled, coordination between different lock objects (for thread synchronization purposes). In this section, we will discuss a thought experiment commonly known as the Dining Philosophers problem, in order to illustrate the concept of deadlock and its causes; from there, you will learn how to simulate the problem in a Python concurrent program.

The Dining Philosophers problem

The Dining Philosophers problem was first introduced by Edgar Dijkstra (who, as you learned in *Chapter 8*, *Advanced Introduction to Concurrent and Parallel Programming* was a leading pioneer in concurrent programming) in 1965. The problem was first demonstrated using different technical terms (resource contention in computer systems), and was later rephrased by Tony Hoare, a British computer scientist and the inventor of the quicksort sorting algorithm. The problem statement is as follows.

Five philosophers sit around a table, and each has a bowl of food in front of them. Placed between these five bowls of food are five forks, so each philosopher has a fork on their left side, and one on their right side. This setup is demonstrated by the following diagram:

An illustration of the Dining Philosophers problem

Each silent philosopher is to alternate between thinking and eating. Each philosopher is required to have both of the forks around them to be able to pick up the food from their individual bowl, and no fork can be shared between two or more different philosophers. When a philosopher finishes eating a specific amount of food, they are to place both of the forks back in their respective, original locations. At this point, the philosophers around that philosopher will be able to use those forks.

Since the philosophers are silent and cannot communicate with each other, they have no method to let each other know they need the forks to eat. In other words, the only way for a philosopher to eat is to have both of the forks already available to them. The question of this problem is to design a set of instructions for the philosophers to efficiently switch between eating and thinking, so that each philosopher is provided with enough food.

Now, a potential approach to this problem would be the following set of instructions:

1. A philosopher must think until the fork on their left side becomes available. When that happens, the philosopher is to pick it up.
2. A philosopher must think until the fork on their right side becomes available. When that happens, the philosopher is to pick it up.
3. If a philosopher is holding two forks, they will eat a specific amount of food from the bowl in front of them, and then the following will apply:
   - Afterwards, the philosopher has to put the right fork down in its original place
   - Afterwards, the philosopher has to put the left fork down in its original place
4. The process repeats from the first bullet point.

It is quite clear how this set of instructions can lead to a situation where no progress can be made; namely, if at the beginning, all of the philosophers start to execute their instructions at the same time. Since all of the forks are on the table at the beginning, and are therefore available to be picked up by nearby philosophers, each philosopher will be able to execute the first instruction (picking up the fork on their left side).

Now, after this step, each philosopher will be holding a fork with their left hand, and no forks will be left on the table. Since no philosopher has both forks in their hands, they cannot proceed to eat their food. Furthermore, the set of instructions that they were given specifies that only after a philosopher has eaten a specific amount of food can they put their forks down on the table. This means that as long as a philosopher has not eaten, they will not release any fork that they are holding.

So, as each philosopher is holding only one fork with their left hand, they cannot proceed to eat or put down the fork they are holding. The only time a philosopher gets to eat their food is when their neighboring philosopher puts their fork down, which is only possible if they can eat their own food; this creates a never-ending circle of conditions that can never be satisfied. This situation is, in essence, the nature of a deadlock, in which all of the elements of a system are stuck in place, and no progress can be made.

Deadlock in a concurrent system

With the example of the Dining Philosophers problem in mind, let us consider the formal concept of deadlock, and the relevant theories around it. Given a concurrent program with multiple threads or processes, the execution flow enters a situation of deadlock if a process (or thread) is waiting on a resource that is being held and utilized by another process, which is, in turn, waiting for another resource that is held by a different process. In other words, processes cannot proceed with their execution instructions while waiting for resources that can only be released after the execution is completed; therefore, these processes are unable to change their execution states.

Deadlock is also defined by the conditions that a concurrent program needs to have at the same time in order for deadlock to occur. These conditions were first proposed by the computer scientist Edward G. Coffman, Jr., and are therefore known as the Coffman conditions. These conditions are as follows:

- At least one resource has to be in a non-shareable state. This means that that resource is being held by an individual process (or thread), and cannot be accessed by others; the resource can only be accessed and held by a single process (or thread) at any given time. This condition is also known as mutual exclusion.
- There exists one process (or thread) that is simultaneously accessing a resource and waiting for another held by other processes (or threads). In other words, this process (or thread) needs access to two resources in order to execute its instructions, one of which it is already holding, the other of which it is waiting for from other processes (or threads). This condition is called hold and wait.
- Resources can only be released by a process (or a thread) holding them if there are specific instructions for the process (or thread) to do so. This is to say that unless the process (or thread) voluntarily and actively releases the resource, that resource remains in a non-shareable state. This is the no preemption condition.
- The final condition is called circular wait. As suggested by the name, this condition specifies that there exists a set of processes (or threads) such that the first process (or thread) in the set is in a waiting state for a resource to be released by the second process (or thread), which, in turn, needs to be waiting for the third process (or thread); finally, the last process (or thread) in the set is waiting for the first one.

Let us quickly take a look at a basic example of deadlock. Consider a concurrent program in which there are two different processes (process **A** and process **B**), and two different resources (resource **R1** and resource **R2**), as follows:

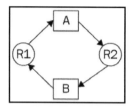

Sample deadlock diagram

Neither of the resources can be shared across separate processes, and each process needs to access both resources to execute its instructions. Take process **A**, for example. It is already holding resource **R1**, but its also needs **R2** to proceed with its execution. However, **R2** cannot be acquired by process **A**, as it is being held by process **B**. So, process **A** cannot proceed. The same goes for process **B**, which is holding **R2** and needs **R1** to proceed. **R1** is, in turn, held by process **A**.

Python simulation

In this section, we will implement the preceding situation in an actual Python program. Specifically, we will have two locks (we will call them lock A and lock B), and two separate threads interacting with the locks (thread A and thread B). In our program, we will set up a situation in which thread A has acquired lock A and is waiting to acquire lock B, which has already been acquired by thread B, which is, in turn, waiting for lock A to be released.

If you have already downloaded the code for this book from the GitHub page, go ahead and navigate to the `Chapter18` folder. Let us consider the `Chapter18/example1.py` file, as follows:

```
# Chapter18/example1.py

import threading
import time

def thread_a():
    print('Thread A is starting...')

    print('Thread A waiting to acquire lock A.')
    lock_a.acquire()
    print('Thread A has acquired lock A, performing some calculation...')
```

```
        time.sleep(2)

        print('Thread A waiting to acquire lock B.')
        lock_b.acquire()
        print('Thread A has acquired lock B, performing some calculation...')
        time.sleep(2)

        print('Thread A releasing both locks.')
        lock_a.release()
        lock_b.release()
    def thread_b():
        print('Thread B is starting...')

        print('Thread B waiting to acquire lock B.')
        lock_b.acquire()
        print('Thread B has acquired lock B, performing some calculation...')
        time.sleep(5)

        print('Thread B waiting to acquire lock A.')
        lock_a.acquire()
        print('Thread B has acquired lock A, performing some calculation...')
        time.sleep(5)

        print('Thread B releasing both locks.')
        lock_b.release()
        lock_a.release()

lock_a = threading.Lock()
lock_b = threading.Lock()

thread1 = threading.Thread(target=thread_a)
thread2 = threading.Thread(target=thread_b)

thread1.start()
thread2.start()

thread1.join()
thread2.join()

print('Finished.')
```

In this script, the `thread_a()` and `thread_b()` functions specify our thread A and thread B, respectively. In our main program, we also have two `threading.Lock` objects: lock A and lock B. The general structure of the thread instructions is as follows:

1. Start the thread
2. Try to acquire the lock with the same name as the thread (thread A will try to acquire lock A, and thread B will try to acquire lock B)
3. Perform some calculations
4. Try to acquire the other lock (thread A will try to acquire lock B, and thread B will try to acquire lock A)
5. Perform some other calculations
6. Release both locks
7. End the thread

Note that we are using the `time.sleep()` function to simulate the action of some calculations being processed.

First of all, we are starting both thread A and thread B almost simultaneously, within the main program. With the structure of the thread instruction set in mind, we can see that at this point, both threads will be initiated; thread A will try to acquire lock A, and will succeed in doing so, since lock A is still available at this point. The same goes for thread B and lock B. The two threads will then go on to perform some calculations on their own.

Let us consider the current state of our program: lock A has been acquired by thread A, and lock B has been acquired by thread B. After their respective calculation processes are complete, thread A will then try to acquire lock B, and thread B will try to acquire lock A. We can easily see that this is the beginning of our deadlock situation: since lock B is already being held by thread B, and cannot be acquired by thread A, thread B, for the same reason, cannot acquire lock A.

Both of the threads will now wait infinitely, in order to acquire their respective second lock. However, the only way a lock can be released is for a thread to continue its execution instructions and release all of the locks it has at the end. Our program will therefore be stuck in its execution at this point, and no further progress will be made.

The following diagram further illustrates the process of how the deadlock unfolds, in sequence:

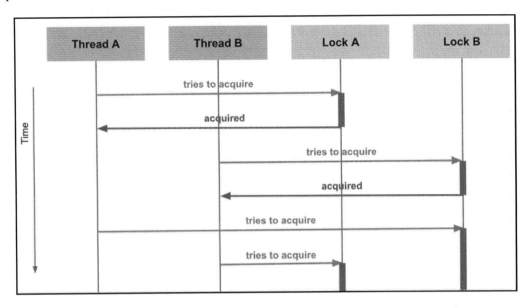

Deadlock sequence diagram

Now, let's see the deadlock that we have created in action. Run the script, and you should obtain the following output:

```
> python example1.py
Thread A is starting...
Thread A waiting to acquire lock A.
Thread B is starting...
Thread A has acquired lock A, performing some calculation...
Thread B waiting to acquire lock B.
Thread B has acquired lock B, performing some calculation...
Thread A waiting to acquire lock B.
Thread B waiting to acquire lock A.
```

As we discussed, since each thread is trying to acquire a lock that is currently held by the other thread, and the only way for a lock to be released is for a thread to continue its execution. This is a deadlock, and your program will hang infinitely, never reaching the final print statement in the last line of the program.

Approaches to deadlock situations

As we have seen, deadlock can lead our concurrent programs to an infinite hang, which is undesirable in every way. In this section, we will be discussing potential approaches to prevent deadlocks from occurring. Intuitively, each approach looks to eliminate one of the four Coffman conditions from our program, in order to prevent deadlocks.

Implementing ranking among resources

From both the Dining Philosophers problem and our Python example, we can see that the last condition of the four Coffman conditions, circular wait, is at the heart of the problem of deadlock. It specifies that the different processes (or threads) in our concurrent program wait for resources held by other processes (or threads) in a circular manner. Giving this a closer look, we can see that the root cause for this condition is the order (or lack thereof) in which the processes (or threads) access the resources.

In the Dining Philosophers problem, each philosopher is instructed to pick up the fork on their left side first, while in our Python example, the threads always try to acquire the locks with the same name before performing any calculations. As you have seen, when the philosophers want to start eating at the same time, they will pick up their respective left forks, and will be stuck in an infinite wait; similarly, when the two threads start their execution at the same time, they will acquire their individual locks, and, again, they will wait for the other locks infinitely.

The conclusion that we can infer from this is that if, instead of accessing the resources arbitrarily, the processes (or threads) were to access them in a predetermined, static order, the circular nature of the way that they acquire and wait for the resources will be eliminated. So, for our two-lock Python example, instead of having thread A try to acquire lock A and thread B try to acquire lock B in their respective execution instructions, we will require that both threads try to acquire the locks in the same order. For example, both threads will now try to acquire lock A first, perform some calculations, try to acquire lock B, perform further calculations, and finally, release both threads.

This change is implemented in the `Chapter18/example2.py` file, as follows:

```
# Chapter18/example2.py

import threading
import time

def thread_a():
    print('Thread A is starting...')
```

```
    print('Thread A waiting to acquire lock A.')
    lock_a.acquire()
    print('Thread A has acquired lock A, performing some calculation...')
    time.sleep(2)

    print('Thread A waiting to acquire lock B.')
    lock_b.acquire()
    print('Thread A has acquired lock B, performing some calculation...')
    time.sleep(2)

    print('Thread A releasing both locks.')
    lock_a.release()
    lock_b.release()

def thread_b():
    print('Thread B is starting...')

    print('Thread B waiting to acquire lock A.')
    lock_a.acquire()
    print('Thread B has acquired lock A, performing some calculation...')
    time.sleep(5)

    print('Thread B waiting to acquire lock B.')
    lock_b.acquire()
    print('Thread B has acquired lock B, performing some calculation...')
    time.sleep(5)

    print('Thread B releasing both locks.')
    lock_b.release()
    lock_a.release()

lock_a = threading.Lock()
lock_b = threading.Lock()

thread1 = threading.Thread(target=thread_a)
thread2 = threading.Thread(target=thread_b)

thread1.start()
thread2.start()

thread1.join()
thread2.join()

print('Finished.')
```

This version of the script is now able to finish its execution, and should produce the following output:

```
> python3 example2.py
Thread A is starting...
Thread A waiting to acquire lock A.
Thread A has acquired lock A, performing some calculation...
Thread B is starting...
Thread B waiting to acquire lock A.
Thread A waiting to acquire lock B.
Thread A has acquired lock B, performing some calculation...
Thread A releasing both locks.
Thread B has acquired lock A, performing some calculation...
Thread B waiting to acquire lock B.
Thread B has acquired lock B, performing some calculation...
Thread B releasing both locks.
Finished.
```

This approach efficiently eliminates the problem of deadlock in our two-lock example, but how well does it hold up for the Dining Philosophers problem? To answer this question, let's try to simulate the problem and the solution in Python by ourselves. The Chapter18/example3.py file contains the implementation of the Dining Philosophers problem in Python, as follows:

```python
# Chapter18/example3.py

import threading

# The philosopher thread
def philosopher(left, right):
    while True:
        with left:
            with right:
                print(f'Philosopher at {threading.currentThread()}
                    is eating.')

# The chopsticks
N_FORKS = 5
forks = [threading.Lock() for n in range(N_FORKS)]

# Create all of the philosophers
phils = [threading.Thread(
    target=philosopher,
    args=(forks[n], forks[(n + 1) % N_FORKS])
) for n in range(N_FORKS)]

# Run all of the philosophers
```

```
for p in phils:
    p.start()
```

Here, we have the `philospher()` function as the underlying logic for our separate threads. It takes in two `Threading.Lock` objects and simulates the previously discussed eating procedure, with two context managers. In our main program, we create a list of five lock objects, named `forks`, and a list of five threads, named `phils`, with the specification that the first thread will take in the first and second locks, the second thread will take in the second and third locks, and so on; and the fifth thread will take in the fifth and first locks (in order). Finally, we start all five threads simultaneously.

Run the script, and it can easily be observed that deadlock occurs almost immediately. The following is my output, up until the program hangs infinitely:

```
> python3 example3.py
Philosopher at <Thread(Thread-1, started 123145445048320)> is eating.
Philosopher at <Thread(Thread-1, started 123145445048320)> is eating.
Philosopher at <Thread(Thread-1, started 123145445048320)> is eating.
Philosopher at <Thread(Thread-1, started 123145445048320)> is eating.
Philosopher at <Thread(Thread-1, started 123145445048320)> is eating.
Philosopher at <Thread(Thread-1, started 123145445048320)> is eating.
Philosopher at <Thread(Thread-3, started 123145455558656)> is eating.
Philosopher at <Thread(Thread-1, started 123145445048320)> is eating.
Philosopher at <Thread(Thread-3, started 123145455558656)> is eating.
Philosopher at <Thread(Thread-3, started 123145455558656)> is eating.
Philosopher at <Thread(Thread-3, started 123145455558656)> is eating.
Philosopher at <Thread(Thread-3, started 123145455558656)> is eating.
Philosopher at <Thread(Thread-5, started 123145466068992)> is eating.
Philosopher at <Thread(Thread-3, started 123145455558656)> is eating.
Philosopher at <Thread(Thread-3, started 123145455558656)> is eating.
```

The question that naturally follows is: how can we implement an order in which the locks are acquired in the `philosopher()` function? We will be using the built-in `id()` function in Python, which returns the unique, constant identity of the parameter, as the keys to sort the lock objects. We will also implement a custom context manager, in order to factor out this sorting logic in a separate class. Navigate to `Chapter18/example4.py` for this specific implementation, as follows:

```
# Chapter18/example4.py

class acquire(object):
    def __init__(self, *locks):
        self.locks = sorted(locks, key=lambda x: id(x))

    def __enter__(self):
        for lock in self.locks:
```

```
                lock.acquire()

        def __exit__(self, ty, val, tb):
            for lock in reversed(self.locks):
                lock.release()
            return False

    # The philosopher thread
    def philosopher(left, right):
        while True:
            with acquire(left,right):
                print(f'Philosopher at {threading.currentThread()}
                    is eating.')
```

With the main program remaining in the same, this script will produce an output showing that this solution of ranking can effectively address the Dining Philosophers problem.

However, there is a problem with this approach when it is applied to some particular cases. Keeping the high-level idea of concurrency in mind, we know that one of our main goals when applying concurrency to our programs is to improve the speed. Let us go back to our two-lock example and examine the execution time of our program with resource ranking implemented. Take a look at the `Chapter18/example5.py` file; it is simply the two-lock program with ranked (or ordered) locking implemented, combined with a timer that is added to keep track of how much time it takes for the two threads to finish executing.

After running the script, your output should look similar to the following:

```
> python3 example5.py
Thread A is starting...
Thread A waiting to acquire lock A.
Thread B is starting...
Thread A has acquired lock A, performing some calculation...
Thread B waiting to acquire lock A.
Thread A waiting to acquire lock B.
Thread A has acquired lock B, performing some calculation...
Thread A releasing both locks.
Thread B has acquired lock A, performing some calculation...
Thread B waiting to acquire lock B.
Thread B has acquired lock B, performing some calculation...
Thread B releasing both locks.
Took 14.01 seconds.
Finished.
```

You can see that the combined execution of both threads took around 14 seconds. However, if we take a closer look at the specific instructions in the two threads, we can see that aside from interacting with the locks, thread A would take around 4 seconds to do its calculations (simulated by two `time.sleep(2)` commands), while thread B would take around 10 seconds (two `time.sleep(5)` commands).

Does this mean that our program is taking as long as it would if we were to execute the two threads sequentially? We will test this theory with our `Chapter18/example6.py` file, in which we specify that each thread should execute its instructions one at a time, in our main program:

```
# Chapter18/example6.py

lock_a = threading.Lock()
lock_b = threading.Lock()

thread1 = threading.Thread(target=thread_a)
thread2 = threading.Thread(target=thread_b)

start = timer()

thread1.start()
thread1.join()

thread2.start()
thread2.join()

print('Took %.2f seconds.' % (timer() - start))
print('Finished.')
```

Run this script, and you will see that this sequential version of our two-lock program will take the same amount of time as its concurrent counterpart:

```
> python3 example6.py
Thread A is starting...
Thread A waiting to acquire lock A.
Thread A has acquired lock A, performing some calculation...
Thread A waiting to acquire lock B.
Thread A has acquired lock B, performing some calculation...
Thread A releasing both locks.
Thread B is starting...
Thread B waiting to acquire lock A.
Thread B has acquired lock A, performing some calculation...
Thread B waiting to acquire lock B.
Thread B has acquired lock B, performing some calculation...
Thread B releasing both locks.
```

```
Took 14.01 seconds.
Finished.
```

This interesting phenomenon is a direct result of the heavy requirements that we have placed on the locks in the program. In other words, since each thread has to acquire both locks to complete its execution, each lock cannot be acquired by more than one thread at any given time, and finally, the locks are required to be acquired in a specific order, and the execution of individual threads cannot happen simultaneously. If we were to go back and examine the output produced by the `Chapter18/example5.py` file, it would be apparent that thread B could not start its calculations after thread A released both locks at the end of its execution.

It is quite intuitive, then, to arrive at the conclusion that if you placed enough locks on the resources of your concurrent program, it would become entirely sequential in its execution, and, combined with the overhead of concurrent programming functionalities, it would have an even worse speed than the purely sequential version of the program. However, we did not see in the Dining Philosophers problem (simulated in Python) this sequentiality created by locks. This is because in the two-thread problem, two locks were enough to sequentialize the program execution, while five were not enough to do the same for the Dining Philosophers problem.

We will explore another instance of this phenomenon in *Chapter 20*, *Race Conditions*.

Ignoring locks and sharing resources

Locks are undoubtedly an important tool in synchronization tasks, and in concurrent programming in general. However, if the use of locks leads to an undesirable situation, such as a deadlock, then it is quite natural for us to explore the option of simply not using locks in our concurrent programs. By ignoring locks, our program's resources effectively become shareable among different processes/threads in a concurrent program, thus eliminating the first of the four Coffman conditions: mutual exclusion.

This approach to the problem of deadlock can be straightforward to implement; let us try with the two preceding examples. In the two-lock example, we simply remove the code specifying any interaction with the lock objects both inside the thread functions and in the main program. In other words, we are not utilizing a locking mechanism anymore. The `Chapter18/example7.py` file contains the implementation of this approach, as follows:

```
# Chapter18/example7.py

import threading
import time
```

```
from timeit import default_timer as timer

def thread_a():
    print('Thread A is starting...')

    print('Thread A is performing some calculation...')
    time.sleep(2)

    print('Thread A is performing some calculation...')
    time.sleep(2)

def thread_b():
    print('Thread B is starting...')

    print('Thread B is performing some calculation...')
    time.sleep(5)

    print('Thread B is performing some calculation...')
    time.sleep(5)

thread1 = threading.Thread(target=thread_a)
thread2 = threading.Thread(target=thread_b)

start = timer()

thread1.start()
thread2.start()

thread1.join()
thread2.join()

print('Took %.2f seconds.' % (timer() - start))

print('Finished.')
```

Run the script, and your output should look similar to the following:

```
> python3 example7.py
Thread A is starting...
Thread A is performing some calculation...
Thread B is starting...
Thread B is performing some calculation...
Thread A is performing some calculation...
Thread B is performing some calculation...
Took 10.00 seconds.
Finished.
```

It is clear that since we are not using locks to restrict access to any calculation processes, the executions of the two threads have now become entirely independent of one another, and the threads were therefore run completely in parallel. For this reason, we also obtained a better speed: since the threads ran in parallel, the total time that the whole program took was the same as the time that the longer task of the two threads took (in other words, thread B, with 10 seconds).

What about the Dining Philosophers problem? It seems that we can also conclude that without locks (the forks), the problem can be solved easily. Since the resources (food) are unique to each philosopher (in other words, no philosopher should eat another philosopher's food), it should be the case that each philosopher can proceed with their execution without worrying about the others. By ignoring the locks, each can be executed in parallel, similar to what we saw in our two-lock example.

Doing this, however, means that we are completely misunderstanding the problem. We know that locks are utilized so that processes and threads can access the shared resources in a program in a systematic, coordinated way, to avoid mishandling the data. Therefore, removing any locking mechanisms in a concurrent program means that the likelihood of the shared resources, which are now free from access limitations, being manipulated in an uncoordinated way (and therefore, becoming corrupted) increases significantly.

So, by ignoring locks, it is relatively likely that we will need to completely redesign and restructure our concurrent program. If the shared resources still need to be accessed and manipulated in an organized way, other synchronization methods will need to be implemented. The logic of our processes and threads might need to be altered to appropriately interact with this new synchronization method, the execution time might be negatively affected by this change in the structure of the program, and other potential synchronization problems might also arise.

An additional note about locks

While the approach of dismissing locking mechanisms in our program to eliminate deadlocks might raise some questions and concerns, it does effectively reveal a new point for us about lock objects in Python: it is possible for an element of a concurrent program to completely bypass the locks when accessing a given resource. In other words, lock objects only prevent different processes/threads from accessing and manipulating a shared resource if those processes or threads actually acquire the lock objects.

Locks, then, do not actually lock anything. They are simply flags that help to indicate whether a resource should be accessed at a given time; if a poorly instructed, or even malicious, process/thread attempts to access that resource without checking the lock object exists, it will most likely be able to do that without difficulty. In other words, locks are not at all connected to the resources that they are supposed to lock, and they most certainly do not block processes/threads from accessing those resources.

The simple use of locks is therefore inefficient to design and implement a secure, dynamic, concurrent data structure. To achieve that, we would need to either add more concrete links between the locks and their corresponding resources, or utilize a different synchronization tool altogether (for example, atomic message queues).

Concluding note on deadlock solutions

You have seen two of the most common approaches to the problem of deadlock. Each addresses one of the four Coffman conditions, and, while both (somewhat) successfully prevent deadlocks from occurring in our examples, each raises different, additional problems and concerns. It is therefore important to truly understand the nature of your concurrent programs, in order to know which of the two is applicable, if either of them are.

It is also possible that some programs, through deadlock, are revealed to us as unsuitable to be made concurrent; some programs are better left sequential, and will be made worse with forced concurrency. As we have discussed, while concurrency provides significant improvements in many areas of our applications, some are inherently inappropriate for the application of concurrent programming. In situations of deadlock, developers should be ready to consider different approaches to designing a concurrent program, and should not be reluctant to implement another method when one concurrent approach does not work.

The concept of livelock

The concept of livelock is connected to deadlock; some even consider it an alternate version of deadlock. In a livelock situation, the processes (or threads) in the concurrent program are able to switch their states; in fact, they switch states constantly. Yet, they simply switch back and forth infinitely, and no progress is made. We will now consider an actual scenario of livelock.

Suppose that a pair of spouses are eating dinner together at a table. They only have one fork to share with each other, so only one of them can eat at any given point. Additionally, the spouses are really polite to each other, so even if one spouse is hungry and wants to eat their food, they will leave the fork on the table if their partner is also hungry. This specification is at the heart of creating a livelock for this problem: when both spouses are hungry, each will wait for the other to eat first, creating a infinite loop in which each spouse switches between wanting to eat and waiting for the other spouse to eat.

Let's simulate this problem in Python. Navigate to `Chapter18/example8.py`, and take a look at the `Spouse` class:

```python
# Chapter18/example8.py

class Spouse(threading.Thread):

    def __init__(self, name, partner):
        threading.Thread.__init__(self)
        self.name = name
        self.partner = partner
        self.hungry = True

    def run(self):
        while self.hungry:
            print('%s is hungry and wants to eat.' % self.name)

            if self.partner.hungry:
                print('%s is waiting for their partner to eat first...'
                    % self.name)
            else:
                with fork:
                    print('%s has stared eating.' % self.name)
                    time.sleep(5)

                    print('%s is now full.' % self.name)
                    self.hungry = False
```

This class inherits from the `threading.Thread` class and implements the logic that we discussed previously. It takes in a name for the `Spouse` instance and another `Spouse` object as its partner; when initialized, a `Spouse` object is also always hungry (the `hungry` attribute is always set to `True`). The `run()` function in the class specifies the logic when the thread is started: as long as the `Spouse` object's `hungry` attribute is set to `True`, the object will attempt to use the fork, which is a lock object, to eat. However, it always checks to see whether its partner also has its `hungry` attribute set to `True`, in which case, it will not proceed to acquire the lock, and will instead wait for its partner to do it.

In our main program, we create the fork as a lock object first; then, we create two `Spouse` thread objects, which are each other's `partner` attributes. Finally, we start both threads, and run the program until both threads finish executing:

```
# Chapter18/example8.py

fork = threading.Lock()

partner1 = Spouse('Wife', None)
partner2 = Spouse('Husband', partner1)
partner1.partner = partner2

partner1.start()
partner2.start()

partner1.join()
partner2.join()

print('Finished.')
```

Run the script, and you will see that, as we discussed, each thread will go into an infinite loop, switching between wanting to eat and waiting for its partner to eat; the program will run forever, until Python is interrupted. The following code shows the first few lines of the output that I obtained:

```
> python3 example8.py
Wife is hungry and wants to eat.
Wife is waiting for their partner to eat first...
Husband is hungry and wants to eat.
Wife is hungry and wants to eat.
Husband is waiting for their partner to eat first...
Wife is waiting for their partner to eat first...
Husband is hungry and wants to eat.
Wife is hungry and wants to eat.
Husband is waiting for their partner to eat first...
Wife is waiting for their partner to eat first...
Husband is hungry and wants to eat.
Wife is hungry and wants to eat.
Husband is waiting for their partner to eat first...
...
```

Summary

In the field of computer science, deadlock refers to a specific situation in concurrent programming, in which no progress is made and the program is locked in its current state. In most cases, this phenomenon is caused by a lack of, or mishandled, coordination between different lock objects, and it can be illustrated with the Dining Philosophers problem.

Potential approaches to preventing deadlocks from occurring include imposing an order for the lock objects and sharing non-shareable resources by ignoring lock objects. Each solution addresses one of the four Coffman conditions, and, while both solutions can successfully prevent deadlocks, each raises different, additional problems and concerns.

Connected to the concept of deadlock is livelock. In a livelock situation, processes (or threads) in the concurrent program are able to switch their states, but they simply switch back and forth infinitely, and no progress is made. In the next chapter, we will discuss another common problem in concurrent programming: starvation.

Questions

- What can lead to a deadlock situation, and why is it undesirable?
- How is the Dining Philosophers problem related to the problem of deadlock?
- What are the four Coffman conditions?
- How can resource ranking solve the problem of deadlock? What other problems can occur when this is implemented?
- How can ignoring locks solve the problem of deadlock? What other problems can occur when this is implemented?
- How is livelock related to deadlock?

Further reading

For more information, you can refer to the following links:

- *Parallel Programming with Python*, by Jan. Palach, Packt Publishing Ltd, 2014
- *Python Parallel Programming Cookbook*, by Giancarlo Zaccone, Packt Publishing Ltd, 2015
- *Python Thread Deadlock Avoidance* (`dabeaz.blogspot.com/2009/11/python-thread-deadlock-avoidance_20`)

20
Starvation

In this chapter, we will discuss the concept of starvation and its potential causes in concurrent programming. We will cover a number of readers-writers problems, which are prime examples of starvation, and we will simulate them in example Python code. This chapter will also cover the relationship between deadlock and starvation, as well as some potential solutions for starvation.

The following topics will be covered in this chapter:

- The basic idea behind starvation, its root causes, and some more relevant concepts
- A detailed analysis of the readers-writers problem, which is used to illustrate the complexity of starvation in a concurrent system

Technical requirements

The following is a list of prerequisites for this chapter:

- Ensure that you have Python 3 installed on your computer
- Download the GitHub repository at `https://github.com/PacktPublishing/AdvancedPythonProgramming`
- During this chapter, we will be working with the subfolder titled `Chapter20`
- Check out the following video to see the Code in Action: `http://bit.ly/2r3caw8`

The concept of starvation

Starvation is a problem in concurrent systems, in which a process (or a thread) cannot gain access to the necessary resources in order to proceed with its execution and, therefore, cannot make any progress. In this section, we will look into the characteristics of a starvation situation, analyze the most common causes of starvation, and finally, consider a sample program that exemplifies starvation.

What is starvation?

It is quite common for a concurrent program to implement some sort of ordering between the different processes in its execution. For example, consider a program that has three separate processes, as follows:

- One is responsible for handling extremely pressing instructions that need to be run as soon as the necessary resources become available
- Another process is responsible for other important executions, which are not as essential as the tasks in the first process
- The last one handles miscellaneous, very infrequent tasks

Furthermore, these three process need to utilize the same resources in order to execute their respective instructions.

Intuitively, we have every reason to implement a specification that allows the first process to have the highest priority of execution and access to resources, then the second process, and then the last process, with the lowest priority. However, imagine situations in which the first two processes (with higher priorities) run so often that the third process cannot execute its instructions; anytime the third process needs to run, it checks to see whether the resources are available to be used and finds out that one of the other, higher-priority processes is using them.

This is a situation of starvation: the third process is given no opportunity to execute and, therefore, no progress can be made with that process. In a typical concurrent program, it is quite common to have more than three processes at different priority levels, yet the situation is fundamentally similar: some processes are given more opportunities to run and, therefore, they are constantly executing. Others have lower priorities and cannot access the necessary resources to execute.

Scheduling

In the next few subsections, we will be discussing the potential candidates that cause starvation situations. Most of the time, a poorly coordinated set of scheduling instructions is the main cause of starvation. For example, a considerably naive algorithm that deals with three separate tasks might implement constant communication and interaction between the first two tasks.

This setup leads to the fact that the execution flow of the algorithm switches solely between the first and second tasks, while the third finds itself idle and unable to make any progress with its execution; in this case, because it is starved of CPU execution flow. Intuitively, we can identify the root of the problem as the fact that the algorithm allows the first two tasks to always dominate the CPU, and hence, effectively prevents any other task to also utilize the CPU. A characteristic of a good scheduling algorithm is the ability to distribute the execution flow and allocate the resources equally and appropriately.

As mentioned previously, many concurrent systems and programs implement a specific order of priority, in terms of process and thread execution. This implementation of ordered scheduling may very likely lead to the starvation of processes and threads of lower priorities and can result in a condition called **priority inversion**.

Suppose that, in your concurrent program, you have process A of the highest priority, process B of a medium priority, and finally, process C of the lowest priority; process C would most likely be put in the situation of starvation. Additionally, if the execution of process A, the prioritized process, is dependent on the completion of process C, which is already in starvation, then process A might never be able to complete its execution, either, even though it is given the highest priority in the concurrent program.

The following diagram further illustrates the concept of priority inversion: a high-priority task running from the time **t2** to **t3** needs to access some resources, which are being utilized by a low-priority task:

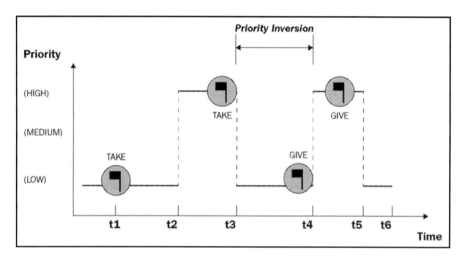

Diagram of priority inversion

To reiterate, combining starvation and priority inversion can lead to a situation where even the high-priority tasks are unable to execute their instructions.

Causes of starvation

With the complexity of designing a scheduling algorithm in mind, let us discuss the specific causes of starvation. The situations that we described in the preceding section indicate some potential causes of the situation of starvation. However, starvation can arise from a number of sources, as follows:

- Processes (or threads) with high priorities dominate the execution flow in the CPU, and hence, low-priority processes (or threads) are not given the opportunity to execute their own instructions.
- Processes (or threads) with high priorities dominate the usage of non-shareable resources, and hence, low-priority processes (or threads) are not given the opportunity to execute their own instructions. This situation is similar to the first one, but addresses the priority of accessing resources, instead of the priority of the execution itself.

- Processes (or threads) with low priorities are waiting for resources to execute their instructions, but, as soon as the resources become available, other processes (or threads) with higher priorities are immediately given access to them, so the low-priority processes (or threads) wait infinitely.

There are other causes of starvation, as well, but the preceding are the most common root causes.

Starvation's relationship to deadlock

Interestingly, deadlock situations can also lead to starvation, as the definition of starvation states that if there is a process (or a thread) that is unable to make any progress because it cannot gain access to the necessary process, the process (or thread) is experiencing starvation.

Recall our example of deadlock, the Dining Philosophers problem, illustrated as follows:

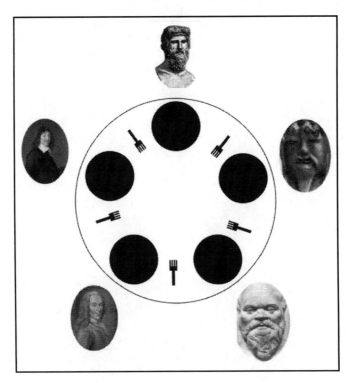

An illustration of the Dining Philosophers problem

When deadlock occurs for this situation, no philosopher can obtain the necessary resources to execute their instructions (each philosopher is required to have two forks to start eating). Each philosopher that is in a deadlock is therefore also in a state of starvation.

The readers-writers problem

The readers-writers problem is one of the classic and most complex examples in the field of computer science, illustrating problems that might occur in a concurrent program. Throughout the analysis of the different variations of the readers-writers problem, we will reveal more about starvation, as well as its common causes. We will also simulate the problem in Python, so that a deeper understanding of the problem can be gained.

Problem statement

In a readers-writers problem, first and foremost, we have a shared resource, which, in most cases, is a text file. Different threads interact with that text file; each is either a reader or a writer. A **reader** is a thread that simply accesses the shared resource (the text file) and reads in the data included in that file, while a **writer** is a thread that accesses, and possibly mutates, the contents of the text file.

We know that writers and readers cannot access the shared resources simultaneously since if a thread is writing data to the file, no other thread should be accessing the file to read any data from it. The goal of the readers-writers problem is therefore to find a correct and efficient way to design and coordinate the scheduling of these reader and writer thread. A successful implementation of that goal is not only that the program as a whole executes in the most optimized way, but also that all threads are given sufficient opportunity to execute their instructions and no starvation can occur. Additionally, the shared resource (the text file) needs to be handled appropriately, so that no data will be corrupted.

The following diagram further illustrates the setup of the readers-writers problem:

Diagram of readers-writers problem

The first readers-writers problem

As we mentioned, the problem asks us to come up with a scheduling algorithm, so that readers and writers can access the text file appropriately and efficiently, without mishandling/corrupting the data that is included. A naive solution to this problem is to impose a lock on the text file, so that it becomes a non-shareable resource; this means that only one thread (either a reader or a writer) can access (and potentially manipulate) the text file at any given time.

Yet, this approach simply equates to a sequential program: if the shared resource can be utilized by only one thread at a given time, none of the processing time between different threads can be overlapped, and effectively, the execution becomes sequential. Therefore, this is not an optimal solution, as it is taking advantage of concurrent programming.

One insight regarding the reader threads can lead to a more optimal solution to this problem: since readers simply read in the text file and do not alter the data in it, multiple readers can be allowed to access the text file simultaneously. Indeed, even if more than one reader is fetching data from the text file at the same time, the data is not being changed in any way, and the consistency and accuracy of the data is therefore maintained.

Following this approach, we will implement a specification in which no reader will be kept waiting if the shared resource is being opened for reading by another reader. Specifically, in addition to a lock on the shared resource, we will also have a counter for the number of readers currently accessing the resource. If, at any point in the program, that counter goes from zero to one (in other words, at least one reader is starting to access the resource), we will lock the resource from the writers; similarly, whenever the counter decreases to zero (in other words, no reader is asking for access to the resource), we will release the lock on the resource, so that writers can access it.

This specification is efficient for the readers, in the sense that, once the first reader has accessed the resource and placed a lock on it, no writers can access it, and the subsequent readers will not have to re-lock it until the last reader finishes reading the resource.

Let us try to implement this solution in Python. If you have already downloaded the code for this book from the GitHub page, go ahead and navigate to the `Chapter20` folder. Let us take a look at the `Chapter20/example1.py` file; specifically, the `writer()` and `reader()` functions, as follows:

```
# Chapter20/example1.py

def writer():
    global text

    while True:
        with resource:
            print(f'Writing being done by
                    {threading.current_thread().name}.')
            text += f'Writing was done by
                    {threading.current_thread().name}. '

def reader():
    global rcount

    while True:
        with rcounter:
            rcount += 1
            if rcount == 1:
                resource.acquire()
```

```
print(f'Reading being done by
        {threading.current_thread().name}:')
print(text)

with rcounter:
    rcount -= 1
    if rcount == 0:
        resource.release()
```

In the preceding script, the `writer()` function, which is to be called by a `threading.Thread` instance (in other words, a separate thread), specifies the logic of the writer threads that we discussed previously: accessing the shared resource (in this case, the global variable, `text`, which is simply a Python string) and writing some data to the resource. Note that we are putting all of its instructions inside a `while` loop, to simulate the constant nature of the application (writers and readers constantly try to access the shared resource).

We can also see the reader logic in the `reader()` function. Before asking for access to the shared resource, each reader will increment a counter for the number of readers that are currently active and trying to access the resource. Similarly, after reading data off the file, each reader needs to decrement the number of readers. During this process, if a reader is the first reader to access the file (in other words, when the counter is one), it will put a lock on the file, so that no writers can access it; conversely, when a reader is the last reader to read the file, it has to release that lock.

One note about the handling of that counter of readers: you might have noticed that we are using a lock object named `rcounter` when incrementing/decrementing the counter variable (`rcount`). This is a method that is used to avoid a race condition, which is another common concurrency-related problem, for the counter variable; specifically, without the lock, multiple threads can be accessing and altering the counter variable at the same time, but the only way to ensure the integrity of the data is for this counter variable to be handled sequentially. We will discuss race conditions (and the practice that is used to avoid them) in more detail in the next chapter.

Going back to our current script, in the main program, we will set up the `text` variable, the counter for readers, and two lock objects (for the reader counter and the shared resource, respectively). We are also initializing and starting three reader threads and two writer threads, as follows:

```
# Chapter20/example1.py

text = 'This is some text. '
rcount = 0
```

```
rcounter = threading.Lock()
resource = threading.Lock()

threads = [threading.Thread(target=reader) for i in range(3)] +
[threading.Thread(target=writer) for i in range(2)]

for thread in threads:
    thread.start()
```

It is important to note that, since the instructions of the reader and writer threads are both wrapped in `while` loops, the script, when started, will run infinitely. You should cancel the Python execution after around 3-4 seconds, when enough output has been produced so that the general behavior of the program can be observed.

The following code shows the first few lines of output that I obtained after running the script:

```
> python3 example1.py
Reading being done by Thread-1:
This is some text.
Reading being done by Thread-2:
Reading being done by Thread-1:
This is some text.
This is some text.
Reading being done by Thread-2:
Reading being done by Thread-1:
This is some text.
This is some text.
Reading being done by Thread-3:
Reading being done by Thread-1:
This is some text.
This is some text.
...
```

As you can see, there is a specific pattern in the preceding output: all of the threads that were accessing the shared resource were readers. In fact, throughout my entire output, no writer was able to access the file, and therefore, the `text` variable only contains the initial string, `This is some text.`, and was not altered in any way. The output that you obtain should also have the same pattern (the shared resource not being altered).

In this case, the writers are experiencing starvation, as none of them are able to access and use the resource. This is a direct result of our scheduling algorithm; since multiple readers are allowed to access the text file simultaneously, if there are multiple readers accessing the text file frequently enough, it will create a continuous stream of readers going through the text file, giving no room for a writer to attempt to access the file.

This scheduling algorithm inadvertently gives priority to the readers over the writers, and is therefore called **readers-preference**. So, this design is undesirable.

The second readers-writers problem

The problem with the first approach is that, when a reader is accessing the text file and a writer is waiting for the file to be unlocked, if another reader starts its execution and wants to access the file, it will be given priority over the writer that has already been waiting. Additionally, if more and more readers keep requesting access to the file, the writer will be waiting infinitely, and that was what we observed in our first code example.

To address this problem, we will implement the specification that, once a writer makes a request to access the file, no reader should be able to jump in line and access the file before that writer. To do this, we will have an additional lock object in our program, to specify whether a writer is waiting for the file, and consequently, whether a reader thread can attempt to read the file; we will call this lock `read_try`.

Similar to how the first of the readers accessing the text file always locks it from the writers, we will now have the first writer of the multiple that are waiting to access the file lock `read_try`, so that no reader can, again, jump in line before those writers that requested access before it. As we discussed in reference to the readers, since we are keeping track of the number of writers waiting for the text file, we will need to implement a counter for the number of writers, and its corresponding lock, in our program.

The `Chapter20/example2.py` file contains the code for this implementation, as follows:

```
# Chapter20/example2.py

import threading

def writer():
    global text
    global wcount

    while True:
        with wcounter:
            wcount += 1
            if wcount == 1:
                read_try.acquire()

        with resource:
            print(f'Writing being done by
                    {threading.current_thread().name}.')
            text += f'Writing was done by
```

```
                    {threading.current_thread().name}. '

        with wcounter:
            wcount -= 1
            if wcount == 0:
                read_try.release()

def reader():
    global rcount

    while True:
        with read_try:
            with rcounter:
                rcount += 1
                if rcount == 1:
                    resource.acquire()

            print(f'Reading being done by
                {threading.current_thread().name}:')
            print(text)

            with rcounter:
                rcount -= 1
                if rcount == 0:
                    resource.release()

text = 'This is some text. '
wcount = 0
rcount = 0

wcounter = threading.Lock()
rcounter = threading.Lock()
resource = threading.Lock()
read_try = threading.Lock()

threads = [threading.Thread(target=reader) for i in range(3)] +
          [threading.Thread(target=writer) for i in range(2)]

for thread in threads:
    thread.start()
```

Compared to our first solution to the problem, the main program remains relatively the same (except for the initialization of the read_try lock, the wcount counter, and its lock, wcounter), but in our writer() function, we are locking read_try as soon as there is at least one writer waiting to access the file; when the last writer finishes its execution, it will release the lock, so that any reader waiting for the file can now access it.

Again, to see the output produced by the program, we will have it run for 3-4 seconds, and then cancel the execution, as the program would otherwise run forever. The following is the output that I obtained via this script:

```
> python3 example2.py
Reading being done by Thread-1:
This is some text.
Reading being done by Thread-1:
This is some text.
Writing being done by Thread-4.
Writing being done by Thread-5.
Writing being done by Thread-4.
Writing being done by Thread-4.
Writing being done by Thread-4.
Writing being done by Thread-5.
Writing being done by Thread-4.
...
```

It can be observed that, while some readers were able to access the text file (indicated by the first four lines of my output), once a writer gained access to the shared resource, no reader was able to access it anymore. The rest of my output included messages about writing instructions: Writing being done by, and so on. As opposed to what we saw in the first solution of the readers-writers problem, this solution is giving priority to writers, and, as a consequence, the readers are starved. This is therefore called **writers-preference**.

The priority that writers were given over readers resulted from the fact that, while only the first and the last writers have to acquire and release the read_try lock, respectively, each and every reader wanting to access the text file have to interact with that lock object individually. Once read_try is locked by a writer, no reader can even attempt to execute its instructions, let alone try to access the text file.

There are cases in which some readers are able to gain access to the text file, if the readers are initialized and executed before the writers (for example, in our program, the readers were the first three elements, and the writers were the last two, in our list of threads). However, once a writer is able to access the file and acquire the read_try lock during its execution, starvation will most likely occur for the readers.

This solution is also not desirable, as it gives higher priority to the writer threads in our program.

The third readers-writers problem

You have seen that both of the solutions that we tried to implement can result in starvation, by not giving equal priorities to the separate threads; one can starve the writers, and the other can starve the readers. A balance between these two approaches might give us an implementation with equal priorities among the readers and writers, and hence, solve the problem of starvation.

Recall this: in our second approach, we are placing a lock on a reader's attempt to access the text file, requiring that no writer will be starved once it starts waiting for the file. In this solution, we will implement a lock that also utilizes this logic, but is then applied to both readers and writers. All of the threads will then be subjected to the constraints of the lock, and equal priority will hence be achieved among the separate threads.

Specifically, this is a lock that specifies whether a thread will be given access to the text file at a given moment; we will call this the **service lock**. Each writer or reader has to try to acquire this service lock before executing any of its instructions. A writer, having obtained this service lock, will also attempt to obtain the resource lock and release the service lock immediately thereafter. The writer will then execute its writing logic and finally release the resource lock at the end of its execution.

Let us take a look at the `writer()` function in the `Chapter20/example3.py` file for our implementation in Python, as follows:

```python
# Chapter20/example3.py

def writer():
    global text

    while True:
        with service:
            resource.acquire()

        print(f'Writing being done by
            {threading.current_thread().name}.')
        text += f'Writing was done by
            {threading.current_thread().name}. '

        resource.release()
```

A reader, on the other hand, will also need to acquire the service lock first. Since we are still allowing multiple readers to access the resource at the same time, we are implementing the reader counter and its corresponding lock.

The reader will acquire the service lock and the counter lock, increment the reader counter (and potentially, lock the resource), and then release the service lock and counter lock, sequentially. Now, it will actually read data off the text file, and finally, it will decrement the reader counter, and will potentially release the resource lock, if it is the last reader to access the file at that time.

The `reader()` function contains this specification, as follows:

```
# Chapter20/example3.py

def reader():
    global rcount

    while True:
        with service:
            rcounter.acquire()
            rcount += 1
            if rcount == 1:
                resource.acquire()
        rcounter.release()

        print(f'Reading being done by
                {threading.current_thread().name}:')
        #print(text)

        with rcounter:
            rcount -= 1
            if rcount == 0:
                resource.release()
```

Finally, in our main program, we initialize the text string, the reader counter, all of the necessary locks, and the reader and writer threads, as follows:

```
# Chapter20/example3.py

text = 'This is some text. '
rcount = 0

rcounter = threading.Lock()
resource = threading.Lock()
service = threading.Lock()

threads = [threading.Thread(target=reader) for i in range(3)] +
[threading.Thread(target=writer) for i in range(2)]

for thread in threads:
    thread.start()
```

Note that, we are commenting the code that prints out the current content of the text file in the `reader()` function for readability for our output later on. Run the program for 3-4 seconds, and then cancel it. The following output is what I obtained on my personal computer:

```
> python3 example3.py
Reading being done by Thread-3:
Writing being done by Thread-4.
Reading being done by Thread-1:
Writing being done by Thread-5.
Reading being done by Thread-2:
Reading being done by Thread-3:
Writing being done by Thread-4.
. . .
```

The pattern that we have with this current output is that the readers and writers are able to access the shared resource cooperatively and efficiently; all of the readers and writers are executing their instructions, and no thread is being starved by this scheduling algorithm.

Note that as you work with a reader-writer problem in your concurrent program, you do not have to reinvent the wheel regarding the approaches that we just discussed. PyPI actually has an external library called `readerwriterlock` that contains the implementation of the three approaches in Python, as well as supports for timeouts. Navigate to `https://pypi.org/project/readerwriterlock/` to find out more about the library and its documentation.

Solutions to starvation

Through an analysis of different approaches to the readers-writers problem, you have seen the key to solving starvation: since some threads will be starved if they are not given a high priority in accessing the shared resources, implementing fairness in the execution of all of the threads will prevent starvation from occurring. Fairness, in this case, does not require a program to forgo any order or priority that it has imposed on the different threads; but to implement fairness, a program needs to ensure that all threads are given sufficient opportunities to execute their instructions.

Keeping this idea in mind, we can potentially address the problem of starvation by implementing one (or a combination) of the following approaches:

- **Increasing the priority of low-priority threads**: As we did with the writer threads in the second approach and the reader threads in the third approach to the readers-writers problem, prioritizing the threads that would otherwise not have any opportunity to access the shared resource can successfully eliminate starvation.

- **First-in-first-out thread queue**: To ensure that a thread that started waiting for the shared resource before another thread will be able to acquire the resource before the other thread, we can keep track of the threads requesting access in a first-in-first-out queue.

- **Other methods**: Several methods can also be implemented to balance the selection frequency of different threads. For example, a priority queue that also gives gradually increasing priority to threads that have been waiting in the queue for a long time, or if a thread has been able to access the shared resource for many times, it will be given less priority, and so on.

Solving starvation in your concurrent program can be a rather complex and involved process, and a deep understanding of its scheduling algorithm, combined with an understanding of how processes and threads interact with the shared resources, is necessary during the process. As you saw in the example of the readers-writers problem, it can also take several implementations and revisions of different approaches to arrive at a good solution to starvation.

Summary

Starvation is a problem in concurrent systems in which a process (or thread) cannot gain access to the necessary resources to proceed with its execution and, therefore, cannot make any progress. Most of the time, a poorly coordinated set of scheduling instructions is the main cause of starvation; deadlock situations can also lead to starvation.

The readers-writers problem is one of the classic and most complex examples in the field of computer science, illustrating problems that might occur in a concurrent program. Through an analysis of different approaches to the readers-writers problem, you have gained insight regarding how starvation can be solved with different scheduling algorithms. Fairness is an essential element of a good scheduling algorithm, and, by making sure that the priority is distributed appropriately among different processes and threads, starvation can be eliminated.

In the next chapter, we will discuss the last of the three common problems of concurrent programming: race conditions. We will cover the basic foundation and causes of race conditions, relevant concepts, and the connection of race conditions to other concurrency-related problems.

Questions

- What is starvation, and why is it undesirable in a concurrent program?
- What are the underlying causes of starvation? What are the common high-level causes of starvation that can manifest from the underlying cause?
- What is the connection between deadlock and starvation?
- What is the readers-writers problem?
- What is the first approach to the readers-writers problem? Why does starvation arise in that situation?
- What is the second approach to the readers-writers problem? Why does starvation arise in that situation?
- What is the third approach to the readers-writers problem? Why does it successfully address starvation?
- What are some common solutions to starvation?

Further reading

- *Parallel Programming with Python*, by Jan Palach, Packt Publishing Ltd, 2014
- *Python Parallel Programming Cookbook*, by Giancarlo Zaccone, Packt Publishing Ltd, 2015
- *Starvation and Fairness* (`tutorials.jenkov.com/java-concurrency/starvation-and-fairness`), by Jakob Jenkov
- *Faster Fair Solution for the Reader-Writer Problem*, V.Popov and O.Mazonka

21
Race Conditions

In this chapter, we will discuss the concept of race conditions and their potential causes in the context of concurrency. The definition of critical section, which is a concept highly relevant to race conditions and concurrent programming, will also be covered. We will use some example code in Python to simulate race conditions and the solutions commonly used to address them. Finally, real-life applications that commonly deal with race conditions will be discussed.

The following topics will be covered in this chapter:

- The basic concept of a race condition, and how it occurs in concurrent applications, along with the definition of critical sections
- A simulation of a race condition in Python and how to implement race condition solutions
- The real-life computer science concepts that commonly interact and work with race conditions

Technical requirements

Following is the list of prerequisites needed for this chapter:

- Ensure that you have Python 3 installed on your computer
- Download the GitHub repository at https://github.com/PacktPublishing/AdvancedPythonProgramming
- During this chapter, we will be working with the subfolder titled Chapter21
- Check out the following video to see the Code in Action: http://bit.ly/2AdYWRj

The concept of race conditions

A race condition is typically defined as a phenomenon during which the output of a system is indeterminate and dependent on the scheduling algorithm and the order in which tasks are scheduled and executed. When the data becomes mishandled and corrupted during this process, a race condition becomes a bug in the system. Given the nature of this problem, it is quite common for a race condition to occur in concurrent systems, which emphasize scheduling and coordinating independent tasks.

A race condition can occur in both an electronic hardware system and a software application; in this chapter, we will only be discussing race conditions in the context of software development—specifically, concurrent software applications. This section will cover the theoretical foundations of race conditions and their root causes and the concept of critical sections.

Critical sections

Critical sections indicate shared resources that are accessed by multiple processes or threads in a concurrent application, which can lead to unexpected, and even erroneous, behavior. We have seen that there are multiple methods to protect the integrity of the data contained in these resources, and we call these protected sections **critical sections**.

As you can imagine, the data in these critical sections, when interacted with and altered concurrently or in parallel, can become mishandled or corrupted. This is especially true when the threads and processes interacting with it are poorly coordinated and scheduled. The logical conclusion, therefore, is to not allow multiple agents to go into a critical section at the same time. We call this concept **mutual exclusion**.

We will discuss the relationship between critical sections and the causes of race conditions in the next subsection.

How race conditions occur

Let's consider a simple concurrent program, in order to understand what can give rise to a race condition. Suppose that the program has a shared resource and two separate threads (thread 1 and thread 2) that will access and interact with that resource. Specifically, the shared resource is a number and, as per their respective execution instructions, each thread is to read in that number, increment it by 1, and finally, update the value of the shared resource with the incremented number.

Suppose that the shared number is originally 2, and then, thread 1 accesses and interacts with the number; the shared resource then becomes 3. After thread 1 successfully alters and exits the resource, thread 2 begins to execute its instructions, and the shared resource that is a number is updated to 4. Throughout this process, the number was originally 2, was incremented twice (each time by a separate thread), and held a value of 4 at the end. The shared number was not mishandled and corrupted in this case.

Imagine, then, a scenario in which the shared number is still 2 at the beginning, yet both of the threads access the number at the same time. Now, each of the threads reads in the number 2 from the shared resource, each increments the number 2 to 3 individually, and then, each writes the number 3 back to the shared resource. Even though the shared resource was accessed and interacted with by a thread twice, it only held a value of 3 at the end of the process.

This is an example of a race condition occurring in a concurrent program: since the second thread to access a shared resource does it before the first thread finishes its execution (in other words, writing the new value to the shared resource), the second thread fails to take in the updated resource value. This leads to the fact that, when the second thread writes to the resource, the value that is processed and updated by the first thread is overwritten. At the end of the execution of the two threads, the shared resource has technically only been updated by the second thread.

The following diagram further illustrates the contrast between a correct data handling process and a situation with a race condition:

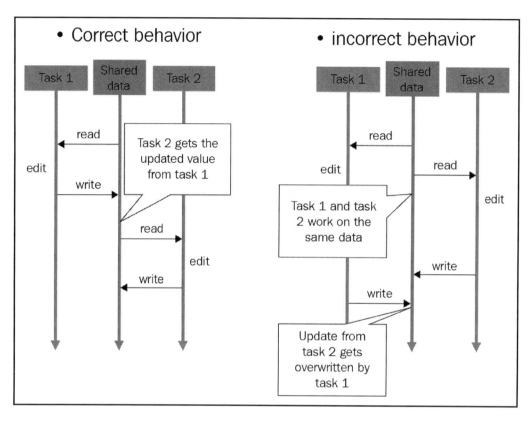

Mishandling shared data

Intuitively, we can see that a race condition can result in the mishandling and corruption of data. In the preceding example, we can see that a race condition can occur with only two separate threads accessing a common resource, causing the shared resource to be updated incorrectly and hold an incorrect value at the end of the program. We know that most real-life concurrent applications contain significantly more threads and processes and more shared resources, and the more threads/processes that interact with the shared resource, the more likely it is that a race condition will occur.

Simulating race conditions in Python

Before we discuss a solution that we can implement to solve the problem of race conditions, let's try to simulate the problem in Python. If you have already downloaded the code for this book from the GitHub page, go ahead and navigate to the Chapter21 folder. Let's take a look at the Chapter21/example1.py file—specifically, the update() function, as follows:

```
# Chapter21/example1.py

import random
import time

def update():
    global counter

    current_counter = counter # reading in shared resource
    time.sleep(random.randint(0, 1)) # simulating heavy calculations
    counter = current_counter + 1 # updating shared resource
```

The goal of the preceding update() function is to increment a global variable called counter, and it is to be called by a separate thread in our script. Inside the function, we are interacting with a shared resource—in this case, counter. We then assign the value of counter to another local variable, called current_counter (this is to simulate the process of reading data from more complex data structures for the shared resources).

Next, we will pause the execution of the function by using the time.sleep() method. The length of the period during which the program will pause is pseudo-randomly chosen between 0 and 1, generated by the function call, random.randint(0, 1), so the program will either pause for one second or not at all. Finally, we assign the newly computed value of current_counter (which is its one-increment) to the original shared resource (the counter variable).

Now, we can move on to our main program:

```
# Chapter21/example1.py

import threading

counter = 0

threads = [threading.Thread(target=update) for i in range(20)]

for thread in threads:
    thread.start()
```

```
for thread in threads:
    thread.join()

print(f'Final counter: {counter}.')
print('Finished.')
```

Here, we are initializing the `counter` global variable with a set of `threading.Thread` objects, in order to execute the `update()` function concurrently; we are initializing twenty thread objects, to increment our shared counter twenty times. After starting and joining all of the threads that we have, we can finally print out the end value of our shared `counter` variable.

Theoretically, a well-designed concurrent program will successfully increment the share counter twenty times in total, and, since its original value is 0, the end value of the counter should be 20 at the end of the program. However, as you run this script, the `counter` variable that you obtain will most likely not hold an end value of 20. The following is my own output, obtained from running the script:

```
> python3 example1.py
Final counter: 9.
Finished.
```

This output indicates that the counter was only successfully incremented nine times. This is a direct result of a race condition that our concurrent program has. This race condition occurs when a specific thread spends time reading in and processing the data from the shared resource (specifically, for one second, using the `time.sleep()` method), and another thread reads in the current value of the `counter` variable, which, at this point, has not been updated by the first thread, since it has not completed its execution.

Interestingly, if a thread does not spend anytime processing the data (in other words, when 0 is chosen by the pseudo-random `random.randint()` method), the value of the shared resource can potentially be updated just in time for the next thread to read and process it. This phenomenon is illustrated by the fact that the end value of the counter varies within different runs of the program. For example, the following is the output that I obtained after running the script three times. The output from the first run is as follows:

```
> python3 example1.py
Final counter: 9.
Finished.
```

The output from the second run is as follows:

```
> python3 example1.py
Final counter: 12.
Finished.
```

The output from the third run is as follows:

```
> python3 example1.py
Final counter: 5.
Finished.
```

Again, the final value of the counter is dependent on the number of threads that spend one second pausing and the number of threads not pausing at all. Since these two numbers are, in turn, dependent on the `random.randint()` method, the final value of the counter changes between different runs of the program. We will still have a race condition in our program, except for when we can ensure that the final value of the counter is always 20 (the counter being successfully incremented twenty times, in total).

Locks as a solution to race conditions

In this section, we will discuss the most common solution to race conditions: locks. Intuitively, since the race conditions that we observed arose when multiple threads or processes accessed and wrote to a shared resource simultaneously, the key idea to solving race conditions is to isolate the executions of different threads/processes, especially when interacting with a shared resource. Specifically, we need to make sure that a thread/process can only access the shared resource after any other threads/processes interacting with the resource have finished their interactions with that resource.

The effectiveness of locks

With locks, we can turn a shared resource in a concurrent program into a critical section, whose integrity of data is guaranteed to be protected. A critical section guarantees the mutual exclusion of a shared resource, and cannot be accessed concurrently by multiple processes or threads; this will prevent any protected data from being updated or altered with conflicting information, resulting from race conditions.

In the following diagram, **Thread B** is blocked from accessing the shared resource—the critical section, named `var`—by a mutex (mutual exclusion) lock, because **Thread A** is already accessing the resource:

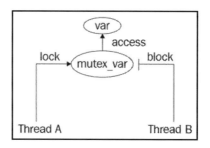

Locks prevent simultaneous access to a critical section

Now, we will specify that, in order to gain access to a critical section in a concurrent program, a thread or process needs to acquire a lock object that is associated with the critical section; similarly, that thread or process also needs to release that lock upon leaving the critical section. This setup will effectively prevent multiple accesses to the critical section, and will therefore prevent race conditions. The following diagram illustrates the execution flow of multiple threads interacting with multiple critical sections, with the implementation of locks in place:

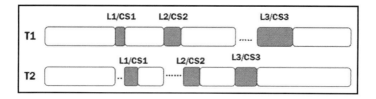

Locks and critical sections in multiple threads

As you can see in the diagram, threads **T1** and **T2** both interact with three critical sections in their respective execution instructions: **CS1**, **CS2**, and **CS3**. Here, **T1** and **T2** attempt to access **CS1** at almost the same time, and, since **CS1** is protected with lock **L1**, only **T1** is able to acquire lock **L1**, and hence, access/interact with the critical section, while **T2** has to spend time waiting for **T1** to exit out of the critical section and release the lock before accessing the section itself. Similarly, for the critical sections, **CS2** and **CS3**, although both threads require access to a critical section at the same time, only one can process it, while the other has to wait to acquire the lock associated with the critical section.

Implementation in Python

Now, let's implement the specification in the preceding example, in order to solve the problem of race conditions. Navigate to the Chapter21/example2.py file and consider our corrected update() function, as follows:

```
# Chapter21/example2.py

import random
import time

def update():
    global counter

    with count_lock:
        current_counter = counter # reading in shared resource
        time.sleep(random.randint(0, 1)) # simulating heavy calculations
        counter = current_counter + 1
```

You can see that all of the execution instructions of a thread specified in the update() function are under the context manager of a lock object named count_lock. So, every time a thread is called to run the function, it will have to first acquire the lock object, before any instructions can be executed. In our main program, we simply create the lock object in addition to what we already had, as follows:

```
# Chapter21/example2.py

import threading

counter = 0
count_lock = threading.Lock()

threads = [threading.Thread(target=update) for i in range(20)]

for thread in threads:
    thread.start()
for thread in threads:
    thread.join()

print(f'Final counter: {counter}.')
print('Finished.')
```

Run the program, and your output should look similar to the following:

```
> python3 example2.py
Final counter: 20.
Finished.
```

You can see that the counter was successfully incremented twenty times and held the correct value at the end of the program. Furthermore, no matter how many times the script is executed, the final value of the counter will always be **20**. This is the advantage of using locks to implement critical sections in your concurrent programs.

The downside of locks

In Chapter 19, *Deadlocks*, we covered an interesting phenomenon, in which the use of locks can lead to undesirable results. Specifically, we found out that, with enough locks implemented in a concurrent program, the whole program can become sequential. Let's analyze this concept with our current program. Consider the Chapter21/example3.py file, as follows:

```python
# ch21/example3.py

import threading
import random; random.seed(0)
import time

def update(pause_period):
    global counter

    with count_lock:
        current_counter = counter # reading in shared resource
        time.sleep(pause_period) # simulating heavy calculations
        counter = current_counter + 1 # updating shared resource

pause_periods = [random.randint(0, 1) for i in range(20)]

###################################################################################

counter = 0
count_lock = threading.Lock()

start = time.perf_counter()
for i in range(20):
    update(pause_periods[i])

print('--Sequential version--')
```

```
print(f'Final counter: {counter}.')
print(f'Took {time.perf_counter() - start : .2f} seconds.')

################################################################

counter = 0

threads = [threading.Thread(target=update, args=(pause_periods[i],)) for i
in range(20)]

start = time.perf_counter()
for thread in threads:
    thread.start()
for thread in threads:
    thread.join()

print('--Concurrent version--')
print(f'Final counter: {counter}.')
print(f'Took {time.perf_counter() - start : .2f} seconds.')

################################################################

print('Finished.')
```

Turning a concurrent program sequential

The goal of this script is to compare the speed of our current concurrent program with its sequential version. Here, we are still using the same update() function, with locks, and we are running it twenty times, both sequentially and concurrently, like we did earlier. We are also creating a list of determined periods of pausing, so that these periods are consistent between when we simulate the sequential version and when we simulate the concurrent version (for this reason, the update() function now takes in a parameter that specifies the period of pausing each time it is called):

```
pause_periods = [random.randint(0, 1) for i in range(20)]
```

During the next step of the program, we simply call the update() function inside a for loop, with twenty iterations, keeping track of the time it takes for the loop to finish. Note that, even though this is to simulate the sequential version of the program, the update() function still needs the lock object to be created prior, so we are initializing it here:

```
counter = 0
count_lock = threading.Lock()

start = time.perf_counter()
```

```
for i in range(20):
    update(pause_periods[i])

print('--Sequential version--')
print(f'Final counter: {counter}.')
print(f'Took {time.perf_counter() - start : .2f} seconds.')
```

The last step is to reset the counter and run the concurrent version of the program that we already implemented. Again, we need to pass in the corresponding pause period while initializing each of the threads that run the update() function. We are also keeping track of the time it takes for this concurrent version of the program to run:

```
counter = 0

threads = [threading.Thread(target=update, args=(pause_periods[i],)) for i
in range(20)]

start = time.perf_counter()
for thread in threads:
    thread.start()
for thread in threads:
    thread.join()

print('--Concurrent version--')
print(f'Final counter: {counter}.')
print(f'Took {time.perf_counter() - start : .2f} seconds.')
```

Now, after you have run the script, you will observe that both the sequential version and the concurrent version of our program took the same amount of time to run. Specifically, the following is the output that I obtained; in this case, they both took approximately 12 seconds. The actual time that your program takes might be different, but the speed of the two versions should still be equal:

```
> python3 example3.py
--Sequential version--
Final counter: 20.
Took 12.03 seconds.
--Concurrent version--
Final counter: 20.
Took 12.03 seconds.
Finished.
```

So, our concurrent program is taking just as much time as its sequential version, which negates one of the biggest purposes of implementing concurrency in a program: improving speed. But why would concurrent and traditional sequential applications with the same sets of instructions and elements also have the same speed? Should the concurrent program always produce a faster speed than the sequential one?

Recall that, in our program, the critical section is being protected by a lock object, and no multiple threads can access it at the same time. Since all of the execution of the program (incrementing the counter for twenty times) depends on a thread accessing the critical section, the placement of the lock object on the critical section means that only one thread can be executing at a given time. With this specification, the executions of any two threads cannot overlap with each other, and no additional speed can be gained from this implementation of concurrency.

This is the phenomenon that we encountered when analyzing the problem of deadlock: if enough locks are placed in a concurrent program, that program will become entirely sequential. This is a reason why locks are sometimes undesirable solutions to problems in concurrent programming. However, this situation only happens if all of the execution of the concurrent program is dependent upon interacting with the critical section. Most of the time, reading and manipulating the data of a shared resource is only a portion of the entire program and, therefore, concurrency still provides the intended additional speed for our program.

Locks do not lock anything

An additional aspect of locks is the fact that they do not actually lock anything. The only way that a lock object is utilized, with respect to a specific shared resource, is for the threads and processes interacting with that resource to also interact with the lock. In other words, if those threads and processes choose to not check with the lock before accessing and altering the shared resource, the lock object itself cannot stop them from doing so.

In our examples, you have seen that, to implement the acquiring/releasing process of a lock object, the instructions of a thread or process will be wrapped around by a lock context manager; this specification is dependent on the implementation of the thread/process execution logic and not the resource. That is because the lock objects that we have seen are not connected to the resources that they are supposed to protect in any way. So, if the thread/process execution logic does not require any interaction with the lock object associated with the shared resource, that thread or process can simply gain access to the resource without difficulty, potentially resulting in the mismanipulation and corruption of data.

This is not only true in the scope of having multiple threads and processes in a single concurrent program. Suppose that we have a concurrent system consisting of multiple components that all interact and manipulate the data of a resource shared across the system, and this resource is associated with a lock object; it follows that, if any of these components fail to interact with that lock, it can simply bypass the protection implemented by the lock and access the shared resource. More importantly, this characteristic of locks also has implications regarding the security of a concurrent program. If an outside, malicious agent is connected to the system (say, a malicious client interacting with a server) and intends to corrupt the data shared across the system, that agent can be instructed to simply ignore the lock object and access that data in an intrusive way.

The view that locks don't lock anything was popularized by Raymond Hettinger, a Python core developer who worked on the implementation of various elements in Python concurrent programming. It is argued that using lock objects alone does not guarantee a secure implementation of concurrent data structures and systems. Locks need to be concretely linked to the resources that they are to protect, and nothing should be able to access a resource without first acquiring the lock that is associated with it. Alternatively, other concurrent synchronization tools, such as atomic message queues, can provide a solution to this problem.

Race conditions in real life

You have now learned about the concept of race conditions, how they are caused in concurrent systems, and how to effectively prevent them. In this section, we will provide an overarching view of how race conditions can occur in real-life examples, within the various sub-fields of computer science. Specifically, we will be discussing the topics of security, file management, and networking.

Security

Concurrent programming can have significant implications in terms of the security of the system in question. Recall that a race condition arises between the process of reading and altering the data of a resource; a race condition in an authenticating system can cause the corruption of data between the **time of check** (when the credentials of an agent are checked) and the **time of use** (when the agent can utilize the resource). This problem is also known as a **Time-Of-Check-To-Time-Of-Use** (**TOCTTOU**) bug, which is undoubtedly detrimental to security systems.

Careless protection of shared resources when handling race conditions, as we briefly touched upon during the last section, can provide external agents with access to those supposedly protected resources. Those agents can then change the data of the resources to create **privilege escalation** (in simple terms, to give themselves more illegal access to more shared resources), or they can simply corrupt the data, causing the whole system to malfunction.

Interestingly, race conditions can also be used to implement computer security. As race conditions result from the uncoordinated access of multiple threads/processes to a shared resources, the specification in which a race condition occurs is significantly random. For example, in our own Python example, you saw that, when simulating a race condition, the final value of the counter varies between different executions of the program; this is (partly) because of the unpredictable nature of the situation, in which multiple threads are running and accessing the shared resources. (I say partly, since the randomness also results from the random pausing periods that we generate in each execution of the program.) So, race conditions are sometimes intentionally provoked, and the information obtained when the race condition occurs can be used to generate digital fingerprints for security processes—this information, again, is significantly random, and is therefore valuable for security purposes.

Operating systems

Race conditions can occur in the context of file and memory management in an operating system, when two separate programs attempt to access the same resource, such as memory space. Imagine a situation where two processes from different programs have been running for a significant amount of time, and, even though they were originally initialized apart from each other in terms of memory space, enough data has been accumulated and the stack of execution of one process now collides with that of the other process. This can lead to the two processes sharing the same portion of memory space and can ultimately result in unpredictable consequences.

Another aspect of the complexity of race conditions is illustrated by the Unix version 7 operating system—specifically, in the `mkdir` command. Typically, the `mkdir` command is used to create a new directory in the Unix operating system; this is done by calling the `mknod` command to create the actual directory and the `chown` command to specify the owner of that directory. Because there are two separate commands to be run and a definite gap exists between when the first command is finished and the second is called, this can cause a race condition.

During the gap between the two commands, if someone can delete the new directory created by the `mknod` command and link the reference to another file, when the `chown` command is run, the ownership of that file will be changed. By exploiting this vulnerability, someone can theoretically change the ownership of any file in an operating system so that someone can create a new directory. The following diagram further illustrates this exploitation:

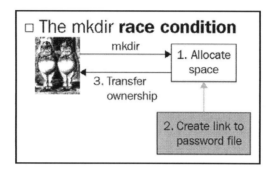

Diagram of mkdir race condition

Networking

In networking, race conditions can take the form of giving multiple users unique privileges in a network. Specifically, say a given server should only have exactly one user with admin privileges. If two users, who are both eligible to become the server admin, request access to those privileges at the same time, then it is possible for both of them to gain that access. This is because, at the point when both of the user requests are received by the server, neither of the users have been granted admin privileges yet, and the server thinks that admin privileges can still be given out.

This form of a race condition is quite common when a network is highly optimized for parallel processing (for example, non-blocking sockets), without a careful consideration of the resources shared across the network.

Summary

A race condition is defined as a phenomenon during which the output of a system is indeterminate and is dependent on the scheduling algorithm and the order in which tasks are scheduled and executed. Critical sections indicate shared resources that are accessed by multiple processes or threads in a concurrent application, which can lead to unexpected, and even erroneous, behavior. A race condition occurs when two or more threads/processes access and alter a shared resource simultaneously, resulting in mishandled and corrupted data. Race conditions also have significant implications in real-life applications, such as security, operating systems, and networking.

Since the race conditions that we observed arose when multiple threads or processes accessed and wrote to a shared resource simultaneously, the key idea for solving race conditions is to isolate the execution of different threads/processes, especially when interacting with a shared resource. With locks, we can turn a shared resource in a concurrent program into a critical section, whose integrity of data is guaranteed to be protected. However, there are a number of disadvantages to using locks: with enough locks implemented in a concurrent program, the whole program might become sequential; locks don't lock anything.

In the next chapter, we will consider one of the biggest problems in Python concurrent programming: the infamous **Global Interpreter Lock (GIL)**. You will learn about the basic idea behind the GIL, its purposes, and how to effectively work with it in concurrent Python applications.

Questions

- What is a critical section?
- What is a race condition and why is it undesirable in a concurrent program?
- What is the underlying cause of race conditions?
- How can locks solve the problem of race conditions?
- Why are locks sometimes undesirable in a concurrent program?
- What is the significance of race conditions in real-life systems and applications?

Further reading

For more information, you can refer to the following links:

- *Parallel Programming with Python*, by Jan Palach, Packt Publishing Ltd, 2014
- *Python Parallel Programming Cookbook*, by Giancarlo Zaccone, Packt Publishing Ltd, 2015
- *Race Conditions and Critical Sections* (tutorials.jenkov.com/java-concurrency/race-conditions-and-critical-sections), by Jakob Jenkov
- *Race conditions, files, and security flaws; or the tortoise and the hare redux*, by Matt Bishop, Technical Report CSE-95-98(1995)
- *Computer and Information Security, Chapter 11, Software Flaws and Malware 1 Illustration* (slideplayer.com/slide/10319860/)

22
The Global Interpreter Lock

One of the major players in Python concurrent programming is the **Global Interpreter Lock (GIL)**. In this chapter, we will cover the definition and purposes of the GIL, and how it affects concurrent Python applications. The problems that the GIL poses for Python concurrent systems and the controversy around its implementation will also be discussed. Finally, we will mention some thoughts on how Python programmers and developers should think about, and interact with, the GIL.

The following topics will be covered in this chapter:

- A brief introduction to the GIL: what gave rise to it, and the problems it causes
- Efforts in removing/fixing the GIL in Python
- How to effectively work with the GIL in Python concurrent programs

Technical requirements

The following is a list of prerequisites for this chapter:

- Ensure that you have Python 3 installed on your computer
- Download the GitHub repository at `https://github.com/PacktPublishing/AdvancedPythonProgramming`
- During this chapter, we will be working with the subfolder named `Chapter22`
- Check out the following video to see the Code in Action: `http://bit.ly/2DFDYhC`

An introduction to the Global Interpreter Lock

The GIL is quite popular in the Python concurrent programming community. Designed as a lock that will only allow one thread to access and control the Python interpreter at any given time, the GIL in Python is often known as the infamous GIL that prevents multithreaded programs from reaching their fully optimized speed. In this section, we will discuss the concept behind the GIL, and its goals: why it was designed and implemented, and how it affected multithreaded programming in Python.

An analysis of memory management in Python

Before we jump into the specifics of the GIL and its effects, let's consider the problems that Python core developers encountered during the early days of Python, and that gave rise to a need for the GIL. Specifically, there is a significant difference between Python programming and programming in other popular languages, in terms of managing objects in the memory space.

For example, in the programming language C++, a variable is actually a location in the memory space where a value will be written. This setup leads to the fact that, when a non-pointer variable is assigned with a specific value, the programming language will effectively copy that specific value to the memory location (that is, the variable). Additionally, when a variable is assigned with another variable (which is not a pointer), the memory location of the latter will be copied to that of the former; no further connection between these two variables will be maintained after the assignment.

On the other hand, Python considers a variable as simply a name, while the actual values of its variables are isolated in another region in the memory space. When a value is assigned to a variable, the variable is effectively given a reference to the location in the memory space of the value (even though the term referencing is not used in the same sense as C++ referencing). Memory management in Python is therefore fundamentally different from the model of putting a value into a memory space that we see in C++.

This means that when an assignment instruction is executed, Python simply interacts with references and switches them around—not the actual values themselves. Also, for this reason, multiple variables can be referenced by the same value, and the changes made by one variable will be reflected throughout all of the other associated variables.

Let's analyze this feature in Python. If you have already downloaded the code for this book from the GitHub page, go ahead and navigate to the `Chapter22` folder. Let's take a look at the `Chapter22/example1.py` file, as follows:

```
# Chapter22/example1.py

import sys

print(f'Reference count when direct-referencing: {sys.getrefcount([7])}.')

a = [7]
print(f'Reference count when referenced once: {sys.getrefcount(a)}.')

b = a
print(f'Reference count when referenced twice: {sys.getrefcount(a)}.')

###################################################################

a[0] = 8
print(f'Variable a after a is changed: {a}.')
print(f'Variable b after a is changed: {b}.')

print('Finished.')
```

In this example, we are looking at the management of the value `[7]` (a list of one element: the integer 7). We mentioned that values in Python are stored independently of variables, and value management in Python simply references variables to the appropriate values. The `sys.getrefcount()` method in Python takes in an object and returns the counter of all references that the value associated to that object has. Here, we are calling `sys.getrefcount()` three times: on the actual value, `[7]`; the variable a that is assigned with the value; and finally, the variable b that is assigned with the variable a.

Additionally, we are exploring the process of mutating the value by using a variable referenced with it and the resulting values of all of the variables associated to that value. Specifically, we are mutating the first element of the list via variable a, and printing out the values of both a and b. Run the script, and your output should be similar to the following:

```
> python3 example1.py
Reference count when direct-referencing: 1.
Reference count when referenced once: 2.
Reference count when referenced twice: 3.
Variable a after a is changed: [8].
Variable b after a is changed: [8].
Finished.
```

As you can see, this output is consistent with what we discussed: for the first `sys.getrefcount()` function call, there is only one reference count for the value `[7]`, which is created when we directly reference it; when we assign the list to variable `a`, the value has two references, since `a` is now associated with the value; finally, when `a` is assigned to `b`, `[7]` is additionally referenced by `b`, and the reference count is now three.

In the output of the second part of the program, we can see that, when we changed the value of which variable `a` references, `[7]` was mutated instead of the variable `a`. As a result, variable `b`, which was referencing the same value as `a`, also had its value changed.

The following diagram illustrates this process. In Python programs, variables (`a` and `b`) simply make references to the actual values (objects), and an assignment statement between two variables (for example, `a = b`) instructs Python to have the two variables reference the same object (as opposed to copying the actual value to another memory location, like in C++):

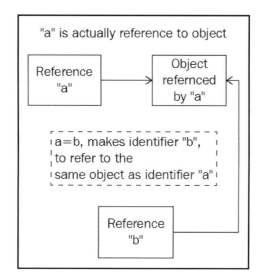

Diagram of Python's referencing scheme

The problem that the GIL addresses

Keeping Python's implementation of memory and variable management in mind, we can see that references to a given value in Python are constantly changing in a program, and keeping track of the reference count for a value is therefore highly important.

Now, applying what you learned in *Chapter 21*, *Race Conditions*, you should know that in a Python concurrent program, this reference count is a shared resource that needs protection from race conditions. In other words, this reference count is a critical section, which, if handled carelessly, will result in an incorrect interpretation of how many variables are referencing a particular value. This will cause memory leaks that will make Python programs significantly inefficient, and may even release a memory that is actually being referenced by some variables, losing that value forever.

As you learned in the previous chapter, a solution to making sure that race conditions will not occur with regard to a particular shared resource is to place a lock on that resource, effectively allowing one thread, at the most, to access the resource at any given time within a concurrent program. We also discussed that, if enough locks are placed in a concurrent program, that program will become entirely sequential, and no additional speed will be gained by implementing concurrency.

The GIL is a solution to the combination of the two preceding problems, being one single lock on the entire execution of Python. The GIL must first be acquired by any Python instruction that wants to be executed (CPU-bound tasks), preventing a race condition from occurring for any reference count.

In the early days of the development of the Python language, other solutions to the problem described here were also proposed, but the GIL was the most efficient and simple to implement, by far. Since the GIL is a lightweight, overarching lock for the entire execution of Python, no other lock needs to be implemented to guarantee the integrity of other critical sections, keeping the performance overhead of Python programs at a minimum.

Problems raised by the GIL

Intuitively, with a lock guarding all CPU-bound tasks in Python, a concurrent program will not be able to become fully multithreading. The GIL effectively prevents CPU-bound tasks from being executed in parallel across multiple threads. To understand the effect of this feature of the GIL, let's consider an example in Python; navigate to Chapter22/example2.py, as follows:

```python
# Chapter22/example2.py

import time
import threading

COUNT = 50000000

def countdown(n):
    while n > 0:
        n -= 1

###########################################################################

start = time.time()
countdown(COUNT)

print('Sequential program finished.')
print(f'Took {time.time() - start : .2f} seconds.')

###########################################################################

thread1 = threading.Thread(target=countdown, args=(COUNT // 2,))
thread2 = threading.Thread(target=countdown, args=(COUNT // 2,))

start = time.time()
thread1.start()
thread2.start()
thread1.join()
thread2.join()

print('Concurrent program finished.')
print(f'Took {time.time() - start : .2f} seconds.')
```

In this example, we are comparing the speed of executing a particular program in Python sequentially and concurrently, via multithreading. Specifically, we have a function named `countdown()` that simulates a heavy CPU-bound task, which takes in a number, n, and decrements it until it becomes zero or negative. We then call `countdown()` on 50,000,000 once, as a sequential program. Finally, we call the function twice, each in a separate thread, on 25,000,000, which is exactly half of 50,000,000; this is the multithreading version of the program. We are also keeping track of the time it takes for Python to run both the sequential program and the multithreading program.

Theoretically, the multithreading version of the program should take half as long as the sequential version, as the task is effectively being split in half and run in parallel, via the two threads that we created. However, the output produced by the program would suggest otherwise. The following output is what I obtained through running the script:

```
> python3 example2.py
Sequential program finished.
Took 2.80 seconds.
Concurrent program finished.
Took 2.74 seconds.
```

Contrary to what we predicted, the concurrent version of the countdown took almost as long as the sequential version; multithreading did not offer any considerable speedup for our program. This is a direct effect of having the GIL guarding CPU-bound tasks, as multiple threads are not allowed to run simultaneously. Sometimes, a multithreading program can take even longer to complete its execution than its sequential counterpart, since there is also the overhead of acquiring and releasing the GIL.

This is undoubtedly a significant problem for multithreading, and for concurrent programming in Python in general, because as long as a program contains CPU-bound instructions, those instructions will, in fact, be sequential in the execution of the program. However, instructions that are not CPU-bound happen outside the GIL, and thus, they are not affected by the GIL (for example, I/O-bound instructions).

The potential removal of the GIL from Python

You have learned that the GIL sets a significant constraint on our multithreading programs in Python, especially those with CPU-bound tasks. For this reason, many Python developers have come to view the GIL in a negative light, and the term *"the infamous GIL"* has started to become popular; it is not surprising that some have even advocated the complete removal of the GIL from the Python language.

In fact, multiple attempts to remove the GIL have been made by prominent Python users. However, the GIL is so deeply implanted in the implementation of the language, and the execution of most libraries and packages that are not thread-safe is so significantly dependent on the GIL, that the removal of the GIL will actually engender bugs as well as backward incompatibility issues for your Python programs. A number of Python developers and researchers tried to completely omit the GIL from Python execution, and most existing C extensions, which depend heavily on the functionalities of the GIL, stopped working.

Now there are other viable solutions to address the problems that we have discussed; in other words, the GIL is in every way replaceable. However, most of these solutions contain so many complex instructions that they actually decrease the performance of sequential and I/O-bound programs, which are not affected by the GIL. So, these solutions will slow down single-threaded or multithreaded I/O programs, which actually make up a large percentage of existing Python applications. Interestingly, the creator of Python, Guido van Rossum, also commented on this topic in his article, *It isn't Easy to Remove the GIL*:

> *"I'd welcome a set of patches into Py3k only if the performance for a single-threaded program (and for a multi-threaded but I/O-bound program) does not decrease."*

Unfortunately, this request has not been achieved by any of the proposed alternatives to the GIL. The GIL remains an integral part of the Python language.

How to work with the GIL

There are a few ways to deal with the GIL in your Python applications, which will be addressed as follows.

Implementing multiprocessing, rather than multithreading

This is perhaps the most popular and easiest method to circumvent the GIL and achieve optimal speed in a concurrent program. As the GIL only prevents multiple threads from executing CPU-bound tasks simultaneously, processes executing over multiple cores of a system, each having its own memory space, are completely immune to the GIL.

Specifically, considering the preceding countdown example, let's compare the performance of that CPU-bound program when it is sequential, multithreading, and multiprocessing. Navigate to the `Chapter22/example3.py` file; the first part of the program is identical to what we saw earlier, but at the end we add in an implementation of a multiprocessing solution for the problem of counting down from 50,000,000, using two separate processes:

```python
# Chapter22/example3.py

import time
import threading
from multiprocessing import Pool

COUNT = 50000000

def countdown(n):
    while n > 0:
        n -= 1

if __name__ == '__main__':

    ###########################################################################
    # Sequential

    start = time.time()
    countdown(COUNT)

    print('Sequential program finished.')
    print(f'Took {time.time() - start : .2f} seconds.')
    print()

    ###########################################################################
    # Multithreading

    thread1 = threading.Thread(target=countdown, args=(COUNT // 2,))
    thread2 = threading.Thread(target=countdown, args=(COUNT // 2,))

    start = time.time()
    thread1.start()
```

```
thread2.start()
thread1.join()
thread2.join()

print('Multithreading program finished.')
print(f'Took {time.time() - start : .2f} seconds.')
print()

##################################################################
# Multiprocessing

pool = Pool(processes=2)
start = time.time()
pool.apply_async(countdown, args=(COUNT//2,))
pool.apply_async(countdown, args=(COUNT//2,))
pool.close()
pool.join()

print('Multiprocessing program finished.')
print(f'Took {time.time() - start : .2f} seconds.')
```

After running the program, my output was as follows:

```
> python3 example3.py
Sequential program finished.
Took 2.95 seconds.

Multithreading program finished.
Took 2.69 seconds.

Multiprocessing program finished.
Took 1.54 seconds.
```

There is still a minimal difference in speed between the sequential and multithreading versions of the program. However, the multiprocessing version was able to cut that speed by almost half in its execution; as discussed in earlier chapters; since processes are fairly heavy weight, multiprocessing instructions contain significant overhead, which is the reason why the speed of the multiprocessing program was not exactly half of the sequential program.

Getting around the GIL with native extensions

There are Python native extensions that are written in C/C++, and are therefore able to avoid the limitations that the GIL sets out; one example is the most popular Python scientific computing package, NumPy. Within these extensions, manual releases of the GIL can be made, so that the execution can simply bypass the lock. However, these releases need to be implemented carefully and accompanied by the reassertion of the GIL before the execution goes back to the main Python execution.

Utilizing a different Python interpreter

The GIL only exists in CPython, which is the most common interpreter for the language by far, and is built in C. However, there are other interpreters for Python, such as Jython (written in Java) and IronPython (written in C++), that can be used to avoid the GIL and its affects on multithreading programs. Keep in mind that these interpreters are not as widely used as CPython, and some packages and libraries might not be compatible with one or both of them.

Summary

While the GIL in Python offers a simple and intuitive solution to one of the more difficult problems in the language, it also raises a number of problems of its own, concerning the ability to run multiple threads in a Python program to process CPU-bound tasks. Multiple attempts have been made to remove the GIL from the main implementation of Python, but none have been able to achieve it while maintaining the effectiveness of processing non-CPU-bound tasks, which are affected by the GIL.

In Python, multiple methods are available to provide options for working with the GIL. All in all, while it possesses considerable notoriety among the Python programming community, the GIL only affects a certain portion of the Python ecosystem, and can be seen as a necessary evil that is too essential to remove from the language. Python developers should learn to coexist with the GIL, and work around it in their concurrent programs.

In the last four chapters, we discussed some of the most well-known and common problems in concurrent programming in Python. In the last section of the book, we will be looking at some of the more advanced functionalities of concurrency that Python provides. In the next chapter, you will learn about the design of lock-free and lock-based concurrent data structures.

Questions

- What are the differences in memory management between Python and C++?
- What problem does the GIL solve for Python?
- What problem does the GIL create for Python?
- What are some of the approaches to circumventing the GIL in Python programs?

Further reading

For more information, you can refer to the following links:

- *What is the Python Global Interpreter Lock (GIL)?* (`realpython.com/python-gil/`), Abhinav Ajitsaria
- *The Python GIL Visualized* (`dabeaz.blogspot.com/2010/01/python-gil-visualized`), Dave Beazley
- *Copy Operations in Python* (`pythontic.com/modules/copy/introduction`)
- *It isn't Easy to Remove the GIL* (`www.artima.com/weblogs/viewpost.jsp?thread=214235`), Guido Van Rossum
- *Parallel Programming with Python*, by Jan Palach, Packt Publishing Ltd, 2014
- *Learning Concurrency in Python: Build highly efficient, robust, and concurrent applications*, Elliot Forbes (2017)

23
The Factory Pattern

Design patterns are reusable programming solutions that have been used in various real-world contexts, and have proved to produce expected results. They are shared among programmers and continue being improved over time. This topic is popular thanks to the book by Erich Gamma, Richard Helm, Ralph Johnson, and John Vlissides, titled *Design Patterns: Elements of Reusable Object-Oriented Software*.

 Gang of Four: The book by Erich Gamma, Richard Helm, Ralph Johnson, and John Vlissides is also called the *Gang of Four* book for short (or *GOF book* for even shorter).

Here is a quote about design patterns from the *Gang of Four book*:

A design pattern systematically names, motivates, and explains a general design that addresses a recurring design problem in object-oriented systems. It describes the problem, the solution, when to apply the solution, and its consequences. It also gives implementation hints and examples. The solution is a general arrangement of objects and classes that solve the problem. The solution is customized and implemented to solve the problem in a particular context.

There are several categories of design patterns used in **object-oriented programming**, depending on the type of problem they address and/or the types of solutions they help us build. In their book, the *Gang of Four* present 23 design patterns, split into three categories: **creational**, **structural**, and **behavioral**.

Creational design patterns are the first category we will cover throughout this chapter, and *Chapters 24*, *The Builder Pattern* and *Chapter 25*, *Other Creational Patterns*. These patterns deal with different aspects of object creation. Their goal is to provide better alternatives for situations where direct object creation, which in Python happens within the __init__() function, is not convenient.

See `https://docs.python.org/3/tutorial/classes.html` for a quick overview of object classes and the special `__init__()` method Python uses to initialize a new class instance.

We will start with the first creational design pattern from the *Gang of Four* book: the factory design pattern. In the factory design pattern, a **client** (meaning client code) asks for an object without knowing where the object is coming from (that is, which class is used to generate it). The idea behind a factory is to simplify the object creation process. It is easier to track which objects are created if this is done through a central function, compared to letting a client create objects using a direct class instantiation. A factory reduces the complexity of maintaining an application by decoupling the code that creates an object from the code that uses it.

Factories typically come in two forms—the **factory method**, which is a method (or simply a function for a Python developer) that returns a different object per input parameter, and the **abstract factory**, which is a group of factory methods used to create a family of related objects.

In this chapter, we will discuss:

- The factory method
- The abstract factory

The factory method

The factory method is based on a single function written to handle our object creation task. We execute it, passing a parameter that provides information about what we want, and, as a result, the wanted object is created.

Interestingly, when using the factory method, we are not required to know any details about how the resulting object is implemented and where it is coming from.

Real-world examples

An example of the factory method pattern used in reality is in the context of a plastic toy construction kit. The molding material used to construct plastic toys is the same, but different toys (different figures or shapes) can be produced using the right plastic molds. This is like having a factory method in which the input is the name of the toy that we want (for example, *duck* or *car*) and the output (after the molding) is the plastic toy that was requested.

In the software world, the Django web framework uses the factory method pattern for creating the fields of a web form. The `forms` module, included in Django, supports the creation of different kinds of fields (for example, `CharField`, `EmailField`, and so on). And parts of their behavior can be customized using attributes such as `max_length` or `required` (j.mp/djangofac). As an illustration, there follows a snippet that a developer could write for a form (the `PersonForm` form containing the fields `name` and `birth_date`) as part of a Django application's UI code:

```
from django import forms

class PersonForm(forms.Form):
    name = forms.CharField(max_length=100)
    birth_date = forms.DateField(required=False)
```

Use cases

If you realize that you cannot track the objects created by your application because the code that creates them is in many different places instead of in a single function/method, you should consider using the factory method pattern. The factory method centralizes object creation and tracking your objects becomes much easier. Note that it is absolutely fine to create more than one factory method, and this is how it is typically done in practice. Each factory method logically groups the creation of objects that have similarities. For example, one factory method might be responsible for connecting you to different databases (MySQL, SQLite), another factory method might be responsible for creating the geometrical object that you request (circle, triangle), and so on.

The factory method is also useful when you want to decouple object creation from object usage. We are not coupled/bound to a specific class when creating an object; we just provide partial information about what we want by calling a function. This means that introducing changes to the function is easy and does not require any changes to the code that uses it.

Another use case worth mentioning is related to improving the performance and memory usage of an application. A factory method can improve the performance and memory usage by creating new objects only if it is absolutely necessary. When we create objects using a direct class instantiation, extra memory is allocated every time a new object is created (unless the class uses caching internally, which is usually not the case). We can see that in practice in the following code (file id.py), it creates two instances of the same class, A, and uses the id() function to compare their **memory addresses**. The addresses are also printed in the output so that we can inspect them. The fact that the memory addresses are different means that two distinct objects are created as follows:

```
class A:
    pass

if __name__ == '__main__':
    a = A()
    b = A()
    print(id(a) == id(b))
    print(a, b)
```

Executing the python id.py command on my computer results in the following output:

```
False
<__main__.A object at 0x7f5771de8f60> <__main__.A object at 0x7f5771df2208>
```

Note that the addresses that you see if you execute the file are not the same as the ones I see because they depend on the current memory layout and allocation. But the result must be the same—the two addresses should be different. There's one exception that happens if you write and execute the code in the Python **Read-Eval-Print Loop** (**REPL**)—or simply put, the interactive prompt—but that's a REPL-specific optimization which does not happen normally.

Implementing the factory method

Data comes in many forms. There are two main file categories for storing/retrieving data: human-readable files and binary files. Examples of human-readable files are XML, RSS/Atom, YAML, and JSON. Examples of binary files are the .sq3 file format used by SQLite and the .mp3 audio file format used to listen to music.

In this example, we will focus on two popular human-readable formats—XML and JSON. Although human-readable files are generally slower to parse than binary files, they make data exchange, inspection, and modification much easier. For this reason, it is advised that you work with human-readable files, unless there are other restrictions that do not allow it (mainly unacceptable performance and proprietary binary formats).

In this case, we have some input data stored in an XML and a JSON file, and we want to parse them and retrieve some information. At the same time, we want to centralize the client's connection to those (and all future) external services. We will use the factory method to solve this problem. The example focuses only on XML and JSON, but adding support for more services should be straightforward.

First, let's take a look at the data files.

The JSON file, `movies.json`, is an example (found on GitHub) of a dataset containing information about American movies (title, year, director name, genre, and so on). This is actually a big file but here is an extract, simplified for better readability, to show how its content is organized:

```
[
  {"title":"After Dark in Central Park",
   "year":1900,
   "director":null, "cast":null, "genre":null},
  {"title":"Boarding School Girls' Pajama Parade",
   "year":1900,
   "director":null, "cast":null, "genre":null},
  {"title":"Buffalo Bill's Wild West Parad",
   "year":1900,
   "director":null, "cast":null, "genre":null},
  {"title":"Caught",
   "year":1900,
   "director":null, "cast":null, "genre":null},
  {"title":"Clowns Spinning Hats",
   "year":1900,
   "director":null, "cast":null, "genre":null},
{"title":"Capture of Boer Battery by British",
   "year":1900,
   "director":"James H. White", "cast":null, "genre":"Short documentary"},
  {"title":"The Enchanted Drawing",
   "year":1900,
   "director":"J. Stuart Blackton", "cast":null,"genre":null},
  {"title":"Family Troubles",
   "year":1900,
   "director":null, "cast":null, "genre":null},
  {"title":"Feeding Sea Lions",
   "year":1900,
```

```
"director":null, "cast":"Paul Boyton", "genre":null}
]
```

The XML file, `person.xml`, is based on a Wikipedia example (`j.mp/wikijson`), and contains information about individuals (`firstName`, `lastName`, `gender`, and so on) as follows:

1. We start with the enclosing tag of the persons XML container:

   ```
   <persons>
   ```

2. Then, an XML element representing a person's data code is presented as follows:

   ```
   <person>
     <firstName>John</firstName>
     <lastName>Smith</lastName>
     <age>25</age>
     <address>
       <streetAddress>21 2nd Street</streetAddress>
       <city>New York</city>
       <state>NY</state>
       <postalCode>10021</postalCode>
     </address>
     <phoneNumbers>
       <phoneNumber type="home">212 555-1234</phoneNumber>
       <phoneNumber type="fax">646 555-4567</phoneNumber>
     </phoneNumbers>
     <gender>
       <type>male</type>
     </gender>
   </person>
   ```

3. An XML element representing another person's data is shown by the following code:

   ```
   <person>
     <firstName>Jimy</firstName>
     <lastName>Liar</lastName>
     <age>19</age>
     <address>
       <streetAddress>18 2nd Street</streetAddress>
       <city>New York</city>
       <state>NY</state>
       <postalCode>10021</postalCode>
     </address>
     <phoneNumbers>
     <phoneNumber type="home">212 555-1234</phoneNumber>
     </phoneNumbers>
   ```

```
  <gender>
    <type>male</type>
  </gender>
</person>
```

4. An XML element representing a third person's data is shown by the code:

```
<person>
  <firstName>Patty</firstName>
  <lastName>Liar</lastName>
  <age>20</age>
  <address>
    <streetAddress>18 2nd Street</streetAddress>
    <city>New York</city>
    <state>NY</state>
    <postalCode>10021</postalCode>
  </address>
  <phoneNumbers>
    <phoneNumber type="home">212 555-1234</phoneNumber>
    <phoneNumber type="mobile">001 452-8819</phoneNumber>
  </phoneNumbers>
  <gender>
    <type>female</type>
  </gender>
</person>
```

5. Finally, we close the XML container:

```
</persons>
```

We will use two libraries that are part of the Python distribution for working with JSON and XML, `json` and `xml.etree.ElementTree`, as follows:

```
import json
import xml.etree.ElementTree as etree
```

The `JSONDataExtractor` class parses the JSON file and has a `parsed_data()` method that returns all data as a dictionary (`dict`). The property decorator is used to make `parsed_data()` appear as a normal attribute instead of a method, as follows:

```
class JSONDataExtractor:
  def __init__(self, filepath):
    self.data = dict()
    with open(filepath, mode='r', encoding='utf-8') as
    f:self.data = json.load(f)
    @property
    def parsed_data(self):
        return self.data
```

The `XMLDataExtractor` class parses the XML file and has a `parsed_data()` method that returns all data as a list of `xml.etree.Element` as follows:

```
class XMLDataExtractor:
  def __init__(self, filepath):
  self.tree =  etree.parse(filepath)
  @property
  def parsed_data(self):
  return self.tree
```

The `dataextraction_factory()` function is a factory method. It returns an instance of `JSONDataExtractor` or `XMLDataExtractor` depending on the extension of the input file path as follows:

```
def dataextraction_factory(filepath):
    if filepath.endswith('json'):
        extractor = JSONDataExtractor
    elif filepath.endswith('xml'):
        extractor = XMLDataExtractor
    else:
        raise ValueError('Cannot extract data from {}'.format(filepath))
    return extractor(filepath)
```

The `extract_data_from()` function is a wrapper of `dataextraction_factory()`. It adds exception handling as follows:

```
def extract_data_from(filepath):
    factory_obj = None
    try:
        factory_obj = dataextraction_factory(filepath)
    except ValueError as e:
        print(e)
    return factory_obj
```

The `main()` function demonstrates how the factory method design pattern can be used. The first part makes sure that exception handling is effective, as follows:

```
def main():
    sqlite_factory = extract_data_from('data/person.sq3')
    print()
```

The next part shows how to work with the JSON files using the factory method. Based on the parsing, the title, year, director name, and genre of the movie can be shown (when the value is not empty), as follows:

```
json_factory = extract_data_from('data/movies.json')
json_data = json_factory.parsed_data
print(f'Found: {len(json_data)} movies')
for movie in json_data:
  print(f"Title: {movie['title']}")
  year = movie['year']
  if year:
  print(f"Year: {year}")
  director = movie['director']
  if director:
  print(f"Director: {director}")
  genre = movie['genre']
  if genre:
  print(f"Genre: {genre}")
  print()
```

The final part shows you how to work with the XML files using the factory method. XPath is used to find all person elements that have the last name `Liar` (using `liars = xml_data.findall(f".//person[lastName='Liar']")`). For each matched person, the basic name and phone number information are shown, as follows:

```
xml_factory = extract_data_from('data/person.xml')
xml_data = xml_factory.parsed_data
liars = xml_data.findall(f".//person[lastName='Liar']")
print(f'found: {len(liars)} persons')
for liar in liars:
    firstname = liar.find('firstName').text
    print(f'first name: {firstname}')
    lastname = liar.find('lastName').text
    print(f'last name: {lastname}')
    [print(f"phone number ({p.attrib['type']}):", p.text)
    for p in liar.find('phoneNumbers')]
    print()
```

Here is the summary of the implementation (you can find the code in the `factory_method.py` file):

1. We start by importing the modules we need (`json` and `ElementTree`).
2. We define the JSON data extractor class (`JSONDataExtractor`).
3. We define the XML data extractor class (`XMLDataExtractor`).
4. We add the factory function, `dataextraction_factory()`, for getting the right data extractor class.
5. We also add our wrapper for handling exceptions, the `extract_data_from()` function.
6. Finally, we have the `main()` function, followed by Python's conventional trick for calling it when invoking this file from the command line. The following are the aspects of the `main` function:
   - We try to extract data from an SQL file (`data/person.sq3`), to show how the exception is handled
   - We extract data from a JSON file and parse the result
   - We extract data from an XML file and parse the result

The following is the type of output (for the different cases) you will get by calling the `python factory_method.py` command.

First, there is an exception message when trying to access an SQLite (`.sq3`) file:

```
Cannot extract data from data/person.sq3
```

Then, we get the following result from processing the `movies` file (JSON):

```
Found: 9 movies
Title: After Dark in Central Park
Year: 1900

Title: Boarding School Girls' Pajama Parade
Year: 1900

Title: Buffalo Bill's Wild West Parad
Year: 1900

Title: Caught
Year: 1900

Title: Clowns Spinning Hats
Year: 1900

Title: Capture of Boer Battery by British
Year: 1900
Director: James H. White
Genre: Short documentary

Title: The Enchanted Drawing
Year: 1900
Director: J. Stuart Blackton

Title: Family Troubles
Year: 1900

Title: Feeding Sea Lions
Year: 1900
```

Finally, we get this result from processing the `person` XML file to find the people whose last name is `Liar`:

```
found: 2 persons
first name: Jimy
last name: Liar
phone number (home): 212 555-1234

first name: Patty
last name: Liar
phone number (home): 212 555-1234
phone number (mobile): 001 452-8819
```

Notice that although `JSONDataExtractor` and `XMLDataExtractor` have the same interfaces, what is returned by `parsed_data()` is not handled in a uniform way. Different Python code must be used to work with each **data extractor**. Although it would be nice to be able to use the same code for all extractors, this is not realistic for the most part, unless we use some kind of common mapping for the data, which is very often provided by external data providers. Assuming that you can use exactly the same code for handling the XML and JSON files, what changes are required to support a third format, for example, SQLite? Find an SQLite file, or create your own and try it.

The abstract factory

The abstract factory design pattern is a generalization of the factory method. Basically, an abstract factory is a (logical) group of factory methods, where each factory method is responsible for generating a different kind of object.

We are going to discuss some examples, use cases, and a possible implementation.

Real-world examples

The abstract factory is used in car manufacturing. The same machinery is used for stamping the parts (doors, panels, hoods, fenders, and mirrors) of different car models. The model that is assembled by the machinery is configurable and easy to change at any time.

In the software category, the `factory_boy` (`https://github.com/FactoryBoy/factory_boy`) package provides an abstract factory implementation for creating Django models in tests. It is used for creating instances of models that support **test-specific attributes**. This is important because, this way, your tests become readable and you avoid sharing unnecessary code.

 Django models are special classes used by the framework to help store and interact with data in the database (tables). See the Django documentation (`https://docs.djangoproject.com`) for more details.

Use cases

Since the abstract factory pattern is a generalization of the factory method pattern, it offers the same benefits, it makes tracking an object creation easier, it decouples object creation from object usage, and it gives us the potential to improve the memory usage and performance of our application.

But, a question is raised: How do we know when to use the factory method versus using an abstract factory? The answer is that we usually start with the factory method which is simpler. If we find out that our application requires many factory methods, which it makes sense to combine to create a family of objects, we end up with an abstract factory.

A benefit of the abstract factory that is usually not very visible from a user's point of view when using the factory method is that it gives us the ability to modify the behavior of our application dynamically (at runtime) by changing the active factory method. The classic example is the ability to change the look and feel of an application (for example, Apple-like, Windows-like, and so on) for the user while the application is in use, without the need to terminate it and start it again.

Implementing the abstract factory pattern

To demonstrate the abstract factory pattern, I will reuse one of my favorite examples, included in the book, *Python 3 Patterns, Recipes and Idioms*, by Bruce Eckel. Imagine that we are creating a game or we want to include a mini-game as part of our application to entertain our users. We want to include at least two games, one for children and one for adults. We will decide which game to create and launch at runtime, based on user input. An abstract factory takes care of the game creation part.

Let's start with the kid's game. It is called **FrogWorld**. The main hero is a frog who enjoys eating bugs. Every hero needs a good name, and in our case, the name is given by the user at runtime. The `interact_with()` method is used to describe the interaction of the frog with an obstacle (for example, a bug, puzzle, and other frogs) as follows:

```
class Frog:
    def __init__(self, name):
        self.name = name

    def __str__(self):
        return self.name

    def interact_with(self, obstacle):
        act = obstacle.action()
        msg = f'{self} the Frog encounters {obstacle} and {act}!'
        print(msg)
```

There can be many different kinds of obstacles but for our example, an obstacle can only be a bug. When the frog encounters a bug, only one action is supported. It eats it:

```
class Bug:
    def __str__(self):
        return 'a bug'

    def action(self):
        return 'eats it'
```

The `FrogWorld` class is an abstract factory. Its main responsibilities are creating the main character and the obstacle(s) in the game. Keeping the creation methods separate and their names generic (for example, `make_character()` and `make_obstacle()`) allows us to change the active factory (and therefore the active game) dynamically without any code changes. In a statically typed language, the abstract factory would be an abstract class/interface with empty methods, but in Python, this is not required because the types are checked at runtime (`j.mp/ginstromdp`). The code is as follows:

```
class FrogWorld:
    def __init__(self, name):
        print(self)
        self.player_name = name

    def __str__(self):
        return '\n\n\t------ Frog World -------'

    def make_character(self):
        return Frog(self.player_name)
```

```
    def make_obstacle(self):
        return Bug()
```

The **WizardWorld** game is similar. The only difference is that the wizard battles against monsters such as `orks` instead of eating bugs!

Here is the definition of the `Wizard` class, which is similar to the `Frog` one:

```
class Wizard:
    def __init__(self, name):
        self.name = name

    def __str__(self):
        return self.name

    def interact_with(self, obstacle):
        act = obstacle.action()
        msg = f'{self} the Wizard battles against {obstacle}
        and {act}!'
        print(msg)
```

Then, the definition of the `Ork` class is as follows:

```
class Ork:
    def __str__(self):
        return 'an evil ork'

    def action(self):
        return 'kills it'
```

We also need to define the `WizardWorld` class, similar to the `FrogWorld` one that we have discussed; the obstacle, in this case, is an `Ork` instance:

```
class WizardWorld:
    def __init__(self, name):
        print(self)
        self.player_name = name

    def __str__(self):
        return '\n\n\t------ Wizard World -------'

    def make_character(self):
        return Wizard(self.player_name)

    def make_obstacle(self):
        return Ork()
```

The `GameEnvironment` class is the main entry point of our game. It accepts the factory as an input and uses it to create the world of the game. The `play()` method initiates the interaction between the created hero and the obstacle, as follows:

```
class GameEnvironment:
    def __init__(self, factory):
        self.hero = factory.make_character()
        self.obstacle = factory.make_obstacle()

    def play(self):
        self.hero.interact_with(self.obstacle)
```

The `validate_age()` function prompts the user to give a valid age. If the age is not valid, it returns a tuple with the first element set to `False`. If the age is fine, the first element of the tuple is set to `True` and that's the case where we actually care about the second element of the tuple, which is the age given by the user, as follows:

```
def validate_age(name):
    try:
        age = input(f'Welcome {name}. How old are you? ')
        age = int(age)
    except ValueError as err:
        print(f"Age {age} is invalid, please try again...")
        return (False, age)
    return (True, age)
```

Last but not least comes the `main()` function. It asks for the user's name and age, and decides which game should be played, given the age of the user, as follows:

```
def main():
    name = input("Hello. What's your name? ")
    valid_input = False
    while not valid_input:
        valid_input, age = validate_age(name)
    game = FrogWorld if age < 18 else WizardWorld
    environment = GameEnvironment(game(name))
    environment.play()
```

The summary for the implementation we just discussed (see the complete code in the `abstract_factory.py` file) is as follows:

1. We define the `Frog` and `Bug` classes for the FrogWorld game.
2. We add the `FrogWorld` class, where we use our `Frog` and `Bug` classes.

3. We define the `Wizard` and `Ork` classes for the WizardWorld game.
4. We add the `WizardWorld` class, where we use our `Wizard` and `Ork` classes.
5. We define the `GameEnvironment` class.
6. We add the `validate_age()` function.
7. Finally, we have the `main()` function, followed by the conventional trick for calling it. The following are the aspects of this function:
   - We get the user's input for name and age
   - We decide which game class to use based on the user's age
   - We instantiate the right game class, and then the `GameEnvironment` class
   - We call `.play()` on the environment object to play the game

Let's call this program using the `python abstract_factory.py` command, and see some sample output.

The sample output for a teenager is as follows:

```
Hello. What's your name? Billy
Welcome Billy. How old are you? 12


        ------ Frog World -------
Billy the Frog encounters a bug and eats it!
```

The sample output for an adult is as follows:

```
Hello. What's your name? Charles
Welcome Charles. How old are you? 25


        ------ Wizard World -------
Charles the Wizard battles against an evil ork and kills it!
```

Try extending the game to make it more complete. You can go as far as you want; create many obstacles, many enemies, and whatever else you like.

Summary

In this chapter, we have seen how to use the factory method and the abstract factory design patterns. Both patterns are used when we want to track object creation, decouple object creation from object usage, or even improve the performance and resource usage of an application. Improving the performance was not demonstrated in this chapter. You might consider trying it as a good exercise.

The factory method design pattern is implemented as a single function that doesn't belong to any class and is responsible for the creation of a single kind of object (a shape, a connection point, and so on). We saw how the factory method relates to toy construction, mentioned how it is used by Django for creating different form fields, and discussed other possible use cases for it. As an example, we implemented a factory method that provided access to the XML and JSON files.

The abstract factory design pattern is implemented as a number of factory methods that belong to a single class and are used to create a family of related objects (the parts of a car, the environment of a game, and so forth). We mentioned how the abstract factory is related to car manufacturing, how the `django_factory` package for Django makes use of it to create clean tests, and then we covered its common use cases. Our implementation example of the abstract factory is a mini-game that shows how we can use many related factories in a single class.

In the next chapter, we will discuss the builder pattern, which is another creational pattern that can be used for fine-tuning the creation of complex objects.

24
The Builder Pattern

In the previous chapter, we covered the first two creational patterns, the factory method and abstract factory, which both offer approaches to improve the way we create objects in nontrivial cases.

Now, imagine that we want to create an object that is composed of multiple parts and the composition needs to be done step by step. The object is not complete unless all its parts are fully created. That's where the builder design pattern can help us. The builder pattern separates the construction of a complex object from its representation. By keeping the construction separate from the representation, the same construction can be used to create several different representations (j.mp/builderpat).

A practical example can help us understand what the purpose of the builder pattern is. Suppose that we want to create an HTML page generator. The basic structure (construction part) of an HTML page is always the same: it begins with <html> and finishes with </html>, inside the HTML section are the <head> and </head> elements, inside the head section are the <title> and </title> elements, and so forth. But the representation of the page can differ. Each page has its own title, its own headings, and different <body> contents. Moreover, the page is usually built in steps: one function adds the title, another adds the main heading, another the footer, and so on. Only after the whole structure of a page is complete can it be shown to the client using a final render function. We can take it even further and extend the HTML generator so that it can generate totally different HTML pages. One page might contain tables, another page might contain image galleries, yet another page contains the contact form, and so on.

The HTML page generation problem can be solved using the builder pattern. In this pattern, there are two main participants:

- **The builder**: The component responsible for creating the various parts of a complex object. In this example, these parts are the title, heading, body, and the footer of the page.
- **The director**: The component that controls the building process using a `builder` instance. It calls the builder's functions for setting the title, the heading, and so on. And, using a different `builder` instance allows us to create a different HTML page without touching any of the code of the director.

In this chapter, we will discuss:

- Real-world examples
- Use cases
- Implementation

Real-world examples

In our everyday life, the builder design pattern is used in fast-food restaurants. The same procedure is always used to prepare a burger and the packaging (box and paper bag), even if there are many different kinds of burgers (classic, cheeseburger, and more) and different packages (small-sized box, medium-sized box, and so forth). The difference between a classic burger and a cheeseburger is in the representation, and not in the construction procedure. In this case, the **director** is the cashier who gives instructions about what needs to be prepared to the crew, and the **builder** is the person from the crew that takes care of the specific order.

We can also find software examples:

- The HTML example that was mentioned at the beginning of the chapter is actually used by django-widgy (`https://wid.gy/`), a third-party tree editor for Django that can be used as a **content management system** (**CMS**). The django-widgy editor contains a page builder that can be used for creating HTML pages with different layouts.

- The django-query-builder library (`https://github.com/ambitioninc/django-query-builder`) is another third-party Django library that relies on the builder pattern. This library can be used for building SQL queries dynamically, allowing you to control all aspects of a query and create a different range of queries, from simple to very complex ones.

Use cases

We use the builder pattern when we know that an object must be created in multiple steps, and different representations of the same construction are required. These requirements exist in many applications such as page generators (for example, the HTML page generator mentioned in this chapter), document converters, and **user interface** (**UI**) form creators (`j.mp/pipbuild`).

Some online resources mention that the builder pattern can also be used as a solution to the telescopic constructor problem. The telescopic constructor problem occurs when we are forced to create a new constructor for supporting different ways of creating an object. The problem is that we end up with many constructors and long parameter lists, which are hard to manage. An example of the telescopic constructor is listed at the Stack Overflow website (`j.mp/sobuilder`). Fortunately, this problem does not exist in Python, because it can be solved in at least two ways:

- With named parameters (`j.mp/sobuipython`)
- With argument list unpacking (`j.mp/arglistpy`)

At this point, the distinction between the builder pattern and the factory pattern might not be very clear. The main difference is that a factory pattern creates an object in a single step, whereas a builder pattern creates an object in multiple steps, and almost always through the use of a director. Some targeted implementations of the builder pattern, such as Java's StringBuilder, bypass the use of a director, but that's the exception to the rule.

Another difference is that while a factory pattern returns a created object immediately, in the builder pattern the client code explicitly asks the director to return the final object when it needs it (`j.mp/builderpat`).

The new computer analogy might help you to distinguish between a builder pattern and a factory pattern. Assume that you want to buy a new computer. If you decide to buy a specific, preconfigured computer model, for example, the latest Apple 1.4 GHz Mac Mini, you use the factory pattern. All the hardware specifications are already predefined by the manufacturer, who knows what to do without consulting you. The manufacturer typically receives just a single instruction. Code-wise, this would look like the following (apple_factory.py):

```python
MINI14 = '1.4GHz Mac mini'

class AppleFactory:
    class MacMini14:
        def __init__(self):
            self.memory = 4 # in gigabytes
            self.hdd = 500 # in gigabytes
            self.gpu = 'Intel HD Graphics 5000'

        def __str__(self):
            info = (f'Model: {MINI14}',
                    f'Memory: {self.memory}GB',
                    f'Hard Disk: {self.hdd}GB',
                    f'Graphics Card: {self.gpu}')
            return '\n'.join(info)

    def build_computer(self, model):
        if model == MINI14:
            return self.MacMini14()
        else:
            msg = f"I don't know how to build {model}"
            print(msg)
```

Now, we add the main part of the program, the snippet which uses the AppleFactory class:

```python
if __name__ == '__main__':
    afac = AppleFactory()
    mac_mini = afac.build_computer(MINI14)
    print(mac_mini)
```

Notice the nested `MacMini14` class. This is a neat way of forbidding the direct instantiation of a class.

Another option would be to buy a custom PC. In this case, you use the builder pattern. You are the director that gives orders to the manufacturer (`builder`) about your ideal computer specifications. Code-wise, this looks like the following (`computer_builder.py`):

- We define the `Computer` class as follows:

```
class Computer:
    def __init__(self, serial_number):
        self.serial = serial_number
        self.memory = None # in gigabytes
        self.hdd = None # in gigabytes
        self.gpu = None

    def __str__(self):
        info = (f'Memory: {self.memory}GB',
                f'Hard Disk: {self.hdd}GB',
                f'Graphics Card: {self.gpu}')
        return '\n'.join(info)
```

- We define the `ComputerBuilder` class:

```
class ComputerBuilder:
    def __init__(self):
        self.computer = Computer('AG23385193')

    def configure_memory(self, amount):
        self.computer.memory = amount

    def configure_hdd(self, amount):
        self.computer.hdd = amount

    def configure_gpu(self, gpu_model):
        self.computer.gpu = gpu_model
```

- We define the `HardwareEngineer` class as follows:

```
class HardwareEngineer:
    def __init__(self):
        self.builder = None

    def construct_computer(self, memory, hdd, gpu):
        self.builder = ComputerBuilder()
        steps = (self.builder.configure_memory(memory),
                 self.builder.configure_hdd(hdd),
                 self.builder.configure_gpu(gpu))
        [step for step in steps]

    @property
    def computer(self):
        return self.builder.computer
```

- We end our code with the `main()` function, followed by the trick to call it when the file is called from the command line:

```
def main():
    engineer = HardwareEngineer()
    engineer.construct_computer(hdd=500,
                                memory=8,
                                gpu='GeForce GTX 650 Ti')
    computer = engineer.computer
    print(computer)

if __name__ == '__main__':
    main()
```

The basic changes are the introduction of a builder, `ComputerBuilder`, a director, `HardwareEngineer`, and the step-by-step construction of a computer, which now supports different configurations (notice that `memory`, `hdd`, and `gpu` are parameters and are not preconfigured). What do we need to do if we want to support the construction of tablets? Implement this as an exercise.

You might also want to change the computer's `serial_number` into something that is different for each computer, because as it is now, it means that all computers will have the same serial number (which is impractical).

Implementation

Let's see how we can use the builder design pattern to make a pizza-ordering application. The pizza example is particularly interesting because a pizza is prepared in steps that should follow a specific order. To add the sauce, you first need to prepare the dough. To add the topping, you first need to add the sauce. And you can't start baking the pizza unless both the sauce and the topping are placed on the dough. Moreover, each pizza usually requires a different baking time, depending on the thickness of its dough and the topping used.

We start by importing the required modules and declaring a few Enum parameters (j.mp/pytenum) plus a constant that is used many times in the application. The STEP_DELAY constant is used to add a time delay between the different steps of preparing a pizza (prepare the dough, add the sauce, and so on) as follows:

```
from enum import Enum
import time
PizzaProgress = Enum('PizzaProgress', 'queued preparation baking ready')
PizzaDough = Enum('PizzaDough', 'thin thick')
PizzaSauce = Enum('PizzaSauce', 'tomato creme_fraiche')
PizzaTopping = Enum('PizzaTopping',
         'mozzarella double_mozzarella bacon ham mushrooms red_onion
oregano')
STEP_DELAY = 3 # in seconds for the sake of the example
```

Our end product is a pizza, which is described by the Pizza class. When using the builder pattern, the end product does not have many responsibilities, since it is not supposed to be instantiated directly. A builder creates an instance of the end product and makes sure that it is properly prepared. That's why the Pizza class is so minimal. It basically initializes all data to sane default values. An exception is the prepare_dough() method.

The prepare_dough() method is defined in the Pizza class instead of a builder for two reasons. First, to clarify the fact that the end product is typically minimal, which does not mean that you should never assign it any responsibilities. Second, to promote code reuse through composition.

So, we define our Pizza class as follows:

```
class Pizza:
    def __init__(self, name):
        self.name = name
        self.dough = None
        self.sauce = None
        self.topping = []
```

```
def __str__(self):
    return self.name

def prepare_dough(self, dough):
    self.dough = dough
    print(f'preparing the {self.dough.name} dough of your {self}...')
    time.sleep(STEP_DELAY)
    print(f'done with the {self.dough.name} dough')
```

There are two builders: one for creating a margarita pizza (`MargaritaBuilder`) and another for creating a creamy bacon pizza (`CreamyBaconBuilder`). Each builder creates a `Pizza` instance and contains methods that follow the pizza-making procedure: `prepare_dough()`, `add_sauce()`, `add_topping()`, and `bake()`. To be precise, `prepare_dough()` is just a wrapper to the `prepare_dough()` method of the `Pizza` class.

Notice how each builder takes care of all the pizza-specific details. For example, the topping of the margarita pizza is double mozzarella and oregano, while the topping of the creamy bacon pizza is mozzarella, bacon, ham, mushrooms, red onion, and oregano.

This part of our code is laid out as follows:

- We define the `MargaritaBuilder` class as follows:

```
class MargaritaBuilder:
    def __init__(self):
        self.pizza = Pizza('margarita')
        self.progress = PizzaProgress.queued
        self.baking_time = 5 # in seconds for the sake of
        the example

    def prepare_dough(self):
        self.progress = PizzaProgress.preparation
        self.pizza.prepare_dough(PizzaDough.thin)

    def add_sauce(self):
        print('adding the tomato sauce to your margarita...')
        self.pizza.sauce = PizzaSauce.tomato
        time.sleep(STEP_DELAY)
        print('done with the tomato sauce')

    def add_topping(self):
        topping_desc = 'double mozzarella, oregano'
        topping_items = (PizzaTopping.double_mozzarella,
        PizzaTopping.oregano)
        print(f'adding the topping ({topping_desc}) to your
        margarita')
        self.pizza.topping.append([t for t in topping_items])
```

```
        time.sleep(STEP_DELAY)
        print(f'done with the topping ({topping_desc})')

    def bake(self):
        self.progress = PizzaProgress.baking
        print(f'baking your margarita for {self.baking_time}
        seconds')
        time.sleep(self.baking_time)
        self.progress = PizzaProgress.ready
        print('your margarita is ready')
```

- We define the `CreamyBaconBuilder` class as follows:

```
class CreamyBaconBuilder:
    def __init__(self):
        self.pizza = Pizza('creamy bacon')
        self.progress = PizzaProgress.queued
        self.baking_time = 7 # in seconds for the sake of
        the example

    def prepare_dough(self):
        self.progress = PizzaProgress.preparation
        self.pizza.prepare_dough(PizzaDough.thick)

    def add_sauce(self):
        print('adding the crème fraîche sauce to your creamy
        bacon')
        self.pizza.sauce = PizzaSauce.creme_fraiche
        time.sleep(STEP_DELAY)
        print('done with the crème fraîche sauce')

    def add_topping(self):
        topping_desc = 'mozzarella, bacon, ham, mushrooms,
        red onion, oregano'
        topping_items =  (PizzaTopping.mozzarella,
                          PizzaTopping.bacon,
                          PizzaTopping.ham,
                          PizzaTopping.mushrooms,
                          PizzaTopping.red_onion,
                          PizzaTopping.oregano)
        print(f'adding the topping ({topping_desc}) to your
        creamy bacon')
        self.pizza.topping.append([t for t in topping_items])
        time.sleep(STEP_DELAY)
        print(f'done with the topping ({topping_desc})')

    def bake(self):
        self.progress = PizzaProgress.baking
```

```
print(f'baking your creamy bacon for {self.baking_time}
seconds')
time.sleep(self.baking_time)
self.progress = PizzaProgress.ready
print('your creamy bacon is ready')
```

The director in this example is the waiter. The core of the `Waiter` class is the `construct_pizza()` method, which accepts a builder as a parameter and executes all the pizza-preparation steps in the right order. Choosing the appropriate builder, which can even be done at runtime, gives us the ability to create different pizza styles without modifying any of the code of the director (`Waiter`). The `Waiter` class also contains the `pizza()` method, which returns the end product (prepared pizza) as a variable to the caller as follows:

```
class Waiter:
    def __init__(self):
        self.builder = None

    def construct_pizza(self, builder):
        self.builder = builder
        steps = (builder.prepare_dough,
                 builder.add_sauce,
                 builder.add_topping,
                 builder.bake)
        [step() for step in steps]

    @property
    def pizza(self):
        return self.builder.pizza
```

The `validate_style()` function is similar to the `validate_age()` function as described in *Chapter 23*, *The Factory Pattern*. It is used to make sure that the user gives valid input, which in this case is a character that is mapped to a pizza builder. The m character uses the `MargaritaBuilder` class and the c character uses the `CreamyBaconBuilder` class. These mappings are in the builder parameter. A tuple is returned, with the first element set to `True` if the input is valid, or `False` if it is invalid as follows:

```
def validate_style(builders):
    try:
        input_msg = 'What pizza would you like, [m]argarita or
        [c]reamy bacon? '
        pizza_style = input(input_msg)
        builder = builders[pizza_style]()
        valid_input = True
    except KeyError:
        error_msg = 'Sorry, only margarita (key m) and creamy
```

```
                bacon (key c) are available'
            print(error_msg)
            return (False, None)
        return (True, builder)
```

The last part is the `main()` function. The `main()` function contains code for instantiating a pizza builder. The pizza builder is then used by the `Waiter` director for preparing the pizza. The created pizza can be delivered to the client at any later point:

```
def main():
    builders = dict(m=MargaritaBuilder, c=CreamyBaconBuilder)
    valid_input = False
    while not valid_input:
        valid_input, builder = validate_style(builders)
    print()
    waiter = Waiter()
    waiter.construct_pizza(builder)
    pizza = waiter.pizza
    print()
    print(f'Enjoy your {pizza}!')
```

Here is the summary of the implementation (see the complete code in the `builder.py` file):

1. We start with a couple of imports we need, for the standard `Enum` class and `time` module.
2. We declare the variables for a few constants: `PizzaProgress`, `PizzaDough`, `PizzaSauce`, `PizzaTopping`, and `STEP_DELAY`.
3. We define our `Pizza` class.
4. We define the classes for two builders, `MargaritaBuilder` and `CreamyBaconBuilder`.
5. We define our `Waiter` class.
6. We add the `validate_style()` function to improve things regarding exception handling.
7. Finally, we have the `main()` function, followed by the snippet for calling it when the program is run. In the `main` function, the following happens:
   - We make it possible to choose the pizza builder based on the user's input, after validation via the `validate_style()` function.
   - The pizza builder is used by the waiter for preparing the pizza.
   - The created pizza is then delivered.

Here is the output produced by calling the `python builder.py` command to execute this example program:

```
What pizza would you like, [m]argarita or [c]reamy bacon? r
Sorry, only margarita (key m) and creamy bacon (key c) are available
What pizza would you like, [m]argarita or [c]reamy bacon? m

preparing the thin dough of your margarita...
done with the thin dough
adding the tomato sauce to your margarita...
done with the tomato sauce
adding the topping (double mozzarella, oregano) to your margarita
done with the topping (double mozzarella, oregano)
baking your margarita for 5 seconds
your margarita is ready

Enjoy your margarita!
```

But... supporting only two pizza types is a shame. Feel like getting a Hawaiian pizza builder? Consider using inheritance after thinking about the advantages and disadvantages. Check the ingredients of a typical Hawaiian pizza and decide which class you need to extend: `MargaritaBuilder` or `CreamyBaconBuilder`?. Perhaps both (`j.mp/pymulti`)?

In his book, *Effective Java (2nd edition)*, Joshua Bloch describes an interesting variation of the builder pattern where calls to builder methods are chained. This is accomplished by defining the builder itself as an inner class and returning itself from each of the setter-like methods on it. The `build()` method returns the final object. This pattern is called the **fluent builder**. Here's a Python implementation, which was kindly provided by a reviewer of the book:

```python
class Pizza:
    def __init__(self, builder):
        self.garlic = builder.garlic
        self.extra_cheese = builder.extra_cheese

    def __str__(self):
        garlic = 'yes' if self.garlic else 'no'
        cheese = 'yes' if self.extra_cheese else 'no'
        info = (f'Garlic: {garlic}', f'Extra cheese: {cheese}')
        return '\n'.join(info)

class PizzaBuilder:
    def __init__(self):
        self.extra_cheese = False
        self.garlic = False
```

```
        def add_garlic(self):
            self.garlic = True
            return self

        def add_extra_cheese(self):
            self.extra_cheese = True
            return self

        def build(self):
            return Pizza(self)

if __name__ == '__main__':
    pizza = Pizza.PizzaBuilder().add_garlic().add_extra_cheese().build()
    print(pizza)
```

Adapt the pizza example to make use of the fluent builder pattern. Which version of the two do you prefer? What are the pros and cons of each version?

Summary

In this chapter, we have seen how to use the builder design pattern. We use the builder pattern for creating an object in situations where using the factory pattern (either a factory method or an abstract factory) is not a good option. A builder pattern is usually a better candidate than a factory pattern when the following applies:

- We want to create a complex object (an object composed of many parts and created in different steps that might need to follow a specific order).
- Different representations of an object are required, and we want to keep the construction of an object decoupled from its representation.
- We want to create an object at one point in time, but access it at a later point.

We saw how the builder pattern is used in fast-food restaurants for preparing meals, and how two third-party Django packages, `django-widgy`, and `django-query-builder`, use it for generating HTML pages and dynamic SQL queries, respectively. We focused on the differences between a builder pattern and a factory pattern, and provided a preconfigured (factory) and customer (builder) computer order analogy to clarify them.

In the *Implementation* section, we looked at how to create a pizza-ordering application with preparation dependencies. There were many recommended and interesting exercises in this chapter, including implementing a fluent builder.

In the next chapter, you will learn about other useful creational patterns.

25
Other Creational Patterns

In the previous chapter, we covered a third creational pattern, that is, builder, which offers a nice way of creating the various parts of a complex object. Besides the factory method, the abstract factory, and the builder patterns covered so far, there are other creational patterns that are interesting to discuss, such as the **prototype** pattern and the **singleton** pattern.

What is the prototype pattern? The prototype pattern is useful when one needs to create objects based on an existing object by using a **cloning** technique.

As you may have guessed, the idea is to use a copy of that object's complete structure to produce the new object. We will see that this is almost natural in Python because we have a **copy feature** that helps greatly in using this technique.

What is the singleton pattern? The singleton pattern offers a way to implement a class from which you can only create one object, hence the name singleton. As you will understand with our exploration of this pattern, or while doing your own research, there have always been discussions about this pattern, and some even consider it an **anti-pattern**.

Besides that, what is interesting is that it is useful when we need to create one and only one object, for example to store and maintain a global state for our program, and in Python it can be implemented using some special built-in features.

In this chapter, we will discuss:

- The prototype pattern
- The singleton pattern

The prototype pattern

Sometimes, we need to create an exact copy of an object. For instance, assume that you want to create an application for storing, sharing, and editing presentation and marketing content for products promoted by a group of salespeople. Think of the popular distribution model called **direct selling** or **network marketing**, the home-based activity where individuals partner with a company to distribute products within their social network, using promotional tools (brochures, PowerPoint presentations, videos, and so on).

Let's say a user, Bob, leads a team of distributors within a network marketing organization. They use a presentation video on a daily basis to introduce the product to their prospects. At some point, Bob gets his friend, Alice, to join him and she also uses the same video (one of the governing principles is to follow the system or, as they say, *Duplicate what already works*). But Alice soon finds prospects that could join her team and help her business grow, if only the video was in French, or at least subtitled. *What should they do?* The original presentation video cannot be used for the different custom needs that may arise.

To help everyone, the system could allow the distributors with certain rank or trust levels, such as Bob, to create independent copies of the original presentation video, as long as the new version is validated by the **compliance team** of the **backing company** before public use. Each copy is called a clone; it is an exact copy of the original object at a specific point in time.

So Bob, with the validation of the compliance team, which is part of the process, makes a copy of the presentation video to address the new need and hands it over to Alice. She could then adapt that version by adding French subtitles.

With cloning, Bob and Alice can have their own copy of a video, and as such, changes by each one of them will not affect the other person's version of the material. In the alternative situation, which is what actually happens by default, each person would hold a reference to the same (reference) object; changes made by Bob would impact Alice and vice versa.

The prototype design pattern helps us with creating object clones. In its simplest version, this pattern is just a `clone()` function that accepts an object as an input parameter and returns a clone of it. In Python, this can be done using the `copy.deepcopy()` function.

Real-world examples

A non-computer example that comes to mind is the sheep named Dolly that was created by researchers in Scotland by cloning a cell from a mammary gland.

There are many Python applications that make use of the prototype pattern (j.mp/pythonprot), but it is almost never referred to as "prototype" since cloning' objects is a built-in feature of the language.

Use cases

The prototype pattern is useful when we have an existing object that needs to stay untouched, and we want to create an exact copy of it, allowing changes in some parts of the copy.

There is also the frequent need for duplicating an object that is populated from a database and has references to other database-based objects. It is costly (multiple queries to a database) to clone such a complex object, so a prototype is a convenient way to solve the problem.

Implementation

Nowadays, some organizations, even of small size, deal with many websites and apps via their infrastructure/DevOps teams, hosting providers, or cloud service providers.

When you have to manage multiple websites, there is a point where it becomes difficult to follow. You need to access information quickly such as IP addresses that are involved, domain names and their expiration dates, and maybe details about the DNS parameters. So you need a kind of inventory tool.

Let's imagine how these teams deal with this type of data for daily activities, and touch on the implementation of a piece of software that helps consolidate and maintain the data (other than in Excel spreadsheets).

First, we need to import Python's standard copy module, as follows:

```
import copy
```

At the heart of this system, we will have a Website class for holding all the useful information such as the name, the domain name, the description, the author of a website we are managing, and so on.

In the __init__() method of the class, only some parameters are fixed: `name`, `domain`, `description`, and `author`. But we also want flexibility, and client code can pass more parameters in the form of keywords (`name=value`) using the `kwargs` variable-length collection (a Python dictionary).

Note that there is a Python idiom to set an arbitrary attribute named `attr` with a value `val` on an object `obj`, using the `setattr()` built-in function: `setattr(obj, attr, val)`.

So, we are using this technique for the optional attributes of our class, at the end of the initialization method, this way:

```
for key in kwargs:
    setattr(self, key, kwargs[key])
```

So our `Website` class is defined as follows:

```
class Website:
    def __init__(self, name, domain, description, author, **kwargs):
        '''Examples of optional attributes (kwargs):
          category, creation_date, technologies, keywords.
        '''
        self.name = name
        self.domain = domain
        self.description = description
        self.author = author
        for key in kwargs:
            setattr(self, key, kwargs[key])

    def __str__(self):
        summary = [f'Website "{self.name}"\n',]
        infos = vars(self).items()
        ordered_infos = sorted(infos)
        for attr, val in ordered_infos:
            if attr == 'name':
                continue
            summary.append(f'{attr}: {val}\n')
        return ''.join(summary)
```

Next, the `Prototype` class implements the prototype design pattern.

The heart of the `Prototype` class is the `clone()` method, which is in charge of cloning the object using the `copy.deepcopy()` function. Since cloning means we allow setting values for optional attributes, notice how we use the `setattr()` technique here with the `attrs` dictionary.

Also, for more convenience, the `Prototype` class contains the `register()` and `unregister()` methods, which can be used to keep track of the cloned objects in a dictionary:

```python
class Prototype:
    def __init__(self):
        self.objects = dict()

    def register(self, identifier, obj):
        self.objects[identifier] = obj

    def unregister(self, identifier):
        del self.objects[identifier]

    def clone(self, identifier, **attrs):
        found = self.objects.get(identifier)
        if not found:
            raise ValueError(f'Incorrect object identifier: {identifier}')
        obj = copy.deepcopy(found)
        for key in attrs:
            setattr(obj, key, attrs[key])

        return obj
```

In the `main()` function, as shown in the following code, we can clone a first `Website` instance, `site1`, to get a second object' `site2`. Basically, we instantiate the `Prototype` class and we use its `.clone()` method. That is what the following code shows:

```python
def main():
    keywords = ('python', 'data', 'apis', 'automation')
    site1 = Website('ContentGardening',
            domain='contentgardening.com',
            description='Automation and data-driven apps',
            author='Kamon Ayeva',
            category='Blog',
            keywords=keywords)

    prototype = Prototype()
    identifier = 'ka-cg-1'
    prototype.register(identifier, site1)
    site2 = prototype.clone(identifier,
```

```
name='ContentGardeningPlayground',
domain='play.contentgardening.com',
description='Experimentation for techniques featured
on the blog',
category='Membership site',
creation_date='2018-08-01')
```

To end that function, we can use the `id()` function which returns the memory address of an object, for comparing both objects' addresses, as follows. When we clone an object using a deep copy, the memory addresses of the clone must be different from the memory addresses of the original object:

```
for site in (site1, site2):
    print(site)
print(f'ID site1 : {id(site1)} != ID site2 : {id(site2)}')
```

You will find the program's full code in the `prototype.py` file. Here is a summary of what we do in the code:

1. We start by importing the `copy` module.
2. We define the `Website` class, with its initialization method (`__init__()`) and its string representation method (`__str__()`) as shown earlier.
3. We define our `Prototype` class as shown earlier.
4. Then, we have the `main()` function, where we do the following:
    - We define the `keywords` list we need
    - We create the instance of the `Website` class, called `site1` (we use the `keywords` list here)
    - We create the `Prototype` object and we use its `register()` method to register `site1` with its identifier (this helps us keep track of the cloned objects in a dictionary)
    - We clone the `site1` object to get `site2`
    - We display the result (both `Website` objects)

A sample output when I execute the `python prototype.py` command on my machine is as follows:

```
Website "ContentGardening"
author: Kamon Ayeva
category: Blog
description: Automation and data-driven apps
domain: contentgardening.com
keywords: ('python', 'data', 'apis', 'automation')

Website "ContentGardeningPlayground"
author: Kamon Ayeva
category: Membership site
creation_date: 2018-08-01
description: Experimentation for techniques featured on the blog
domain: play.contentgardening.com
keywords: ('python', 'data', 'apis', 'automation')

ID site1 : 2209666079432 != ID site2 : 2209666114000
```

Indeed, `Prototype` works as expected. We can see the information about the original `Website` object and its clone.

Looking at the output of the `id()` function, we can see that the two addresses are different.

Singleton

The singleton pattern restricts the instantiation of a class to *one* object, which is useful when you need one object to coordinate actions for the system.

The basic idea is that only one instance of a particular class, doing a job, is created for the needs of the program. To ensure that this works, we need mechanisms that prevent the instantiation of the class more than once and also prevent cloning.

Real-world examples

In a real-life scenario, we can think of the captain of a ship or a boat. On the ship, he is the one in charge. He is responsible for important decisions, and a number of requests are directed to him because of this responsibility.

In software, the Plone CMS has, at its core, an implementation of the singleton. There are actually several singleton objects available at the root of a Plone site, called **tools**, each in charge of providing a specific set of features for the site. For example, the **Catalog tool** deals with content indexation and search features (built-in search engines for small sites where you don't need to integrate products like ElasticSearch), the **Membership tool** deals with things related to user profiles, and the **Registry tool** provides a configuration registry to store and maintain different kinds of configuration properties for the Plone site. Each tool is global to the site, created from a specific `singleton` class, and you can't create another instance of that `singleton` class in the context of the site.

Use cases

The singleton design pattern is useful when you need to create only one object or you need some sort of object capable of maintaining a global state for your program.

Other possible use cases are:

- Controlling concurrent access to a shared resource. For example, the class managing the connection to a database.
- A service or resource that is transversal in the sense that it can be accessed from different parts of the application or by different users and do its work. For example, the class at the core of the logging system or utility.

Implementation

Let's implement a program to fetch content from web pages, inspired by the tutorial from Michael Ford (`https://docs.python.org/3/howto/urllib2.html`). We have only take the simple part since the focus is to illustrate our pattern more than it is to build a special web-scraping tool.

We will use the `urllib` module to connect to web pages using their URLs; the core of the program would be the `URLFetcher` class that takes care of doing the work via a `fetch()` method.

We want to be able to track the list of web pages that were tracked, hence the use of the singleton pattern: we need a single object to maintain that global state.

First, our naive version, inspired by the tutorial but modified to help us track the list of URLs that were fetched, would be:

```
import urllib.parse
import urllib.request

class URLFetcher:

    def __init__(self):
        self.urls = []
    def fetch(self, url):
        req = urllib.request.Request(url)
        with urllib.request.urlopen(req) as response:
            if response.code == 200:
                the_page = response.read()
                print(the_page)
                urls = self.urls
                urls.append(url)
                self.urls = urls
```

As an exercise, add the usual if __name__ == '__main__' block with a few lines of code to call the .fetch() method on an instance of URLFetcher.

But then, does our class implement a singleton? Here is a clue. To create a singleton, we need to make sure one can only create one instance of it. So, to see if our class implements a singleton or not, we could use a trick which consists of comparing two instances using the is operator.

You may have guessed the second exercise. Put the following code in your if __name__ == '__main__' block instead of what you previously had:

```
f1 = URLFetcher()
f2 = URLFetcher()
print(f1 is f2)
```

As an alternative, use the concise but still elegant form:

```
print(URLFetcher() is URLFetcher())
```

With this change, when executing the program, you should get False as the output.

Okay! This means that the first try does not yet give us a singleton. Remember, we want to manage a global state, using one and only one instance of the class for the program. The current version of the class does not yet implement a singleton.

After checking the literature and the forums on the web, you will find that there are several techniques, each with pros and cons, and some are probably outdated.

Since many use Python 3 nowadays, the recommended technique we will choose is the **metaclass** technique. We first implement a metaclass for the singleton, meaning the class (or type) of the classes that implement the singleton pattern, as follows:

```python
class SingletonType(type):
    _instances = {}
    def __call__(cls, *args, **kwargs):
        if cls not in cls._instances:
            cls._instances[cls] = super(SingletonType,
            cls).__call__(*args, **kwargs)
        return cls._instances[cls]
```

Now, we will rewrite our URLFetcher class to use that metaclass. We also add a dump_url_registry() method, which is useful to get the current list of URLs tracked:

```python
class URLFetcher(metaclass=SingletonType):

    def fetch(self, url):
        req = urllib.request.Request(url)
        with urllib.request.urlopen(req) as response:
            if response.code == 200:
                the_page = response.read()
                print(the_page)
                urls = self.urls
                urls.append(url)
                self.urls = urls

    def dump_url_registry(self):
        return ', '.join(self.urls)

if __name__ == '__main__':
    print(URLFetcher() is URLFetcher())
```

This time, you get True by executing the program.

Let's complete the program to do what we wanted, using a `main()` function that we will call:

```
def main():

    MY_URLS = ['http://www.voidspace.org.uk',
               'http://google.com',
               'http://python.org',
               'https://www.python.org/error',
               ]

    print(URLFetcher() is URLFetcher())

    fetcher = URLFetcher()
    for url in MY_URLS:
        try:
            fetcher.fetch(url)
        except Exception as e:
            print(e)
    print('-------')
    done_urls = fetcher.dump_url_registry()
    print(f'Done URLs: {done_urls}')
```

You will find the program's full code in the `singleton.py` file. Here is a summary of what we do:

1. We start with our needed module imports (`urllib.parse` and `urllib.request`)
2. As shown earlier, we define the `SingletonType` class, with its special `__call__()` method
3. As shown earlier, we define `URLFetcher`, the class implementing the fetcher for the web pages, initializing it with the `urls` attribute; as discussed, we add its `fetch()` and `dump_url_registry()` methods
4. Then, we add our `main()` function
5. Lastly, we add Python's conventional snippet used to call the `main` function

A sample output when executing the `python singleton.py` command is as follows:

```
fo/python-dev" title="">python-dev list</a></li>\n    \n          <li class="tier-2 element-4" role="treeitem"><a href="/d
ev/core-mentorship/" title="">Core Mentorship</a></li>\n     \n</ul>\n\n         \n    </li>\n    \n</ul>\n\n\n
        <a id="back-to-top-2" class="jump-link" href="#python-network"><span aria-hidden="true" class="icon-arrow-up"><
span>&#9650;</span></span> Back to Top</a>\n                    \n\n                  </div><!-- end .container -->\n
        </div> <!-- end .main-footer-links -->\n\n\n              <div class="site-base">\n                  <div class="contai
ner">\n               \n                         <ul class="footer-links navigation menu do-not-print" role="tree">\n
            <li class="tier-1 element-1"><a href="/about/help/">Help &amp; <span class="say-no-more">General</s
pan> Contact</a></li>\n                         <li class="tier-1 element-2"><a href="/community/diversity/">Diversity <s
pan class="say-no-more">Initiatives</span></a></li>\n               <li class="tier-1 element-3"><a href="https
://github.com/python/pythondotorg/issues">Submit Website Bug</a></li>\n                        <li class="tier-1 element
-4">\n                         <a href="https://status.python.org/">Status <span class="python-status-indicator-defau
lt" id="python-status-indicator"></span></a>\n                    </li>\n                    </ul>\n\n\n
        <div class="copyright">\n                            <p><small>\n                            <span class="pre">Copyrig
ht &copy;2001-2018.</span>\n                             <span class="pre"><a href="/psf-landing/">Python Software
Foundation</a></span>\n                             <span class="pre"><a href="/about/legal/">Legal Statements</a><
/span>\n                             <span class="pre"><a href="/privacy/">Privacy Policy</a></span>\n
             <span class="pre"><a href="/psf/sponsorship/sponsors/">Powered by Rackspace</a></span>\n
        </small></p>\n                  </div>\n\n            </div><!-- end .container -->\n                    </di
v><!-- end .site-base -->\n\n         </footer>\n\n    </div><!-- end #touchnav-wrapper -->\n\n   \n   <script src="//a
jax.googleapis.com/ajax/libs/jquery/1.8.2/jquery.min.js"></script>\n    <script>window.jQuery || document.write('<scrip
t src="/static/js/libs/jquery-1.8.2.min.js"><\\/script>')</script>\n\n    <script src="/static/js/libs/masonry.pkgd.min
.js"></script>\n\n    <script type="text/javascript" src="/static/js/main-min.js" charset="utf-8"></script>\n    \n\n
<!--[if lte IE 7]>\n    <script type="text/javascript" src="/static/js/plugins/IE8-min.js" charset="utf-8"></script>\n
    \n   \n   <![endif]-->\n\n    <!--[if lte IE 8]>\n    <script type="text/javascript" src="/static/js/plugins/getCom
putedStyle-min.js" charset="utf-8"></script>\n    \n   \n   <![endif]-->\n\n   \n\n   \n   \n\n</body>\n</html>\n'
HTTP Error 404: OK
-------
Done URLs: http://www.voidspace.org.uk, http://google.com, http://python.org
```

We can see that we get the expected result: both the content of the pages that the program was able to connect to and the list of URLs the operation was successful for.

We see that the URL, `https://www.python.org/error`, does not come in the list returned by `fetcher.dump_url_registry()`; indeed, it is an erroneous URL and the `urlllib` request to it gets a **404** response code.

 The link to the preceding URL is not supposed to work; that's exactly the point.

Summary

In this chapter, we have seen how to use two other creational design patterns: the prototype and the singleton.

A prototype is used for creating exact copies of objects. In the general case of creating a copy of an object, what happens is that you make a new reference to the same object, a method called a **shallow copy**. But, if you need to duplicate the object, which is the case with a prototype, you make **a deep copy**.

As seen in the implementation example we discussed, using a prototype in Python is natural and based on built-in features, so it is not something even mentioned.

The singleton pattern can be implemented by making the singleton class use a metaclass, its type, having previously defined the said metaclass. As required, the metaclass's __call__() method holds the code that ensures that only one instance of the class can be created.

The next chapter is about the adapter pattern, a structural design pattern that can be used to make two incompatible software interfaces compatible.

26
The Adapter Pattern

In the previous chapters, we have covered creational patterns, object-oriented programming patterns that help us with object creation procedures. The next category of patterns we want to present is *structural design patterns*.

A structural design pattern proposes a way of composing objects for creating new functionality. The first of these patterns we will cover is the *adapter* pattern.

The *adapter* pattern is a structural design pattern that helps us make two incompatible interfaces compatible. What does that really mean? If we have an old component and we want to use it in a new system, or a new component that we want to use in an old system, the two can rarely communicate without requiring any code changes. But, changing the code is not always possible, either because we don't have access to it, or because it is impractical. In such cases, we can write an extra layer that makes all the required modifications for enabling the communication between the two interfaces. This layer is called an **adapter**.

In general, if you want to use an interface that expects `function_a()`, but you only have `function_b()`, you can use an adapter to convert (adapt) `function_b()` to `function_a()`.

In this chapter, we will discuss the following:

- Real-world examples
- Use cases
- Implementation

Real-world examples

When you are traveling from most European countries to the UK or USA, or the other way around, you need to use a plug adapter for charging your laptop. The same kind of adapter is needed for connecting some devices to your computer: the USB adapter.

In the software category, the Zope application server (`http://www.zope.org`) is known for its **Zope Component Architecture (ZCA)**, which contributed an implementation of interfaces and adapters used by several big Python web projects. Pyramid, built by former Zope developers, is a Python web framework that took good ideas from Zope to provide a more modular approach for developing web apps. Pyramid uses adapters for making it possible for existing objects to conform to specific APIs without the need to modify them. Another project from the Zope ecosystem, *Plone CMS*, uses adapters under the hood.

Use cases

Usually, one of the two incompatible interfaces is either foreign or old/legacy. If the interface is foreign, it means that we have no access to the source code. If it is old, it is usually impractical to refactor it.

Using an adapter for making things work after they have been implemented is a good approach because it does not require access to the source code of the foreign interface. It is also often a pragmatic solution if we have to reuse some legacy code.

Implementation

Let's look at a relatively simple application to illustrate **adaptation**: a club's activities, mainly the need to organize performances and events for the entertainment of its clients, by hiring talented artists.

At the core, we have a `Club` class that represents the club where hired artists perform some evenings. The `organize_performance()` method is the main action that the club can perform. The code is as follows:

```python
class Club:
    def __init__(self, name):
        self.name = name

    def __str__(self):
        return f'the club {self.name}'

    def organize_event(self):
        return 'hires an artist to perform for the people'
```

Most of the time, our club hires a DJ to perform, but our application addresses the need to organize a diversity of performances, by a musician or music band, by a dancer, a one-man or one-woman show, and so on.

Via our research to try and reuse existing code, we find an open source contributed library that brings us two interesting classes: `Musician` and `Dancer`. In the `Musician` class, the main action is performed by the `play()` method. In the `Dancer` class, it is performed by the `dance()` method.

In our example, to indicate that these two classes are external, we place them in a separate module. The code is as follows for the `Musician` class:

```
class Musician:
 def __init__(self, name):
 self.name = name

 def __str__(self):
 return f'the musician {self.name}'

  def play(self):
 return 'plays music'
```

Then, the `Dancer` class is defined as follows:

```
class Dancer:
    def __init__(self, name):
        self.name = name
    def __str__(self):
        return f'the dancer {self.name}'
    def dance(self):
        return 'does a dance performance'
```

The client code, using these classes, only knows how to call the `organize_performance()` method (on the `Club` class); it has no idea about `play()` or `dance()` (on the respective classes from the external library).

How can we make the code work without changing the `Musician` and `Dancer` classes?

Adapters to the rescue! We create a generic `Adapter` class that allows us to adapt a number of objects with different interfaces, into one unified interface. The `obj` argument of the `__init__()` method is the object that we want to adapt, and `adapted_methods` is a dictionary containing key/value pairs matching the method the client calls and the method that should be called.

The code for the `Adapter` class is as follows:

```
class Adapter:
    def __init__(self, obj, adapted_methods):
        self.obj = obj
        self.__dict__.update(adapted_methods)
```

```
    def __str__(self):
        return str(self.obj)
```

When dealing with the different instances of the classes, we have two cases:

- The compatible object that belongs to the `Club` class needs no adaptation. We can treat it as is.
- The incompatible objects need to be adapted first, using the `Adapter` class.

The result is that the client code can continue using the known `organize_performance()` method on all objects without the need to be aware of any interface differences between the used classes. Consider the following code:

```
def main():
    objects = [Club('Jazz Cafe'), Musician('Roy Ayers'), Dancer('Shane
Sparks')]
    for obj in objects:
        if hasattr(obj, 'play') or hasattr(obj, 'dance'):
            if hasattr(obj, 'play'):
                adapted_methods = dict(organize_event=obj.play)
            elif hasattr(obj, 'dance'):
                adapted_methods = dict(organize_event=obj.dance)
            # referencing the adapted object here
            obj = Adapter(obj, adapted_methods)
        print(f'{obj} {obj.organize_event()}')
```

Let's recapitulate the complete code of our adapter pattern implementation:

1. We define the `Musician` and `Dancer` classes (in `external.py`).
2. Then, we need to import those classes from the external module (in `adapter.py`):

   ```
   from external import Musician, Dance
   ```

3. We then define the `Adapter` class (in `adapter.py`).
4. We add the `main()` function, as shown earlier, and the usual trick to call it (in `adapter.py`).

Here is the output when executing the `python adapter.py` command, as usual:

```
the club Jazz Cafe hires an artist to perform for the people
the musician Roy Ayers plays music
the dancer Shane Sparks does a dance performance
```

As you can see, we managed to make the Musician and Dancer classes compatible with the interface expected by the client, without changing their source code.

Summary

This chapter covered the adapter design pattern. We use the adapter pattern for making two (or more) incompatible interfaces compatible. We use adapters every day for interconnecting devices, charging them, and so on.

The adapter makes things work after they have been implemented. The Pyramid web framework, the Plone CMS, and other Zope-based or related frameworks use the adapter pattern for achieving interface compatibility.

In the *Implementation* section, we saw how to achieve interface conformance using the adapter pattern without modifying the source code of the incompatible model. This is achieved through a generic Adapter class that does the work for us.

In the next chapter, we will cover the decorator pattern.

27
The Decorator Pattern

As we saw in the previous chapter, using an **adapter**, a first structural design pattern, you can adapt an object implementing a given interface to implement another interface. This is called **interface adaptation** and includes the kinds of patterns that encourage composition over inheritance, and it could bring benefits when you have to maintain a large codebase.

A second interesting structural pattern to learn about is the **decorator** pattern, which allows a programmer to add responsibilities to an object dynamically, and in a transparent manner (without affecting other objects).

There is another reason why this pattern is interesting to us, as you will see in a minute.

As Python developers, we can write decorators in a **Pythonic** way (meaning using the language's features), thanks to the built-in decorator feature (`https://docs.python.org/3/reference/compound_stmts.html#function`). What exactly is this feature? A Python decorator is a **callable** (function, method, or class) that gets a function object `func_in` as input, and returns another function object `func_out`. It is a commonly used technique for extending the behavior of a function, method, or class.

But, this feature should not be completely new to you. We have already seen how to use the built-in **property** decorator that makes a method appear as a variable in both *Chapter 23, The Factory Pattern*, and *Chapter 24, The Builder Pattern*. And there are several other useful built-in decorators in Python. In the *Implementation* section of this chapter, we will learn how to implement and use our own decorators.

Note that there is no one-to-one relationship between the decorator pattern and Python's decorator feature. Python decorators can actually do much more than the decorator pattern. One of the things they can be used for is to implement the decorator pattern (`j.mp/moinpydec`).

In this chapter, we will discuss:

- Real-world examples
- Use cases
- Implementation

Real-world examples

The decorator pattern is generally used for extending the functionality of an object. In everyday life, examples of such extensions are: adding a silencer to a gun, using different camera lenses, and so on.

In the Django Framework, which uses decorators a lot, we have the `View` decorators which can be used for (`j.mp/djangodec`) the following:

- Restricting access to views based on the HTTP request
- Controlling the caching behavior on specific views
- Controlling compression on a per-view basis
- Controlling caching based on specific HTTP request headers

Both the Pyramid Framework and the Zope application server also use decorators to achieve various goals:

- Registering a function as an event subscriber
- Protecting a method with a specific permission
- Implementing the adapter pattern

Use cases

The decorator pattern shines when used for implementing cross-cutting concerns (`j.mp/wikicrosscut`). Examples of cross-cutting concerns are as follows:

- Data validation
- Caching
- Logging

- Monitoring
- Debugging
- Business rules
- Encryption

In general, all parts of an application that are generic and can be applied to many other parts of it are considered to be cross-cutting concerns.

Another popular example of using the decorator pattern is **graphical user interface (GUI)** toolkits. In a GUI toolkit, we want to be able to add features such as borders, shadows, colors, and scrolling to individual components/widgets.

Implementation

Python decorators are generic and very powerful. You can find many examples of how they can be used at the decorator library of `python.org` (j.mp/pydeclib). In this section, we will see how we can implement a memoization decorator (j.mp/memoi). All recursive functions can benefit from memoization, so let's try a function `number_sum()` that returns the sum of the first *n* numbers. Note that this function is already available in the `math` module as `fsum()`, but let's pretend it is not.

First, let's look at the naive implementation (the `number_sum_naive.py` file):

```python
def number_sum(n):
    '''Returns the sum of the first n numbers'''
    assert(n >= 0), 'n must be >= 0'
    if n == 0:
        return 0
    else:
        return n + number_sum(n-1)


if __name__ == '__main__':
    from timeit import Timer
    t = Timer('number_sum(30)', 'from __main__ import number_sum')
    print('Time: ', t.timeit())
```

A sample execution of this example shows how slow this implementation is. It takes 15 seconds to calculate the sum of the first 30 numbers. We get the following output when executing the `python number_sum_naive.py` command:

```
Time: 15.69870145995352
```

Let's see if using memoization can help us improve the performance number. In the following code, we use a `dict` for caching the already computed sums. We also change the parameter passed to the `number_sum()` function. We want to calculate the sum of the first 300 numbers instead of only the first 30.

Here is the new version of the code, using memoization:

```
sum_cache = {0:0}
def number_sum(n):
    '''Returns the sum of the first n numbers'''
    assert(n >= 0), 'n must be >= 0'
    if n in sum_cache:
        return sum_cache[n]
    res = n + number_sum(n-1)
    # Add the value to the cache
    sum_cache[n] = res
    return res
if __name__ == '__main__':
    from timeit import Timer
    t = Timer('number_sum(300)', 'from __main__ import number_sum')
    print('Time: ', t.timeit())
```

Executing the memoization-based code shows that performance improves dramatically, and is acceptable even for computing large values.

A sample execution, using `python number_sum.py`, is as follows:

```
Time: 0.5695815602065222
```

But there are already a few problems with this approach. While the performance is not an issue any longer, the code is not as clean as it is when not using memoization. And what happens if we decide to extend the code with more math functions and turn it into a module? We can think of several functions that would be useful for our module, for problems such as Pascal's triangle or the Fibonacci numbers suite algorithm.

So, if we wanted a function in the same module as `number_sum()`, for the Fibonacci numbers suite, using the same memoization technique, we would add code, as follows:

```
cache_fib = {0:0, 1:1}

def fibonacci(n):
    '''Returns the suite of Fibonacci numbers'''
    assert(n >= 0), 'n must be >= 0'
    if n in cache_fib:
        return cache_fib[n]
    res = fibonacci(n-1) + fibonacci(n-2)
    cache_fib[n] = res
    return res
```

Do you notice the problem already? We ended up with a new `dict` called `cache_fib` which acts as our cache for the `fibonacci()` function, and a function that is more complex than it would be without using memoization. Our module is becoming unnecessarily complex. Is it possible to write these functions keeping them as simple as the naive versions, but achieving a performance similar to the performance of the functions that use memoization?

Fortunately, it is, and the solution is to use the decorator pattern.

First, we create a `memoize()` decorator as shown in the following example. Our decorator accepts the function `fn` that needs to be memoized, as an input. It uses a `dict` named `cache` as the cached data container. The `functools.wraps()` function is used for convenience when creating decorators. It is not mandatory but a good practice to use it, since it makes sure that the documentation, and the signature of the function that is decorated, are preserved (j.mp/funcwraps). The argument list `*args` is required in this case because the functions that we want to decorate accepts input arguments (such as the n argument for our two functions):

```
import functools

def memoize(fn):
    cache = dict()

    @functools.wraps(fn)
    def memoizer(*args):
        if args not in cache:
            cache[args] = fn(*args)
        return cache[args]

    return memoizer
```

Now, we can use our `memoize()` decorator with the naive version of our functions. This has the benefit of readable code without performance impact. We apply a decorator using what is known as decoration (or a decoration line). A decoration uses the `@name` syntax, where `name` is the name of the decorator that we want to use. It is nothing more than syntactic sugar for simplifying the usage of decorators. We can even bypass this syntax and execute our decorator manually, but that is left as an exercise for you.

So the `memoize()` decorator can be used with our recursive functions as follows:

```python
@memoize
def number_sum(n):
    '''Returns the sum of the first n numbers'''
    assert(n >= 0), 'n must be >= 0'
    if n == 0:
        return 0
    else:
        return n + number_sum(n-1)

@memoize
def fibonacci(n):
    '''Returns the suite of Fibonacci numbers'''
    assert(n >= 0), 'n must be >= 0'
    if n in (0, 1):
        return n
    else:
        return fibonacci(n-1) + fibonacci(n-2)
```

In the last part of the code, via the `main()` function, we show how to use the decorated functions and measure their performance. The `to_execute` variable is used to hold a list of tuples containing the reference to each function and the corresponding `timeit.Timer()` call (to execute it while measuring the time spent), thus avoiding code repetition. Note how the `__name__` and `__doc__` method attributes show the proper function names and documentation values, respectively. Try removing the `@functools.wraps(fn)` decoration from `memoize()`, and see if this is still the case.

Here is the last part of the code:

```python
def main():
    from timeit import Timer

    to_execute = [
        (number_sum,
         Timer('number_sum(300)', 'from __main__ import number_sum')),
        (fibonacci,
         Timer('fibonacci(100)', 'from __main__ import fibonacci'))
    ]
```

```
    for item in to_execute:
        fn = item[0]
        print(f'Function "{fn.__name__}": {fn.__doc__}')
        t = item[1]
        print(f'Time: {t.timeit()}')
        print()

if __name__ == '__main__':
    main()
```

Let's recapitulate how we write the complete code of our math module (file `mymath.py`):

1. After the import of Python's `functools` module that we will be using, we define the `memoize()` decorator function
2. Then, we define the `number_sum()` function, decorated using `memoize()`
3. We also define the `fibonacci()` function, as decorated
4. Finally, we add the `main()` function, as shown earlier, and the usual trick to call it

Here is a sample output when executing the `python mymath.py` command:

```
Function "number_sum": Returns the sum of the first n numbers
Time: 0.65116599080041739

Function "fibonacci": Returns the suite of Fibonacci numbers
Time: 0.6524761144050873
```

The execution times might differ in your case.

Nice. We ended up with readable code and acceptable performance. Now, you might argue that this is not the decorator pattern, since we don't apply it at runtime. The truth is that a decorated function cannot be undecorated, but you can still decide at runtime if the decorator will be executed or not. That's an interesting exercise left for you.

Use a decorator that acts as a wrapper, which decides whether or not the real decorator is executed based on some condition.

Another interesting property of decorators that is not covered in this chapter is that you can decorate a function with more than one decorator. So here's another exercise: create a decorator that helps you to debug recursive functions, and apply it on `number_sum()` and `fibonacci()`. In what order are the multiple decorators executed?

Summary

This chapter covered the decorator pattern and its relationship to the Python programming language. We use the decorator pattern as a convenient way of extending the behavior of an object without using inheritance. Python, with its built-in decorator feature, extends the decorator concept even more, by allowing us to extend the behavior of any callable (function, method, or class) without using inheritance or composition.

We have seen a few examples of real-world objects that are decorated, such as cameras. From a software point of view, both Django and Pyramid use decorators to achieve different goals, such as controlling HTTP compression and caching.

The decorator pattern is a great solution for implementing cross-cutting concerns because they are generic and do not fit well into the OOP paradigm. We mentioned several categories of cross-cutting concerns in the *Use cases* section. In fact, in the *Implementation* section, a cross-cutting concern was demonstrated: memoization. We saw how decorators can help us to keep our functions clean, without sacrificing performance.

The next chapter covers the bridge pattern.

28
The Bridge Pattern

In the previous two chapters, we covered our first structural pattern, *adapter*, which is used to make two incompatible interfaces compatible, and *decorator*, which allows us to add responsibilities to an object in a dynamic way. There are more similar patterns. Let's continue with the series!

A third structural pattern to look at is the *bridge* pattern. We can actually compare the *bridge* and the *adapter* patterns, looking at the way both work. While *adapter* is used later to make unrelated classes work together, as we saw in the implementation example we discussed in Chapter 26, *The Adapter Pattern*, the *bridge* pattern is designed up-front to decouple an implementation from its abstraction, as we are going to see.

In this chapter, we will discuss:

- Real-world examples
- Use cases
- Implementation

Real-world examples

In our *modern*, everyday lives, an example of the bridge pattern I can think of is from the *digital economy*: information products. Nowadays, the information product or *infoproduct* is part of the resources one can find online for training, self-improvement, or one's ideas and business development. The purpose of an information product that you find on certain marketplaces, or the website of the provider, is to deliver information on a given topic in such a way that it is easy to access and consume. The provided material can be a PDF document or ebook, an ebook series, a video, a video series, an online course, a subscription-based newsletter, or a combination of all those formats.

In the software realm, *device drivers* are often cited as an example of the bridge pattern, when the developers of an OS defines the interface for device vendors to implement it.

Use cases

Using the bridge pattern is a good idea when you want to share an implementation among multiple objects. Basically, instead of implementing several specialized classes, defining all that is required within each class, you can define the following special components:

- An abstraction that applies to all the classes
- A separate interface for the different objects involved

An implementation example we are about to see will illustrate this approach.

Implementation

Let's assume we are building an application where the user is going to manage and deliver content after fetching it from diverse sources, which could be:

- A web page (based on its URL)
- A resource accessed on an FTP server
- A file on the local file system
- A database server

So, here is the idea: instead of implementing several content classes, each holding the methods responsible for getting the content pieces, assembling them, and showing them inside the application, we can define an abstraction for the *Resource Content* and a separate interface for the objects that are responsible for fetching the content. Let's try it!

We begin with the class for our *Resource Content* abstraction, called `ResourceContent`. Then, we will need to define the interface for implementation classes that help fetch content, that is, the `ResourceContentFetcher` class. This concept is called **the Implementor**.

The first trick we use here is that, via an attribute (`_imp`) on the `ResourceContent` class, we maintain a reference to the object which represents the *Implementor*:

```
class ResourceContent:
    """
    Define the abstraction's interface.
```

```
Maintain a reference to an object which represents the Implementor.
"""

def __init__(self, imp):
    self._imp = imp

def show_content(self, path):
    self._imp.fetch(path)
```

As you may know now, we define the equivalent of an interface in Python using two features of the language, the `metaclass` feature (which helps define the *type of a type*), and **abstract base classes (ABC)**:

```
class ResourceContentFetcher(metaclass=abc.ABCMeta):
    """
    Define the interface for implementation classes that fetch content.
    """
    @abc.abstractmethod
    def fetch(path):
        pass
```

Now, we can add an `implementation` class to fetch content from a web page or resource:

```
class URLFetcher(ResourceContentFetcher):
    """
    Implement the Implementor interface and define its concrete
    implementation.
    """
    def fetch(self, path):
        # path is an URL
        req = urllib.request.Request(path)
        with urllib.request.urlopen(req) as response:
            if response.code == 200:
                the_page = response.read()
                print(the_page)
```

We can also add an `implementation` class to fetch content from a file on the local filesystem:

```
class LocalFileFetcher(ResourceContentFetcher):
    """
    Implement the Implementor interface and define its concrete
    implementation.
    """

    def fetch(self, path):
        # path is the filepath to a text file
        with open(path) as f:
            print(r.read())
```

Based on that, our `main` function to show content using both *content fetchers* could look like the following:

```
def main():
    url_fetcher = URLFetcher()
    iface = ResourceContent(url_fetcher)
    iface.show_content('http://python.org')

    print('====================')
    localfs_fetcher = LocalFileFetcher()
    iface = ResourceContent(localfs_fetcher)
    iface.show_content('file.txt')
```

Let's see a summary for the complete code of our example (the `bridge.py` file):

1. We import the three modules we need for the program (`abc`, `urllib.parse`, and `urllib.request`).
2. We define the `ResourceContent` class for the interface of the *abstraction*.
3. We define the `ResourceContentFetcher` class for the *Implementator*.
4. We define two `implementation` classes:
    - `URLFetcher` for fetching content from an URL
    - `LocalFileFetcher` for fetching content from the local filesystem
    - Finally, we add the `main()` function, as shown earlier, and the usual trick to call it

Here is a sample output when executing the `python bridge.py` command:

```
et Python">Community News</a></li>\n   \n          <li class="tier-2 element-3" role="treeitem"><a href="http://pyfound.blog
\n   \n   \n       <li class="tier-2 element-4" role="treeitem"><a href="http://pycon.blogspot.com/" title="PyCon Blog">PyCon
/li>\n   \n     <li class="tier-1 element-7">\n          <a href="/events/" >Events</a>\n        \n      \n\n<ul class=
-2 element-1" role="treeitem"><a href="/events/python-events" title="">Python Events</a></li>\n   \n      <li class="tie
ts/python-user-group/" title="">User Group Events</a></li>\n   \n        <li class="tier-2 element-3" role="treeitem"><a h
thon Events Archive</a></li>\n   \n        <li class="tier-2 element-4" role="treeitem"><a href="/events/python-user-group
></li>\n   \n      <li class="tier-2 element-5" role="treeitem"><a href="https://wiki.python.org/moin/PythonEventsCalend
ent</a></li>\n     \n\n</ul>\n\n       \n   </li>\n    \n      <li class="tier-1 element-8">\n       <a href="/dev/" >Contrib
s="subnav menu">\n   \n       <li class="tier-2 element-1" role="treeitem"><a href="https://devguide.python.org/" title="
    <li class="tier-2 element-2" role="treeitem"><a href="https://bugs.python.org/" title="">Issue Tracker</a></li>\n   \n
eitem"><a href="https://mail.python.org/mailman/listinfo/python-dev" title="">python-dev list</a></li>\n   \n       <li c
ef="/dev/core-mentorship/" title="">Core Mentorship</a></li>\n   \n</ul>\n\n      \n    </li>\n   \n</ul>\n\n\n
-link" href="#python-network"><span aria-hidden="true" class="icon-arrow-up"><span>&#9650;</span></span> Back to Top</a>\n
<!-- end .container -->\n        \n        </div> <!-- end .main-footer-links -->\n\n        <div class="site-base">\n
  help/">Help &amp; <span class="say-no-more">General</span> Contact</a></li>\n              <li class="tier-1 elem
ity <span class="say-no-more">Initiatives</span></a></li>\n          <li class="tier-1 element-3"><a href="ht
Submit Website Bug</a></li>\n          <li class="tier-1 element-4">\n           <a href="ht
"python-status-indicator-default" id="python-status-indicator"></span></a>\n        </li>\n
copyright">\n              <p><small>\n               <span class="pre">Copyright &copy;2001-2018.</
n class="pre"><a href="/psf-landing/">Python Software Foundation</a></span>\n            <span class=
s</a></span>\n           <span class="pre"><a href="/privacy/">Privacy Policy</a></span>\n
href="/psf/sponsorship/sponsors/">Powered by Rackspace</a></span>\n           </small></p>\n
ontainer -->\n        </div><!-- end .site-base -->\n\n      </div><!-- end #touchnav-wrapper -->\n\
/ajax/libs/jquery/1.8.2/jquery.min.js"></script>\n    <script>window.jQuery || document.write('\'<script src="/static/js/lib
>\n\n    <script src="/static/js/libs/masonry.pkgd.min.js"></script>\n\n   <script type="text/javascript" src="/static/js/
n\n    <!--[if lte IE 7]>\n    <script type="text/javascript" src="/static/js/plugins/IE8-min.js" charset="utf-8"></script>
lte IE 8]>\n    <script type="text/javascript" src="/static/js/plugins/getComputedStyle-min.js" charset="utf-8"></script>\
\n    \n\n</body>\n</html>\n'
========================
 Lorem ipsum dolor sit amet, consectetur adipiscing elit. Proin in nibh in enim euismod mattis placerat in velit. Donec mal
ncidunt porttitor euismod. Etiam non odio sodales, tincidunt elit ac, sodales nisi. Donec massa felis, pharetra ut libero n
sem non erat ultricies finibus. Donec sed blandit arcu. Aliquam erat volutpat. Donec aliquam ipsum risus, et accumsan nibh
tae rutrum. Sed ullamcorper leo sed orci efficitur rhoncus.

Duis vitae dolor vestibulum nibh semper faucibus. Vivamus libero quam, ultrices quis sapien vel, blandit ultricies purus. N
 non ligula. Duis ullamcorper, nulla quis luctus commodo, massa lorem tristique orci, quis aliquam diam est semper nisi. Ma
n convallis tellus iaculis. Fusce quis purus nibh. Nulla tempor est vel metus sodales, in dapibus risus molestie. Donec tri
ue ut vehicula mauris. Vivamus pellentesque, tellus in dictum vehicula, justo ex volutpat sem, at cursus nisl elit non ex.
rnare vitae mi a vestibulum. Suspendisse potenti. Donec sed ligula ac enim mattis posuere.
```

This is a basic illustration of how, using the bridge pattern in your design, you can extract content from different sources and integrate the results in the same data manipulation system or user interface.

Summary

In this chapter, we discussed the bridge pattern. Sharing similarities with the adapter pattern, the bridge pattern is different from it, in the sense that it is used up-front to define an abstraction and its implementation in a decoupled way so that both can vary independently.

The bridge pattern is useful when writing software for problem domains such as operation systems and device drivers, GUIs, and website builders where we have multiple themes and we need to change the theme of a website based on certain properties.

To help you understand this pattern, we discussed an example in the domain of content extraction and management, where we defined an interface for the abstraction, an interface for the implementor, and two implementations.

In the next chapter, we are going to cover the facade pattern.

29
The Facade Pattern

In the previous chapter, we covered a third structural pattern, the bridge pattern, which helps to define an abstraction and its implementation in a decoupled way, so that both can vary independently.

As systems evolve, they can get very complex. It is not unusual to end up with a very large (and sometimes confusing) collection of classes and interactions. In many cases, we don't want to expose this complexity to the client. This is where our next structural pattern comes to the rescue: **facade**.

The facade design pattern helps us to hide the internal complexity of our systems and expose only what is necessary to the client through a simplified interface. In essence, facade is an abstraction layer implemented over an existing complex system.

Let's take the example of the computer to illustrate things. A computer is a complex machine that depends on several parts to be fully functional. To keep things simple, the word "computer", in this case, refers to an IBM derivative that uses a von Neumann architecture. Booting a computer is a particularly complex procedure. The CPU, main memory, and hard disk need to be up and running, the boot loader must be loaded from the hard disk to the main memory, the CPU must boot the operating system kernel, and so forth. Instead of exposing all this complexity to the client, we create a facade that encapsulates the whole procedure, making sure that all steps are executed in the right order.

In terms of object design and programming, we should have several classes, but only the `Computer` class needs to be exposed to the client code. The client will only have to execute the `start()` method of the `Computer` class, for example, and all the other complex parts are taken care of by the facade `Computer` class.

In this chapter, we will discuss:

- Real-world examples
- Use cases
- Implementation

Real-world examples

The facade pattern is quite common in life. When you call a bank or a company, you are usually first connected to the customer service department. The customer service employee acts as a facade between you and the actual department (billing, technical support, general assistance, and so on), and the employee that will help you with your specific problem.

As another example, a key used to turn on a car or motorcycle can also be considered a facade. It is a simple way of activating a system that is very complex internally. And, of course, the same is true for other complex electronic devices that we can activate with a single button, such as computers.

In software, the `django-oscar-datacash` module is a Django third-party module that integrates with the **DataCash** payment gateway. The module has a gateway class that provides fine-grained access to the various DataCash APIs. On top of that, it also offers a facade class that provides a less granular API (for those who don't want to mess with the details), and the ability to save transactions for auditing purposes.

Use cases

The most usual reason to use the facade pattern is for providing a single, simple entry point to a complex system. By introducing facade, the client code can use a system by simply calling a single method/function. At the same time, the internal system does not lose any functionality, it just encapsulates it.

Not exposing the internal functionality of a system to the client code gives us an extra benefit: we can introduce changes to the system, but the client code remains unaware of and unaffected by the changes. No modifications are required to the client code.

Facade is also useful if you have more than one layer in your system. You can introduce one facade entry point per layer, and let all layers communicate with each other through their facades. That promotes **loose coupling** and keeps the layers as independent as possible.

Implementation

Assume that we want to create an operating system using a multi-server approach, similar to how it is done in MINIX 3 (j.mp/minix3) or GNU Hurd (j.mp/gnuhurd). A multiserver operating system has a minimal kernel, called the **microkernel**, which runs in privileged mode. All the other services of the system are following a server architecture (driver server, process server, file server, and so forth). Each server belongs to a different memory address space and runs on top of the microkernel in user mode. The pros of this approach are that the operating system can become more fault-tolerant, reliable, and secure. For example, since all drivers are running in user mode on a driver server, a bug in a driver cannot crash the whole system, nor can it affect the other servers. The cons of this approach are the performance overhead and the complexity of system programming, because the communication between a server and the microkernel, as well as between the independent servers, happens using message passing. Message passing is more complex than the shared memory model used in monolithic kernels such as Linux (j.mp/helenosm).

We begin with a `Server` interface. An `Enum` parameter describes the different possible states of a server. We use the ABC module to forbid direct instantiation of the `Server` interface and make the fundamental `boot()` and `kill()` methods mandatory, assuming that different actions are needed to be taken for booting, killing, and restarting each server. If you have not used the ABC module before, note the following important things:

- We need to subclass `ABCMeta` using the `metaclass` keyword.
- We use the `@abstractmethod` decorator for stating which methods should be implemented (mandatory) by all subclasses of server.

Try removing the `boot()` or `kill()` method of a subclass and see what happens. Do the same after removing the `@abstractmethod` decorator also. Do things work as you expected?

Let's consider the following code:

```
State = Enum('State', 'new running sleeping restart zombie')
class Server(metaclass=ABCMeta):
    @abstractmethod
    def __init__(self):
        pass
    def __str__(self):
        return self.name
    @abstractmethod
    def boot(self):
        pass
    @abstractmethod
```

```
        def kill(self, restart=True):
            pass
```

A modular operating system can have a great number of interesting servers: a file server, a process server, an authentication server, a network server, a graphical/window server, and so forth. The following example includes two stub servers: the `FileServer` and the `ProcessServer`. Apart from the methods required to be implemented by the `Server` interface, each server can have its own specific methods. For instance, the `FileServer` has a `create_file()` method for creating files, and the `ProcessServer` has a `create_process()` method for creating processes.

The `FileServer` class is as follows:

```
class FileServer(Server):
    def __init__(self):
        '''actions required for initializing the file server'''
        self.name = 'FileServer'
        self.state = State.new

    def boot(self):
        print(f'booting the {self}')
        '''actions required for booting the file server'''
        self.state = State.running

    def kill(self, restart=True):
        print(f'Killing {self}')
        '''actions required for killing the file server'''
        self.state = State.restart if restart else State.zombie

    def create_file(self, user, name, permissions):
        '''check validity of permissions, user rights, etc.'''
        print(f"trying to create the file '{name}' for user '{user}' with
permissions {permissions}")
```

The `ProcessServer` class is as follows:

```
class ProcessServer(Server):
    def __init__(self):
        '''actions required for initializing the process server'''
        self.name = 'ProcessServer'
        self.state = State.new

    def boot(self):
        print(f'booting the {self}')
        '''actions required for booting the process server'''
        self.state = State.running
```

```
    def kill(self, restart=True):
        print(f'Killing {self}')
        '''actions required for killing the process server'''
        self.state = State.restart if restart else State.zombie

    def create_process(self, user, name):
        '''check user rights, generate PID, etc.'''
        print(f"trying to create the process '{name}' for user '{user}'")
```

The OperatingSystem class is a facade. In its __init__(), all the necessary server instances are created. The start() method, used by the client code, is the entry point to the system. More wrapper methods can be added, if necessary, as access points to the services of the servers, such as the wrappers, create_file() and create_process(). From the client's point of view, all those services are provided by the OperatingSystem class. The client should not be confused by unnecessary details such as the existence of servers and the responsibility of each server.

The code for the OperatingSystem class is as follows:

```
class OperatingSystem:
    '''The Facade'''
    def __init__(self):
        self.fs = FileServer()
        self.ps = ProcessServer()

    def start(self):
        [i.boot() for i in (self.fs, self.ps)]

    def create_file(self, user, name, permissions):
        return self.fs.create_file(user, name, permissions)

    def create_process(self, user, name):
        return self.ps.create_process(user, name)
```

As you are going to see in a minute, when we present a summary of the example, there are many dummy classes and servers. They are there to give you an idea about the required abstractions (User, Process, File, and so forth) and servers (WindowServer, NetworkServer, and so forth) for making the system functional. A recommended exercise is to implement at least one service of the system (for example, file creation). Feel free to change the interface and the signature of the methods to fit your needs. Make sure that after your changes, the client code does not need to know anything other than the façade OperatingSystem class.

We are going to recapitulate the details of our implementation example; the full code is in the `facade.py` file:

1. We start with the imports we need:

    ```
    from enum import Enum
    from abc import ABCMeta, abstractmethod
    ```

2. We define the `State` constant using `Enum`, as shown earlier.
3. We then add the `User`, `Process`, and `File` classes, which do nothing in this minimal but functional example:

    ```
    class User:
        pass

    class Process:
        pass

    class File:
        pass
    ```

4. We define the base `Server` class, as shown earlier.
5. We then define the `FileServer` class and the `ProcessServer` class, which are both subclasses of `Server`.
6. We add two other dummy classes, `WindowServer` and `NetworkServer`:

    ```
    class WindowServer:
        pass

    class NetworkServer:
        pass
    ```

7. Then we define our facade class, `OperatingSystem`, as shown earlier.
8. Finally, here is the main part of the code, where we use the facade we have defined:

    ```
    def main():
        os = OperatingSystem()
        os.start()
        os.create_file('foo', 'hello', '-rw-r-r')
        os.create_process('bar', 'ls /tmp')

    if __name__ == '__main__':
        main()
    ```

As you can see, executing the `python facade.py` command shows the starting message of our two stub servers:

```
booting the FileServer
booting the ProcessServer
trying to create the file 'hello' for user 'foo' with permissions -rw-r-r
trying to create the process 'ls /tmp' for user 'bar'
```

The facade `OperatingSystem` class does a good job. The client code can create files and processes without needing to know internal details about the operating system, such as the existence of multiple servers. To be precise, the client code can call the methods for creating files and processes, but they are currently dummy. As an interesting exercise, you can implement one of the two methods, or even both.

Summary

In this chapter, we have learned how to use the facade pattern. This pattern is ideal for providing a simple interface to client code that wants to use a complex system but does not need to be aware of the system's complexity. A computer is a facade since all we need to do to use it is press a single button for turning it on. All the rest of the hardware complexity is handled transparently by the BIOS, the boot loader, and the other components of the system software. There are more real-life examples of facade, such as when we are connected to the customer service department of a bank or a company, and the keys that we use to turn a vehicle on.

We discussed a Django third-party module that uses Facade: `django-oscar-datacash`. It uses the facade pattern to provide a simple DataCash API and the ability to save transactions.

We covered the basic use cases of facade and ended the chapter with an implementation of the interface used by a multiserver operating system. A facade is an elegant way of hiding the complexity of a system because, in most cases, the client code should not be aware of such details.

In the next chapter, we will cover other structural design patterns.

30
Other Structural Patterns

Besides the patterns covered in previous chapters, there are other structural patterns we can cover: **flyweight**, **model-view-controller** (**MVC**), and **proxy**.

What is the flyweight pattern? Object-oriented systems can face performance issues due to the overhead of object creation. Performance issues usually appear in embedded systems with limited resources, such as smartphones and tablets. They can also appear in large and complex systems where we need to create a very large number of objects (and possibly users) that need to coexist at the same time. The *flyweight* pattern teaches programmers how to minimize memory usage by sharing resources with similar objects as much as possible.

The MVC pattern is useful mainly in application development and helps developers improve the maintainability of their applications by avoiding mixing the business logic with the user interface.

In some applications, we want to execute one or more important actions before accessing an object, and this is where the proxy pattern comes in. An example is the accessing of sensitive information. Before allowing any user to access sensitive information, we want to make sure that the user has sufficient privileges. The important action is not necessarily related to security issues. Lazy initialization (`j.mp/wikilazy`) is another case; we want to delay the creation of a computationally expensive object until the first time the user actually needs to use it. The idea of the proxy pattern is to help with performing such an action before accessing the actual object.

In this chapter, we will discuss:

- The flyweight pattern
- The MVC pattern
- The proxy pattern

The flyweight pattern

Whenever we create a new object, extra memory needs to be allocated. Although virtual memory provides us, theoretically, with unlimited memory, the reality is different. If all the physical memory of a system gets exhausted, it will start swapping pages with the secondary storage, usually a **hard disk drive** (**HDD**), which, in most cases, is unacceptable due to the performance differences between the main memory and HDD. **Solid-state drives** (**SSDs**) generally have better performance than HDDs, but not everybody is expected to use SSDs. So, SSDs are not going to totally replace HDDs anytime soon.

Apart from memory usage, performance is also a consideration. Graphics software, including computer games, should be able to render 3-D information (for example, a forest with thousands of trees, a village full of soldiers, or an urban area with a lot of cars) extremely quickly. If each object in a 3-D terrain is created individually and no data sharing is used, the performance will be prohibitive.

As software engineers, we should solve software problems by writing better software, instead of forcing the customer to buy extra or better hardware. The flyweight design pattern is a technique used to minimize memory usage and improve performance by introducing data sharing between similar objects (`j.mp/wflyw`). A flyweight is a shared object that contains state-independent, immutable (also known as **intrinsic**) data. The state-dependent, mutable (also known as **extrinsic**) data should not be part of flyweight because this is information that cannot be shared, since it differs per object. If flyweight needs extrinsic data, it should be provided explicitly by the client code.

An example might help to clarify how the flyweight pattern can be practically used. Let's assume that we are creating a performance-critical game, for example, a **first-person shooter** (**FPS**). In FPS games, the players (soldiers) share some states, such as representation and behavior. In *Counter-Strike*, for instance, all soldiers on the same team (counter-terrorists versus terrorists) look the same (representation). In the same game, all soldiers (on both teams) have some common actions, such as jump, duck, and so forth (behavior). This means that we can create a flyweight that will contain all of the common data. Of course, the soldiers also have a lot of data that is different per soldier and will not be a part of the flyweight, such as weapons, health, location, and so on.

Real-world examples

Flyweight is an optimization design pattern, therefore, it is not easy to find a good noncomputing example of it. We can think of flyweight as caching in real life. For example, many bookstores have dedicated shelves with the newest and most popular publications. This is a cache. First, you can take a look at the dedicated shelves for the book you are looking for, and if you cannot find it, you can ask the bookseller to assist you.

The Exaile music player uses flyweight to reuse objects (in this case, music tracks) that are identified by the same URL. There's no point in creating a new object if it has the same URL as an existing object, so the same object is reused to save resources.

Peppy, a XEmacs-like editor implemented in Python, uses the flyweight pattern to store the state of a major mode status bar. That's because unless modified by the user, all status bars share the same properties.

Use cases

Flyweight is all about improving performance and memory usage. All embedded systems (phones, tablets, games consoles, microcontrollers, and so forth) and performance-critical applications (games, 3-D graphics processing, real-time systems, and so forth) can benefit from it.

The *Gang of Four* (*GoF*) book lists the following requirements that need to be satisfied to effectively use the flyweight pattern:

- The application needs to use a large number of objects.
- There are so many objects that it's too expensive to store/render them. Once the mutable state is removed (because if it is required, it should be passed explicitly to flyweight by the client code), many groups of distinct objects can be replaced by relatively few shared objects.
- Object identity is not important for the application. We cannot rely on object identity because object sharing causes identity comparisons to fail (objects that appear different to the client code end up having the same identity).

Implementation

Let's see how we can implement the example mentioned previously for cars in an area. We will create a small car park to illustrate the idea, making sure that the whole output is readable in a single terminal page. However, no matter how large you make the car park, the memory allocation stays the same.

Before diving into the code, let's spend a moment noting the differences between the memoization and the flyweight pattern. **Memoization** is an optimization technique that uses a cache to avoid recomputing results that were already computed in an earlier execution step. Memoization does not focus on a specific programming paradigm such as **object-oriented programming** (OOP). In Python, memoization can be applied to both methods and simple functions. Flyweight is an OOP-specific optimization design pattern that focuses on sharing object data.

First, we need an Enum parameter that describes the three different types of car that are in the car park:

```
CarType = Enum('CarType', 'subcompact compact suv')
```

Then, we will define the class at the core of our implementation: Car. The pool variable is the object pool (in other words, our cache). Notice that pool is a class attribute (a variable shared by all instances).

Using the __new__() special method, which is called before __init__(), we are converting the Car class to a metaclass that supports self-references. This means that cls references the Car class. When the client code creates an instance of Car, they pass the type of the car as car_type. The type of the car is used to check if a car of the same type has already been created. If that's the case, the previously created object is returned; otherwise, the new car type is added to the pool and returned:

```
class Car:
    pool = dict()

    def __new__(cls, car_type):
        obj = cls.pool.get(car_type, None)
        if not obj:
            obj = object.__new__(cls)
            cls.pool[car_type] = obj
            obj.car_type = car_type
        return obj
```

The `render()` method is what will be used to render a car on the screen. Notice how all the mutable information not known by flyweight needs to be explicitly passed by the client code. In this case, a random `color` and the coordinates of a location (of form x, y) are used for each car.

Also, note that to make `render()` more useful, it is necessary to ensure that no cars are rendered on top of each other. Consider this as an exercise. If you want to make rendering more fun, you can use a graphics toolkit such as Tkinter, Pygame, or Kivy.

The `render()` method is defined as follows:

```
def render(self, color, x, y):
    type = self.car_type
    msg = f'render a car of type {type} and color {color} at ({x},
{y})'
    print(msg)
```

The `main()` function shows how we can use the flyweight pattern. The color of a car is a random value from a predefined list of colors. The coordinates use random values between 1 and 100. Although 18 cars are rendered, memory is allocated only for three. The last line of the output proves that when using flyweight, we cannot rely on object identity. The `id()` function returns the memory address of an object. This is not the default behavior in Python because by default, `id()` returns a unique ID (actually the memory address of an object as an integer) for each object. In our case, even if two objects appear to be different, they actually have the same identity if they belong to the same **flyweight family** (in this case, the family is defined by `car_type`). Of course, different identity comparisons can still be used for objects of different families, but that is possible only if the client knows the implementation details.

Our example `main()` function's code is as follows:

```
def main():
    rnd = random.Random()
    colors = 'white black silver gray red blue brown beige yellow
green'.split()
    min_point, max_point = 0, 100
    car_counter = 0

    for _ in range(10):
        c1 = Car(CarType.subcompact)
        c1.render(random.choice(colors),
                rnd.randint(min_point, max_point),
                rnd.randint(min_point, max_point))
        car_counter += 1
```

```
for _ in range(3):
    c2 = Car(CarType.compact)
    c2.render(random.choice(colors),
              rnd.randint(min_point, max_point),
              rnd.randint(min_point, max_point))
    car_counter += 1

for _ in range(5):
    c3 = Car(CarType.suv)
    c3.render(random.choice(colors),
              rnd.randint(min_point, max_point),
              rnd.randint(min_point, max_point))
    car_counter += 1

print(f'cars rendered: {car_counter}')
print(f'cars actually created: {len(Car.pool)}')

c4 = Car(CarType.subcompact)
c5 = Car(CarType.subcompact)
c6 = Car(CarType.suv)
print(f'{id(c4)} == {id(c5)}? {id(c4) == id(c5)}')
print(f'{id(c5)} == {id(c6)}? {id(c5) == id(c6)}')
```

Here is the full code listing (the `flyweight.py` file) to show you how the flyweight pattern is implemented and used:

1. We need a couple of imports:

   ```
   import random
   from enum import Enum
   ```

2. The `Enum` for the types of cars is shown here:

   ```
   CarType = Enum('CarType', 'subcompact compact suv')
   ```

3. Then we have the `Car` class, with its `pool` attribute and the `__new__()` and `render()` methods:

   ```
   class Car:
       pool = dict()

       def __new__(cls, car_type):
           obj = cls.pool.get(car_type, None)
           if not obj:
               obj = object.__new__(cls)
               cls.pool[car_type] = obj
               obj.car_type = car_type
           return obj
   ```

```
    def render(self, color, x, y):
        type = self.car_type
        msg = f'render a car of type {type} and color {color} at
({x}, {y})'
        print(msg)
```

4. In the first part of the `main` function, we define some variables and render a set of cars of type `subcompact`:

```
def main():
    rnd = random.Random()
    colors = 'white black silver gray red blue brown beige yellow
green'.split()
    min_point, max_point = 0, 100
    car_counter = 0

    for _ in range(10):
        c1 = Car(CarType.subcompact)
        c1.render(random.choice(colors),
                rnd.randint(min_point, max_point),
                rnd.randint(min_point, max_point))
        car_counter += 1
```

5. The second part of the `main` function is as follows:

```
    for _ in range(3):
        c2 = Car(CarType.compact)
        c2.render(random.choice(colors),
                rnd.randint(min_point, max_point),
                rnd.randint(min_point, max_point))
        car_counter += 1
```

6. The third part of the `main` function is as follows:

```
    for _ in range(5):    c3 = Car(CarType.suv)
        c3.render(random.choice(colors),
                rnd.randint(min_point, max_point),
                rnd.randint(min_point, max_point))
        car_counter += 1

    print(f'cars rendered: {car_counter}')
    print(f'cars actually created: {len(Car.pool)}')
```

7. Finally, here is the fourth part of the `main` function:

```
c4 = Car(CarType.subcompact)
c5 = Car(CarType.subcompact)
c6 = Car(CarType.suv)
print(f'{id(c4)} == {id(c5)}? {id(c4) == id(c5)}')
print(f'{id(c5)} == {id(c6)}? {id(c5) == id(c6)}')
```

8. We do not forget our usual __name__ == '__main__' trick and good practice, as follows:

```
if __name__ == '__main__':
    main()
```

The execution of the `python flyweight` command shows the type, random color, and coordinates of the rendered objects, as well as the identity comparison results between flyweight objects of the same/different families:

```
render a tree of type TreeType.apple_tree and age 28 at (27, 14)
render a tree of type TreeType.apple_tree and age 10 at (15, 47)
render a tree of type TreeType.apple_tree and age 29 at (41, 29)
render a tree of type TreeType.apple_tree and age 26 at (80, 57)
render a tree of type TreeType.apple_tree and age 11 at (6, 66)
render a tree of type TreeType.apple_tree and age 24 at (0, 1)
render a tree of type TreeType.apple_tree and age 24 at (33, 96)
render a tree of type TreeType.apple_tree and age 15 at (24, 87)
render a tree of type TreeType.apple_tree and age 6 at (0, 87)
render a tree of type TreeType.apple_tree and age 9 at (40, 45)
render a tree of type TreeType.cherry_tree and age 24 at (27, 86)
render a tree of type TreeType.cherry_tree and age 30 at (75, 76)
render a tree of type TreeType.cherry_tree and age 15 at (78, 74)
render a tree of type TreeType.peach_tree and age 30 at (11, 24)
render a tree of type TreeType.peach_tree and age 24 at (21, 7)
render a tree of type TreeType.peach_tree and age 10 at (13, 89)
render a tree of type TreeType.peach_tree and age 2 at (85, 93)
render a tree of type TreeType.peach_tree and age 27 at (81, 79)
trees rendered: 18
trees actually created: 3
3085454594848 == 3085454594848? True
3085454594848 == 3085454560616? False
```

Do not expect to see the same output since the colors and coordinates are random, and the object identities depend on the memory map.

The model-view-controller pattern

One of the design principles related to software engineering is the **separation of concerns** (**SoC**) principle. The idea behind the SoC principle is to split an application into distinct sections, where each section addresses a separate concern. Examples of such concerns are the layers used in a layered design (data access layer, business logic layer, presentation layer, and so forth). Using the SoC principle simplifies the development and maintenance of software applications.

The MVC pattern is nothing more than the SoC principle applied to OOP. The name of the pattern comes from the three main components used to split a software application: the model, the view, and the controller. MVC is considered an architectural pattern rather than a design pattern. The difference between an architectural and a design pattern is that the former has a broader scope than the latter. Nevertheless, MVC is too important to skip just for this reason. Even if we will never have to implement it from scratch, we need to be familiar with it because all common frameworks use MVC or a slightly different version of it (more on this later).

The model is the core component. It represents knowledge. It contains and manages the (business) logic, data, state, and rules of an application. The view is a visual representation of the model. Examples of views are a computer GUI, the text output of a computer terminal, a smartphone's application GUI, a PDF document, a pie chart, a bar chart, and so forth. The view only displays the data; it doesn't handle it. The controller is the link/glue between the model and view. All communication between the model and the view happens through a controller.

A typical use of an application that uses MVC, after the initial screen is rendered to the user is as follows:

1. The user triggers a view by clicking (typing, touching, and so on) a button
2. The view informs the controller of the user's action
3. The controller processes user input and interacts with the model
4. The model performs all the necessary validation and state changes and informs the controller about what should be done
5. The controller instructs the view to update and display the output appropriately, following the instructions that are given by the model

You might be wondering, why the controller part is necessary? Can't we just skip it? We could, but then we would lose a big benefit that MVC provides: the ability to use more than one view (even at the same time, if that's what we want) without modifying the model. To achieve decoupling between the model and its representation, every view typically needs its own controller. If the model communicated directly with a specific view, we wouldn't be able to use multiple views (or at least, not in a clean and modular way).

Real-world examples

MVC is the SoC principle applied to OOP. The SoC principle is used a lot in real life. For example, if you build a new house, you usually assign different professionals to: 1) install the plumbing and electricity; and, 2) paint the house.

Another example is a restaurant. In a restaurant, the waiters receive orders and serve dishes to the customers, but the meals are cooked by the chefs.

In web development, several frameworks use the MVC idea:

- The Web2py Framework (`j.mp/webtopy`) is a lightweight Python Framework that embraces the MVC pattern. If you have never tried Web2py, I encourage you to do it since it is extremely simple to install. There are many examples that demonstrate how MVC can be used in Web2py on the project's web page.
- Django is also an MVC Framework, although it uses different naming conventions. The controller is called view, and the view is called **template**. Django uses the name **Model-Template-View** (**MTV**). According to the designers of Django, the view describes what data is seen by the user, and therefore, it uses the name view as the Python callback function for a particular URL. The term **template** in Django is used to separate content from representation. It describes how the data is seen by the user, not which data is seen.

Use cases

MVC is a very generic and useful design pattern. In fact, all popular web frameworks (Django, Rails, and Symfony or Yii) and application frameworks (iPhone SDK, Android, and QT) make use of MVC or a variation of it—**model-view-adapter** (**MVA**), **model-view-presenter** (**MVP**), and so forth. However, even if we don't use any of these frameworks, it makes sense to implement the pattern on our own because of the benefits it provides, which are as follows:

- The separation between the view and model allows graphics designers to focus on the UI part and programmers to focus on development, without interfering with each other.
- Because of the loose coupling between the view and model, each part can be modified/extended without affecting the other. For example, adding a new view is trivial. Just implement a new controller for it.
- Maintaining each part is easier because the responsibilities are clear.

When implementing MVC from scratch, be sure that you create smart models, thin controllers, and dumb views.

A model is considered smart because it does the following:

- Contains all the validation/business rules/logic
- Handles the state of the application
- Has access to application data (database, cloud, and so on)
- Does not depend on the UI

A controller is considered thin because it does the following:

- Updates the model when the user interacts with the view
- Updates the view when the model changes
- Processes the data before delivering it to the model/view, if necessary
- Does not display the data
- Does not access the application data directly
- Does not contain validation/business rules/logic

A view is considered dumb because it does the following:

- Displays the data
- Allows the user to interact with it
- Does only minimal processing, usually provided by a template language (for example, using simple variables and loop controls)
- Does not store any data
- Does not access the application data directly
- Does not contain validation/business rules/logic

If you are implementing MVC from scratch and want to find out if you did it right, you can try answering some key questions:

- If your application has a GUI, is it skinnable? How easily can you change the skin/look and feel of it? Can you give the user the ability to change the skin of your application during runtime? If this is not simple, it means that something is going wrong with your MVC implementation.
- If your application has no GUI (for instance, if it's a terminal application), how hard is it to add GUI support? Or, if adding a GUI is irrelevant, is it easy to add views to display the results in a chart (pie chart, bar chart, and so on) or a document (PDF, spreadsheet, and so on)? If these changes are not trivial (a matter of creating a new controller with a view attached to it, without modifying the model), MVC is not implemented properly.

If you make sure that these conditions are satisfied, your application will be more flexible and maintainable compared to an application that does not use MVC.

Implementation

I could use any of the common frameworks to demonstrate how to use MVC, but I feel that the picture will be incomplete. So, I decided to show you how to implement MVC from scratch, using a very simple example: a quote printer. The idea is extremely simple. The user enters a number and sees the quote related to that number. The quotes are stored in a quotes tuple. This is the data that normally exists in a database, file, and so on, and only the model has direct access to it.

Let's consider the example in the following code:

```
quotes =
(
  'A man is not complete until he is married. Then he is finished.',
```

```
    'As I said before, I never repeat myself.',
    'Behind a successful man is an exhausted woman.',
    'Black holes really suck...',
    'Facts are stubborn things.'
)
```

The model is minimalistic; it only has a `get_quote()` method that returns the quote (string) of the quotes tuple based on its index *n*. Note that *n* can be less than or equal to zero, due to the way indexing works in Python. Improving this behavior is given as an exercise for you at the end of this section:

```
class QuoteModel:
    def get_quote(self, n):
        try:
            value = quotes[n]
        except IndexError as err:
            value = 'Not found!'
        return value
```

The view has three methods: `show()`, which is used to print a quote (or the message **Not found!**) on the screen, `error()`, which is used to print an error message on the screen, and `select_quote()`, which reads the user's selection. This can be seen in the following code:

```
class QuoteTerminalView:
    def show(self, quote):
        print(f'And the quote is: "{quote}"')
    def error(self, msg):
        print(f'Error: {msg}')
    def select_quote(self):
        return input('Which quote number would you like to see? ')
```

The controller does the coordination. The `__init__()` method initializes the model and view. The `run()` method validates the quoted index given by the user, gets the quote from the model, and passes it back to the view to be displayed as shown in the following code:

```
class QuoteTerminalController:
    def __init__(self):
        self.model = QuoteModel()
        self.view = QuoteTerminalView()
    def run(self):
        valid_input = False
        while not valid_input:
            try:
                n = self.view.select_quote()
                n = int(n)
                valid_input = True
            except ValueError as err:
```

```
                self.view.error(f"Incorrect index '{n}'")
        quote = self.model.get_quote(n)
        self.view.show(quote)
```

Last but not least, the `main()` function initializes and fires the controller as shown in the following code:

```
def main():
    controller = QuoteTerminalController()
    while True:
        controller.run()
```

The following is the full code of the example (the `mvc.py` file):

- We start by defining a variable for the list of quotes as shown in the following code snippet:

```
quotes =
(
  'A man is not complete until he is
finished.',
  'As I said before, I never repeat myself.',
  'Behind a successful man is an exhausted woman.',
  'Black holes really suck...',
  'Facts are stubborn things.'
)
```

- Here is the code for the model class, `QuoteModel`:

```
class QuoteModel:
    def get_quote(self, n):
        try:
            value = quotes[n]
        except IndexError as err:
            value = 'Not found!'
        return value
```

- Here is the code for the view class, `QuoteTerminalView`:

```
class QuoteTerminalView:
    def show(self, quote):
        print(f'And the quote is: "{quote}"')

    def error(self, msg):
        print(f'Error: {msg}')

    def select_quote(self):
        return input('Which quote number would you like to see?
')
```

- Here is the code for the controller class, `QuoteTerminalController`:

```
class QuoteTerminalController:
    def __init__(self):
        self.model = QuoteModel()
        self.view = QuoteTerminalView()
    def run(self):
        valid_input = False
        while not valid_input:
            try:
                n = self.view.select_quote()
                n = int(n)
                valid_input = True
            except ValueError as err:
                self.view.error(f"Incorrect index '{n}'")
        quote = self.model.get_quote(n)
        self.view.show(quote)
```

- Here is the end of our example code with the `main()` function:

```
def main():
    controller = QuoteTerminalController()
    while True:
        controller.run()


if __name__ == '__main__':
    main()
```

A sample execution of the `python mvc.py` command shows how the program prints quotes to the user:

```
Which quote number would you like to see? 2
And the quote is: "Behind a successful man is an exhausted woman."
Which quote number would you like to see? 4
And the quote is: "Facts are stubborn things."
Which quote number would you like to see? 1
And the quote is: "As I said before, I never repeat myself."
Which quote number would you like to see? 6
And the quote is: "Not found!"
Which quote number would you like to see? 3
And the quote is: "Black holes really suck..."
Which quote number would you like to see? 0
And the quote is: "A man is not complete until he is married. Then he is finished."
Which quote number would you like to see? _
```

The proxy pattern

The proxy design pattern gets its name from the proxy (also known as **surrogate**) object used to perform an important action before accessing the actual object. There are four different well-known proxy types (`j.mp/proxypat`). They are as follows:

- A **remote proxy**, which acts as the local representation of an object that really exists in a different address space (for example, a network server).
- A **virtual proxy**, which uses lazy initialization to defer the creation of a computationally expensive object until the moment it is actually needed.
- A **protection/protective proxy**, which controls access to a sensitive object.
- A **smart (reference) proxy**, which performs extra actions when an object is accessed. Examples of such actions are reference counting and thread-safety checks.

I find virtual proxies very useful so let's see an example of how we can implement them in Python right now. In the *Implementation* section, you will learn how to create protective proxies.

There are many ways to create a virtual proxy in Python, but I always like focusing on the idiomatic/Pythonic implementations. The code shown here is based on the great answer by Cyclone, a user of the site `stackoverflow.com` (`j.mp/solazyinit`). To avoid confusion, I should clarify that in this section, the terms *property*, *variable*, and *attribute* are used interchangeably. First, we create a `LazyProperty` class that can be used as a decorator. When it decorates a property, `LazyProperty` loads the property lazily (on the first use), instead of instantly. The `__init__()` method creates two variables that are used as aliases to the method that initializes a property. The `method` variable is an alias to the actual method, and the `method_name` variable is an alias to the method's name. To get a better understanding of how the two aliases are used, print their value to the output (uncomment the two commented lines in the following code):

```
class LazyProperty:
    def __init__(self, method):
        self.method = method
        self.method_name = method.__name__
        # print(f"function overriden: {self.fget}")
        # print(f"function's name: {self.func_name}")
```

The `LazyProperty` class is actually a descriptor (`j.mp/pydesc`). Descriptors are the recommended mechanisms to use in Python to override the default behavior of its attribute access methods: `__get__()`, `__set__()`, and `__delete__()`. The `LazyProperty` class overrides only `__set__()` because that is the only access method it needs to override. In other words, we don't have to override all access methods. The `__get__()` method accesses the value of the property the underlying method wants to assign, and uses `setattr()` to do the assignment manually. What `__get()__` actually does is very neat: it replaces the method with the value! This means that not only is the property lazily loaded, it can also be set only once. We will see what this means in a moment. Again, uncomment the commented line in the following code to get some extra information:

```
def __get__(self, obj, cls):
    if not obj:
        return None
    value = self.method(obj)
    # print(f'value {value}')
    setattr(obj, self.method_name, value)
    return value
```

The `Test` class shows how we can use the `LazyProperty` class. There are three attributes: x, y, and _resource. We want the _resource variable to be loaded lazily; thus, we initialize it to `None` as shown in the following code:

```
class Test:
    def __init__(self):
```

```
        self.x = 'foo'
        self.y = 'bar'
        self._resource = None
```

The `resource()` method is decorated with the `LazyProperty` class. For demonstration purposes, the `LazyProperty` class initializes the `_resource` attribute as a tuple, as shown in the following code. Normally, this would be a slow/expensive initialization (database, graphics, and so on):

```
@LazyProperty
def resource(self):
    print(f'initializing self._resource which is: {self._resource}')
    self._resource = tuple(range(5)) # expensive
    return self._resource
```

The `main()` function, as follows, shows how lazy initialization behaves:

```
def main():
    t = Test()
    print(t.x)
    print(t.y)
    # do more work...
    print(t.resource)
    print(t.resource)
```

Notice how overriding the `__get()__` access method makes it possible to treat the `resource()` method as a simple attribute (we can use `t.resource` instead of `t.resource()`).

In the execution output of this example (the `lazy.py` file), we can see that:

- The `_resource` variable is indeed initialized not by the time the `t` instance is created, but the first time that we use `t.resource`.
- The second time `t.resource` is used, the variable is not initialized again. That's why the initialization string initializing `self._resource` is shown only once.

Here is the output we get when executing the `python lazy.py` command:

```
foo
bar
initializing self._resource which is: None
(0, 1, 2, 3, 4)
(0, 1, 2, 3, 4)
```

There are two basic, different kinds of lazy initialization in OOP. They are as follows:

- **At the instance level**: This means that an object's property is initialized lazily, but the property has an object scope. Each instance (object) of the same class has its own (different) copy of the property.
- **At the class or module level**: In this case, we do not want a different copy per instance, but all the instances share the same property, which is lazily initialized. This case is not covered in this chapter. If you find it interesting, consider it as an exercise.

Real-world examples

Chip (also known as **Chip and PIN**) cards (`j.mp/wichpin`) offer a good example of how a protective proxy is used in real life. The debit/credit card contains a chip that first needs to be read by the ATM or card reader. After the chip is verified, a password (PIN) is required to complete the transaction. This means that you cannot make any transactions without physically presenting the card and knowing the PIN.

A bank check that is used instead of cash to make purchases and deals is an example of a remote proxy. The check gives access to a bank account.

In software, the `weakref` module of Python contains a `proxy()` method that accepts an input object and returns a smart proxy to it. Weak references are the recommended way to add reference-counting support to an object.

Use cases

Since there are at least four common proxy types, the proxy design pattern has many use cases, as follows:

- It is used when creating a distributed system using either a private network or the cloud. In a distributed system, some objects exist in the local memory and some objects exist in the memory of remote computers. If we don't want the client code to be aware of such differences, we can create a remote proxy that hides/encapsulates them, making the distributed nature of the application transparent.
- It is used when our application is suffering from performance issues due to the early creation of expensive objects. Introducing lazy initialization using a virtual proxy to create the objects only at the moment they are actually required can give us significant performance improvements.

- It is used to check if a user has sufficient privileges to access a piece of information. If our application handles sensitive information (for example, medical data), we want to make sure that the user trying to access/modify it is allowed to do so. A protection/protective proxy can handle all security-related actions.
- It is used when our application (or library, toolkit, framework, and so forth) uses multiple threads and we want to move the burden of thread safety from the client code to the application. In this case, we can create a smart proxy to hide the thread-safety complexities from the client.
- An **object-relational mapping (ORM)** API is also an example of how to use a remote proxy. Many popular web frameworks, including Django, use an ORM to provide OOP-like access to a relational database. An ORM acts as a proxy to a relational database that can be actually located anywhere, either at a local or remote server.

Implementation

To demonstrate the proxy pattern, we will implement a simple protection proxy to view and add users. The service provides two options:

- **Viewing the list of users**: This operation does not require special privileges
- **Adding a new user**: This operation requires the client to provide a special secret message

The `SensitiveInfo` class contains the information that we want to protect. The users variable is the list of existing users. The `read()` method prints the list of the users. The `add()` method adds a new user to the list.

Let's consider the following code:

```python
class SensitiveInfo:
    def __init__(self):
        self.users = ['nick', 'tom', 'ben', 'mike']
    def read(self):
        nb = len(self.users)
        print(f"There are {nb} users: {' '.join(self.users)}")
    def add(self, user):
        self.users.append(user)
        print(f'Added user {user}')
```

The `Info` class is a protection proxy of `SensitiveInfo`. The `secret` variable is the message required to be known/provided by the client code to add a new user. Note that this is just an example. In reality, you should never do the following:

- Store passwords in the source code
- Store passwords in a clear-text form
- Use a weak (for example, MD5) or custom form of encryption

In the `Info` class, as we can see next, the `read()` method is a wrapper to `SensitiveInfo.read()` and the `add()` method ensures that a new user can be added only if the client code knows the secret message:

```python
class Info:
    '''protection proxy to SensitiveInfo'''
    def __init__(self):
        self.protected = SensitiveInfo()
        self.secret = '0xdeadbeef'
    def read(self):
        self.protected.read()
    def add(self, user):
        sec = input('what is the secret? ')
        self.protected.add(user) if sec == self.secret else print("That's
wrong!")
```

The `main()` function shows how the proxy pattern can be used by the client code. The client code creates an instance of the `Info` class and uses the displayed menu to read the list, add a new user, or exit the application. Let's consider the following code:

```python
def main():
    info = Info()
    while True:
        print('1. read list |==| 2. add user |==| 3. quit')
        key = input('choose option: ')
        if key == '1':
            info.read()
        elif key == '2':
            name = input('choose username: ')
            info.add(name)
        elif key == '3':
            exit()
        else:
            print(f'unknown option: {key}')
```

Let's recapitulate the full code of the `proxy.py` file:

1. First, we define the `LazyProperty` class:

```python
class LazyProperty:
    def __init__(self, method):
        self.method = method
        self.method_name = method.__name__
        # print(f"function overriden: {self.fget}")
        # print(f"function's name: {self.func_name}")
    def __get__(self, obj, cls):
        if not obj:
            return None
        value = self.method(obj)
        # print(f'value {value}')
        setattr(obj, self.method_name, value)
        return value
```

2. Then, we have the code for the `Test` class, as follows:

```python
class Test:
    def __init__(self):
        self.x = 'foo'
        self.y = 'bar'
        self._resource = None
    @LazyProperty
    def resource(self):
        print(f'initializing self._resource which is:
{self._resource}')
        self._resource = tuple(range(5))  # expensive
        return self._resource
```

3. Finally, here is the `main()` function and the end of the code:

```python
def main():
    t = Test()
    print(t.x)
    print(t.y)
    # do more work...
    print(t.resource)
    print(t.resource)

if __name__ == '__main__':
    main()
```

4. We can see here a sample output of the program when executing the `python proxy.py` command:

```
1. read list |==| 2. add user |==| 3. quit
choose option: 1
There are 4 users: nick tom ben mike
1. read list |==| 2. add user |==| 3. quit
choose option: 2
choose username: bill
what is the secret? 12345
That's wrong!
1. read list |==| 2. add user |==| 3. quit
choose option: 2
choose username: bill
what is the secret? 0xdeadbeef
Added user bill
1. read list |==| 2. add user |==| 3. quit
choose option: 1
There are 5 users: nick tom ben mike bill
1. read list |==| 2. add user |==| 3. quit
```

Have you already spotted flaws or missing features that can improve our proxy example? I have a few suggestions. They are as follows:

- This example has a very big security flaw. Nothing prevents the client code from bypassing the security of the application by creating an instance of `SensitiveInfo` directly. Improve the example to prevent this situation. One way is to use the `abc` module to forbid direct instantiation of `SensitiveInfo`. What are other code changes required in this case?
- A basic security rule is that we should never store clear-text passwords. Storing a password safely is not very hard as long as we know which libraries to use (`j.mp/hashsec`). If you have an interest in security, try to implement a secure way to store the secret message externally (for example, in a file or database).
- The application only supports adding new users, but what about removing an existing user? Add a `remove()` method.

Summary

In this chapter, we covered three other structural design patterns: flyweight, MVC, and proxy.

We can use flyweight when we want to improve the memory usage and possibly the performance of our application. This is quite important in all systems with limited resources (think of embedded systems), and systems that focus on performance, such as graphics software and electronic games.

In general, we use flyweight when an application needs to create a large number of computationally expensive objects that share many properties. The important point is to separate the immutable (shared) properties from the mutable. We implemented a tree renderer that supports three different tree families. By providing the mutable `age` and `x, y` properties explicitly to the `render()` method, we managed to create only three different objects instead of eighteen. Although that might not seem like a big win, imagine if the trees were 2,000 instead of 18.

MVC is a very important design pattern used to structure an application in three parts: the model, the view, and the controller. Each part has clear roles and responsibilities. The model has access to the data and manages the state of the application. The view is a representation of the model. The view does not need to be graphical; textual output is also considered a totally fine view. The controller is the link between the model and the view. Proper use of MVC guarantees that we end up with an application that is easy to maintain and extend.

We discussed several use cases of the proxy pattern, including performance, security, and how to offer simple APIs to users. In the first code example, we created a virtual proxy (using decorators and descriptors), allowing us to initialize object properties in a lazy manner. In the second code example, we implemented a protection proxy to handle users. This example can be improved in many ways, especially regarding its security flaws and the fact that the list of users is not persistent.

In the next chapter, we will start exploring behavioral design patterns. Behavioral patterns cope with object interconnection and algorithms. The first behavioral pattern that will be covered is a chain of responsibility.

31
The Chain of Responsibility Pattern

When developing an application, most of the time we know which method should satisfy a particular request in advance. However, this is not always the case. For example, think of any broadcast computer network, such as the original Ethernet implementation (j.mp/wikishared). In broadcast computer networks, all requests are sent to all nodes (broadcast domains are excluded for simplicity), but only the nodes that are interested in a sent request process it.

All computers that participate in a broadcast network are connected to each other using a common medium such as the cable that connects all nodes. If a node is not interested or does not know how to handle a request, it can perform the following actions:

- Ignore the request and do nothing
- Forward the request to the next node

The way in which the node reacts to a request is an implementation detail. However, we can use the analogy of a broadcast computer network to understand what the Chain of Responsibility pattern is all about. The Chain of Responsibility pattern is used when we want to give a chance to multiple objects to satisfy a single request, or when we don't know in advance which object (from a chain of objects) should process a specific request.

To illustrate the principle, imagine a chain (linked list, tree, or any other convenient data structure) of objects, and the following flow:

1. We start by sending a request to the first object in the chain
2. The object decides whether it should satisfy the request or not
3. The object forwards the request to the next object
4. This procedure is repeated until we reach the end of the chain

At the application level, instead of talking about cables and network nodes, we can focus on objects and the flow of a request. The following diagram shows how the client code sends a request to all processing elements of an application:

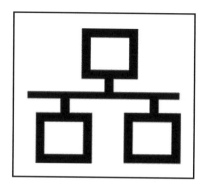

Note that the client code only knows about the first processing element, instead of having references to all of them, and each processing element only knows about its immediate next neighbor (called the **successor**), not about every other processing element. This is usually a one-way relationship, which in programming terms means a singly linked list in contrast to a doubly linked list; a singly linked list does not allow navigation in both ways, while a doubly linked list allows that. This chain organization is used for a good reason. It achieves decoupling between the sender (client) and the receivers (processing elements).

In this chapter, we will discuss:

- Real-world examples
- Use cases
- Implementation

Real-world examples

ATMs and, in general, any kind of machine that accepts/returns banknotes or coins (for example, a snack-vending machine) use the Chain of Responsibility pattern.

There is always a single slot for all banknotes, as shown in the following diagram, courtesy of `sourcemaking.com` (`www.sourcemaking.com`):

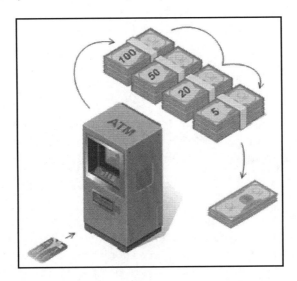

When a banknote is dropped, it is routed to the appropriate receptacle. When it is returned, it is taken from the appropriate receptacle. We can think of the single slot as the shared communication medium and the different receptacles as the processing elements. The result contains cash from one or more receptacles. For example, in the preceding diagram, we see what happens when we request $175 from the ATM.

In software, the servlet filters of Java are pieces of code that are executed before an HTTP request arrives at a target. When using servlet filters, there is a chain of filters. Each filter performs a different action (user authentication, logging, data compression, and so forth), and either forwards the request to the next filter until the chain is exhausted, or it breaks the flow if there is an error—for example, the authentication failed three consecutive times (`j.mp/soservl`).

Another software example, Apple's Cocoa and Cocoa Touch frameworks, use the Chain of Responsibility to handle events. When a view receives an event that it doesn't know how to handle, it forwards the event to its superview. This goes on until a view is capable of handling the event or the chain of views is exhausted (`j.mp/chaincocoa`).

Use cases

By using the Chain of Responsibility pattern, we provide a chance to a number of different objects to satisfy a specific request. This is useful when we don't know which object should satisfy a request in advance. An example is a purchase system. In purchase systems, there are many approval authorities. One approval authority might be able to approve orders up to a certain value, let's say $100. If the order is for more than $100, the order is sent to the next approval authority in the chain that can approve orders up to $200, and so forth.

Another case where the Chain of Responsibility is useful is when we know that more than one object might need to process a single request. This is what happens in event-based programming. A single event, such as a left-mouse click, can be caught by more than one listener.

It is important to note that the Chain of Responsibility pattern is not very useful if all the requests can be taken care of by a single processing element, unless we really don't know which element that is. The value of this pattern is the decoupling that it offers. Instead of having a many-to-many relationship between a client and all processing elements (and the same is true regarding the relationship between a processing element and all other processing elements), a client only needs to know how to communicate with the start (head) of the chain.

The following diagram illustrates the difference between tight and loose coupling. The idea behind loosely coupled systems is to simplify maintenance and make it easier for us to understand how they function (`j.mp/loosecoup`):

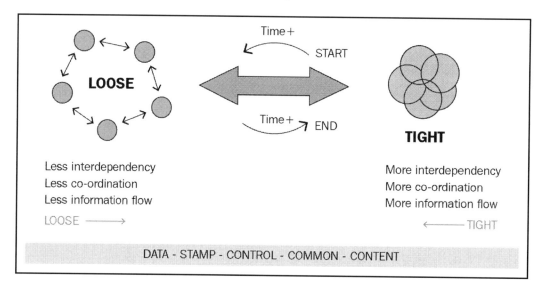

Implementation

There are many ways to implement a Chain of Responsibility in Python, but my favorite implementation is the one by Vespe Savikko (`https://legacy.python.org/workshops/1997-10/proceedings/savikko.html`). Vespe's implementation uses dynamic dispatching in a Pythonic style to handle requests (`http://j.mp/ddispatch`).

Let's implement a simple, event-based system using Vespe's implementation as a guide. The following is the UML class diagram of the system:

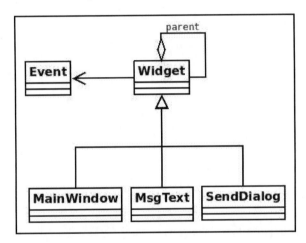

The `Event` class describes an event. We'll keep it simple, so in our case, an event has only a `name`:

```
class Event:
    def __init__(self, name):
        self.name = name

    def __str__(self):
        return self.name
```

The `Widget` class is the core class of the application. The **parent** aggregation shown in the UML diagram indicates that each widget can have a reference to a `parent` object, which by convention, we assume is a `Widget` instance. Note, however, that according to the rules of inheritance, an instance of any of the subclasses of `Widget` (for example, an instance of `MsgText`) is also an instance of `Widget`. The default value of `parent` is `None`:

```
class Widget:
    def __init__(self, parent=None):
        self.parent = parent
```

The `handle()` method uses dynamic dispatching through `hasattr()` and `getattr()` to decide who is the handler of a specific request (event). If the widget that is asked to handle an event does not support it, there are two fallback mechanisms. If the widget has a parent, then the `handle()` method of the parent is executed. If the widget has no parent but a `handle_default()` method, `handle_default()` is executed:

```
def handle(self, event):
    handler = f'handle_{event}'
    if hasattr(self, handler):
    method = getattr(self, handler)
    method(event)
    elif self.parent is not None:
    self.parent.handle(event)
    elif hasattr(self, 'handle_default'):
    self.handle_default(event)
```

At this point, you might have realized why the `Widget` and `Event` classes are only associated (no aggregation or composition relationships) in the UML class diagram. The association is used to show that the `Widget` class knows about the `Event` class but does not have any strict references to it, since an event needs to be passed only as a parameter to `handle()`.

`MainWIndow`, `MsgText`, and `SendDialog` are all widgets with different behaviors. Not all these three widgets are expected to be able to handle the same events, and even if they can handle the same event, they might behave differently. `MainWindow` can handle only the close and default events:

```
class MainWindow(Widget):
    def handle_close(self, event):
        print(f'MainWindow: {event}')

    def handle_default(self, event):
        print(f'MainWindow Default: {event}')
```

`SendDialog` can handle only the paint event:

```
class SendDialog(Widget):
    def handle_paint(self, event):
        print(f'SendDialog: {event}')
```

Finally, `MsgText` can handle only the down event:

```
class MsgText(Widget):
    def handle_down(self, event):
        print(f'MsgText: {event}')
```

The `main()` function shows how we can create a few widgets and events, and how the widgets react to those events. All events are sent to all the widgets. Note the parent relationship of each widget. The `sd` object (an instance of `SendDialog`) has as its parent the `mw` object (an instance of `MainWindow`). However, not all objects need to have a parent that is an instance of `MainWindow`. For example, the `msg` object (an instance of `MsgText`) has the `sd` object as a parent:

```python
def main():
    mw = MainWindow()
    sd = SendDialog(mw)
    msg = MsgText(sd)

    for e in ('down', 'paint', 'unhandled', 'close'):
        evt = Event(e)
        print(f'Sending event -{evt}- to MainWindow')
        mw.handle(evt)
        print(f'Sending event -{evt}- to SendDialog')
        sd.handle(evt)
        print(f'Sending event -{evt}- to MsgText')
        msg.handle(evt)
```

The following is the full code of the example (`chain.py`):

1. We define the `Event` class:

    ```python
    class Event:
        def __init__(self, name):
            self.name = name

        def __str__(self):
            return self.name
    ```

2. Then, we define the `Widget` class:

    ```python
    class Widget:
        def __init__(self, parent=None):
            self.parent = parent

        def handle(self, event):
            handler = f'handle_{event}'
            if hasattr(self, handler):
                method = getattr(self, handler)
                method(event)
            elif self.parent is not None:
                self.parent.handle(event)
            elif hasattr(self, 'handle_default'):
                self.handle_default(event)
    ```

3. We add the specialized widget classes, `MainWindow`, `SendDialog`, and `MsgText`:

```python
class MainWindow(Widget):
    def handle_close(self, event):
        print(f'MainWindow: {event}')

    def handle_default(self, event):
        print(f'MainWindow Default: {event}')

class SendDialog(Widget):
    def handle_paint(self, event):
        print(f'SendDialog: {event}')

class MsgText(Widget):
    def handle_down(self, event):
        print(f'MsgText: {event}')
```

4. Finally, we have the code for the `main()` function and the usual snippet where we call it:

```python
def main():
    mw = MainWindow()
    sd = SendDialog(mw)
    msg = MsgText(sd)

    for e in ('down', 'paint', 'unhandled', 'close'):
        evt = Event(e)
        print(f'Sending event -{evt}- to MainWindow')
        mw.handle(evt)
        print(f'Sending event -{evt}- to SendDialog')
        sd.handle(evt)
        print(f'Sending event -{evt}- to MsgText')
        msg.handle(evt)

if __name__ == '__main__':
    main()
```

5. Executing the `python chain.py` command gives us the following output:

```
Sending event -down- to MainWindow
MainWindow Default: down
Sending event -down- to SendDialog
MainWindow Default: down
Sending event -down- to MsgText
MsgText: down
Sending event -paint- to MainWindow
MainWindow Default: paint
Sending event -paint- to SendDialog
SendDialog: paint
Sending event -paint- to MsgText
SendDialog: paint
Sending event -unhandled- to MainWindow
MainWindow Default: unhandled
Sending event -unhandled- to SendDialog
MainWindow Default: unhandled
Sending event -unhandled- to MsgText
MainWindow Default: unhandled
Sending event -close- to MainWindow
MainWindow: close
Sending event -close- to SendDialog
MainWindow: close
Sending event -close- to MsgText
MainWindow: close
```

There are some interesting things that we can see in the output. For instance, sending a `down` event to `MainWindow` ends up being handled by the default `MainWindow` handler. Another nice case is that although a `close` event cannot be handled directly by `SendDialog` and `MsgText`, all the `close` events end up being handled properly by `MainWindow`. That's the beauty of using the parent relationship as a fallback mechanism.

If you want to spend some more creative time on the event example, you can replace the dumb `print` statements and add some actual behavior to the listed events. Of course, you are not limited to the listed events. Just add your favorite event and make it do something useful!

Another exercise is to add a `MsgText` instance during runtime that has `MainWindow` as the parent. Is this hard? Do the same for an event (add a new event to an existing widget). Which is harder?

Summary

In this chapter, we covered the Chain of Responsibility design pattern. This pattern is useful to model requests and/or handle events when the number and type of handlers aren't known in advance. Examples of systems that fit well with Chain of Responsibility are event-based systems, purchase systems, and shipping systems.

In the Chain of Responsibility pattern, the sender has direct access to the first node of a chain. If the request cannot be satisfied by the first node, it forwards it to the next node. This continues until either the request is satisfied by a node or the whole chain is traversed. This design is used to achieve loose coupling between the sender and the receiver(s).

ATMs are an example of Chain of Responsibility. The single slot that is used for all banknotes can be considered the head of the chain. From here, depending on the transaction, one or more receptacles are used to process the transaction. The receptacles can be considered to be the processing elements of the chain.

Java's servlet filters use the Chain of Responsibility pattern to perform different actions (for example, compression and authentication) on an HTTP request. Apple's Cocoa Frameworks use the same pattern to handle events such as button presses and finger gestures.

32
The Command Pattern

Most applications nowadays have an **undo** operation. It is hard to imagine, but undo did not exist in any software for many years. Undo was introduced in 1974 (j.mp/wiundo), but Fortran and Lisp, two programming languages that are still widely used, were created in 1957 and 1958, respectively (j.mp/proghist)! I wouldn't like to have been an application user during those years. Making a mistake meant that the user had no easy way to fix it.

Enough with the history. We want to know how we can implement the undo functionality in our applications. And since you have read the title of this chapter, you already know which design pattern is recommended to implement undo: the Command pattern.

The Command design pattern helps us encapsulate an operation (undo, redo, copy, paste, and so forth) as an object. What this simply means is that we create a class that contains all the logic and the methods required to implement the operation. The advantages of doing this are as follows (j.mp/cmdpattern):

- We don't have to execute a command directly. It can be executed at will.
- The object that invokes the command is decoupled from the object that knows how to perform it. The invoker does not need to know any implementation details about the command.
- If it makes sense, multiple commands can be grouped to allow the invoker to execute them in order. This is useful, for instance, when implementing a multilevel undo command.

In this chapter, we will discuss:

- Real-world examples
- Use cases
- Implementation

Real-world examples

When we go to a restaurant for dinner, we give the order to the waiter. The check (usually paper) that they use to write the order on is an example of a command. After writing the order, the waiter places it in the check queue that is executed by the cook. Each check is independent and can be used to execute many different commands, for example, one command for each item that will be cooked.

As you would expect, we also have several examples in software. Here are two I can think of:

- PyQt is the Python binding of the QT toolkit. PyQt contains a `QAction` class that models an action as a command. Extra optional information is supported for every action, such as description, tooltip, shortcut, and more (`j.mp/qaction`).
- Git Cola (`j.mp/git-cola`), a Git GUI written in Python, uses the Command pattern to modify the model, amend a commit, apply a different election, check out, and so forth (`j.mp/git-cola-code`).

Use cases

Many developers use the undo example as the only use case of the Command pattern. The truth is that undo is the killer feature of the Command pattern. However, the Command pattern can actually do much more (`j.mp/commddp`):

- **GUI buttons and menu items**: The PyQt example that was already mentioned uses the Command pattern to implement actions on buttons and menu items.
- **Other operations**: Apart from undo, commands can be used to implement any operation. A few examples are cut, copy, paste, redo, and capitalize text.
- **Transactional behavior and logging**: Transactional behavior and logging are important to keep a persistent log of changes. They are used by operating systems to recover from system crashes, relational databases to implement transactions, filesystems to implement snapshots, and installers (wizards) to revert canceled installations.
- **Macros**: By macros, in this case, we mean a sequence of actions that can be recorded and executed on demand at any point in time. Popular editors such as Emacs and Vim support macros.

Implementation

In this section, we will use the Command pattern to implement the most basic file utilities:

- Creating a file and optionally writing text (a string) to it
- Reading the contents of a file
- Renaming a file
- Deleting a file

We will not implement these utilities from scratch, since Python already offers good implementations of them in the `os` module. What we want is to add an extra abstraction level on top of them so that they can be treated as commands. By doing this, we get all the advantages offered by commands.

From the operations shown, renaming a file and creating a file support undo. Deleting a file and reading the contents of a file do no support undo. Undo can actually be implemented on delete file operations. One technique is to use a special trash/wastebasket directory that stores all the deleted files, so that they can be restored when the user requests it. This is the default behavior used on all modern desktop environments and is left as an exercise.

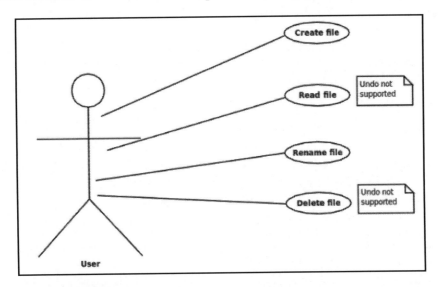

Each command has two parts:

- **The initialization part**: It is taken care of by the __init__() method and contains all the information required by the command to be able to do something useful (the path of a file, the contents that will be written to the file, and so forth).

- **The execution part**: It is taken care of by the `execute()` method. We call the `execute()` method when we want to actually run a command. This is not necessarily right after initializing it.

Let's start with the rename utility, which is implemented using the `RenameFile` class. The `__init__()` method accepts the source (`src`) and destination (`dest`) file paths as parameters (strings). If no path separators are used, the current directory is used to create the file. An example of using a path separator is passing the `/tmp/file1` string as `src` and the `/home/user/file2` string as `dest`. Another example, where we would not use a path, is passing `file1` as `src` and `file2` as `dest`:

```
class RenameFile:
    def __init__(self, src, dest):
        self.src = src
        self.dest = dest
```

We add the `execute()` method to the class. This method does the actual renaming using `os.rename()`. The `verbose` variable corresponds to a global **flag**, which, when activated (by default, it is activated) gives feedback to the user about the operation that is performed. You can deactivate it if you prefer silent commands. Note that although `print()` is good enough for an example, normally something more mature and powerful can be used, for example, the logging module (`j.mp/py3log`):

```
def execute(self):
    if verbose:
        print(f"[renaming '{self.src}' to '{self.dest}']")
    os.rename(self.src, self.dest)
```

Our rename utility (`RenameFile`) supports the undo operation through its `undo()` method. In this case, we use `os.rename()` again to revert the name of the file to its original value:

```
def undo(self):
    if verbose:
        print(f"[renaming '{self.dest}' back to '{self.src}']")
    os.rename(self.dest, self.src)
```

In this example, deleting a file is implemented in a function, instead of a class. That is to show it is not mandatory to create a new class for every command that you want to add (more on that will be covered later). The `delete_file()` function accepts a file path as a string and uses `os.remove()` to delete it:

```
def delete_file(path):
    if verbose:
        print(f"deleting file {path}")
    os.remove(path)
```

Back to using classes again. The `CreateFile` class is used to create a file. The `__init__()` method for that class accepts the familiar `path` parameter and a `txt` parameter for the content (a string) that will be written to the file. If nothing is passed as `txt`, the default `hello world` text is written to the file. Normally, the sane default behavior is to create an empty file, but for the needs of this example, I decided to write a default string in it.

The definition of the `CreateFile` class starts as follows:

```
class CreateFile:

    def __init__(self, path, txt='hello world\n'):
        self.path = path
        self.txt = txt
```

Then we add an `execute()` method, in which we use the `with` statement and Python's `open()` built-in function to open the file (`mode='w'` means write mode), and the `write()` function to write the `txt` string to it, as follows:

```
    def execute(self):
        if verbose:
            print(f"[creating file '{self.path}']")
        with open(self.path, mode='w', encoding='utf-8') as out_file:
            out_file.write(self.txt)
```

The undo for the operation of creating a file is to delete that file. So, the `undo()` method, which we add to the class, simply uses the `delete_file()` function to achieve that, as follows:

```
    def undo(self):
        delete_file(self.path)
```

The last utility gives us the ability to read the contents of a file. The `execute()` method of the `ReadFile` class uses `open()` again, this time in read mode, and just prints the content of the file using `print()`.

The `ReadFile` class is defined as follows:

```
class ReadFile:

    def __init__(self, path):
        self.path = path

    def execute(self):
        if verbose:
            print(f"[reading file '{self.path}']")
```

```
        with open(self.path, mode='r', encoding='utf-8') as in_file:
            print(in_file.read(), end='')
```

The `main()` function makes use of the utilities we have defined. The `orig_name` and `new_name` parameters are the original and new name of the file that is created and renamed. A commands list is used to add (and configure) all the commands that we want to execute at a later point. Note that the commands are not executed unless we explicitly call `execute()` for each command:

```
def main():
    orig_name, new_name = 'file1', 'file2'
    commands = (
        CreateFile(orig_name),
        ReadFile(orig_name),
        RenameFile(orig_name, new_name)
    )
    [c.execute() for c in commands]
```

The next step is to ask the users if they want to undo the executed commands or not. The user selects whether the commands will be undone or not. If they choose to undo them, `undo()` is executed for all commands in the commands list. However, since not all commands support undo, exception handling is used to catch (and ignore) the `AttributeError` exception generated when the `undo()` method is missing. The code would look like the following:

```
answer = input('reverse the executed commands? [y/n] ')
if answer not in 'yY':
    print(f"the result is {new_name}")
    exit()
for c in reversed(commands):
    try:
    c.undo()
except AttributeError as e:
    print("Error", str(e))
```

Using exception handling for such cases is an acceptable practice, but if you don't like it, you can check explicitly whether a command supports the undo operation by adding a **Boolean** method, for example, `supports_undo()` or `can_be_undone()`. Again, that is not mandatory.

Here's the full code of the example (`command.py`):

1. We import the `os` module and we define the constant we need:

```
import os
verbose = True
```

2. Here, we define the class for the rename file operation:

```python
class RenameFile:

    def __init__(self, src, dest):
        self.src = src
        self.dest = dest
    def execute(self):
        if verbose:
            print(f"[renaming '{self.src}' to '{self.dest}']")
        os.rename(self.src, self.dest)

    def undo(self):
        if verbose:
            print(f"[renaming '{self.dest}' back to '{self.src}']")
        os.rename(self.dest, self.src)
```

3. Here, we define the class for the create file operation:

```python
class CreateFile:

    def __init__(self, path, txt='hello world\n'):
        self.path = path
        self.txt = txt

    def execute(self):
        if verbose:
            print(f"[creating file '{self.path}']")
        with open(self.path, mode='w', encoding='utf-8') as out_file:
            out_file.write(self.txt)
    def undo(self):
        delete_file(self.path)
```

4. We also define the class for the read file operation, as follows:

```python
class ReadFile:

    def __init__(self, path):
        self.path = path

    def execute(self):
        if verbose:
            print(f"[reading file '{self.path}']")
        with open(self.path, mode='r', encoding='utf-8') as in_file:
            print(in_file.read(), end='')
```

5. And for the delete file operation, we decide to use a function (and not a class), as follows:

```python
def delete_file(path):
    if verbose:
        print(f"deleting file {path}")
    os.remove(path)
```

6. Here is the main part of the program now:

```python
def main():

    orig_name, new_name = 'file1', 'file2'
    commands = (
        CreateFile(orig_name),
        ReadFile(orig_name),
        RenameFile(orig_name, new_name)
    )
    [c.execute() for c in commands]
    answer = input('reverse the executed commands? [y/n] ')
    if answer not in 'yY':
        print(f"the result is {new_name}")
        exit()
    for c in reversed(commands):
        try:
            c.undo()
        except AttributeError as e:
            print("Error", str(e))
if __name__ == "__main__":
    main()
```

Let's see two sample executions using the python command.py command line.

In the first one, there is no undo of commands:

```
[creating file 'file1']
[reading file 'file1']
hello world
[renaming 'file1' to 'file2']
reverse the executed commands? [y/n] y
[renaming 'file2' back to 'file1']
Error 'ReadFile' object has no attribute 'undo'
deleting file file1
```

In the second one, we have the undo of commands:

```
[creating file 'file1']
[reading file 'file1']
hello world
[renaming 'file1' to 'file2']
reverse the executed commands? [y/n] n
the result is file2
```

But wait! Let's see what can be improved in our command implementation example. Among the things to consider are the following:

- What happens if we try to rename a file that doesn't exist?
- What about files that exist but cannot be renamed because we don't have the proper filesystem permissions?

We can try improving the utilities by doing some kind of error handling. Checking the return status of the functions in the os module can be useful. We could check if the file exists before trying the delete action, using the os.path.exists() function.

Also, the file creation utility creates a file using the default file permissions as decided by the filesystem. For example, in POSIX systems, the permissions are -rw-rw-r--. You might want to give the ability to the user to provide their own permissions by passing the appropriate parameter to CreateFile. How can you do that? Hint: one way is by using os.fdopen().

And now, here's something for you to think about. I mentioned earlier that a command does not necessarily need to be a class. That's how the delete utility was implemented; there is just a delete_file() function. What are the advantages and disadvantages of this approach? Here's a hint: Is it possible to put a delete command in the commands list as was done for the rest of the commands? We know that functions are first-class citizens in Python, so we can do something such as the following (see the first-class.py file):

```python
import os
verbose = True

class CreateFile:

    def __init__(self, path, txt='hello world\n'):
        self.path = path
        self.txt = txt

    def execute(self):
```

```
            if verbose:
                print(f"[creating file '{self.path}']")
            with open(self.path, mode='w', encoding='utf-8') as out_file:
                out_file.write(self.txt)
        def undo(self):
            try:
                delete_file(self.path)
            except:
                print('delete action not successful...')
                print('... file was probably already deleted.')

    def delete_file(path):
        if verbose:
            print(f"deleting file {path}...")
        os.remove(path)
    def main():

        orig_name = 'file1'
        df=delete_file

        commands = [CreateFile(orig_name),]
        commands.append(df)
        for c in commands:
            try:
                c.execute()
            except AttributeError as e:
                df(orig_name)
        for c in reversed(commands):
            try:
                c.undo()
            except AttributeError as e:
                pass
    if __name__ == "__main__":
        main()
```

Although this variant of the implementation example works, there are still some issues:

- The code is not uniform. We rely too much on exception handling, which is not the normal flow of a program. While all the other commands we implemented have an `execute()` method, in this case, there is no `execute()`.

- Currently, the delete file utility has no undo support. What happens if we eventually decide to add undo support for it? Normally, we add an `undo()` method in the class that represents the command. However, in this case, there is no class. We could create another function to handle undo, but creating a class is a better approach.

Summary

In this chapter, we covered the Command pattern. Using this design pattern, we can encapsulate an operation, such as copy/paste, as an object. This offers many benefits, as follows:

- We can execute a command whenever we want, and not necessarily at creation time
- The client code that executes a command does not need to know any details about how it is implemented
- We can group commands and execute them in a specific order

Executing a command is like ordering at a restaurant. Each customer's order is an independent command that enters many stages and is finally executed by the cook.

Many GUI frameworks, including PyQt, use the Command pattern to model actions that can be triggered by one or more events and can be customized. However, Command is not limited to frameworks; normal applications such as git-cola also use it for the benefits it offers.

Although the most advertised feature of command by far is undo, it has more uses. In general, any operation that can be executed at the user's will at runtime is a good candidate to use the Command pattern. The command pattern is also great for grouping multiple commands. It's useful for implementing macros, multilevel undoing, and transactions. A transaction should either succeed, which means that all operations of it should succeed (the commit operation), or it should fail completely if at least one of its operations fails (the rollback operation). If you want to take the Command pattern to the next level, you can work on an example that involves grouping commands as transactions.

To demonstrate command, we implemented some basic file utilities on top of Python's os module. Our utilities supported undo and had a uniform interface, which makes grouping commands easy.

The next chapter covers the Observer pattern.

33
The Observer Pattern

When we need to update a group of objects when the state of another object changes, a popular solution is offered by the **Model-View-Controller (MVC)** pattern. Assume that we are using the data of the same *model* in two *views*, for instance in a pie chart and in a spreadsheet. Whenever the model is modified, both the views need to be updated. That's the role of the Observer design pattern.

The Observer pattern describes a publish-subscribe relationship between a single object, the publisher, which is also known as the **subject** or **observable**, and one or more objects, the subscribers, also known as **observers**.

In the case of MVC, the publisher is the model and the subscribers are the views. There are other examples and we will discuss them throughout this chapter.

The ideas behind Observer are the same as those behind the separation of concerns principle, that is, to increase decoupling between the publisher and subscribers, and to make it easy to add/remove subscribers at runtime.

In this chapter, we will discuss:

- Real-world examples
- Use cases
- Implementation

Real-world examples

In reality, an auction resembles the Observer pattern. Every auction bidder has a number paddle that is raised whenever they want to place a bid. Whenever the paddle is raised by a bidder, the auctioneer acts as the subject by updating the price of the bid and broadcasting the new price to all bidders (subscribers).

In software, we can cite at least two examples:

- Kivy, the Python Framework for developing user interfaces, has a module called **Properties**, which implements the Observer pattern. Using this technique, you can specify what should happen when a property's value changes.
- The RabbitMQ library can be used to add asynchronous messaging support to an application. Several messaging protocols are supported, such as HTTP and AMQP. RabbitMQ can be used in a Python application to implement a publish-subscribe pattern, which is nothing more than the Observer design pattern (`j.mp/rabbitmqobs`).

Use cases

We generally use the Observer pattern when we want to inform/update *one or more objects* (observers/subscribers) about a change that happened on *a given object* (subject/publisher/observable). The number of observers, as well as who those observers are may vary and can be changed dynamically.

We can think of many cases where Observer can be useful. One such use case is **news feeds**. With RSS, Atom, or other related formats, you follow a feed, and every time it is updated, you receive a notification about the update.

The same concept exists in social networking. If you are connected to another person using a social networking service, and your connection updates something, you are notified about it. It doesn't matter if the connection is a Twitter user that you follow, a real friend on Facebook, or a business colleague on LinkedIn.

Event-driven systems are another example where Observer is usually used. In such systems, you have *listeners* that *listen* for specific events. The listeners are triggered when an event they are listening to is created. This can be typing a specific key (on the keyboard), moving the mouse, and more. The event plays the role of the publisher and the listeners play the role of the observers. The key point in this case is that multiple listeners (observers) can be attached to a single event (publisher).

Implementation

In this section, we will implement a data formatter. The ideas described here are based on the ActiveState Python Observer code recipe (`https://code.activestate.com/`). There is a default formatter that shows a value in the decimal format. However, we can add/register more formatters. In this example, we will add a hex and binary formatter. Every time the value of the default formatter is updated, the registered formatters are notified and take action. In this case, the action is to show the new value in the relevant format.

Observer is actually one of the patterns where inheritance makes sense. We can have a base `Publisher` class that contains the common functionality of adding, removing, and notifying observers. Our `DefaultFormatter` class derives from `Publisher` and adds the formatter-specific functionality. And, we can dynamically add and remove observers on demand.

We begin with the `Publisher` class. The observers are kept in the observers list. The `add()` method registers a new observer, or throws an error if it already exists. The `remove()` method unregisters an existing observer, or throws an exception if it does not exist. Finally, the `notify()` method informs all observers about a change:

```
class Publisher:
    def __init__(self):
        self.observers = []

    def add(self, observer):
        if observer not in self.observers:
            self.observers.append(observer)
        else:
            print(f'Failed to add: {observer}')

    def remove(self, observer):
        try:
            self.observers.remove(observer)
        except ValueError:
            print(f'Failed to remove: {observer}')

    def notify(self):
        [o.notify(self) for o in self.observers]
```

Let's continue with the `DefaultFormatter` class. The first thing that its __init__() does is call the __init__() method of the base class, since this is not done automatically in Python.

A `DefaultFormatter` instance has a name to make it easier for us to track its status. We use name mangling in the _data variable to state that it should not be accessed directly. Note that this is always possible in Python but fellow developers have no excuse for doing so, since the code already states that they shouldn't. There is a serious reason for using name mangling in this case. Stay tuned. `DefaultFormatter` treats the _data variable as an integer, and the default value is zero:

```
class DefaultFormatter(Publisher):
    def __init__(self, name):
        Publisher.__init__(self)
        self.name = name
        self._data = 0
```

The `__str__()` method returns information about the name of the publisher and the value of the _data attribute. `type(self).__name__` is a handy trick to get the name of a class without hardcoding it. It is one of those tricks that makes your code easier to maintain:

```
def __str__(self):
    return f"{type(self).__name__}: '{self.name}' has data =
    {self._data}"
```

There are two `data()` methods. The first one uses the `@property` decorator to give read access to the _data variable. Using this, we can just execute `object.data` instead of `object.data()`:

```
@property
def data(self):
    return self._data
```

The second `data()` method is more interesting. It uses the `@setter` decorator, which is called every time the assignment (=) operator is used to assign a new value to the _data variable. This method also tries to cast a new value to an integer, and does exception handling in case this operation fails:

```
@data.setter
def data(self, new_value):
    try:
        self._data = int(new_value)
    except ValueError as e:
        print(f'Error: {e}')
    else:
        self.notify()
```

The next step is to add the observers. The functionality of `HexFormatter` and `BinaryFormatter` is very similar. The only difference between them is how they format the value of data received by the publisher, that is, in hexadecimal and binary, respectively:

```
class HexFormatterObs:
    def notify(self, publisher):
        value = hex(publisher.data)
        print(f"{type(self).__name__}: '{publisher.name}' has now hex data = {value}")

class BinaryFormatterObs:
    def notify(self, publisher):
        value = bin(publisher.data)
        print(f"{type(self).__name__}: '{publisher.name}' has now bin data = {value}")
```

To help us use those classes, the `main()` function initially creates a `DefaultFormatter` instance named `test1` and, afterwards, attaches (and detaches) the two available observers. We also have some exception handling to make sure that the application does not crash when erroneous data is passed by the user.

The code is as follows:

```
def main():
    df = DefaultFormatter('test1')
    print(df)

    print()
    hf = HexFormatterObs()
    df.add(hf)
    df.data = 3
    print(df)

    print()
    bf = BinaryFormatterObs()
    df.add(bf)
    df.data = 21
    print(df)
```

Moreover, tasks such as trying to add the same observer twice or removing an observer that does not exist should cause no crashes:

```
    print()
    df.remove(hf)
    df.data = 40
    print(df)
```

```
print()
df.remove(hf)
df.add(bf)

df.data = 'hello'
print(df)

print()
df.data = 15.8
print(df)
```

Let's now recapitulate the full code of the example (the `observer.py` file):

1. We define the `Publisher` class:

```
class Publisher:
    def __init__(self):
        self.observers = []
    def add(self, observer):
        if observer not in self.observers:
            self.observers.append(observer)
        else:
            print(f'Failed to add: {observer}')
    def remove(self, observer):
        try:
            self.observers.remove(observer)
        except ValueError:
            print(f'Failed to remove: {observer}')
    def notify(self):
        [o.notify(self) for o in self.observers]
```

2. We define the `DefaultFormatter` class, with its special `__init__` and `__str__` methods:

```
class DefaultFormatter(Publisher):
    def __init__(self, name):
        Publisher.__init__(self)
        self.name = name
        self._data = 0
    def __str__(self):
        return f"{type(self).__name__}: '{self.name}' has data =
{self._data}"
```

3. We add the `data` property getter and setter methods to the `DefaultFormatter` class:

```
@property
def data(self):
```

```
        return self._data
    @data.setter
    def data(self, new_value):
        try:
            self._data = int(new_value)
        except ValueError as e:
          print(f'Error: {e}')
        else:
          self.notify()
```

4. We define our two observer classes, as follows:

```
class HexFormatterObs:
    def notify(self, publisher):
        value = hex(publisher.data)
        print(f"{type(self).__name__}: '{publisher.name}' has now
        hex data = {value}")
class BinaryFormatterObs:
    def notify(self, publisher):
        value = bin(publisher.data)
        print(f"{type(self).__name__}: '{publisher.name}' has now
        bin data = {value}")
```

5. Now, we take care of the main part of the program; the first part of the main() function is as follows:

```
def main():
    df = DefaultFormatter('test1')
    print(df)
    print()
    hf = HexFormatterObs()
    df.add(hf)
    df.data = 3
    print(df)
    print()
    bf = BinaryFormatterObs()
    df.add(bf)
    df.data = 21
    print(df)
```

6. Here is the end of the main() function:

```
    print()
    df.remove(hf)
    df.data = 40
    print(df)
    print()
    df.remove(hf)
```

```
        df.add(bf)
        df.data = 'hello'
        print(df)
        print()
        df.data = 15.8
        print(df)
```

7. We do not forget the usual snippet that calls the `main()` function:

```
if __name__ == '__main__':
    main()
```

Executing the `python observer.py` command gives the following output:

```
DefaultFormatter: 'test1' has data = 0

HexFormatterObs: 'test1' has now hex data = 0x3
DefaultFormatter: 'test1' has data = 3

HexFormatterObs: 'test1' has now hex data = 0x15
BinaryFormatterObs: 'test1' has now bin data = 0b10101
DefaultFormatter: 'test1' has data = 21

BinaryFormatterObs: 'test1' has now bin data = 0b101000
DefaultFormatter: 'test1' has data = 40

Failed to remove: <__main__.HexFormatterObs object at 0x0000023707F90D30>
Failed to add: <__main__.BinaryFormatterObs object at 0x0000023707F90D68>
Error: invalid literal for int() with base 10: 'hello'
DefaultFormatter: 'test1' has data = 40

BinaryFormatterObs: 'test1' has now bin data = 0b1111
DefaultFormatter: 'test1' has data = 15
```

What we see in the output is that as the extra observers are added, more (and relevant) output is shown, and when an observer is removed, it is not notified any longer. That's exactly what we want: runtime notifications that we are able to enable/disable on demand.

The defensive programming part of the application also seems to work fine. Trying to do funny things, such as removing an observer that does not exist or adding the same observer twice, is not allowed. The messages shown are not very user-friendly, but I leave that up to you as an exercise. Runtime failures such as trying to pass a string when the API expects a number are also properly handled without causing the application to crash/terminate.

This example would be much more interesting if it were interactive. Even a simple menu that allows the user to attach/detach observers at runtime and to modify the value of `DefaultFormatter` would be nice because the runtime aspect becomes much more visible. Feel free to do it.

Another nice exercise is to add more observers. For example, you can add an octal formatter, a Roman numeral formatter, or any other observer that uses your favorite representation. Be creative!

Summary

In this chapter, we covered the Observer design pattern. We use Observer when we want to be able to inform/notify all stakeholders (an object or a group of objects) when the state of an object changes. An important feature of Observer is that the number of subscribers/observers, as well as who the subscribers are, may vary and can be changed at runtime.

To understand Observer, you can think of an auction, with the bidders being the subscribers and the auctioneer being the publisher. This pattern is used quite a lot in the software world.

As specific examples of software using Observer, we mentioned the following:

- Kivy, the framework for developing innovative user interfaces, with its *Properties* concept and module.
- The Python bindings of RabbitMQ. We referred to a specific example of RabbitMQ used to implement the publish-subscribe (also known as Observer) pattern.

In the implementation example, we saw how to use Observer to create data formatters that can be attached and detached at runtime to enrich the behavior of an object. Hopefully, you will find the recommended exercises interesting.

Appendix

Chapter 8

What is the idea behind concurrency, and why is it useful?

Concurrency is about designing and structuring program commands and instructions so that different sections of the program can be executed in an efficient order, while sharing the same resources.

What are the differences between concurrent programming and sequential programming?

In sequential programming, the commands and instructions are executed one at the time, in a sequential order. In concurrent programming, some sections might be executed in an efficient way for better execution time.

What are the differences between concurrent programming and parallel programming?

In parallel programming, the separate sections of a program are independent of one another; they do not interact with one another, and therefore, they can be executed simultaneously. In concurrent programming, the separate tasks share the same resources, and some form of coordination between them is therefore required.

Can every program be made concurrent or parallel?

No.

What are embarrassingly parallel tasks?

Embarrassingly parallel tasks can be divided into separate, independent sections, with little or no effort.

What are inherently sequential tasks?

Tasks wherein the order of execution of individual sections is crucial to the results of the tasks, which cannot be made concurrent or parallel to obtain better execution time, are called inherently sequential.

What does I/O bound mean?

This is a condition in which the time it takes to complete a computation is determined mainly by the time spent waiting for input/output operations to be completed.

How is concurrent processing currently being used in the real world?

Concurrency can be found almost everywhere: desktop and mobile applications, video games, web and internet development, artificial intelligence, and so on.

Chapter 9

What is Amdahl's law? What problem does Amdahl's law look to solve?

Amdahl's law provides an estimate of the theoretical speedup in latency of the execution of a task at fixed workload that can be expected of a system whose resources are improved.

Explain the formula of Amdahl's Law, along with its components.

The formula for Amdahl's Law is as follows:

$$S = \frac{1}{B + \frac{1-B}{j}}$$

In the preceding formula, the following applies:

- S is the theoretical speedup in consideration.
- B is the portion of the whole task that is inherently sequential.
- j is the number of processors being utilized.

According to Amdahl's Law, would speedup increase indefinitely as resources in the system improved?

No; as the number of processors becomes larger, the efficiency gained through the improvement decreases.

What is the relationship between Amdahl's Law and the law of diminishing returns?

You have seen that in specific situations (namely, when only the number of processors increases), Amdahl's Law resembles the law of diminishing returns. Specifically, as the number of processors becomes larger, the efficiency gained through the improvement decreases, and the speedup curve flattens out.

Chapter 10

What is a thread? What are the core differences between a thread and a process?

A thread of execution is the smallest unit of programming commands. More than one thread can be implemented within a same process, usually executing concurrently and accessing/sharing the same resources, such as memory, while separate processes do not do this.

What are the API options provided by the `thread` **module in Python?**

The main feature of the `thread` module is its fast and efficient method of creating new threads to execute functions: the `thread.start_new_thread()` function. Aside from this, the module only supports a number of low-level ways of working with multithreaded primitives and sharing their global data space. Additionally, simple lock objects (for example, mutexes and semaphores) are provided for synchronization purposes.

What are the API options provided by the `threading` **module in Python?**

In addition to all of the functionalities for working with threads that the `thread` module provides, the `threading` module also supports a number of extra methods, as follows:

- `threading.activeCount()`: This function returns the number of currently active thread objects in the program.
- `threading.currentThread()`: This function returns the number of thread objects in the current thread control from the caller.
- `threading.enumerate()`: This function returns a list of all of the currently active thread objects in the program.

What are the processes of creating new threads via the `thread` **and** `threading` **modules?**

The processes for creating new threads using the `thread` and `threading` module is as follows:

- In the `thread` module, new threads are created to execute functions concurrently. The way to do this is by using the `thread.start_new_thread()` function: `thread.start_new_thread(function, args[, kwargs])`.

- To create and customize a new thread using the threading module, there are specific steps that need to be followed:
    1. Define a subclass of the threading.Thread class in our program
    2. Override the default __init__(self [,args]) method inside the subclass to add custom arguments for the class
    3. Override the default run(self [,args]) method inside the subclass to customize the behavior of the thread class when a new thread is initialized and started

What is the idea behind thread synchronization using locks?

In a given program, when a thread is accessing/executing the critical section of the program, any other threads need to wait until that thread finishes executing. The typical goal of thread synchronization is to avoid any potential data discrepancies when multiple threads access their shared resource; allowing only one thread to execute the critical section at a time guarantees that no data conflicts can occur in our multithreaded applications. One of the most common ways to apply thread synchronization is through the implementation of a locking mechanism.

What is the process of implementing thread synchronization using locks in Python?

In our threading module, the threading.Lock class provides a simple and intuitive approach to creating and working with locks. Its main usage includes the following methods:

- threading.Lock(): This method initializes and returns a new lock object.
- acquire(blocking): When this method is called, all threads will run synchronously (that is, only one thread can execute the critical section at a time).
- release(): When this method is called, the lock is released.

What is the idea behind the queue data structure?

A queue is an abstract data structure that is a collection of different elements maintained in a specific order; these elements can be other objects in a program.

What is the main application of queuing in concurrent programming?

The concept of a queue is even more prevalent in the subfield of concurrent programming, as the order of elements maintained inside a queue plays an important role when a multithreaded program handles and manipulates its shared resources.

What are the core differences between a regular queue and a priority queue?

The priority queue abstract data structure is similar to the queue data structure, but each of the elements of a priority queue, as the name suggests, has a priority associated with it; in other words, when an element is added to a priority queue, its priority needs to be specified. Unlike in regular queues, the dequeuing principle of a priority queue relies on the priority of the elements: the elements with higher priority are processed before those with lower priority.

Chapter 11

What is a file descriptor, and in what ways can it be handled in Python?

A file descriptor is used as a handle on an opened external file in a program. In Python, a file descriptor is handled by either using `open()` and `close()` functions or using the `with` statement; for example:

- `f = open(filename, 'r'); ... ; f.close()`
- `with open(filename, 'r') as f: ...`

What problem arises when file descriptors are not handled carefully?

Systems can only handle a certain number of opened external files in one running process. When that limit is passed, the handles on the opened files will be compromised and file descriptor leakage will occur.

What is a lock, and in what ways can it be handled in Python?

A lock is a mechanism in concurrent and parallel programming that performs thread synchronization. In Python, a `threading.Lock` object can be handled by either using the `acquire()` and `release()` methods or using the `with` statement; for example:

- `my_lock.acquire(); ... ; my_lock.release()`
- `with my_lock: ...`

What problem arises when locks are not handled carefully?

When an exception occurs while a lock is acquired, the lock can never be released and acquired again if it is not handled carefully, causing a common problem in concurrent and parallel programming called deadlock.

What is the idea behind context managers?

Context managers are in charge of the context of resources within a program; they define and handle the interaction of other entities with those resources, and perform cleanup tasks after the program exits the context.

What options does the `with` statement in Python provide, in terms of context management?

The `with` statement in Python offers an intuitive and convenient way to manage resources while ensuring that errors and exceptions are handled correctly. Aside from better error handling and guaranteed cleanup tasks, the `with` statement also provides extra readability from your programs, which is one of the strongest features that Python offers to its developers.

Chapter 12

What is HTML?

HTML stands for **Hypertext Markup Language**, which is the standard and most common markup language for developing web pages and web applications.

What are HTTP requests?

Most of the communication done via the internet (more specifically, the World Wide Web) utilizes HTTP. In HTTP, request methods are used to convey information on what data is being requested and should be sent back from a server.

What are HTTP response status codes?

HTTP response status codes are three-digit numbers that signify the state of communication between a server and its client. They are sorted into five categories, each indicating a specific state of communication.

How does the `requests` module help with making web requests?

The `requests` module manages the communication between a Python program and a web server through HTTP requests.

What is a ping test and how is one typically designed?

A ping test is a tool typically used by web administrators to make sure that their sites are still available to clients. A ping test does this by making requests to the websites under consideration and analyzes the returned response status codes

Why is concurrency applicable in making web requests?

Both the process of making different requests to a web server and the process of parsing and processing downloaded HTML source code are independent across separate requests.

What are the considerations that need to be made when developing web scraping applications?

The following considerations should be made when developing applications that make concurrent web requests:

- The terms of service and data-collecting policies
- Error handling
- Updating your program regularly
- Avoiding over-scraping

Chapter 13

What is a process? What are the core differences between a process and a thread?

A process is an instance of a specific computer program or software that is being executed by the operating system. A process contains both the program code and its current activities and interactions with other entities. More than one thread can be implemented within the same process to access and share memory or other resources, while different processes do not interact in this way.

What is multiprocessing? What are the core differences between multiprocessing and multithreading?

Multiprocessing refers to the execution of multiple concurrent processes from an operating system, in which each process is executed on a separate CPU, as opposed to a single process at any given time. Multithreading, on the other hand, is the execution of multiple threads, which can be within the same process.

What are the API options provided by the multiprocessing module?

The `multiprocessing` module provides APIs to the `Process` class, which contains the implementation of a process while offering methods to spawn and interact with processes using an API similar to the `threading` module. The module also provides the `Pool` class, which is mainly used to implement a pool of processes, each of which will carry out the tasks submitted.

What are the core differences between the `Process` class and the `Pool` class from the multiprocessing module?

The `Pool` class implements a pool of processes, each of which will carry out tasks submitted to a `Pool` object. Generally, the `Pool` class is more convenient than the `Process` class, especially if the results returned from your concurrent application should be ordered.

What are the options to determine the current process in a Python program?

The `multiprocessing` module provides the `current_process()` method, which will return the `Process` object that is currently running at any point of a program. Another way to keep track of running processes in your program is to look at the individual process IDs through the `os` module.

What are daemon processes? What are their purposes, in terms of waiting for processes in a multiprocessing program?

Daemon processes run in the background and do not block the main program from exiting. This specification is common when there is not an easy way for the main program to tell if it is appropriate to interrupt the process at any given time, or when exiting the main program without completing the worker does not affect the end result.

How can you terminate a process? Why is it sometimes acceptable to terminate processes?

The `terminate()` method from the `multiprocessing.Process` class offers a way to quickly terminate a process. If the processes in your program never interact with the shared resources, the `terminate()` method is considerably useful, especially if a process appears to be unresponsive or deadlocked.

What are the ways to facilitate interprocess communication in Python?

While locks are one of the most common synchronization primitives used for communication among threads, pipes and queues are the main way to communicate between different processes. Specifically, they provide message passing options to facilitate communication between processes: pipes for connections between two processes, and queues for multiple producers and consumers.

Chapter 14

What is a reduction operator? What conditions must be satisfied so that an operator can be a reduction operator?

An operator is a reduction operator if it satisfies the following conditions:

- The operator can reduce an array of elements into one scalar value
- The end result (the scalar value) is obtained through creating and computing partial tasks

What properties do reduction operators have that are equivalent to the required conditions?

The communicative and associative properties are considered to be equivalent to the requirements for a reduction operator.

What is the connection between reduction operators and concurrent programming?

Reduction operators require communicative and associative properties. Consequently, their sub-tasks have to be able to be processed independently, which makes concurrency and parallelism applicable.

What are some of the considerations that must be made when working with multiprocessing programs that facilitate interprocess communication in Python?

Some considerations include implementing the poison-pill technique, so that sub-tasks are distributed across all consumer processes; calling `task_done()` on the task queue each time the `get()` function is called, to ensure that the `join()` function will not block indefinitely; and avoiding using the `qsize()` method, which is unreliable and is not implemented on Unix operating systems.

What are some real-life applications of concurrent reduction operators?

Some real-life applications include heavy number-crunching operators and complex programs that utilize logic operators.

Chapter 15

What is an image processing task?

Image processing is the task of analyzing and manipulating digital image files to create new versions of the images, or to extract important data from them.

What is the smallest unit of digital imaging? How is it represented in computers?

The smallest unit of digital imaging is a pixel, which typically contains an RGB value: a tuple of integers between 0 and 255.

What is grayscaling? What purpose does the technique serve?

Grayscaling is the process of converting an image to gray colors by considering only the intensity information of each pixel, represented by the amount of light available. It reduces the dimensionality of the image pixel matrix by mapping traditional three-dimensional color data to one-dimensional gray data.

What is thresholding? What purpose does the technique serve?

Thresholding replaces each pixel in an image with a white pixel if the pixel's intensity is greater than a previously specified threshold, and with a black pixel if the pixel's intensity is less than that threshold. After performing thresholding on an image, each pixel of that image can only hold two possible values, significantly reducing the complexity of image data.

Why should image processing be made concurrent?

Heavy computational number-crunching processes are typically involved when it comes to image processing, as each image is a matrix of integer tuples. However, these processes can be executed independently, which suggests that the whole task should be made concurrent.

What are some good practices for concurrent image processing?

Some good practices for concurrent image processing are as follows:

- Choosing the correct method (out of many)
- Spawning an appropriate amount of processes
- Processing input/output concurrently

Chapter 16

What is the idea behind asynchronous programming?

Asynchronous programming is a model of programming that focuses on coordinating different tasks in an application with the goal that the application will use the least amount of time to finish executing those tasks. An asynchronous program switches from one task to another when it is appropriate to create overlap between the waiting and processing time, and therefore shorten the total time taken to finish the whole program.

How is asynchronous programming different from synchronous programming?

In synchronous programming, the instructions of a program are executed sequentially: a task has to finished executing before the next task in the program starts processing. With asynchronous programming, if the current task takes a significant amount of time to finish, you have the option to specify at one time during the task to switch the execution to another task.

How is asynchronous programming different from threading and multiprocessing?

Asynchronous programming keeps all of the instructions of a program in the same thread and process. The main idea behind asynchronous programming is to have a single executor switch from one task to another if it is more efficient (in terms of execution time) to simply wait for the first task for a while, while processing the second.

Chapter 17

What is asynchronous programming? What advantages does it provide?

Asynchronous programming is a model of programming that takes advantage of coordinating computing tasks to overlap the waiting and processing times. If successfully implemented, asynchronous programming provides both responsiveness and an improvement in speed, as compared to synchronous programming.

What are the main elements in an asynchronous program? How do they interact with each other?

There are three main components of an asynchronous program: the event loop, the coroutines, and the futures. The event loop is in charge of scheduling and managing coroutines by using its task queue; the coroutines are computing tasks that are to be executed asynchronously, and each coroutine has to specify, inside its function, exactly where it will give the execution flow back to the event loop (that is, the task-switching event); the futures are placeholder objects that contain the results obtained from the coroutines.

What are the `async` and `await` keywords? What purposes do they serve?

The `async` and `await` keywords are provided by the Python language as a way to implement asynchronous programming on a low level. The `async` keyword is placed in front of a function, in order to declare it as a coroutine, while the `await` keyword specifies the task-switching events.

What options does the `asyncio` module provide, in terms of the implementation of asynchronous programming?

The `asyncio` module provides an easy-to-use API and an intuitive framework to implement asynchronous programs; additionally, this framework makes the asynchronous code just as readable as synchronous code, which is generally quite rare in asynchronous programming.

What are the improvements, in regards to asynchronous programming, provided in Python 3.7?

Python 3.7 comes with improvements in the API that initiates and runs the main event loop of asynchronous programs, while reserving `async` and `await` as official Python keywords.

What are blocking functions? Why do they pose a problem for traditional asynchronous programming?

Blocking functions have non-stop execution, and therefore, they prevent any attempts to cooperatively switch tasks in an asynchronous program. If forced to release the execution flow back to the event loop, blocking functions will simply halt their execution until it is their turn to run again. While still achieving better responsiveness, in this case, asynchronous programming fails to improve the speed of the program; in fact, the asynchronous version of the program takes longer to finish executing than the synchronous version, most of the time, due to various overheads.

How does `concurrent.futures` **provide a solution to blocking functions for asynchronous programming? What options does it provide?**

The `concurrent.futures` module implements threading and multiprocessing for the execution of coroutines in an asynchronous program. It provides the `ThreadPoolExecutor` and `ProcessPoolExecutor` for asynchronous programming in separate threads and separate processes, respectively.

Chapter 18

What is a communication channel? What is its connection to asynchronous programming?

Communication channels are used to denote both the physical wiring connection between different systems and the logical communication of data that facilitates computer networks. The latter is related to computing, and is more relevant to the idea of asynchronous programming. Asynchronous programming can provide functionalities that complement the process of facilitating communication channels efficiently.

What are the two main parts of the Open Systems Interconnection (OSI) model protocol layers? What purposes do each of them serve?

The media layers contain fairly low-level operations that interact with the underlying process of the communication channel, while the host layers deals with high-level data communication and manipulation.

What is the transport layer? Why is it crucial to communication channels?

The transport layer is often viewed as the conceptual transition between the media layers and the host layers, responsible for sending data along end-to-end connections between different systems.

How does `asyncio` **facilitate the implementation of server-side communication channels?**

Server-wise, the `asyncio` module combines the abstraction of transport with the implementation of an asynchronous program. Specifically, via its `BaseTransport` and `BaseProtocol` classes, `asyncio` provides different ways to customize the underlying architecture of a communication channel.

How does `asyncio` **facilitate the implementation of client-side communication channels?**

Together with the `aiohttp` module and, specifically, `aiohttp.ClientSession`, `asyncio` also offers efficiency and flexibility regarding client-side communication processes, via asynchronously making requests and reading the returned responses.

What is `aiofiles`**?**

The `aiofiles` module, which can work in conjunction with `asyncio` and `aiohttp`, helps to facilitate asynchronous file reading/writing.

Chapter 19

What can lead to a deadlock situation, and why is it undesirable?

A lack of (or mishandled) coordination between different lock objects can cause deadlock, in which no progress can be made and the program is locked in its current state.

How is the dining philosophers problem related to the problem of deadlock?

In the dining philosophers problem, as each philosopher is holding only one fork with their left hand, they cannot proceed to eat or put down the fork they are holding. The only way a philosopher gets to eat their food is for their neighbor philosopher to put their fork down, which is only possible if they can eat their own food; this creates a never-ending circle of conditions that can never be satisfied. This situation is, in essence, the nature of a deadlock, in which all elements of a system are stuck in place and no progress can be made.

What are the four Coffman conditions?

Deadlock is also defined by the necessary conditions that a concurrent program needs to have at the same time, in order for deadlock to occur. These conditions were first proposed by the computer scientist Edward G. Coffman, Jr., and are therefore known as the Coffman conditions. The conditions are as follows:

- At least one resource has to be in a non-shareable state. This means that that resource is being held by an individual process (or thread) and cannot be accessed by others; the resource can only be accessed and held by a single process (or thread) at any given time. This condition is also known as **mutual exclusion**.

- There exists one process (or thread) that is simultaneously accessing a resource and waiting for another held by other processes (or threads). In other words, this process (or thread) needs access to two resources in order to execute its instructions, one of which it is already holding, and the other of which it is waiting for from other processes (or threads). This condition is called **hold and wait**.
- Resources can only be released by a process (or a thread) holding them if there are specific instructions for the process (or thread) to do so. This is to say that unless the process (or thread) voluntarily and actively releases the resource, that resource remains in a non-shareable state. This is the **no preemption** condition.
- The final condition is called **circular wait**. As suggested by the name, this condition specifies that there exists a set of processes (or threads) such that the first process (or thread) in the set is in a waiting state for a resource to be released by the second process (or thread), which, in turn, needs to be waiting for the third process (or thread); finally, the last process (or thread) in the set is waiting for the first one.

How can resource ranking solve the problem of deadlock? What other problems occur when this is implemented?

Instead of accessing the resources arbitrarily, if the processes (or threads) are to access them in a predetermined, static order, the circular nature of the way that they acquire and wait for the resources will be eliminated. However, if you place enough locks on the resources of your concurrent program, it will become entirely sequential in its execution, and, combined with the overhead of concurrent programming functionalities, it will have an even worse speed than the purely sequential version of the program.

How can ignoring locks solve the problem of deadlock? What other problems can occur when this is implemented?

By ignoring locks, our program resources effectively become shareable among different processes/threads in a concurrent program, thus eliminating the first of the four Coffman conditions, **mutual exclusion**. Doing this, however, can be seen as misunderstanding the problem completely. We know that locks are utilized so that processes and threads can access the shared resources in a program in a systematic, coordinated way, to avoid mishandling the data. Removing any locking mechanisms in a concurrent program means that the likelihood of the shared resources, which are now free from accessing limitations, being manipulated in an uncoordinated way (and therefore becoming corrupted) increases significantly.

How is livelock related to deadlock?

In a livelock situation, the processes (or threads) in the concurrent program are able to switch their states, yet they simply switch back and forth infinitely, and no progress can be made.

Chapter 20

What is starvation, and why is it undesirable in a concurrent program?

Starvation is a problem in concurrent systems in which a process (or a thread) cannot gain access to the necessary resources to proceed with its execution, and therefore, cannot make any progress.

What are the underlying causes of starvation? What are the common superficial causes of starvation that can manifest from the underlying cause?

Most of the time, a poorly coordinated set of scheduling instructions is the main cause of starvation. Some high-level causes for starvation might include the following:

- Processes (or threads) with high priorities dominate the execution flow in the CPU, and thus, low-priority processes (or threads) are not given the opportunity to execute their own instructions.
- Processes (or threads) with high priorities dominate the usage of non-shareable resources, and thus, low-priority processes (or threads) are not given the opportunity to execute their own instructions. This situation is similar to the first one, but addresses the priority of accessing resources, instead of the priority of execution itself.
- Processes (or threads) with low priorities are waiting for resources to execute their instructions, but as soon as the resources become available, other processes (or threads) with higher priorities are immediately given access to them, so the low-priority processes (or threads) wait infinitely.

What is the connection between deadlock and starvation?

Deadlock situations can also lead to starvation, as the definition of starvation states that if there exists a process (or a thread) that is unable to make any progress because it cannot gain access to the necessary process, the process (or thread) is experiencing starvation. This is also illustrated in the dining philosophers problem.

What is the readers-writers problem?

The readers-writers problem asks for a scheduling algorithm so that readers and writers can access the text file appropriately and efficiently, without mishandling/corrupting the data included.

What is the first approach to the readers-writers problem? Why does starvation arise in that situation?

The first approach allows for multiple readers to access the text file simultaneously, since readers simply read in the text file and do not alter the data in it. The problem with the first approach is that when a reader is accessing the text file and a writer is waiting for the file to be unlocked, if another reader starts its execution and wants to access the file, it will be given priority over the writer that has already been waiting. Additionally, if more and more readers keep requesting access to the file, the writer will be waiting infinitely.

What is the second approach to the readers-writers problem? Why does starvation arise in that situation?

This approach implements the specification that once a writer makes a request to access the file, no reader should be able to jump in line and access the file before that writer. As opposed to what we see in the first solution to the readers-writers problem, this solution is giving priority to writers and, as a consequence, the readers are starved.

What is the third approach to the readers-writers problem? Why does it successfully address starvation?

This approach implements a lock on both readers and writers. All threads will then be subject to the constants of the lock, and equal priority will thus be achieved among separate threads.

What are some common solutions to starvation?

Some common solutions to starvation include the following:

- Increasing the priority of low-priority threads
- Implementing a first-in-first-out thread queue
- A priority queue that also gives gradually increasing priority to threads that have been waiting in the queue for a long time
- Or if a thread has been able to access the shared resource for many times, it will be given less priority

Chapter 21

What is a critical section?

Critical sections indicate shared resources that are accessed by multiple processes or threads in a concurrent application, which can lead to unexpected, and even erroneous, behaviors.

What is a race condition, and why is it undesirable in a concurrent program?

A race condition occurs when two or more threads/processes access and alter a shared resource simultaneously, resulting in mishandled and corrupted data.

What is the underlying cause of a race condition?

The root cause of a race condition is multiple threads/process reading in and altering a shared resource simultaneously; and, when all of the threads/processes finish their execution, only the result of the last thread/process is registered.

How can locks solve the problem of a race condition?

Since the race conditions arise when multiple threads or processes access and write to a shared resource simultaneously, the solution is to isolate the execution of different threads/processes, especially when interacting with the shared resource. With locks, we can turn a shared resource in a concurrent program into a critical section, whose integrity of data is guaranteed to be protected.

Why are locks sometimes undesirable in a concurrent program?

There are a number of disadvantages to using locks: with enough locks implemented in a concurrent program, the whole program might become entirely sequential; locks don't lock anything.

What are the problems race conditions raise in real-life systems and applications?

The problems race conditions raise in real-life systems and applications are as follows:

- **Security**: A race condition can be both exploited as a security vulnerability (to give external agents illegal access to a system) and used as random key generation, for security processes.

- **Operating systems**: A race condition occurring when two agents (users and applications) interact with the same memory space can lead to unpredictable behaviors.
- **Networking**: In networking, a race condition can lead to giving multiple users powerful privileges in a network.

Chapter 22

What is the difference in memory management between Python and C++?

C++ associates a variable to its value by simply writing the value to the memory location of the variable; Python has its variables reference point to the memory location of the values that they hold. For this reason, Python needs to maintain a reference count for every value in its memory space.

What problem does the GIL solve for Python?

To avoid race conditions, and consequently, the corruption of value reference counts, the GIL is implemented so that only one thread can access and mutate the counts at any given time.

What problem does the GIL create for Python?

The GIL effectively prevents multiple threads from taking advantage of the CPU and executing CPU-bound instructions at the same time. This means that if multiple threads that are meant to be executed concurrently are CPU-bound, they will actually be executed sequentially.

What are some of the approaches to circumventing the GIL in Python programs?

There are a few ways to deal with the GIL in your Python applications; namely, implementing multiprocessing instead of multithreading, and utilizing other, alternative Python interpreters.

Other Books You May Enjoy

If you enjoyed this book, you may be interested in these other books by Packt:

Learn Python Programming - Second Edition
Fabrizio Romano

ISBN: 978-1-78899-666-2

- Get Python up and running on Windows, Mac, and Linux
- Explore fundamental concepts of coding using data structures and control flow
- Write elegant, reusable, and efficient code in any situation
- Understand when to use the functional or OOP approach
- Cover the basics of security and concurrent/asynchronous programming
- Create bulletproof, reliable software by writing tests
- Build a simple website in Django
- Fetch, clean, and manipulate data

Clean Code in Python
Mariano Anaya

ISBN: 978-1-78883-583-1

- Set up tools to effectively work in a development environment
- Explore how the magic methods of Python can help us write better code
- Examine the traits of Python to create advanced object-oriented design
- Understand removal of duplicated code using decorators and descriptors
- Effectively refactor code with the help of unit tests
- Learn to implement the SOLID principles in Python

Leave a Review - Let Other Readers Know What You Think

Please share your thoughts on this book with others by leaving a review on the site that you bought it from. If you purchased the book from Amazon, please leave us an honest review on this book's Amazon page. This is vital so that other potential readers can see and use your unbiased opinion to make purchasing decisions, we can understand what our customers think about our products, and our authors can see your feedback on the title that they have worked with Packt to create. It will only take a few minutes of your time, but is valuable to other potential customers, our authors, and Packt. Thank you!

Index

Z

Zope application server